NEW DIRECTIONS IN SCANDINAVIAN STUDIES

ANDY NESTINGEN, SERIES EDITOR

NEW DIRECTIONS IN SCANDINAVIAN STUDIES

This series offers interdisciplinary approaches to the study of the Nordic region of Scandinavia and the Baltic States and their cultural connections in North America. By redefining the boundaries of Scandinavian studies to include the Baltic States and Scandinavian America, the series presents books that focus on the study of the culture, history, literature, and politics of the North.

Small States in International Relations, edited by
Christine Ingebritsen, Iver B. Neumann, Sieglinde Gstohl, and Jessica Beyer

Danish Cookbooks: Domesticity and National Identity, 1616–1901, by
Carol Gold

Crime and Fantasy in Scandinavia: Fiction, Film, and Social Change, by
Andrew Nestingen

Selected Plays of Marcus Thrane, translated and introduced by
Terje I. Leiren

Munch's Ibsen: A Painter's Visions of a Playwright, by
Joan Templeton

Knut Hamsun: The Dark Side of Literary Brilliance, by
Monika Žagar

Nordic Exposures: Scandinavian Identities in Classical Hollywood Cinema, by
Arne Lunde

Icons of Danish Modernity: Georg Brandes and Asta Nielsen, by
Julie K. Allen

Danish Folktales, Legends, and Other Stories, edited and translated by
Timothy R. Tangherlini

The Power of Song: Nonviolent National Culture in the Baltic Singing Revolution, by
Guntis Šmidchens

Church Resistance to Nazism in Norway, 1940–1945, by
Arne Hassing

Christian Krohg's Naturalism, by
Øystein Sjåstad

Fascism and Modernist Literature in Norway, by
Dean Krouk

Sacred to the Touch: Nordic and Baltic Religious Wood Carving, by
Thomas A. DuBois

Sámi Media and Indigenous Agency in the Arctic North, by
Thomas A. DuBois and Coppélie Cocq

The Swedish Theory of Love: Individualism and Social Trust in Modern Sweden, by
Henrik Berggren and Lars Trägårdh, translated by Stephen Donovan

The Swedish Theory of Love

INDIVIDUALISM AND SOCIAL TRUST
IN MODERN SWEDEN

Henrik Berggren and Lars Trägårdh

Translated by Stephen Donovan

UNIVERSITY OF WASHINGTON PRESS
Seattle

The Swedish Theory of Love was made possible in part by support from the Department of Scandinavian Studies at the University of Washington.

The cost of this translation was defrayed by a subsidy from the Swedish Arts Council, gratefully acknowledged.

Originally published as *Är svensken människa? Gemenskap och oberoende i det moderna Sverige*
© Henrik Berggren, Lars Trägårdh 2006, 2015
Norstedts Förlag, Stockholm
English language edition © 2022 by Stephen Donovan

Composed in SabonLTStd-Roman, typeface designed by Jan Tschichold

26 25 24 23 22   5 4 3 2 1

Printed and bound in the United States of America

All rights reserved. No part of this publication may be reproduced or transmitted in any form or by any means, electronic or mechanical, including photocopy, recording, or any information storage or retrieval system, without permission in writing from the publisher.

UNIVERSITY OF WASHINGTON PRESS
uwapress.uw.edu

Library of Congress Cataloging-in-Publication Data
Names: Berggren, Henrik, author. | Trägårdh, Lars, author. | Donovan, Stephen, 1970– translator.
Title: The Swedish theory of love : individualism and social trust in modern Sweden / Henrik Berggren, and Lars Trägårdh; translated by Stephen Donovan.
Other titles: Är svensken människa? English
Description: Seattle : University of Washington Press, [2022] | Series: New directions in Scandinavian studies | "Är svensken människa? Gemenskap och oberoende I det moderna Sverige © Henrik Berggren, Lars Trägårdh 2006, 2015 Norstedts förlag, Stockholm." | Includes bibliographical references and index.
Identifiers: LCCN 2022013786 | ISBN 9780295750545 (hardback) | ISBN 9780295750552 (paperback) | ISBN 9780295750569 (ebook)
Subjects: LCSH: National characteristics, Swedish. | Sweden—Intellectual life. | Individualism—Sweden—History.
Classification: LCC DL639 .B4513 2022 | DDC 814/.52—dc24
LC record available at https://lccn.loc.gov/2022013786

♾ This paper meets the requirements of ANSI/NISO Z39.48-1992 (Permanence of Paper).

CONTENTS

Preface · vii

Introduction. Humanity's Asocial Sociability and the Swedish Paradox · ix

PART 1: ANATOMY OF A NATION

1. The People of Nifelheim · 3
2. Statist Individualism · 16
3. The Swedish Theory of Love · 33

PART 2: SWEDEN IMAGINED

4. Poverty and Progress · 53
5. Love and Independence · 73
6. Supermen and Other People · 92
7. A Bounded Community · 116
8. Sweden for the Swedes! · 134

PART 3: SWEDEN REALIZED

9. Nationalizing the Child · 161
10. Asocial, Unnatural, Inhuman · 183
11. Just a Housewife · 212
12. Competing Visions of Community · 237
13. A Lutheran Modernity? · 262

Coda. Prospects for Swedish Love: Freedom or Alienation? 295

Acknowledgments 317
Notes 319
Bibliography 343
Index 373

PREFACE

A Homecoming of Sorts

This book began in the mid-1980s when we met as graduate students in history at the University of California, Berkeley. Although we were both Swedish by birth, we also felt very American. One of us had spent parts of his childhood and adolescence in Wisconsin and New York; the other had left Sweden in his late teens to study and eventually settle in California. Having between us accumulated almost a lifetime of experience in both Sweden and the United States, we found our conversations repeatedly coming back to the cultural and political differences between the two countries.

Among our favorite topics was the issue of individualism. There is no denying that American culture has at its heart the idea of self-sufficient individuals making their way in the world by their own efforts. And yet we also felt that there was something lopsided about this "rugged individualism." It concerns itself almost exclusively with a suspicion of the state as a threat to individual freedoms and far less with intermediate institutions that leave Americans more dependent on the family, charities, and communities in civil society than is the case in Sweden.

The extent of this difference between the United States and Sweden was brought home to us very clearly when we applied for financial aid from US universities. To be eligible for support, we had to disclose not only our own but also our parents' economic resources. This felt very strange. As we saw it, we were grown-up, if young, independent adults, and our relationships to our parents, not least the economic ones, were nobody's business but our own. The reason we saw it this way was that in Sweden, state grants and loans are given to students as autonomous individuals and not as dependent family members. As a consequence, in Sweden neither parents nor spouses have any economic say in deciding whether someone goes to college and certainly no influence over whether they major in economics or study medieval ballads.

In this sense, "socialist" Sweden was more individualistic than the United States. This forced us to think more deeply about the different forms individualism can take. Our discussions gained further impetus in the 1990s when we both lived on and off in Germany. We came to realize that Germany differed from both Sweden and the United States. Germany's welfare system was almost as extensive as that in Sweden, but it was geared not toward the individual citizen but the family as a collective unit. At the same time, Germany also presented a contrast to the United States in that the state was considered not a threat to the family or to the intermediate institutions in civil society but, rather, a partner in the distribution of social rights such as education, health care, and elder care.

Ultimately, these rambling exchanges resulted in a book that was published in Sweden in 2006, *Är svensken männniska? Gemenskap och oberoende i det moderna Sverige* (a hard title to translate into English, but literally it means *Is the Swede Human? Community and Independence in Modern Sweden*). The primary subject of the study was Swedish political culture, but our approach was informed by a comparative perspective based on our experiences in the United States and Germany. It was received favorably and went into several reprints.

In 2015 we published a new edition with an added chapter on religion and the legacy of the Lutheran State Church; this edition was also translated into German as *Ist der Schwede ein Mensch?* with the somewhat anodyne subtitle *Was wir von unseren nordischen Nachbarn lernen können und wo wir uns in ihnen täuschen* (*What We Can Learn from Our Nordic Neighbors and What We Have Misunderstood about Them*).

In this English translation, we have with some minor exceptions resisted the temptation to revise the 2006 original text beyond the additions made in the 2015 edition. Readers may thus sometimes sense that the book was conceived and largely written in happier and more optimistic times. The exception is the coda, where we speculate about the future of the Swedish social contract and take the liberty of revisiting our historical account in the light of some of the defining tendencies of the last decade, including increasing inequality, refugee migration, political polarization, and the rise of nationalist and anti-immigrant parties in both Europe and the United States.

INTRODUCTION

*Humanity's Asocial Sociability and
the Swedish Paradox*

It was confusing. When the novel coronavirus hit the world in the spring of 2020, Sweden of all countries chose to ignore the global consensus in favor of lockdowns and severe restrictions. More known for its interventionist welfare policies, Sweden suddenly seemed to have become a European version of Texas by putting individual liberty before the collective good. The liberal *New York Times* dubbed it a "pariah state" and accused Swedish politicians and health officials of keeping Sweden open for economic reasons. At the other end of the political spectrum, right-wing American radicals who demonstrated against government restrictions carried signs calling for their leaders to follow Sweden's example. Perplexing to all, the spectacle—or specter—of a "libertarian welfare state" loomed.

This story is not new but a reversal of an old one. Traditionally the left has held up Sweden as a beacon of social solidarity while the right has lamented the lack of individual freedom. Now Dr. Jekyll had turned into Mr. Hyde—or maybe the other way around, depending on one's political inclinations.

But was it really such a dramatic turnabout? There was always something simplistic about the presentations of Sweden in the US and elsewhere as a model for egalitarianism and social engineering. Though an interpretation ready-made for progressive politics, it has seldom been based on any deeper understanding of Swedish history and culture. Nor does it seem very likely that the libertarians waving yellow-and-blue flags realized that individual liberty in Sweden is made possible not in opposition to a strong state but through an embrace of the world's highest tax rates.

In this book we try to unravel the paradox of Sweden as the home of a curious breed of social(ist) individualists. We argue that Sweden never was the socialist paradise it was long portrayed as nor the libertarian haven that it has been made out to be today. In reality, Sweden is sui generis. Instead of choosing one narrative over another, we try to untangle the complex interplay between historical myth and fact that has formed the Sweden of today.

The central point of departure of our analysis is the tug-of-war between two powerful human impulses: the desire for individual sovereignty and the unavoidable necessity of being part of society. To describe this condition, the eighteenth-century German philosopher Immanuel Kant coined a phrase that has since become a classic concept in social thought: *die ungesellige Geselligkeit*, asocial sociability. We humans, he claimed, have an innate impulse to associate with our own kind. We must be part of a community, not merely to survive but in order to develop our innate abilities. But this requirement, both ethical and necessary, also elicits from the individual a kind of resistance that threatens to dissolve the community.

All human beings, Kant argued, have a predisposition to isolate themselves, rooted in a desire to "arrange everything according to their own fancy." And yet this contradiction is not merely some tragic circumstance that condemns humanity to unending unhappiness. In fact, as the influential nineteenth-century Swedish philosopher and historian Erik Gustaf Geijer forcefully observed, movement between community and autonomy serves to strengthen each element: "The more individuals seek to detach themselves, the more acutely they feel the baleful nature of this necessity, which, even under conditions of reciprocal hatred, forces them to forge ever-closer bonds of mutual dependence."

Confronted by this existential paradox, all societies have sought to find a balance between the imperative of social virtues and the individual's desire for freedom. The solutions offered to this universal dilemma have differed around the world. Some societies have erred on the side of social and political control, minimizing individual freedom. Others have sought to diminish state interference in the private domain and have instead placed their trust in the market as well as in families and the voluntary associations that make up civil society. Sweden is of interest because, we claim, it has created a social contract embracing a strong state in the service of individual autonomy. Without compromising in either way, it has embraced the Kantian paradox.

We have chosen to study this social contract from two directions. At the institutional level, we try to trace the building of institutions at the societal level. We seek to show that the hallmark of modern Sweden—which is not so much a model as a historical product—is its claims to offer citizens freedom from the traditional bonds of community without jeopardizing the moral order of society. In a seeming paradox, it tries to combine high levels of social trust and a faith in collective institutions with an affirmation of individual autonomy that is sometimes taken to an extreme. The name we give to this alliance between state and individual, between community and autonomy, is *statist individualism*.

At the existential level, we try to show what makes this order of things attractive to ordinary citizens at the individual level. After all, the institution building we study has largely coincided with Sweden's democratization, itself a gradual process including at first only men, then later women, children, elderly, and individuals who had hitherto been excluded on the grounds of ethnicity, sexuality, or (dis)ability. While elites who at times fashioned themselves as social engineers played a role, they were not free to act as they pleased since they were subject to frequent electoral judgment. Popular support for this social contract is, we argue, premised on a widespread belief in the importance of being independent of other people, of being autonomous and not subordinate or made indebted—whether that debt be economic, emotional, or social. At the heart of this conviction is the idea that true love and friendship—indeed, any authentic relationship—is built not on mutual dependence but on equality, freedom of choice, and autonomy. We call this *the Swedish theory of love*.

While this book is not formally comparative, we nonetheless examine Sweden from an international perspective, principally in relation to Germany and the United States. These countries, which we know relatively well, offer convenient examples of two distinct moral and political logics that differ in illuminating ways from those of Sweden. On the other hand, while there is much than unites Sweden with Finland, Denmark, and Norway, and while any insistence of national peculiarity always carries a whiff of what Sigmund Freud once called "the narcissism of minor differences," we nonetheless restrict ourselves to writing about Sweden. To be sure, there is a large body of writing on the Nordic model, but these four countries also exhibit important differences and divergences from each other, especially in recent decades—for example, in how they organize social investments (schools, elder care, health care), their politics and policies around immigration and integration, and, most recently, their responses to the COVID-19 pandemic. The case for analyzing Sweden's peculiarity is, if anything, stronger than ever.

The book is organized in three sections. Part 1, "Anatomy of a Nation," outlines our theoretical and analytical framework, with a focus on statist individualism and the Swedish theory of love. Part 2, "Sweden Imagined," traces a national narrative that is, fundamentally, more utopian than reflective of actual institutions and social practices, even if we also point to the legacies of *longue durée* social practices and political structures. These are conceptions of rule of law, of social equality and individual freedom, of children's rights, and of equality between men and women that prefigure and enable later developments. Part 3, "Sweden Realized," turns to the modern embodiment of this imagined community of individual citizens, of the "citizens' home," as the prominent Swedish Prime Minister Per Albin Hansson put it in a famous speech in 1928.[1] This state-building endeavor culminated in an era of radical reform during the 1970s that has ever since been the object of equally vigorous defenses and challenges. In the book's coda, we attempt to take stock and ponder the difficult question of whether this experiment has run its course or remains vital.

PART I

Anatomy of a Nation

CHAPTER I

The People of Nifelheim

In 1946, a slim contribution to the fledgling discipline of cultural psychology asked a provocative question in its title: *Är svensken människa?* (*Is the Swede a Human?*) Its author, a journalist named Sanfrid Neander-Nilsson, dissected Sweden's national character in a succession of chapters with headings like "A People with Ice in their Hearts," "A Divorcing People," and "Do Swedes Hate Children?" His conclusions were grim. "Outside of the major cities," he declares, "the Swedish psyche is mostly dominated by its forest."[1]

Neander-Nilsson likened Swedes to a psychopath whose peculiar moral fabric is "different in kind to that of a normal modern person." Swedes are reluctant to initiate contact, he explained, they suffer agonies of shyness, they are boring, they find life tedious, and their vital impulse largely boils down to a capacity for enduring. Beneath Swedes' icy facade, as he saw it, there lay a dread of fellow human beings, an incomprehensible disinclination to "interact with other people, of whatever kind and of both sexes."[2]

Neander-Nilsson was no less damning about the excruciating efforts of Swedish men and women at love and romance. As he saw it, Swedish men were boorish icy lumps, mere blond Nietzschean beasts. Swedish women were dull animals, passive and sensually frigid, whose lovemaking was a chilly vice rehearsed in an emotional Arctic. He despairingly compared the unvarnished, ice-cold mechanics of Swedish desire with the spontaneity of Latin liaisons. But the worst aspect of this emotional coldness was its consequences for Swedish children. The issue was not simply that "children represent an economic burden for modern people living in a two-room apartment" but that Swedes were peculiar in this respect.[3] It was not a coincidence, Neander-Nilsson claimed, that Swedish, alone of all languages, lacked diminutives—terms of endearment for innocent children—but the symptom of a far deeper problem.

To illustrate his point, Neander-Nilsson related a story that had appeared in the house magazine of the Swedish Population League. It concerned a man who gave notice to his tenant because the latter had refused to tether his son in the backyard (the landlord seems to have been upset by the boy leaving footprints in freshly raked sand). Neander-Nilsson saw the landlord's reaction as typically Swedish. In much the same way as this particular man clearly hated children, he argued, "the entire Swedish people apparently hates children as a whole." With an eye to the Swedish Population League's aim of raising the birth rate, he concluded by asking whether it "is really so strange that so few children are born in a country where the majority of the population dislike children so heartily." The situation was dire. "It is easy to be a dog or a cow in Sweden," Neander-Nilsson declared, "but very hard indeed to be a child."[4]

PROUD AND SHY

Neander-Nilsson had no great love for modern individualism. By the time he wrote *Is the Swede a Human?* he was in his late forties with a patchy career behind him as a journalist and author. As a newly qualified young archaeologist, he had worked as a secretary at the Swedish Institute in Rome in the 1920s. The advent of fascism affected him profoundly, and in the interwar years he published a number of positive accounts of Mussolini's Italy and Hitler's Third Reich. His political sympathies lay with the National League of Sweden (Sveriges nationella förbund), a radical right-wing movement that had broken with the Conservative Party (Högerpartiet), and he went on to promote the league's agenda as both journalist and editor at a number of conservative Swedish dailies.

Even after the end of the Second World War, Neander-Nilsson found it difficult to dissociate himself from the Nazis' blood-and-soil philosophy. The Swedish people, he insisted, had a natural closeness to the forest and deep ties of blood and, when forced to live in cities, were tormented by feelings of despondency: "It is the very relationship to blood and nature, the very sense of blood ties and origins, all that great complex accompanying people's purely physical, natural mode of reproduction which has been subjected to crisis on a mass scale in modern, industrialized Sweden." At the time he wrote his book, he declared Swedes "are unhappy people" who "long to return to nature and the earth, to the warmth of blood and the protection and security of family bonds."[5]

By 1946, this analysis was no longer original. Indeed, Neander-Nilsson's notions of Swedishness were merely the latest incarnation of a far older tradition. Since the early 1800s, when the loss of Finland had established the eastern borders of modern Sweden, authors and intellectuals had used up barrels of ink in trying to describe the qualities that defined the inhabitants of the eastern province of the Scandinavian peninsula. Throughout the nineteenth and early-twentieth centuries, the debate was enlivened by contributions from a succession of cultural luminaries, including Erik Gustaf Geijer, Carl Jonas Love Almqvist, August Strindberg, Ellen Key, and Verner von Heidenstam.[6]

Thus Neander-Nilsson's 1946 critique of Swedish social incompetence built on an earlier discussion of Swedish temperament whose prime mover had been a professor at Uppsala University named Gustaf Sundbärg (figure 1.1). In 1911, Sundbärg published *Det svenska folklynnet* (*The Swedish Temperament*), a book that claimed to define the Swedish national character. According to Sundbärg, who was a statistician by training, Swedish people were characterized by a series of attributes, each of which had both a positive and a negative aspect: inflexible but fair; envious but honest; solitary but independent; shy but proud.[7]

Their most characteristic feature, however, was a deep love of nature, the oft-noted Swedish longing for deserted pine forests and remote woodland streams. This intense relationship with nature was the corollary of their tepid attitude toward other people: "we Swedes love and are interested in nature but not in other people."[8] After itemizing these virtues and failings, Sundbärg decided that the negatives outweighed the positives: there was a lack of joy in Sweden that prompted its citizens to leave their native land in hopes of finding happiness in North America. (*The Swedish Temperament* was published as an appendix to a major enquiry into the causes behind emigration.)[9]

Sundbärg's dismal critique of Swedishness was part of a larger effort to pin down the national character during the turbulent years around the turn of the century, which were marked by the dissolution of the union with Norway and by growing unrest among the laboring masses.

ONE HUNDRED YEARS OF SWEDISH SOLITUDE

1911

1946

1968

1971

2001

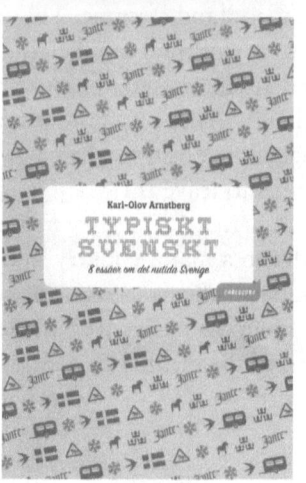
2005

Numerous commentators were expanding upon the basic idea that Swedes had difficulty forming relationships with other people. The more lyrical expressions of this sentiment included Oscar Levertin's gloomy poem "Folket i Nifelheim" ("The People in Nifelheim"), which explains that

> Love is not the song of freedom
> but a sadness shared.
> At once proud and shy,
> The best carry it alone.[10]

In the decades that followed, a string of authors were to develop this uncompromising view of Swedish love and sense of community. In his 1915 study *Folklynnen* (*The National Character*), which ran to nine editions, art historian Carl Laurin followed Sundbärg in counterposing an affinity for nature to an understanding of people. It was "the desire to be entirely one's own" that drove Swedes into the countryside, an expression of their "irrepressible individualism" and "unyielding desire for freedom." This also held true of Swedes who had emigrated to North America. As Abram Ottey declared in 1940 in *The Swedish Race in America*, "Swedish people are known to be individualists. Individualism is one of their defining character traits."[11]

Debates over Swedish national character were often relatively politically innocent in the 1920s, more a topic for chatty articles and literary observations than a matter of identity and national destiny. The conflict between Swedes' love of nature and their love of other people also provided ready material for more lighthearted treatment. In his 1929 volume *Svenskt* (*Swedish*), a physician named Gotthard Söderberg poked fun at Heidenstam's classic recollection of playing as a child on the rocks and cliffs by the sea: "few statements are more true than

---

FIGURE 1.1. Uppsala professor Gustaf Sundbärg's 1911 *Det svenska folklynnet* (*The Swedish Temperament*); journalist Sanfrid Neander-Nilsson's rather desperately titled *Är svensken människa?* (*Is the Swede a Human?*), published in 1946; Englishman Paul Britten Austin's 1968 *On Being Swedish*; British writer Roland Huntford's 1971 *The New Totalitarians* depicts Sweden as a cautionary tale with dystopian overtones; ethnologist Karl-Olov Arnstberg's 2005 essay collection *Typiskt svenskt* (*Typically Swedish*); economic historian Mauricio Rojas's 2001 book *I ensamhetens labyrint* (*In the Labyrinth of Loneliness*) describes the difficulties for those born into another culture but with extensive experience of normative Swedishness.

that Swedes love the stones of their native land. About other Swedes, by contrast, they have very mixed feelings."[12]

The bleaker international climate of the 1930s, including the sense of vulnerability felt by small countries, lent a sharper edge to the question of what constituted Swedishness. In keeping with the spirit of preparedness, commentators often underscored its more positive aspects: the Swedish national character united freedom and orderliness and combined a fierce sense of justice with a firm grasp of the value of individual liberty.

Still, this mood of brooding self-critique continued even during the war. In a 1944 study titled *Svensk Folkkaraktär* (*Swedish National Character*), psychologist and school inspector Georg Brandell took his point of departure in Sundbärg's thesis that Swedes lacked psychological insight and any interest in other people; indeed, Brandell himself admitted to feeling an impulse at the core of his being that he could describe only as *tillknäppthet* ("standoffishness"). But rather than focusing on Swedes' social ineptness, Brandell argued that this antisocial quality was grounded at a deeper level on their "powerful individualism." Swedes were characterized by an overwhelming need "to feel independent and free" and to be unconstrained by suffocating social ties.

Even so, he did not regard the impulse to be free as a uniformly positive character trait. On the contrary, Brandell was extremely concerned that the Nordic race's need for autonomy and freedom had assumed a form that now threatened its survival. The low birth rate, he argued, was deliberate, stemming from a desire to live an independent life free of children and family: "The desire for personal freedom can become so strong that it suppresses all feelings of interpersonal community."[13]

THE USUAL THING: LONELINESS

Shortly after the end of the Second World War, there appeared in 1946 a major essay collection titled *Lasternas bok: Våra kulturfel* (*The Book of Vices: Our Cultural Errors*) whose contributors included literary historian Staffan Björck and author Sven Stolpe. Björck's scathing survey of the image of Swedes in literature echoed Brandell closely: "Literature is awash with studies of lovelessness, the emptiness between man and woman. . . . The prig and the boor join hands in undermining all affection and cast a chill upon every spontaneous impulse."[14]

Testimony to the lack of tenderness among Swedish people was so abundant, Björck reflected, that it forced one to ask whether there was not some deficiency in the national character itself. Indeed, Swedes' love of animals not infrequently took precedence over their love for people. Björck cited novelist Ivar Lo-Johansson: "Swedes are a strange people who feel very strongly about protecting animals and the countryside but fundamentally do not care about people."[15]

However, the self-critical tone of *The Book of Vices* was suppressed, though not entirely extinguished, during the boom period of the welfare state between the 1950s and the mid-1970s. The idea of Swedes being devoid of love was instead taken up by foreign observers and researchers who had visited Sweden to study its successful welfare state. During an unhappy stay in Sweden in the 1960s, an Englishman named George Walton Scott became acquainted with a bleak and lonely land on the edge of Europe:

> The Swedes are a silent people, lost in the city. Their outward dullness, and their inward isolation create in a town like Stockholm a vacuum of human communication. Public manners in towns are for the most part atrocious, people push rudely on trams, and bump against you on the pavement without apology. Swedes have been unable to adapt themselves to urban life; they are not used to crowds.[16]

Another Englishman, Paul Britten Austin, drew heavily on Sundbärg for his 1968 description of Swedish culture: "Swedes love and are interested in nature, not other people." This, he argued, had a positive aspect: self-reliance and the ability to enjoy nature without others. But it was also negative in that it led to isolation and loneliness: "*Ensamhet*, loneliness, isolation. A vast Swedish theme, the aching, ubiquitous counterpart, one might say, to Swedish socialism." In support of this view, Austin quoted examples from Swedish culture, particularly the films of Ingmar Bergman. He held up as evidence the archetypal Bergmanesque figure of Isak Borg in *Wild Strawberries* (1957), who asks the Inquisitor what punishment he will be made to suffer for having withdrawn from human companionship. The Inquisitor replies, "The usual thing: loneliness."[17]

Austin was also inspired by a controversial American study titled *Suicide and Scandinavia* that appeared in 1964. Its author, Herbert Hendin, argued that Swedes, from early childhood to old age, were encouraged to be self-reliant and to regard work rather than social relations as the most important space for self-realization. Both social institutions and individual personalities reflected this deeply imprinted cultural practice. Hendin's perspective, which typified the so-called "culture and personality school" of which he was a leading exponent, led Austin in turn to postulate that much of what was thought to be highly modern about Sweden, such as its gender equality policies, was actually the ideological expression of a deeply rooted psychological preference.[18]

Hendin and Austin saw "the strange, self-isolating behavior of Swedes" as ultimately founded upon what Austin considered "certain inadequacies of the Swedish woman as a mother" and what Hendin located more generally in Swedish child-rearing practices.[19] The typically Swedish pattern that they believed they had discovered involved the early separation of mother and child, coupled with the encouragement of self-sufficiency and independence in even very young children. As Hendin explained, this affected Sweden's family policies: "For instance, if Swedes build more and more daycare centers for working mothers, this does not mean that they regard themselves as creating better citizens by separating mothers and children. Rather, it is the case that the Swedish state is responding to women's needs and demands, since they want to go back to work as soon as possible after having children."[20]

In the 1980s and 1990s, studies with a comparative dimension likewise foregrounded the importance that Swedes placed on self-reliance and autonomy. According to Åke Daun, who published a work titled *Svensk mentalitet* (*Swedish Mentality*) in 1989, this aspect was particularly apparent in studies of child rearing and pedagogy. Things treated as self-evident in Sweden—for example, that the concept of social competence means "children's ability to manage on their own"—are deeply alien in southern Europe, Daun argued, where people find it difficult to imagine that children can find happiness anywhere outside of the framework of the family.[21] Ethnologist Karl-Olov Arnstberg offered a similar analysis in his 2005 essay collection *Typiskt svenskt* (*Typically Swedish*), in which he examined the debate that arose when children's income was factored into the assessment of a family's entitlement to social welfare. Opponents frequently argued that the inclusion of such earnings in a family's total income would undermine young people's sense of autonomy.[22]

The premium that Swedes place on self-sufficiency has also been remarked on by researchers within the discipline of family studies. In *Autonomy and Dependence in the Family*, an anthology published in 2002, scholars from Sweden and Turkey compared the ways in which interpersonal dependence within the family is viewed in their respective countries. According to Elisabeth Özdalga, Sweden is characterized by a strong preference for individual autonomy, the institutional basis for which takes the form of state-financed welfare programs.[23] Another scholar, Lennart Stridsberg, observed the same pattern in the business sphere. After comparing American and Swedish entrepreneurs, he concluded that the latter regard the pursuit of self-sufficiency as more important: "Having a large personal fortune is far more important in the United States than it is in Sweden, while personal independence is far more important in Sweden than it is in the United States. In 1988, a study was conducted into the dominant motive for entrepreneurs in eleven different countries. For Swedes, independence—the desire to be able to make all decisions oneself—was paramount."[24]

At least since the 1990s, Sweden's transformation into a country of immigrants has generated a great many descriptions and analyses by observers born into another culture but with extensive experience of normative Swedishness. Here, too, a recurrent theme is the paradoxical individualism of their adoptive country's native inhabitants. In his polemical 2001 book *I ensamhetens labyrint* (*In the Labyrinth of Loneliness*), economic historian and politician Mauricio Rojas described the difficulty of decoding Swedish social norms: "Social conformity is no joke, it is the ideological cement of the community, its price and precondition. The result is a peculiar combination of a very strong attitude towards freedom and territoriality with an equally strong attachment to a community that sets limits and boundaries even while acting as guarantor for that freedom. It is a balancing act between public collectivism and private individualism, groupthink and asserting one's territory, that is extremely difficult for outsiders to understand and master."[25]

In the same vein, the national daily newspaper *Svenska Dagbladet* ran a major feature article in spring 1998 under the headline "The Peculiar Swedes." The article's author had addressed "the foreigners who live in our country" and asked the question, What defines Swedes? The captions to the photographs of the immigrants being interviewed pithily conveyed their view of Sweden: "Unfathomable need for solitude," "Emotionally inaccessible and brooding," "Extreme individualists," "Formal and systematic." One non-native respondent characterized what she called "the Swedish paradox" as "an extraordinarily individualistic society where people are at the same time hugely dependent upon the state. How can anyone hold two such different perspectives in their head at the same time?"²⁶

In autumn 2005, another national newspaper, *Dagens Nyheter*, published a series of articles on the lack of social contacts between immigrants and native Swedes, in which the authors also discussed the considerable frustration at Swedish unsociability. Immigrants who had lived in Sweden for a long time explained that it was nothing personal: Swedes simply didn't socialize much outside their immediate family. One of those interviewed pointed out that in his home country, where many people ran businesses and shops in order to make ends meet, it was imperative to have a broad contact network. In Sweden, it was possible to manage without, which had at least one advantage: "If a Swede wants to be my friend, I know that he or she really likes me. They're not trying to sell me something."²⁷

ASOCIAL SOCIABILITY

There is a recurrent, if not always visible, theme in these analyses of Swedishness: an individualism that boils down to a desire for independence, which at certain times is venerated as a noble-minded desire for freedom but at other times is accused of being an expression of pathological unsociableness. In the words of Ludvig Nordström, romancer of the Viking era, national virtues and national vices are an interplay of "sun and ice in continual growth and continual flux."²⁸

Such ambivalence about the choice between the individual and the collective is hardly exclusive to Sweden. Underlying all writing on national character is the existential dilemma of humanity: the choice between freedom and community. It is an ever-present theme in the Western tradition from Homer to *The Sopranos*. But there is also a political aspect to this conflict: how can a society best strike a balance between these two impulses? From the eighteenth century onward, this question became a pressing social-philosophical issue, thanks in particular to the German Enlightenment philosopher Immanuel Kant.

Kant formulated one of history's most revolutionary ideas: human beings are wholly independent moral subjects. Previous moral philosophers had ascribed to human beings a moral responsibility, the capacity to act for good or for evil. Kant went further, arguing that individuals had the capacity to make their own laws—and for that very reason had a powerful incentive to be law-abiding. This categorical imperative—"act only according to that maxim whereby you can at the same time will that it should become a universal law"—forms the basis of an autonomous morality in which the individual alone must decide what is right or wrong in each particular situation. It is freedom, yes, but freedom with obligations: human beings are, by virtue of their reason, predestined to create law and order in the world. There is a radical notion of equality here, as well as a civic perspective. Kant came from a humble background—his father was a saddle maker—and, despising hierarchies and servility, held up as an ideal the equal, independent individual governed by reason.[29]

But if people were trying to achieve autonomy, how had society come about? For Kant, it was the result of our *asocial sociability*. There is, he argued, a force that drives people to form communities. At the same time, this force is also bound up with a constant and reciprocal resistance that threatens to dissolve the community. We are born with an impulse to attach ourselves to others of our kind. By joining a community, individuals have a greater chance of developing their innate capacities. However, Kant explained further:

> Man has also a marked propensity to *isolate* himself, because he finds in himself the asocial quality to want to arrange everything according to his own ideas. He therefore expects resistance everywhere, just as he knows that he is inclined to resist others. This resistance awakens all the latent forces in man which drive him to overcome his propensity to be lazy, and so, impelled by vainglory, ambition and avarice, he seeks to achieve a standing among his fellows, whom he does not suffer gladly, but whom he cannot *leave*.[30]

And yet, Kant argued, this is not bad news. It was this very asocial sociability that led human beings to take their first steps from barbarism to culture. Over time, the struggle to remain independent despite being part of a community forces people to realize all of their inherent faculties and talents. As it becomes increasingly enlightened, humanity develops its primitive capacity for moral judgment into practically applicable principles, which are ultimately sufficient to form an overarching social morality. From these conflicts emerges a social contract, a *constitution*, which limits citizens' freedoms even as it enables them to coexist peacefully. Kant compared society to a forest: because the trees are competing for sunlight and air, they force one other to search for both elements, with the result that they develop fine, straight trunks.

To read the body of literature on Swedish national character with Kant's notion of asocial sociability in mind is to see the emergence of a political pattern that does not conform to the familiar explanations provided by anthropology and the history of mentalities. There is every reason to be skeptical about speculative claims about stable national characters, even when these are cloaked in the jargon of modern cultural anthropology. But if, so far as is possible, we peel away the normative assertions about which attributes are good and which are bad, what remains is a body of writing on Swedishness that stubbornly—indeed, almost frenetically—wrestles with the Kantian opposition between individual and community: the desire to order everything according to one's own will, and the need to join forces with other like-minded individuals.

The literature on Swedish national character tells a story that is both problematic and potentially tragic-heroic. For Swedes, the ideal state is a Robinson Crusoe–like existence in nature, living as an autonomous individual, free from both mutual dependency and the common considerateness required by close intercourse with others. Yet this is an impossible ideal. Swedish culture and the survival of the nation demand that its solitary inhabitants overcome their solitariness and longing for freedom and come together to form the social bonds that are needed for society to function. At this point a seemingly invisible conflict appears: Swedes must either abandon their own nature in order to adapt to the demands of society or persist in their futile efforts to achieve autonomy within the framework of family and community, efforts that risk driving them into alcoholism and abject melancholy.

The Kantian solution to this conflict is a social contract, an agreement expressed in institutions and founded on the rule of law, regulating the relationship between individual and community. It is also, we argue in the chapters that follow, the answer to the tragic dilemma identified in the literature on Swedish national character. As with all beloved children, the Swedish social contract goes by several different names: *folkhemmet* ("the people's home"), the Swedish Model, and the social-democratic welfare state. Fundamentally, all these concepts are attempts to describe the local institutional solution to humanity's asocial sociability that has developed in a small country on the northern edge of Europe.

We are not claiming that this challenge is unique to Sweden—on the contrary, the problem is universal, and similar solutions exist in other countries. Even so, we argue in this book that the conflict between autonomy and community has been formulated with rare clarity in the debates over the historical and cultural peculiarities of Swedes. This has led in turn to a series of institutional solutions realized systematically in the modern Swedish welfare state, which to a great degree have been designed to ensure the citizens' independence from each other. In the following chapters, our focus therefore shifts from suggestive but fanciful depictions of national character toward more robust expressions of Swedishness—the state, the law—the fundamental institutions that order the mutual relationships between citizens in contemporary Sweden.

CHAPTER 2

Statist Individualism

On the face of it, the defining feature of Sweden's political tradition presents a curious paradox. For all its talk of individual freedoms, the dominance of the Swedish state has been such that historians have sometimes treated it as one of the first and most fully realized examples of an absolute state. Particularly among critical observers of modern Sweden, it is a commonplace that the country's political culture is remarkably *statist*.

In his controversial 1971 book *The New Totalitarians*, British writer Roland Huntford complained about Swedes' worship of the state. Here was a people, he argued, who had voluntarily given up their freedom in exchange for state-guaranteed security and soulless material prosperity. Instead of cherishing democracy and individual freedom, Swedes had gladly placed control of the state in the hands of bureaucrats: "Modern Sweden has fulfilled Aldous Huxley's specifications for the new totalitarianism. A centralized administration rules people who love their servitude, so that technology may be efficiently exploited."[1]

Among foreign commentators, Huntford was far from alone in taking this view. Even those, typically on the left, who took a more balanced view regarded Swedes' enthusiasm for the state as naive. In a 1982 essay titled "Swedish Autumn," the distinguished German journalist Hans Magnus Enzensberger argued that Swedes were the most submissive people in the world. Their faith in governing bodies and other institutions of the state would be unthinkable for the French, Spanish, Italians, or Irish. Even Germans had learned to be suspicious of governmental authorities.[2]

Both Huntford and Enzensberger approached the Swedish social contract as having its starting point in specific cultural values. From a British or a German perspective, however, the Swedish mixture of freedom and conformity is somewhat confusing. In this chapter, we compare the relationship between individual and state in Sweden, Germany, and the United States in order to reveal the inner dynamic of Sweden's political culture, a phenomenon that we call *statist individualism*.[3]

STATE AND CIVIL SOCIETY IN SWEDEN

While not everyone would go as far as Huntford, the perception of the Swedish state as exceptionally powerful has a long pedigree, even within the country's own borders. As early as 1946—well before the 1930s vision of a Swedish welfare model (*folkhemmet*, literally "a home for the people") had become "the strong society" of the 1960s—the influential political scientist and future conservative leader Gunnar Heckscher described Sweden in terms of "corporatism." The twentieth century, he explained, had seen the emergence of a new "social type, less individualistic and more oriented towards cooperation with other individuals and society."[4]

Although Heckscher was careful to differentiate Sweden from dictatorships like fascist Italy, the label "corporatism," with its connotations of a dominant state, stuck. Forty years after Heckscher's analysis, another prominent political scientist, Bo Rothstein, published a study tellingly entitled *Den korporativa staten* (*The Corporatist State*). Like Heckscher, Rothstein stressed that the (more or less) free organizations played a major role in the Swedish variety of democratic corporatism. Nonetheless, it was obvious that the state played the central role: the state represented the general interests of society, which were accorded greater moral dignity than the private concerns and organized special interests that operated freely within civil society.

Notwithstanding these accounts of a state-dominated and corporatist political order, the image has endured of Sweden as a popular democracy whose historical foundations are both broad and deep. One might even speak of a Swedish "exceptionalism," akin to the narratives invoked by Americans and British commentators when explaining the unique character of their own democracies. Enthusiasts like to claim that personal freedom and local self-governance in Sweden are so deeply rooted that the country represents a haven for freedom and democracy in the world. In the 1930s and '40s, commentators routinely traced an unbroken line from medieval peasant uprisings to more-modern national movements. On this reading, Heckscher's and Rothstein's corporatist state takes on the appearance of a popular democratic movement. According to Hilding Johansson—political scientist, Social Democrat, and contemporary of Heckscher—the idea of corporatism was highly misleading in that it underestimated the strength of the popular movements and exaggerated the sovereignty of the state: "In Sweden these organizations are free and self-governing. Most immediately, they pursue their own goals and safeguard the interests of their members. Collaboration with the state is optional."[5]

There are political consequences to whether one views Sweden as a heavily centralized state or an example of responsible and popular self-government. But beyond the rhetoric, and as many scholars have realized, the two perspectives are not mutually exclusive. Ultimately, Johansson and Heckscher agree more than they disagree, since both describe a peaceful coexistence between a strong state and a vital popular democratic movement. Indeed, Sweden seems to give the lie to the idea that the struggle between state and civil society has to be a zero-sum game: a strong state need not necessarily undermine its people's capacity for self-organization.[6]

The contrast is clear when Sweden is compared to other Western countries where the state attracts far greater suspicion and where relations between state, society, and individual have evolved in far more conflictual fashion. What makes Sweden so different? To answer this question, we need to consider developments in two countries that have historically had a major influence on Swedish culture and are often cited in international comparisons: the United States and Germany.

FREEDOM FROM WHOM?

American democracy has its origins in a revolt against the efforts of the British Crown to suppress religious minorities and freethinkers. From Pennsylvania's Quakers to Utah's Mormons, American history has been shaped by the struggle for religious freedom, initially against the Church of England and, later, through the establishment of a political order that limited the power of the newly formed American state over religious communities. Of equal importance was the struggle for freedom from state intervention in the economic sphere, a conflict epitomized by the Boston Tea Party, an endlessly mythologized tax revolt in which sixty disaffected Americans, disguised as Indians, threw hundreds of crates of English tea into the waters of Boston harbor.[7]

The feud between state and civil society in America was also the culmination of a protracted historical conflict in Europe. In England and France, the struggle between king and aristocracy found ideological expression in the development of liberalism. In the spirit of John Locke and Montesquieu, the framework of the American state would be defined by the principle of a division of powers and the desire to heavily restrict the state's power. The best government, Thomas Jefferson explained, was that which prevented its citizens from harming each other but which otherwise let them settle their differences in peace and did not take food out of the mouths of working men. This classical liberal intellectual tradition, based on theories of the primacy of the individual and of property, was thereby fused with another political tradition, that of civic humanism.

Although civic humanism was similarly founded on the ownership of property, it placed greater emphasis on social responsibility and community. Private property was understood as a process of *Bildung*, character formation, rather than as a goal in itself. The sovereign figure here was not the atomized citizen of liberalism but the socially constituted individual who worked for others in a republic of virtue. The history of the United States hinges on a series of recurrent conflicts that can all be traced back to the War of Independence: an attempt to decentralize power, to protect the family and the local community from incursions by the state, to protect locally rooted religious values against the corrupted "reforms" of worldly state authorities. In the words of American historian Barry Allan Shain, "The vast majority of Americans lived voluntarily in morally demanding agricultural communities shaped by Protestant social and moral norms ... defined by overlapping circles of family and community-assisted self-regulation and even self-denial, rather than individual autonomy."[8]

At the heart of this tradition lie the freedoms that states and local communities enjoy with regard to Washington, DC, the seat of the central administration. The rhetorical force of this mistrust of centralized power is considerable. A classic example is the American Civil War. Although a relatively united body of historians regard the issue of slavery as the war's root cause, there are still Southerners who maintain that the real bone of contention was interference by the central authority in states' rights.[9] This struggle points to a fundamental feature of American political culture: the individualism inherent to the ethos of the United States in no way precludes the existence of a firmly held sense of *Gemeinschaft* (community) in the traditional European mold.

Individualism in the United States has primarily been a question of independence, not from other people but from governmental authority. The state is viewed with great suspicion, while emphasis on the inviolability of the private sphere has turned into the individual's comprehensive freedom from the state in the form of negative individual rights and freedoms. At the same time, American individualism has led to citizens becoming more dependent on other, nonstate collective forms: the family, religious communities, charitable organizations, and other more or less organized groups in society.

A comparison of Swedish and American civil societies makes it clear that the differences go beyond mere political rhetoric. Considered as a whole, Sweden and the United States are comparable: both countries rank highly when it comes to social capital and the vitality of civil society. Yet major differences emerge when those figures are examined more closely. Trade unions and sports clubs dominate in Sweden, but in the United States it is the religious communities and social charities that stand out most clearly in the cloud of statistics.[10]

Germany's federal and pluralistic system, which is guided by the principle of subsidiarity, can be traced back to the Thirty Years' War. The ensuing peace treaty established that the Holy Roman Empire should be defined by a weak central power, federalism, extensive local self-determination, and religious diversity.[11] After the unification of Germany in 1871, Otto von Bismarck and his national-liberal Protestant allies sought to nationalize the country with respect to both religion and economy. However, as Britain's ambassador remarks in a dispatch from that period, Bismarck had completely misjudged the power of the Vatican. Despite Bismarck's unwillingness to compromise, the Roman Catholic Church in Germany survived his anti-Catholic policies, the so-called *Kulturkampf*, with its rights intact. Since the 1880s, German domestic policy has continued to be defined by this tension between a central authority and various local, states', church, and private interests.[12] Indeed, Hitler's twelve years in power are the only historical period in which Germany has been a centralized unitary state.

The German tradition has even less to do with individual autonomy than is the case with its American counterpart. Instead, center stage is occupied by the family and the church. In contrast to Sweden's welfare state, the social contract in Germany has been dominated by the corporate bodies in society, a feature that extends not only to traditional religious interests but even the labor movement. The latter has also had a far more antagonistic relationship with the state, not only under Hitler but also during the critical formative period at the end of the nineteenth century when Bismarck's antisocialist laws led to the labor movement being organized as an autonomous "alternative culture" within civil society.[13]

In her autobiography *Bortom de sju bergen* (*Beyond the Seven Hills*), Kaj Fölster, a daughter of the Swedish social scientists Gunnar and Alva Myrdal who settled in Germany, described her encounter with the voluntary sector of the federal republic: "I discover that it is not, as they say, mainly something to which well-heeled ladies with ample leisure time devote themselves, but a truly powerful labor tradition that has deeply influenced German history, particularly in times of adversity."[14]

Individuals in Germany are seen as members of various kinds of preexisting collective entities. The state's relationship to them is indirect and communicated via intermediary institutions that are often private: the family as a legal and economic entity, voluntary organizations (including churches), private insurance companies, and companies as educational bodies (the famous German apprenticeship system). Social care is often managed, in other words, by the organs of civil society. Only in the final instance—if all else fails—can the individual approach the state, often with begging bowl in hand.

SWEDISH KINGS AND PEASANTS

Power struggles between the state, the church, the aristocracy, and the capital-owning class have been central to the political cultures of Germany and the United States. In Sweden, the nobility and the bourgeoisie never succeeded in dominating to the same degree.

Even before the formation of the modern Swedish state, the so-called Engelbrekt uprising (after its leader, Engelbrekt Engelbrektsson) between 1434 and 1436 had established the Swedish peasantry as a political force to be reckoned with. This historical lesson was not lost on the Swedish nobleman Gustav Vasa, who in 1520 headed an insurrection against the Union of Kalmar that bound Sweden, Denmark, and Norway together. To mobilize troops, he traveled around Sweden and roused the sturdy peasants—or so the story goes—to join his fight against the Union's King Christian II in Copenhagen. A gifted propagandist, Gustav Vasa styled himself as champion of the Swedish peasants against their foreign oppressors. With their help, he eventually defeated the Danes and established an independent Swedish state in 1521. He became a powerful monarch, not unlike his contemporary King Henry VIII of England, and nationalized the Church, curtailed the power of the nobility, and imposed—somewhat ungratefully—heavy taxes on the peasantry.

Indeed, Swedish monarchs of the early modern period would, like Gustav Vasa, prove to be fickle friends of the peasants. During the reign of Queen Christina in the first half of the seventeenth century, large tracts of Crown lands tended by tax-paying peasants were granted to nobles for military service or just out of favoritism. For a while, it seemed that Sweden was well on its way toward a classical feudal system. On the other hand, this tendency was checked by the so-called Reduction of King Charles XI in the 1680s when Parliament gave him the power to confiscate noble estates, thereby breaking the power of the aristocracy.

These complexities did not stop the launching of a romantic national narrative, most prominently associated with the historian Erik Gustaf Geijer, of the Swedish state as founded on an alliance between the good king and the free peasants. Like most national narratives it was a mixture of myth and fact. While it is an essential task for the historian to untangle what is true and false in these narratives,[15] it is equally essential to study them as important historical artifacts in themselves, not least since they have proven both durable and politically potent. This idea of Sweden as a homeland of freedom and democracy over time became so enshrined in the literature and history books that any politician hoping to speak for the nation had to operate within this precisely configured discursive field in order to stand any chance of political success.[16]

Furthermore, even as we accept the discursive nature of these narratives, we must also recognize the limits placed on their inventiveness by concrete practices and institutions. The absence of serfdom and the consequent political power of the peasants in Sweden is not, after all, to be dismissed out of hand as a mere discursive figure. Specialists of the early modern period have stressed the advantageous position of the Swedish peasants in a comparative European perspective. As the

British historian Michel Roberts put it, "It may well be that the idealization of the yeoman peasant by such writers as E. G. Geijer has been proved to have but a shaky historical basis," yet in the final analysis "it is still safe to say that the peasant in mediaeval Sweden retained his social and political freedom to a greater degree, played a greater part in the politics of the country, and was altogether a more considerable person, than in any other western European country."[17]

This is not least evidenced by the fact that the traditional social order in Sweden counted four political classes rather than the three that were the norm in most European countries. From 1527, the Swedish Parliament consisted of four so-called estates: nobles, priests, burghers—and peasants. Their political representation in Parliament made it possible for the peasants to form alliances with the king, based on their common suspicion of the nobility and its dual political agenda of, on the one hand, diminishing the power of the king and, on the other, of enslaving the peasants.

Paradoxically, the crown's supremacy rested on what might be called, with only slight exaggeration, a protodemocratic political order. In Eva Österberg's concise formulation, this was less a cult of action than a culture of transaction.[18] The strength of the peasant estate had its counterpart in "the sad history of the Swedish nobility," as the historian and journalist Maciej Zaremba called it in an insightful essay about the "discreet charm" of the self-governing village community and its influence on the conception of democracy that now characterizes the political culture of Sweden's welfare state.[19]

While the nobility may have had a less prominent role in Sweden, the other potential representative of the power-sharing principle had, if anything, even more dismal prospects. In the wake of the Reformation, the crown's rapid and highly successful subjugation of the church allowed the state to effectively transform the Swedish church into a proxy for its own interests. Meanwhile, in Catholic countries and to some extent Britain, the church continued to represent a countervailing force against the state.

Yet Sweden was neither as religiously divided nor as pluralist as the United States or Germany, where church leaders played a significant political role and were often able to defend the rights of local authorities. Not until the nineteenth century did the burgeoning Free Church movement begin to challenge the Swedish state's hold on the various religious communities. Even so, this oppositional stance was quickly toned down. Like other modern popular movements, the free churches found their place within a more cooperative order, and large swaths of their activities were integrated into the state sector.

Historically, Swedish political culture has been characterized by concentration of power and by standardization, as well as by democratic traditions. These latter invited broad participation but left limited space for individual divergence. Their defining features were consensus and social conformity rather than individual rights and minority rights, which presented a striking contrast to the Anglo-Saxon world, where a gentlemanly ideal served as the social norm. In the United States and Britain, democracy aimed to raise the people to the level of the aristocracy. The freedoms that hitherto had been reserved for the few would be given to the great masses, a democratization of noble privilege that formed the basis for the establishment of human rights in the modern era. In Sweden, however, democratization was intended to make the aristocracy and the people into equals by abolishing all privileges and special rights. As a result, rights-based thinking has only a weak foundation in the Swedish tradition.

During the latter half of the nineteenth century, this historical tradition was both strengthened and modernized. In 1866, the system with four estates was replaced by a modern parliament with two chambers, though with a very restricted suffrage. Local self-governance was increased, and reform was begun of the class of officials that Heckscher described as "quite stagnant."[20] A modern, effective, professional, properly paid, and hence uncorrupted administrative bureaucracy was created. Particularly after the representational reforms of 1866, as Rothstein noted, Sweden's administrative apparatus operated "not like a unitary cadre, separate from society and governing from above, but like a well-integrated part of society."[21] Perhaps to a greater degree than most bureaucracies, it sought to live up to Hegel's and Max Weber's ideals of a civil-servant class as rational, impartial, and dedicated to the common interest.

This double legacy—a strong state combined with a village-level understanding of democracy—was taken up by the Swedish Social Democratic Party, whose strength has historically derived from precisely this freighted duality. Social Democrats laid claim to be both a popular movement from below and a party of government from above: the Swedish Social Democratic Party as both "king" *and* people. The policies of the Swedish welfare model, *folkhemmet*, whose principal tenets are social equality and national solidarity, emerged from an encounter between an emancipating state and ordinary people. The old enemy, the nobility, was replaced by the new era's aristocracy of propertied bourgeoisie and industrial elite. Like the nobility, the new industrial barons were vulnerable to accusations of upper-class posturing and insufficient national loyalty. The rhetorical linchpins were therefore already well established when welfare-state socialism with distinct national features emerged in force after 1933.

Seen from this perspective, many of the intermediary institutions of modern society, such as the family, private charitable organizations, companies, and churches, were deeply problematic. In the liberal worldview, these are understood as guarantors of freedom and pluralism and are associated with what is now approvingly designated as *civil society*. In Swedish political culture, in contrast, many of these institutions were associated with an array of negative phenomena: privileges, inequality, hierarchical and patriarchal power structures, and even personal degradation and humiliation. The great exceptions to this rule were the classic popular movements—particularly the labor movement, which, precisely because its associations were seen as popular-democratic, could serve as an instrument for the extension of social welfare in close collaboration with the state.

EQUALITY—OUR DESTINY

But does the fact that Sweden has been shaped by a strong peasant estate in alliance with the state against the nobility really allow us to talk about a peculiarly Swedish kind of individualism? Rather, is it not the case that Sweden's state-Protestant conformism and socially controlling peasant communities are the very antithesis of what many people understand by "individualism"—the chance to choose one's own path, to deviate, to think independently, indeed even to be aristocratic and eccentric?

Individualism is a multifaceted concept. Sometimes it is used pejoratively as a synonym for egoism and selfishness, sometimes as a term of approbation for describing qualities related to integrity and originality. When, in late-eighteenth-century France, the concept of individualism emerged within the framework of a conservative critique of the Enlightenment and the French Revolution, it was highly negative.[22] But the person who made the concept internationally famous—the

French political philosopher Alexis de Tocqueville—used it more evenhandedly, as a way to describe relations between citizens in a democratic society that was imbued with the notion of equality.[23]

After touring the United States in the 1830s, Tocqueville became concerned about the consequences of democracy's breakthrough, particularly in Europe, which had not yet created a modern civil society like that of the United States. If all the old feudal bonds of dependency were torn away, if the aristocracy, the guilds, and their privileges were abolished without any new forms of social community being instituted, individualism would lead to an enormous expansion of the state's power: "As the men who inhabit democratic countries have no superiors, no inferiors, and no habitual or necessary partners in their undertakings, they readily fall back upon themselves and consider themselves as beings apart.... Hence such men can never, without an effort, tear themselves from their private affairs to engage in public business; their natural bias leads them to abandon the latter to the sole visible and permanent representative of the interests of the community; that is to say, to the state."[24]

Although Tocqueville was not opposed to democracy and equality, he had found himself at a dead end after France's July Revolution of 1830. Because his family had belonged to the pre-Revolutionary civil-service nobility, it was unthinkable for him to continue in the service of the July Monarchy. By inclination, however, he was liberal and reformist. This created a dialectical tension between his emotional ties to the old aristocratic order and his democratic impulses. Indeed, Tocqueville is reminiscent of Karl Marx—if one sets aside the historical materialism. History, as Tocqueville saw it, exhibits an implacable movement toward democracy and equality: "it is universal, it is durable, it easily eludes all human interference."[25]

Previously, in feudal society, the power of the state and the sovereign had been held in check by so-called secondary authorities—that is, different privileged groups, principally the aristocracy but also priests, trade guilds, and burghers. The abolition of privileges and increasing social equality were now changing citizens into social atoms without any kind of natural community.

Tocqueville's individuality had very little to do with the originality, distinctive traits, and other inner qualities that distinguish one person from another. In this regard, he parted company with his friend John Stuart Mill, who placed greater emphasis on the individual's right to be original and eccentric. As Mill argued, "Geniuses are by the nature of things more pronounced individuals than ordinary people."[26] For Tocqueville, in contrast, individualism was intimately connected to equality: the concept served to describe the atomistic culture that arose when people were detached from the old communities of superiority and subordination.

In talking about a specifically Swedish individualism, we are drawing in the first instance on Tocqueville. The advantage of doing so is that his interpretation avoids a series of evaluative issues relating to the term's political significance. Rather, he preserves the original meaning of the word *individual*—the smallest unit, that which cannot be further divided—and relates it both to the emerging modern state and to the traditional communities of the ancien régime.

PERFECT INDEPENDENCE

Tocqueville recognized both the possibilities and the dangers of the new democratic individualism. What concerned him most was the enormous potential for centralization and state oppression that comes in the wake of equality and alienation. One of his more celebrated formulas, which is often cited by critics of the welfare state, compactly expressed these personal fears: "As far as I am concerned, when I feel the hand of power weighing down upon my brow, I take no interest in knowing who oppresses me, and I am not more inclined to put my head under the yoke simply because a million arms offer it to me."[27]

But more than half a century before Tocqueville wrote these lines, an almost identical analysis had prompted the Swiss-French philosopher Jean-Jacques Rousseau to welcome the state as a savior: "Each citizen shall be at the same time perfectly independent of all his fellow citizens and excessively dependent on the republic. This result is always achieved by the same means, since it is the power of the state which makes the freedom of its members."[28]

For Tocqueville, the greatest threat was the state and its concentration of power; for Rousseau, an undemocratic and demeaning personal dependence upon one's fellows. Rousseau's desire for a perfect independence from all other citizens had a class-specific aspect, too, in being aimed at precisely the aristocracy that Tocqueville saw as the foundation of civil society.

A succession of formative experiences in Rousseau's life had given him a keen eye for the oppression of subordinates.[29] At the age of thirteen, Rousseau had been forced to leave his childhood home and serve as an apprentice to an engraver, a brutal experience that he described in his *Confessions*: "Accustomed to live on terms of perfect equality, to be witness of no pleasures I could not command, to see no dish I was not to partake of, or be sensible of a desire I might not express; to be able to bring every wish of my heart to my lips—what a transition!—at my master's I was scarce allowed to speak."[30] The young Rousseau later became an advisor to a French nobleman who exploited his talents but humiliated him by treating him like an inferior servant. As a scholar of Rousseau noted, his political philosophy contains more than a whiff of the lackey's hatred for his master.[31]

But the blisters left by the chains of dependence also gave force and depth to Rousseau's ideas, at the heart of which lies a radical notion of the importance of autonomy and independence in human relations. The society of his day was defined not only by unequal relations of property but also by a pervasive falsity in all aspects of social life. Community corrupted. Its members lied, hid their thoughts, dared not say what they meant. For this reason, human beings, as Rousseau explained in one of his most provocative and debated formulations, must be forced to be free. The purpose of the social contract was to protect citizens from "all personal dependence."[32]

This finding might seem paradoxical given that Rousseau was also advocating that all citizens should be subject to "the general will" and its executive organ, the state. Unlike Tocqueville, however, he believed that it made all the difference who put the yoke on one's shoulders: "Since each person gives himself to all, he gives himself to no one; and since there is no associate over whom he does not gain the same rights as others gain over him, each man recovers the equivalent of everything he loses, and in the bargain he acquires more power to preserve what he has."[33]

For Rousseau, people subordinating themselves to another person, whether a king, a ruler, or even an elected representative, was unthinkable. Nonetheless, he was prepared to give the state almost unrestricted power to carry out the will of the people. If we think of "the state" as comprising ordinary and easily corrupted individuals, he can appear naive. For Rousseau, however, the state meant first and foremost the law. And, like Plato, he seems to have placed his hopes in a body of wise and eminent lawmakers. Ironically, Rousseau's position was not so far from the American political system, with its Founding Fathers and latter-day successors in the Supreme Court whose role is to protect the republic from democracy.

ONLY AUTONOMOUS INDIVIDUALS CAN BE EQUAL

Rousseau's insistence that the individual be subordinated to an abstract general will has made him an extremely controversial figure. In the world of liberal ideas, where power sharing and the rights of individuals and minorities occupy center stage, he is regarded with great suspicion. Nevertheless, his influence on the Western philosophical tradition has been immense. And, above all, in relation to our own focus: he is a permanent guest at the table of Swedish politics, though his hosts are not always aware of it. A great many of Sweden's citizens share his conception of equality and independence, concrete gains that they consider well worth the price of a more or less abstract relation of dependency on the national community—in other words, the state.

Hostility to the privileges of nobility has in Sweden resulted in a principle of relentless equivalence that leaves little room for the kind of individuality that comes from difference, such as cultural diversity or the rights held by an individual in relation to state power. Instead, freedom from personal dependence—on noblemen, the church, charity, and the patriarchal family—has become a national virtue, albeit tacitly so. In the process, as Tocqueville warned and as Rousseau welcomed, the state has been the decisive instrument for both the emancipation and the alienation of the individual. Like Rousseau, the welfare state promises to free individuals by conferring on them a perfect independence from other citizens and guaranteeing that they are at no risk of confronting other individuals unless as a result of free choice.

Rousseau and Tocqueville offer a key insight into the Swedish social contract: the strong state does not necessarily derive its legitimacy from a communitarian ideal or an ethnic conception of national community. It can also draw energy from its citizens' desire for social equality and individual autonomy.

If we jettison the idea that the welfare state has shaped the Swedish mentality and instead reverse the equation, we find ourselves faced with a question that has baffled countless disappointed welfare-state tourists, reflective social anthropologists, and frustrated immigrants. How can the citizens of a country where concepts such as solidarity, community, and even socialism occur almost constantly in the national political rhetoric be so detached, so protective of their independence, and so cautious about letting other people into their lives?

The answer is that observers are crediting the Swedish welfare model with a far greater claim to *Gemeinschaft* (community) than was ever promised in reality. In fact, modern Sweden is far more accurately described as a *Gesellschaft* (society) inhabited by individuals who are both very modern and, historically speaking, highly autonomous.[34] What characterizes Swedish society most deeply is not collectivism but an alliance between state and individual that, to an extraordinary degree, has released the individual from dependence on the family and the charity of civil society. In the words of Peter Antman, a Swedish historian of ideas, "Few welfare states have been . . . as consistently organized around the idea of individual autonomy as Sweden's. Almost all our welfare provisions are connected to the individual person, not to the family or to work, as is typically the case in other Western countries. The struggles for full employment and for a high rate of employment both derive from the precept that every person should have power over their own life. . . . Dependency upon other people has declined when those often instrumental services have been located outside of family life."[35]

The principle of equality lies at the forefront of this process of liberation. And equality's central feature is precisely the autonomy of the individual. Only autonomous subjects can meet as equals. In this way, the ostensibly collectivist ideal of equality paradoxically led to a radical individualization of Swedish society. The intermediary associations that had formerly handled health services and nursing care became negatively associated with hierarchical social relations. And this sociopolitical development was increasingly driven by a logic that produced the situation today, in which Swedes have a largely direct and unmediated relationship to the state and are relatively free of any direct dependence on their fellow citizens for money or services.

Sweden is special in this regard. The issue here is not merely a (revealing) discourse on Swedishness but the robustness of Sweden's institutions. A dramatic contrast emerges when Swedish and Scandinavian social and family policies are compared with those of similar countries in Europe and North America. The roots of these policies can be traced far back in time. Even before the Social Democrats came to power, a pattern had been established that differed markedly from what would become the norm in continental Europe as well as from the systems that would define the Anglo-Saxon countries.

The first steps toward a modern welfare state were taken in Germany under Bismarck, where the social insurance system was from the very beginning tied to work, the family, and the institutions of civil society, albeit with the state as a powerful actor in the background. The market would play a greater role in the Anglo-Saxon countries, where private companies, associations, and individuals became the dominant actors.

In Scandinavia, on the other hand, a system developed in which citizenship—or, to use the idiom of the time, membership of *folket* ("the people")—emerged as the determining principle of the right to social insurance. And the state, rather than private insurance companies and employers, became responsible via the public sector for services that were paid for by taxes rather than in fees to insurance companies. This eventually resulted in Sweden's *folkhemmet* policies and the welfare state, but even the first major reform, the state pension adopted by Parliament in 1913, was forged in this pattern.[36]

While this tendency may not be exclusive to Sweden or the Scandinavian countries, the general welfare policies of the Scandinavian welfare states have been more fully realized than in most other countries. Either the state uses the family, employers, and voluntary organizations as intermediaries in order to guarantee the security of its citizens—something that entails a greater risk of an individual falling through the net—or it adopts a system with a greater element of needs testing, something that leads to an increased risk of social stigmatization and exclusion for citizens who have to apply for help.

The Swedish or Scandinavian model is based on the principle that an individual has a direct relationship with the state as regards both duties and rights. The social insurance system exists regardless of the individual's relationship with their family, employer, or more or less well-intentioned charitable bodies. Direct dependence on family, relations, neighbors, employers, and associations of civil society has been minimized.

Conservative and neoliberal critics find this model of welfare provocative for several reasons. They feel either that the state is being given too much power or that individual independence leads to diminished responsibility, welfare dependency, and a weakened work ethic. The list of potential welfare parasites can be extended infinitely: single mothers, work-avoiding welfare cheats, those on more or less elective sick leave, criminals, antisocial bohemians, and their ilk. Defenders of the welfare state, for their part, have emphasized its emancipatory dimension: how the individual is liberated from the traditional family, employers, and other hierarchically organized institutions in civil society. Precisely because the state guarantees social rights to the individual, citizens can be free and autonomous in their dealings with the relations of power that govern both the market and the family.

At the same time, the individualistic dimension is also problematic for supporters of the welfare state. Although there is a powerful symbiosis in the Swedish welfare state between the concepts of autonomy and solidarity, the relationship is not entirely without friction. For socialists, individual autonomy does not have the same value as equality and solidarity; they, too, put the ideal of community first. The values of solidarity and equality predominate in political debate because they can be celebrated without exposing oneself to criticism. By contrast, for a socialist, the drive to achieve independence lies worryingly close to morally dubious impulses such as selfishness, egoism, and (liberal) individualism. Nonetheless, it is our view that this urge—a striving for autonomy rather than the more socially acceptable desire for collective responsibility—is the fundamental driving force of statist individualism's social contract.

This does not mean that Swedish individualism can be reduced to an escape from social relations. In the next chapter we consider statist individualism from the perspective of interpersonal love. As we move from the levels of social engineering and social policy, we quickly see that this is not simply a matter of justice and equality. Statist individualism also affects those concrete and deeply personal relations between individuals: a woman's relationship to her husband; a child's relationship to its parents; an elderly man's desire for a dignified old age; a needy person's differing experiences of charity and social insurance.

CHAPTER 3

The Swedish Theory of Love

Statist individualism has an antisocial aspect: the lone citizen whose freedom is dependent on a powerful state. There is a good deal of romanticizing of solitude and freedom in the images of Swedishness to be found in classic Swedish literature and contemporary popular culture. The idea of the self-reliant and independent citizen has been connected in particular to nature, something that attests to the strength of a political culture tied to the peculiar status of Sweden's freeholding peasants.

It may be axiomatic in many parts of Europe that *Stadtluft macht frei*—city air makes you free—but in Sweden individual freedom is symbolized by the countryside. Only among rustling trees and rushing waterfalls can Swedes find reassurance that they are their true selves. This sentiment is emblematized by a gigantic tapestry that adorns the main chamber of the Swedish Parliament (figure 3.1). Its prospect of sea and bare rocky islets offers a fitting symbol for the national identity of a people who love their country's stony ground above all else.

And yet to place a one-sided emphasis on the power relationship between state and individual would be to misunderstand the moral meaning of Sweden's social contract. Critics of the welfare state often paint a dystopian picture of Swedes as emotionally stunted, alienated cogs in a machine created by social engineers and ruled by state bureaucrats. Such individuals are no longer truly human when portrayed in their most extreme form, be that Gustaf Sundbärg's early-twentieth-century complaints about Swedish unsociability or Roland Huntford's more recent evocation of Sweden as neototalitarian.[1] These bleak

FIGURE 3.1. As Swedish parliamentarians ponder their next speech in the Riksdag, they can gaze at Elisabeth Hasselberg-Olsson's melancholic tapestry *Minnet av ett landskap* (*Memory of a Landscape*), which is devoid of the people who voted them to power but teeming with water and rocks. Photo by Henrik Berggren.

images of conformism and chilly distance may capture one aspect of Swedish culture, but they also fall very wide of the mark. What characterizes Swedish society is not a lack of social relations but a striking degree of voluntary choice in interpersonal relations.

For associations and organizations, Sweden is the promised land. Its welfare state notwithstanding, Sweden is almost uniquely strong as a civil society by virtue of its plethora of voluntary associations. These include political parties, social movements, trade unions, adult education schools, and interest organizations. These are membership groups organized on a democratic basis, which is also true for the many associations established for the less lofty purposes of leisure, sports, and entertainment. Swedes are also active in voluntary social work, and they take care of their relatives and friends to the same extent or more as people in other Western societies.[2]

The decisive issue is not whether Swedes are antisocial or reserved but what guiding moral principle underpins the way Swedes view all interpersonal relationships. We have given a name to this logic that pushes individualistic modernity to an extreme: *the Swedish theory of love*.[3] In Sweden, there exists a notion of pure love, a love built not on mutual dependence but on a foundation of autonomy. Deeply rooted in systems of values as well as social practices, this mode of thinking

KANT AND ROUSSEAU—AGAIN

Once again we find ourselves confronted by Kant's dilemma. Intimate relationships within families, with friends, or within the local community can have unwelcome consequences because the love that creates dependency also undermines freedom, subtly yet inexorably.

This is not least evident when it comes to the child-parent relationship. Children need care, supervision, and emotional investment from their parents, all of which tangibly restrict the latter's mobility and cannot be reciprocated until the child has grown into adulthood and the parents into old age. Of course, things look very different from the child's perspective, and teenagers' struggle for freedom and the issue of children's rights have been among the driving forces behind the welfare state. It is hardly coincidence that Sweden has forcefully pressed for legislation to give children rights, to criminalize corporal punishment, and to create an ombudsman for children.

In similar fashion, gender equality policy has developed not only from a demand for social justice but from the insight that what is intimate and personal also has a political dimension. Women's independence from men is at once a personal, social, and political question. And, later in their life cycle, both men and women risk the dilemma of old age: the demeaning loss of autonomy as the elderly parent becomes dependent on the adult child. Surveys show that older Swedes are relatively satisfied with their situation in comparison with the elderly in other countries.[4] Yet their greatest wish is not to live in closer community with their children. Rather, as gerontologist Marta Szebehely notes, "Old people prefer 'intimacy at a distance' and do not want to depend upon their children."[5] They value their own self-reliance; they want to socialize with their children and grandchildren because they choose to. This ambivalence emerges clearly in a survey commissioned by the Red Cross in autumn 2005: 49 percent of the seniors polled were worried about becoming "dependent on help from other people" and 60 percent welcomed receiving help from family members—of whom only half received it to the degree that they wanted.[6]

Such family dynamics lay bare the dilemma of dependency. Although most people do not want to live without love, they are resistant to love that leads to an asymmetric power relationship. Our hypothesis of a

Swedish theory of love is based on the idea that there are two ways to relate to other people. One is to view mutual dependence as the very essence and beauty of love. In love and in the family, we as individuals become part of a larger entity, one that is stronger and fundamentally greater than the sum total of its individual members. This is the norm in many parts of the world (even if there is clearly a general tendency toward increased individualization): in continental Europe, in the United States with its emphasis on family values, and in many Asian and African countries with their strong kinship ties.

The second way is to begin with autonomy. Only when people are self-sufficient, particularly with regard to money and the law, can they be sure that they are loved by the other person, and love that other person in turn, without the inducement of instrumental motives or the compulsion of a forced relationship from which they cannot detach themselves. In this view, love based on independence is more genuine since it makes no compromises with the individual's free subjectivity but instead builds on a spontaneous encounter between two autonomous people. It is on this theory of love, we contend, that the Swedish social contract is implicitly founded.

If there is a theoretical inspiration for the politics of free love, it is Rousseau. To be sure, he was not a feminist. On the contrary, he celebrated the complementary abilities of men and women. Even so, his strong emphasis on independence has inspired proponents of equality between men and women. Rousseau's philosophy can of course be understood as a deeply personal view. His own demeaning dependence on noblemen and other social superiors who were intellectually inferior to him lent an explosive intensity to his critique of unequal social relations in pre-Revolutionary society. The feudal system had been based on a societal projection of the hierarchical and patriarchal ideals of the family. Like the father in the family, the nobleman was paterfamilias in relation to the serfs and nominally free peasants, who were subject to his command. And the king was patriarch of all. These relations were formulated in terms of both love and power. The master not only exercised his paternalist power to serve his own interests, he also had a duty to protect his subjects and to see that they did not starve or suffer. Although this love could forge strong and heartfelt ties, it often led to hatred and embitterment.

Rousseau saw the connection between personal dependency and the political system with rare clarity. The evil committed by people, he argued, was the result not of selfishness and egoism, but of *weakness*.

The fundamental experience of childhood that made adults willing to subordinate themselves to another's tyranny was the feeling of dependence on others. Child rearing should therefore foster independence and a strong sense of self. As Rousseau declared, "Make man strong and he will be good." Those who depended on other people were incapable of real love. Their healthy love of self, *amour de soi-même*, became deformed into egotistical self-love, *amour propre*. A person became false and manipulative, their emotional life ruled by the material advantages to be obtained from others. In contrast, strong and secure people who loved themselves had no need to exploit other people; love for another became a gift, to be given freely and without an ulterior motive.[7]

One can speculate how much would remain of human relationships if all love were so unselfish. Far from being a utopia, the result might well be an utterly alienated world, full of self-sufficient people with only a scant interest in emotional interaction with others. Tocqueville's fears that social atomism would pave the way for a totalitarian state were not groundless. Nonetheless, more than any other political philosopher, Rousseau put his finger on the existential conditions for politics: oppression, subordination, and exploitation are possible precisely because citizens are social beings who need others. Later in this book, we see just how powerful Rousseau's critique of interpersonal dependency became when it was replanted in Swedish soil, where it inspired Almqvist, Strindberg, and Key to develop a vision of society that would be fully realized only with the expansion of the Swedish welfare state in the 1960s and '70s.

FAMILY AND LOVE

Like statist individualism, the Swedish view of family relationships has its roots in historical experience.[8] In the 1960s, historian John Hajnal discovered differences between family structures and marriage patterns in Europe going back at least as far as the fifteenth century, possibly further.[9] Compared to those of the Mediterranean region and eastern Europe, the forms of family bonding in northwestern Europe were particularly striking.

In the first place, newlyweds often left the parental home to form new households, unlike in southern and eastern Europe where the new family often stayed on in the parents' house. Second, women married later, which meant that husband and wife were closer in age and that a woman typically had her first child relatively late in her childbearing years. Third, it was common for the family's children to be sent off to work in other households, which was only logical given the numbers of newly established family units in need of help.

The social consequences of this marriage pattern were far-reaching. Late marriage meant fewer children, which meant that each child represented a greater emotional investment by parents. Because women were typically older when they married, fewer widows needed to be supported by relatives or poor relief. The long period during which sexually mature young adults lived without any fixed ties also created a need for strong social controls even as it led to the emergence of a more or less independent youth culture. And the practice of sending children and adolescents into service away from the home broadened their perspectives, encouraged the acquisition of new skills, and made it impossible to sustain an honor culture that prevented women from moving about freely without surveillance by the family. According to Austrian social historian Michael Mitterauer, this mobility enjoyed by the young played a key role in making youth into a period when "the individual, the autonomous personality, was developed."[10]

Research on family history in Sweden strongly confirms this pattern. Young people have long enjoyed greater independence in the Scandinavian countries, not only in relation to Southern and Eastern Europe but also in comparison with other regions that exhibit the same marriage patterns as western Europe. According to Jan Stehouwer, a comparison of Nordic and Anglo-Saxon countries reveals substantial differences in relations between generations: "Nordic parents involve themselves far less in the daily lives of their children, and their children, in turn, avoid asking their parents for support and help. Generations do not exhibit the mutual dependency that is found in Anglo-Saxon countries."[11]

At this point we are reminded of the explanation offered by American researcher Herbert Hendin, who posited that Swedish women encouraged their children to be autonomous from an early age. Hendin has been accused of suggesting that Swedish women were not good mothers. From the point of view of Swedish love, however, things understandably look rather different: if independence is a virtue, it is also a virtue to raise children in accordance with this precept.

Hendin was expressing an insight that had been articulated far earlier. In the nineteenth century, a French sociologist named Frédéric Le Play had argued that young Scandinavians enjoyed considerable freedom to choose their profession and were generally allowed to make decisions about their own life. This was a type of family that encouraged "great powers of initiative in the individual" and where "the value of the individual was highly appreciated."[12] At the same time, their contact with the parental home was looser.

Historian David Gaunt has argued that Scandinavia was also unusual in another respect. In societies where resources were scarce and family farming was the usual paradigm, intergenerational relationships needed to be regulated in some fashion. This most often happened by means of a so-called *undantagskontrakt* (retirement contract), which allowed the old farmer and his wife to transfer the farm to their heirs in return for a guaranteed "pension." The intergenerational conflict this created is well illustrated by an example from the late eighteenth century: "From this moment henceforth, the old people shall be as foreign hirelings upon their own land, and if complaint should be made about lack of feeling, let it be noted that it is thus in many places with regard to the treatment of aged parents, particularly when they reach that age when they are no longer able to work and when it can no longer be kept a secret that others wish them a speedy departure to the next life."[13]

In many European countries, citizens were required by law to care for their parents. In Sweden, too, legislation existed to protect the elderly. The ancient laws of the Swedish provinces, for example, state that "a son or daughter who drives away their father or mother shall receive an annual fine of three marks."[14] According to Gaunt, however, retirement-contract arrangements were entered into more voluntarily in Scandinavia than in the rest of Europe. Paradoxically, this conditional freedom for farmers may have made intergenerational conflicts more acute, thereby increasing resistance toward the mutual dependency of children and parents.[15] Although the Scandinavian retirement contract was based on custom and tradition, its starting point was an assumption of responsibility by the individual. This, Gaunt argued, paved the way for "the ideologies of welfare in which the state, rather than the family, stands as guarantor of social security."[16]

The custom of *nattfrieri* (night courting), which permitted young men and women to spend the night together, albeit for the most part decorously, likewise indicates a greater degree of independence between generations, even if similar patterns can be found in other parts of Europe that followed the European marriage pattern.[17] Night courting meant that a boy and a girl could sleep together in her bed without needing their parents' approval or even knowledge. This type of courtship practice was diametrically opposed to the more patriarchal custom that required a young man to ask the father of his intended for her hand in marriage. Night courting was widespread in Finland, Norway, and northern and central Sweden, but not in the southernmost Swedish province of Skåne or in Denmark—in other words, it predominated in areas where feudalism had never existed and the barriers of class were weaker. The risks of misalliance were smaller in northern and central Sweden, Norway, and Finland, and young people could be given greater freedom to choose their partner themselves. Equality and autonomy, it would seem, are values that reinforce each other.[18]

Moreover, according to Gaunt, the Nordic countries also stand out with respect to the relationships between spouses. An underlying patriarchal structure existed, to be sure, but women's standing in Nordic peasant society exhibited a wide degree of variation:

> In the smallholding communities of the Nordic north, almost everyone owned the lands they farmed. Parents did not decide whom their children should marry but let them make their own decision by night courting. Unmarried mothers were commonplace in many parts of the north and were spared the stigmatization and social control which occurred in southern Sweden. The housewife also had a great deal of responsibility for the household and production, while her counterpart in Skåne was hardly permitted to do any work outside the home.[19]

Even the possibilities for dissolving a marriage were greater in the Nordic region than in the other countries of Europe, Protestant as well as Catholic. Since the sixteenth century it had been possible for peasants to apply to church courts for a complete divorce, and it was possible to remarry—at least for the partner who was deemed blameless for the dissolution of the marriage.[20]

THE NORDIC MARRIAGE

This traditionally more individualistic view of family and marriage also seems to have been generally accepted during the modernization process of the twentieth century. During the era of liberal revolutions, agrarian Sweden had fallen behind more politically and economically developed countries such as Britain and France with respect to women's property rights.[21] But despite the bourgeoisie's relatively weak position in Sweden, or perhaps precisely because of it, Sweden took the lead in family reform in the twentieth century. The legacy of Nordic peasant-community traditions proved to be surprisingly fertile ground for an approach to marriage questions that put the interests of the individual before those of the family as a unit.

British historian David Bradley compared the legal traditions relating to marriage in Germany, England, and the Scandinavian countries at the start of the twentieth century—several decades before Gunnar and Alva Myrdal and other social engineers began their reshaping of the Swedish family. In England, Bradley argued, the state during the nineteenth century was weak and passive with regard to family legislation. The family constituted a protected sphere that stood outside the purview of the law and sociopolitical measures. Married women had no distinct legal identity apart from the husband (husband and wife were one person, and the husband was that person). The husband had a legal right to the wife's possessions in marriage. Access to divorce and abortion was extremely limited, and British laws in these areas did not soften until well into the twentieth century.[22]

In Germany at the turn of the twentieth century, the state intervened actively in the family through legislation but not in order to emancipate women or create equality. On the contrary, it assumed that women should be subordinate to their husbands. The law stipulated that "a husband has the right to determine all matters concerning their shared marital life"; the man controlled his wife's property and could even apply for her to be dismissed from her position of employment. Illegitimate children were not entitled to inherit, and the rights to divorce and access to abortion were severely restricted. It was a patriarchal system in which the state and the traditional family configuration formed a joint bulwark against demands for the individual emancipation of women. The principal reason for Germany's activist family policy was concern for the falling birth rate, not social considerations. This conservative view of the relationship between state and family, which dated from the time of Bismarck, was to survive two world wars and ultimately become codified—albeit in modified form—in the family laws of West Germany.[23]

In Scandinavian countries, too, the state was prepared to intervene in the family—in marked difference to the respectful attitude toward the integrity of the family that dominated British legislation. In contrast to Germany, however, the interventions in these countries were carried out on the basis of a liberal attitude toward sexuality and reproduction. In her comparative analysis of family legislation in Europe during the twentieth century, historian Paola Ronfani concluded that the countries of northern Europe adopted a special position. Although it is possible to identify a general development in Europe—a move away from the hierarchical, patriarchal, and authoritarian family toward a view of the family as a contract between equal partners—this tendency was far more visible in legislation in Scandinavia, where it also occurred at an earlier stage. This held true both for women's relationship to men and for the rights of children.[24]

While marriage legislation in the rest of Europe was not reformed until the 1960s, the laws in Scandinavian countries were rewritten as early as the first decades of the century: 1918 in Norway, 1921 in Sweden, and 1925 in Denmark. Between 1909 and 1929, divorce laws and the internal relationship between married couples were reorganized. Divorce was made easier, and women became more or less equal to their husbands, economically and legally. In the 1930s, the position of illegitimate children was strengthened, and legislation relating to homosexuality and abortion was softened. There was a clear movement toward increasing sexual equality and supporting the family socially as well as economically.[25]

Ronfani also observed that in most countries, in the absence of an overarching family policy program, laws were reformed statute by statute. Here again, the exception was Scandinavia—Sweden in particular. Reform-minded politicians exerted themselves to realize the stated goal of "modernizing" marriage so that it could function as an institution while also furthering the individual's desire for self-realization. The major family policy reforms that took place in Sweden in the 1970s were also more radical and consistent than in most other countries, which only later moved—in piecemeal fashion and incompletely—toward adopting a body of legislation derived from the principle of the family as a voluntary contract between free parties.[26]

The pattern of the 1920s and 1930s was repeated in much the same way during the second half of the century. Sweden and other Scandinavian countries took the lead in reforms promoting individual autonomy. Reforms of family law made divorce easier to obtain. The question of guilt was set aside and alimony declined as women were increasingly expected to have their own income.

In this respect, Sweden stands out as radical. Taxation has been consistently individualized, something that continues to be unusual outside Scandinavia. Following a divorce, both parents are given the rights to and the responsibility for raising their children, while most countries in continental Europe proceed from the assumption that the mother will act as the sole caregiver. Children's rights were further strengthened, and in 1979 corporal punishment and other degrading forms of child punishment were outlawed. In 1989, the idea that children have individual rights as autonomous beings, both within and in relation to the family, was inscribed in the UN Convention on the Rights of the Child, which was itself drafted under the influence of the Swedish tradition of children's rights. The rights of homosexuals gained the force of law in Denmark in 1989, Norway in 1993, Sweden in 1994, Iceland in 1996, and the Netherlands in 1998.[27]

The Scandinavian countries are also unique in having adopted a neutral position early on with regard to the treatment of traditional versus de facto families. The relationship between cohabiting partners—known as a *sambo* relationship, a short form of *sammanboende* (cohabitators)—is more or less equivalent to marriage.[28] Here, too, one could speculate about the significance of the comparatively egalitarian Swedish peasant society with its powerful group norms. Its pragmatic but strict rules for family formation—first, in the form of night courting and voluntary agreements between partners within the peasant community, then through so-called Stockholm marriages of unmarried cohabiters—likely exerted a more powerful binding force than those of the church or sexual morality as defined by religion.

Comparative family historiography and the long discourse on Swedish individualism in general indicate that the relationship between the welfare state's family policy and the putative collapse of the family in Sweden is more complicated than most critics claim. Rather than seeing the welfare state and its family policies as the reason for the supposed erosion of the traditional family as a central and vital societal institution, we need to reverse the order of the two components of this causal relationship. Because there already existed a culturally conditioned desire for independence and self-sufficiency, the promotion of reforms that another culture might have regarded as hostile to the family was not merely made possible—it accorded with how Swedish people already lived. Such preparedness at the sociopsychological level may also account for the fairly weak opposition in Sweden to state-funded collective childcare, something that puzzles commentators who are more familiar with, say, the American view of the family and child rearing. Or, as Austin put it, "for an external observer, [the protagonists in the issue of gender roles] seem to give ideological expression to an already existing psychological tradition; a [tradition] which, moreover, is perhaps decisive for the structure of the Swedish psyche."[29]

POWER RELATIONS IN MODERN WELFARE STATES

Before proceeding in part 2 to our historical presentation, let us first summarize the argument of this chapter and chapter 2 in the form of an extended comparison of Sweden with the United States and Germany. To clarify the differences in their respective views of the relationship between individual, family (and civil society), and state, we have drawn up a classification of ideal types. Any schema of this kind relies on simplifications and generalizations, of course, but figure 3.2 nevertheless captures the logic behind each welfare system by illustrating three different outcomes of a sociopolitical triangle dynamic: state and individual united against the family (Sweden), state and family united against

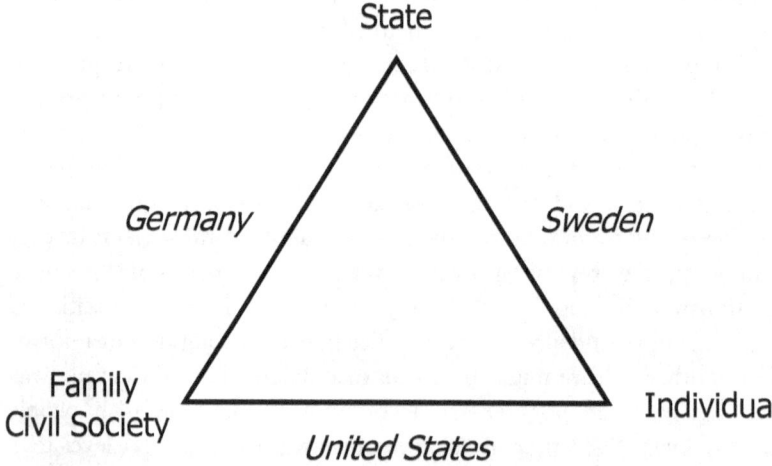

FIGURE 3.2. Power relations in modern welfare states: In Sweden, state and individual unite against the family; in Germany, state and family unite against the individual; in the United States, individual and family unite against the state.

the individual (Germany), and individual and family united against the state (United States).

In Germany, welfare policy proceeds from the family as both the object and the collaborator of the welfare state. The state protects and supports the family as well as other institutions of civil society with the aim that each of these in turn should be able to provide for the welfare of individuals. Although the commitment of the public sector to its citizens' social security is massive, aspects of its implementation have been delegated to actors in family and civil society, ranging from housewives to different kinds of charitable religious organizations. Strong bonds of dependence are regarded as natural, but there is also a consensus that the state bears a large social responsibility, albeit primarily within the framework of the family and according to the logic of subsidiarity—a principle, derived from Catholic social thought, that stresses the role of church and family. To the extent that the state intervenes, it does so on the basis of needs testing. The conditions of eligibility for state assistance often underscore the fact that the recipient is subordinate, dependent, and incapable of coping on their own. However, because the moral norm does not hold up individual autonomy as a superior value, the degree of stigmatization caused by dependency is reduced.[30]

The United States, in contrast, is characterized by a deep-rooted antipathy toward state involvement in any aspect of the private sphere, whether in connection with the individual, the family, or the communities in civil society. While the American welfare state is more comprehensive than both defenders and critics of the American model sometimes like to pretend,[31] its point of departure is that individuals must stand on their own feet, within the parameters of the rules of the market, or rely on the goodwill and available resources of their family or community. The social security network exists primarily to help citizens who are unable to make their way in the market and lack the requisite support from their family or civil society. Both this faith in the individual's right to find happiness and the powerful (and often religiously inflected) ideal of the family make it difficult to implement a more activist and universal welfare policy in the United States.

This passivity can be either conservative or liberal in nature. In the case of the former, it comes down to the view that strong bonds of dependence between people, within the family as well as in civil society, are natural. For individuals unable to cope with various life situations—families with children, the sick, the old, the unemployed—the family as well as religious groups and charitable organizations are expected to offer a helping hand. Its fundamental principle is the insight that people's mutual dependence should serve to elicit help on a voluntary basis. From a liberal perspective, in contrast, the autonomy of the individual is more important than voluntary efforts. Rather than relying on goodwill and compassion, one proceeds by means of businesslike contracts. Citizens join together in mutual insurance funds within civil society that are based on regulated fees and obligations instead of personal relations.

Thus, American conservatives and liberals are united in their communitarian suspicion of overly comprehensive state measures, something that creates a moral tension. Dependence on family and community is more socially acceptable than dependence on the state; individualism and personal freedom are an ideological linchpin tightly linked to antistatism. This leads to a division between "honest poor" and "welfare parasites" and an intense stigmatization of those poor, unemployed, or destitute who do not want, or cannot get, help from family and community but must depend on "welfare."[32]

Sweden resembles Germany with regard to its ambitions for welfare policy in that the state is more or less taken for granted as an actor in the promotion of citizens' prosperity.[33] Yet Sweden differs radically in what it sees as the fundamental unit of society. In Sweden, resources and measures are targeted at the individual citizen, without going through the family or private organizations. In this way, the state protects the individual from any risk of ending up in a relation of dependency on parents, spouses, or charitable organizations. But it also leads to the emancipated citizen becoming more mobile in the labor market, more easily governed through political measures, and more inclined to turn to the market to meet needs that would previously have been satisfied within the family. Social insurance, child benefit allowances, student grants, and other forms of tax-financed social rights accrue to individual citizens even as they increase their dependence on the state.

In some respects, there are similarities in how Sweden and the United States view the individual. As regards gainful work for women, childcare outside of the home, and single parents, both the United States and Sweden rank high from an international perspective. The difference is that in Sweden, the state is expected to support this striving for independence, not only by offering a broad social security net but also by making resources available in a way that makes the individual independent of family, neighbors, employers, community groups, faith-based organizations, and charity organizations. In the United States, on the other hand, the individualist tendency is moderated by a communitarian ethos, shared by liberals and conservatives, and a corresponding antipathy toward an activist state.

The individualistic features of the Swedish welfare state have increasingly become an object of attention: marriage legislation, children's rights, parental leave for both fathers and mothers, and the ban on corporal punishment. For those who see in statist individualism an impending dissolution of the traditional family and general moral collapse, Sweden offers a cautionary tale. For those who see in it a viable strategy for joining a historical tendency toward individualism and radical autonomy to a broader, prosocial social contract, Sweden conversely provides a degree of hope and comfort.

Sweden's peculiarity is also indicated by large-scale, quantitative research projects such as the World Values Study, which since the 1980s has produced a gigantic body of data on different patterns of values within Europe and in the world at large.[34] In measures contrasting "traditional" values linked to family, religion, and ethnic solidarity versus "emancipative" values that emphasize self-realization and individual autonomy, Sweden consistently occupies an extreme position in the upper-right corner of the World Cultural Map constructed by the World Values Survey (figure 3.3).[35]

As Swedish sociologist of religion Thorleif Pettersson noted in his analysis of the data, Swedes are characterized by having "the most atypical and divergent value profile of all."[36] In most areas of life, Swedes prioritize personal independence with respect to familial relations and traditional authority. In a European perspective, Sweden takes an extreme position as regards citizens' acceptance of divorce, view of men and women's equal responsibility to provide income for the household economy, tolerance of other people's sexual preferences, willingness to participate in political actions, and attitude toward the importance of personal responsibility. In contrast, Sweden comes near the bottom of the survey as regards traditional values, such as the expectation that children should love and honor their parents and the number of people who consider themselves religious.[37]

Sweden also stands out in other comparative research into the values, practices, and institutions associated with the family. From a global perspective, the Nordic nations all belong to the cluster of countries that have gone furthest in the process of individualization. But even in this group, Sweden is an outlier.[38]

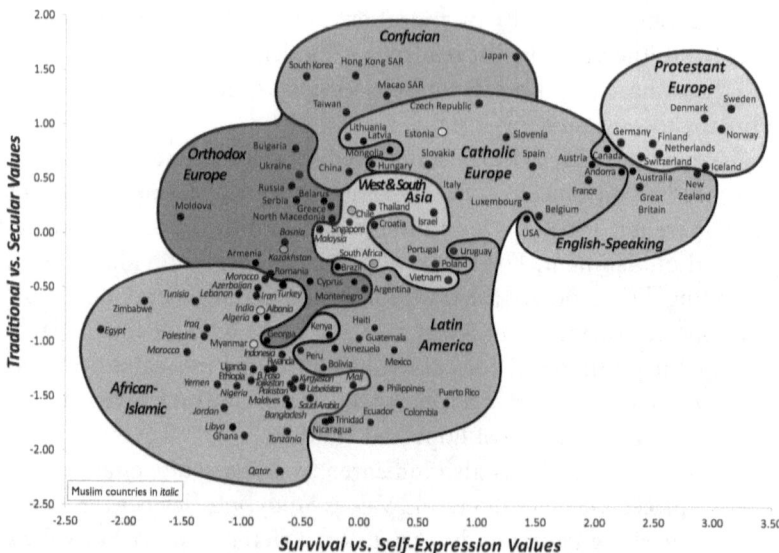

FIGURE 3.3. World Values Survey's 2020 Inglehart-Welzel World Cultural Map, which shows traditional versus secular values in relation to survival versus self-expression values. Source: World Values Survey (2005–2020) www.worldvaluessurvey.org.

Defenders of the welfare state like to claim that the alliance of state and individual has delivered many advantages. Instead of producing stigmatization, state welfare is a public resource, a common social investment that can be used without shame by all citizens throughout their life. Citizens feel safer knowing that there exists a fundamental degree of security, and they are accordingly more flexible and willing to risk change. Swedish citizens can thus invest in education and training, change jobs, get married or divorced, and have children without ever becoming dependent on family, employer, or friends.

Yet Sweden's strong emphasis on individual autonomy has also been criticized. The state's arrogation of traditional interpersonal commitments, it has been argued, is furthering the development of an increasingly cold and loveless society. Institutionalized nursing care is replacing the bonds between people that were once the basis for intimacy and closeness. High divorce rates, loneliness, and poor mental health are often cited as negative consequences of the alliance between state and individual against the family.[39]

Another recurrent criticism focuses less on the existential questions of individualism versus community and instead considers the matter from a power perspective. Autonomy in relation to other people has been purchased at a high price, the argument goes. Not only have the natural communities of civil society been undermined, but citizens have subordinated themselves to the power of the state, a power that is not always exercised tenderly or considerately. In this view, it is possible to draw a straight line from the forced sterilizations of the 1930s and '40s to the fairly weak rights that, even today, Swedes enjoy as individuals in relation to the state.[40]

Whether Sweden's welfare state is viewed from the perspective of Tocqueville or Rousseau, one historical fact about it remains: it represents a solution that is as unusual as it successful to the challenge of how a society should balance the individual's striving for sovereignty with the reciprocity needed to avoid social collapse and Thomas Hobbes's "war of all against all." Democratic, voluntary, and rooted in the nation's history, modern Swedish society is based, we claim, on a social contract that offers maximal individual sovereignty with minimal moral consequences.

The Swedish welfare state is not a solution from above, imposed by fanatical social engineers. On the contrary, the impulse to break with close familial and other ties in civil society has been anchored in popular practices and, moreover, has come to be regarded as an expression of solidarity rather than alienation. In the next chapter, we examine the historical foundations of this singular, even strange achievement.

PART 2

Sweden Imagined

CHAPTER 4

Poverty and Progress

When philosophically inclined Swedes first tried to define Sweden as a nation, their thoughts flew at once to its climate. To them, the conditions for human existence in Sweden were harsh and precarious. "Swedes inhabit a land that is poor and desolate in comparison with those sinful countries in the south which drip with juice and fat," wrote Carl Jonas Love Almqvist in 1838 in *Svenska fattigdomens betydelse* (*The Significance of Poverty in Sweden*). Almqvist echoed Erik Gustaf Geijer's observation, thirteen years earlier, in his book *Svea rikes natur* (*Swedish Nature*), that Scandinavia is a strict and chilly mother: "The polar region extends as far as the Scandinavian peninsula."[1]

Even so, both Geijer and Almqvist regarded such poverty and strictness as positive. Austerity and the very struggle to survive created unusually tough and independent people. "Only a prudent, resilient, and industrious people could settle in the valleys and mountains of Scandinavia," Geijer continued.[2] And the generative power of poverty was, in turn, the central theme of a famous essay Almqvist wrote one year after a disastrous harvest: "To be poor means to be thrown upon one's own resources. . . . Not to perish but to survive: to draw organically from within oneself all that is needed—that is how one endures poverty. Mastering this properly, promptly, independently, and with complete freedom: finding in oneself an inexhaustible source of help, and drawing strength from it with dexterity, craft, and promptitude—this impulse is the fundamental essence of Swedish national character."[3]

Managing by oneself, being self-sufficient and independent—Almqvist named some key tropes of Swedishness that continue to circulate in our own era. His views were seconded by Geijer: "In their industry and endurance, Swedes demonstrate a remarkable ability to meet their own needs while remaining true to themselves: there is no adversity which they cannot overcome: they have mighty resources within themselves which they can call upon when needed; there is no other people among whom natural ingenuity is more widespread than the Swedish peasantry."[4]

Geijer and Almqvist formulated their philosophy of Swedishness in the aftermath of the final defeat of Sweden's imperial ambitions with the loss of its Finnish "eastern kingdom"—which had been an integral part of Sweden since the twelfth century—in 1809. The Napoleonic Wars had brought revolutionary changes to Sweden: a king had been deposed, a new sovereign installed, a new constitution adopted, and the country's borders brusquely redrawn. The ship of state was wallowing on the high seas, explained the Swedish general Georg Carl von Döbeln after Sweden's defeat by Russia—demasted, rudderless, and without sail or compass.[5] Yet defeat and political uncertainty can create favorable conditions for philosophers and poets.

The national trauma of the early 1800s gave rise to a period of introspection in which modern Swedish identity was reevaluated and crystalized. The poet and professor at Lund University Esaias Tegnér called for the creation of an "inner" empire within the new boundaries of Sweden to compensate for the loss of Finland. Although Geijer and Almqvist never mentioned Finland in so many words, their arguments about the value of poverty and of enduring hard times were bound up with this turning point in Swedish history. Greatness, they said, lies not in possessions or power but in the fundamental character traits of a people.

Or, more precisely, of *the* people—because democracy is the other theme in Geijer's and Almqvist's philosophies of Swedishness. The vital impulse of Sweden's identity beats in the heart of its freeholding peasants, according to Geijer and Almqvist. Both disliked the upper class, whom they viewed as less a part of the nation than the common people because they need neither work nor struggle against the bareness of the land itself. Those who are not continually compelled to struggle for survival risk sliding into moral decadence, Geijer wrote: "Sloth destroys the fiery character of the Southerner though outbursts of violent strife; slower, surer, and crueller is the more ignominious gentle death in Scandinavia which our forefathers prayed to their gods to be spared. Beneath our harsh skies this inner lethargy is an easily acquired disease, which blunts all higher faculties, and in consequence of which the innate anxiousness of the Scandinavian character expresses itself only in a fumbling search for light, a loss of any conception of existence, a resulting envy of any seeming advantage, and an inner discord."[6]

Almqvist was even more explicit in his criticism of the upper class's deficient patriotism. The "Swedish gentry," he explained, had dissociated itself from the nation. It was not founded on "a bedrock of Swedish feeling" but had its spiritual home in Germany, France, Britain, or Greece. The nobility, which for the most part had been imported from overseas and which had no natural contact with the people, lacked the ability of the common Swedish people to "find strength in poverty." The great virtue of ordinary Swedes was an almost complete sovereignty that existed nowhere among the nobility. For Swedes, the most important thing was "to always be capable of being poor." Such spiritual freedom gave them the power "at any time to rise up, bound to naught, reliant only upon themselves and nothing else in the world."[7]

To be sure, there was nothing particularly Swedish about holding simple laboring folk up as a Romantic ideal. On the contrary, belief in the intrinsic goodness of poor people was a commonplace among the democratic movements of the day. Geijer and Almqvist were part of a large company of poets and philosophers in the first half of the nineteenth century who connected their political ideals to an idea of the importance of national community. All over Europe and in North America, new national movements were appealing to notions of justice, freedom, and equality, often while claiming that these values were particularly in evidence among their own people.

The revolutionary Giuseppe Mazzini urged his countrymen to realize the dream of a unified and socially progressive Italy. French historian and politician Jules Michelet dug down into his native soil and discovered true Frenchness among his country's industrious rural people. German students and intellectuals went back to the Peasants' War of the 1520s in their search for the roots of a unified German nation. The pastor Nikolaj Grundtvig identified ordinary Danes as descendants of the Norse gods, who would revitalize Denmark after the Napoleonic Wars. And in the United States, printer and journalist Walt Whitman wrote poems about a new people who, though highly modern and self-reliant as individuals, were united in a mystical and American collective destiny.[8]

Discussions of the connection between nationalism and democratic values often emphasize the occasional and sometimes even the contradictory as factors. Marxist historian Eric Hobsbawm argued that equality and liberty are no more logically connected to national feeling than they are to fraternity, the third term of the French Revolution's slogan. In his view, the "nation" is mostly a flag of convenience that serves to gather all those who opposed traditional conservatism and the old aristocratic order. It is an account that associates liberalism primarily with free trade, laissez-faire, and English economists.[9]

Yet this perspective is too narrow. Nineteenth-century liberal nationalism was indeed a heterogeneous movement within which openly liberal positions were forced together with more conservative and religious ideas of various kinds. But there were many who wrestled with a truly political problem: how could a citizenship of equals be reconciled with a functioning social community and a legitimate state? The French Revolution of 1789 had shown the dangers of trying to found a new society solely on abstract rights and unlimited state power.

Few wished to see the return of the executioner's cart or the guillotine. Postrevolutionary democrats, inspired by the Romantic reaction to Enlightenment thinking, particularly the ideas of eighteenth-century Germany philosopher Johann Gottfried Herder about the national specificity of folk culture, sought to anchor their analyses in historical realities and popular community rather than lofty philosophical principles. Famous left-leaning thinkers who were affected by Herder included John Stuart Mill, Henri de Saint-Simon, Benjamin Constant—and Erik Gustaf Geijer.[10]

But the strategy was not without dangers, as Hobsbawm pointed out. Poetry and data need to be in broad agreement if the goal is a philosophical system based on an empirical past but also idealizes members of a particular community as the embodiment of certain civic values. For Geijer, Almqvist, and their spiritual allies in Europe and America, the degree of success depended on their own discursive abilities as well as on actual historical conditions. However much they might wish to, liberal German nationalists in the nineteenth century could not simply conjure up a rosy account of free, emancipated peasants successfully holding their own against aristocrats and monarchs. The defeats in the Peasants' War, the rule of the Prussian nobility, and the the lack of a unified German state collectively created the conditions for a national self-image defined by resentment and the experience of historic defeat, which would in turn be a nursery for future chauvinism and antisemitism.[11]

In the United States, in contrast, it was easier for Walt Whitman and other thinkers inspired by the greatness of the American nation to unite visionary patriotism with radical notions of equality and a powerful individualism. They lived in a country that had successfully broken with the past, a new republic in a new continent. Its fundamental liberal tenets were inscribed in its constitution and shaped the political culture—the task now was to move forward, to make into a reality the intentions that were immanent in the American project. Admittedly, this had led to a bloody civil war that subdued those parts of the nation whose nature was more "European" and feudal—but it had also resulted in the paradox of the United States becoming a recognized power whose claims to influence rested more on universal liberal principles than on the stated interest of the national community.[12]

In Sweden, the prospects for finding democracy and equality in role models from history were somewhat better than those in Germany. The way Geijer and Almqvist talked about independence and individualism resembled more the conversation in America, with one crucial difference: Sweden was not a new country that had been born into revolution and civil war. It would take skill and a good deal of rhetorical sleight of hand to formulate a liberal vision in a politically backward country that lay on the fringes of Europe and still had trade guilds and a parliament of four estates.

ON YOUR OWN

"[The] progress of individual freedom ... is the movement of history itself." These words were penned by Geijer, a conservative history professor and parliamentarian, in the first issue of the journal *Litteraturbladet* in winter 1838. It was his famous defection. In doing so, Geijer sided with the liberal program of the day: universal suffrage, state secondary schools, and reform of the poor-relief system. He recanted his earlier belief in a social order in which people were united by strong mutual bonds of authority and subordination. He rebutted patriarchy with his theory of the primacy of the individual: "The single person and their rights is the be-all and end-all of society."[13]

Just a few years earlier, when reviewing a book on French utopian socialism, he had denied that society could be built on personal freedom. The family, Geijer had declared in 1834, was society's "first element." Next came corporate bodies and the four estates. Equal rights were only for human beings in the abstract; in reality, rights existed only insofar as they were matched by obligations. After his defection, he denied the legitimacy of the institutions of patriarchy: all were founded on "wrongs." Recognition of the personal rights of individuals was needed in order to rectify them. People could as easily "change the course of suns as the eternal laws of such freedom."[14]

Geijer's conversion to a perspective based on the rights of the citizen was an event that caused great excitement. At the time when he changed political course, he was in his mid-fifties. For almost three decades, he had been living and working in Uppsala, a university town that was deeply marked by a Romantic reaction against Enlightenment philosophy. As a poet, philosopher, and historian, he had engaged his ready wit, erudition, and stylistic flair to defend conservative doctrines of the state and to scourge liberal ideas in general. His public position was strong and respected; he taught princes and mingled with the upper echelons of officialdom. But at some point in the 1830s, he had begun to waver in his erstwhile convictions. The July Revolution of 1830 in France was an important, if slow-acting, factor in his change of heart. Geijer followed the debate in English, German, and French newspapers, and despite his initial opposition found himself being impressed by English free-trade liberals as well as by Saint-Simon's more socially compassionate adherents in France. Poverty, overcrowding, and conditions in the "dark satanic mills" raised new questions, sparked debates, and inflamed sympathies.

Conditions closer to home also played their part. The poverty caused by failed harvests in 1837 and a decline in Swedish iron exports both affected Geijer, an ironmaster's son who even in his youth had expressed strong feelings of social compassion. He became increasingly receptive to Sweden's growing liberal opposition, whom he met with during visits to Stockholm in the 1830s. His decision to change sides was thus taken in maturity and after much thought, and he was to hold to his new course until his death in 1847—one year before a new wave of revolutions swept across Europe. Geijer faced accusations of having become an "immoderate and radical democrat." As one critic put it in the conservative newspaper *Dagligt Allehanda*: "Mr G . . . has sunk lower in liberalism than those who have never fallen despite confessing to be a liberal their entire life."[15]

At the same time, Geijer's ideas were too complex for him ever to become a dyed-in-the-wool advocate of liberalism. But his defection would likely not have had the same dramatic historical impact had he not chosen to set down his faith in individual liberty in a famous 1838 poem titled "På nyårsdagen" ("On New Year's Day"). Its image of a solitary sailor in a "fragile vessel," sailing across dangerous stormy seas beneath an endless sky, had a double significance. Not only did it capture Geijer's own feelings about his reappraisal, it underscored the ideological implications of the drastic choice he had made. People were now ultimately alone, despite living in the same society that Geijer, just a few years before, had regarded as firmly grounded on institutions of collective responsibility. They had to forge their own path. Their only company on the journey was a distant God, who "abides in the deep as in the skies."[16]

The degree of discontinuity should not be overstated, however. There were elements of freedom in Geijer's conservatism just as there were conservative aspects to his liberalism. Early-nineteenth-century Scandinavian authors are sometimes presented as antiprogressive Romantics. It is true that that they emphasized the feeling of solidarity between people and nation, advocated a pietistic strand of Christianity and turned their back on faith in abstract reason. Yet Scandinavian Romanticism was nonetheless based on Enlightenment philosophy and the use of reason to solve problems. "All geniuses are practical," as Geijer put it in one of his aphorisms.[17]

Swedish, Norwegian, and Danish intellectuals were not looking out of high palace windows. From their parsonages, they saw not anonymous masses borne down by a feudal yoke but individuals, subjects, personalities—unpolished and uneducated, admittedly, yet quite capable of realizing the full potential of their slumbering virtues. Society would be refashioned not through revolution but by the maturing of its smallest component: individual people. This educational project was patriarchal and Christian, but it was also colored by mythical notions of an ancient Scandinavian "personal freedom."[18]

Geijer's ideals were also grounded in his interpretation of history. In 1811, together with Tegnér and Per Henrik Ling, he founded Götiska förbundet (roughly, the Gothic League), a patriotic society that celebrated Old Norse and whose members wrote prolifically about the Icelandic sagas. Familiar to generations of schoolchildren and criticized by feminists, Geijer's poetry is full of manly virtues, courage, and cruelty. His heroes are strong, silent men who go to their doom resignedly and with dignity—"poetry for martinets and common soldiers," as Swedish historians called it a century later when they settled accounts with those who romanticized the Viking era.[19]

And yet in his poems "Odalbonden" ("The Yeoman"),[20] "Vikingen" ("The Viking"), and "Olav Tryggvason," these and other heroes are connected to his liberal creed. In his two classic poems, one about a Viking whose cabin "became too cramped,"[21] the other about a sturdy yeoman peasant who makes his way to the Svea *ting* (governing assembly) with "his shield upon his arm,"[22] Geijer held up the settled individual against the rootless one. Yet both prize freedom and independence. For the Viking, the sea stands for emancipation from the demands of family and society: the waves hold "no chains, those at sea know no ties." The freeholding peasant, by contrast, does not believe in the "billow's false course": his hopes and faith lie in solid land. But he, too, knows the value of freedom:

> I know only what is *mine*,
> Pay to God and king my dues
> And the rest enjoy[23]

Admittedly, he acknowledged here and there the dark sides of the Viking era: the brutal violence, the autocratic tendencies, and the lawlessness. But these were historical shadows from a lost age whose fundamental values of freedom and equality could now be extricated: "The free man of the heroic early ages was a landowner, warrior, assembly member, worthy in every respect of the Scandinavian yeoman peasant, king in his own house, united with his kin in taking a stand against any insults . . . in matters of equality acknowledging as his master only a man who has been generally approved or who is well-bred, or such as to whom it has fallen by inheritance."[24]

Geijer's "desperate Romanticism," as he later called his Gothicism, was of a piece with his liberalism, if sublimated. In the early years of the century, he was drawn to what he termed "the aesthetic-imaginary tendency," a belief that the world could be reconciled with itself through feeling and imagination. The ancient Norse era offered precisely the mythology needed to balance the Enlightenment's arid faith in reason. "Poetry is the only history before history," Geijer explains.[25] He would later distance himself from this more romantically tinged view of history. But his need to base politics in history remained.

Geijer absorbed the Enlightenment's universalist claim to freedom in the same way as Saint Augustine, the church father, had Christianity: his initial resistance gave depth and strength to his conversion. Freedom was more than a shallow enticement; it was necessary. The solitary sailor on New Year's Eve 1838 is not being driven forward because he wants to be on a desolate sea: it is "the price of his fate." Like Marx, Geijer saw human freedom as a historically determined process. It is this precise blend of general liberal values with a particularist national project that lent a special quality to Geijer's nationalism. As a mythology, it is not unlike the belief that the United States is the promised land of individual freedom. Or perhaps more to the point, since Sweden has not been a country of immigrants, it is more like the idealized image of "freeborn Englishmen" that inspired radicals in Britain.[26]

Before continuing, a more systematic formulation of Geijer's political philosophy can be summarized as four main ideas: (1) the individual is society's smallest constituent element; (2) freedom presupposes equality and independence; (3) the state can emancipate the individual; (4) realization of individual freedom is a state project.

THE INDIVIDUAL IS SOCIETY'S SMALLEST CONSTITUENT UNIT

Geijer's conclusion that the individual is society's smallest constituent element was likely the most painful for him to accept. Prior to his conversion to liberalism, he identified the family as the fundamental social unit. Personal experience gave this conviction a special intensity for him. He had grown up in a large, noisy, and seemingly happy family on a manorial estate in Värmland, a western province bordering Norway. His life was filled with dances, games evenings, and visits to his sprawling extended family. Both Geijer and his brother married their second cousins, and recorded accounts and letters attest to each man's affection for his spouse and parents. Although recent scholarship has managed to establish the existence of gloomier emotions behind the cheerful patriarchal facade, there is little doubt that Geijer believed strongly in the ideal of the family, in principle as well as in practice.[27]

For a long time, Geijer opposed the social atomism that was so integral to Enlightenment thinking. In the article on utopianism mentioned above, the learned professor demonstrates his famously caustic wrath: "We also persist in maintaining that human beings are nothing but so-called *social creatures*. Take them anywhere in the world! You will always have to begin with a *collective entity*."[28]

There is more than a distant echo here of Marx's observation that the smallest social entity is two people. Like Marx, Geijer would appropriate the dialectic in order to unite human emancipation with the social beings of history. Geijer might have recoiled at the consequences of individualism, but he realized that in it lay the fulcrum of his philosophy of society. As he writes, almost as a challenge to himself, in his 1840 essay "The Question of Representation" ("Representationsfrågan"): "To admit [the principles of general human rights] is to be obligated to state them unreservedly and without fear of being charged with exaggeration."[29]

The solution was the *personlighetsprincipen (personality principle)*, the foundation on which Geijer based his radically democratic position regarding the question of universal suffrage.[30] Every person, regardless of class or gender, possessed a unique personality of their own: "It is my unshakeable conviction that there is not one person who is incapable of doing something better than all others. Nor do I believe that there exists a single person from whom I could not learn something. This is my liberalism: to equate all things, whatever they may be." People were thereby liberated from the fusty bonds of feudal servitude to become equal citizens with political rights. But the concept of personhood here also had another meaning. It referred not to people's animal-like existence but to the identity they gained in and through baptism, their admittance into the social community. "I" might be the fundamental unit, but that "I" required an "other I" in order to develop and gain self-awareness and autonomy: "No one can be free without another."[31]

This might seem like a banal idea. As Anders Ehnmark pointed out in his study of Geijer, it is pretty much what most thinkers who wrestle with the problem of individuality come up with. The alternative is complete subjective isolation, a solipsism. What is interesting is that Geijer put so much effort into the rejection of alienating individualism. His writing exhibits a fascination with otherness that is also laced with fear. He was deeply affected by contemporary debates over pauperism," the fears about the new class of impoverished proletarians who were multiplying in the shadows of the new factories and the widening sphere of commerce.

Geijer was likewise greatly impressed by the argument of English philosopher Thomas Hobbes that in a state of nature there is a "war of all against all." Although he made considerable effort to try to show that this dismal thesis was erroneous, he never really managed to convince himself. One of his most frequent formulations was that once upon a time the word "stranger" had meant "enemy."[32]

There is more than a distant echo here of Hegel's philosophical tale about the two strangers in a forest clearing who square up to decide who will be the master and who the slave. Geijer's Romantic poetry abounds in strong, fierce men who do not hesitate to defend their integrity and dignity. Despite its Christian framework, the core of the personality principle is, according to Ehnmark, an encounter defined by conflict. The "I" and the "you" cannot develop without a struggle.[33]

Geijer recognized that emancipation of the individual from the traditional community would place enormous demands on both society and the individual. The latter risks isolation and loneliness; the former is threatened by collapse:

> The more individuals seek to break free and educate themselves independently, the more apparent become ... their commonalities, the clearer becomes the necessity of the collectivity in opposition to the wilfulness of the individual. Were this not a natural law of human freedom, how could one ever imagine human beings giving up their natural freedom in order to live in dependence upon each other. ...
>
> [E]ven if, for the purpose of dissolving all social connections, they turn upon each other in combat and cause their own mutual destruction, before long they will all find themselves caught in a new circle, and the state returns again, as oppressive as before and possibly more so. Because the more individuals long to detach themselves, the more deeply each person feels the baleful necessity, as if in reciprocated hatred, of forcing people to develop an ever-closer mutual dependence.[34]

And the state returns again, as oppressive as before and possibly more so ... Hobbes's mighty dictator Leviathan or, for that matter, Tocqueville's downward-leveling state power is here a deterrent threat. The freedom of the individual leads to a war of all against all, which in turn gives rise to a despotic central power. And yet, continued Geijer, who then summoned up God as a supporting hypothesis, the bitter necessity of dependence can be happily reversed by means of "love"—that is, by making "commonalities" the greatest happiness an individual can choose.

The meaning of Geijer's oracular pronouncement seems to be that we can learn to voluntarily put up with our mutual dependence if we can learn to love the necessity of living together. He counterposed Hobbes's dire autocrat to piety and the moral life. As a happy ending, it is not terribly convincing. An unsympathetic critic—and there have been many—might accuse Geijer of invoking God when he is unable to solve a problem. Like a conveniently rich uncle, religion makes a sudden appearance in the drama's final act. Yet it prompts an essential question: How can a society be both free and good?

FREEDOM PRESUPPOSES EQUALITY AND INDEPENDENCE

Geijer rarely, perhaps never, used the concept of "the individual" in order to describe the private citizen. Wherever possible, he referred to "individual freedom," "the private person," "individuality," "free man," "personality," and "personal right." This is no accident. He disliked the abstract, unhistorical aspect of the word "individual." Geijer's notion of freedom was positive and meant "freedom to," not "freedom from." In the new school of thinking, he wrote, freedom is "a negative concept: being allowed to do something that is not forbidden."[35]

Geijer here allied himself in part with a distinction drawn in the early 1800s by the French liberal Benjamin Constant, between classical and modern freedom. The classical ideal of freedom presupposed the citizen's virtue, a willingness to sacrifice oneself for the common good. This view of freedom stood in contrast to modern freedom—the maximizing of one's own comfort. For his part, Geijer disliked the egoistic modern concept of freedom. He saw clearly the inherent ambivalence of the concept of the individual. On one hand, it could be used to define an active citizen who participates with others in the formation of a just society. On the other, it could refer to the unvarnished egoism that led people to crush their peers in a war of all against all. As a counterpoint to this "new school," Geijer invoked not swishing togas but the rustling leaves of ancient Nordic forests: "For our forefathers, freedom was a carefully defined, positive concept.... In its old designation, free meant someone who, under any imaginable circumstances, answered only to himself or was his own man—unfree denoted any person who did not enjoy this state but instead lay under another's protection."[36]

Freedom meant sovereignty, therefore, and independence from other people. Though as obviously normative and idealizing as the classical concept, it is nonetheless different in crucial respects. This freedom charges individuals with an obligation to realize their innate personality, to elevate themselves above merely catering to their needs and pleasures.

Yet individual autonomy was never entirely subordinated to the requirement for civic virtue. The crucial issue is the right to govern one's own fate. To be sure, the freeholding peasant is ready to do his duty and go to war when the king summons him. But freedom is what remains when God and the king have had their due: to take pleasure in one's own house and land, "and my brothers, like myself, in their own hamlets."[37] The peasant goes to the assembly hall, not in order to show off his civic virtue but because he has grown restless at home and has taken a fancy to it.

Geijer's rhetoric of freedom always has a touch of the peasant's sulkiness. Ehnmark is right in saying that there dwells a citizen within Geijer's peasant and a peasant within Geijer's citizen. But the point is that the two never fully merge with each other. Freedom can be neither idealized as an aristocratic self-sacrifice for the common good nor reduced to egotistical self-interest. There is, rather, a third alternative: giving the community what it is due, with a minimum of fuss, while in all other regards taking care of one's own business without interference—being one's own man.

For Geijer, independence presupposed equality. The meeting of "I" and "you" that formed the core of the personality principle could not take place if either party was subordinate to the other. Geijer's peers were taken unawares by his radical defection in 1838 because they had failed to grasp how uncompromising was his newfound belief in the individual.[38]

In portraying the historical movement toward freedom, Geijer made no exceptions on the basis of gender or class: "Sons were the first to gain independence through war, wives gained theirs through the church, and servants gained their portion of freedom and rights with the advent of the Third Estate [of the French Revolution]."[39] Forcefully and consistently, he now affirms the very philosophy of rights that he had attacked prior to 1838: "Individual suffrage for all morally blameless citizens who have reached their majority is thus the principle upon which I must insist. Justice demands nothing less, as I see it, and this principle can be neither evaded nor denied."

Paradoxically, Geijer's individualism was the more radical because of his avoidance of abstract formulation. He spelled out which groups had to be emancipated: "There was a time when a paterfamilias purchased his wife, determined the life or death of his children, and held his servants in bondage. What other remedy could there be for such a family than the rights of the private person!"[40]

Geijer's discussion of women's right to vote is instructive. As the weaker sex, women were "the original slaves."[41] They had been denied their political rights on the most absurd grounds. A woman's primary task was to raise the new generation to be responsible and self-sufficient, and its subsequent formation by priests and teachers relied on her labors. "It is impossible," Geijer explained, "not to be struck by the unreasonableness of making subservient the very citizens who are expected to bring new members into the body politic."[42] Even so, he did not want women to take part in politics: their task was really a moral one. Geijer may have been stuck in a gendered mode of thinking, but consistency prevented him from denying that women had political rights.

His conclusion, though obviously strained, nonetheless had radical implications: women should indeed be "emancipated" from politics, *not* because they lacked political rights "but because they ought not to want to exercise them."[43] Geijer had put a cautious toe in the door of patriarchal marriage that was about to be kicked wide open.

And precisely because he made positive freedom (the right to sovereignty and personal development for all) rather than negative freedom (the absence of laws and obstacles) the core of his philosophy, Geijer was more radical in relation to social issues. Indeed, he bears more than a passing resemblance to the Tory radicals who at around this time were protesting against the inhuman consequences of liberalism: "A class of slaves is once again being deposited in the bosom of civilization; a class of propertyless and defenceless proletarians, multiplying into an appalling stream." After his defection, and particularly as a member of Parliament, Geijer became deeply engaged in social issues, including the "poor relief" question.[44]

Despite being strongly influenced by Saint-Simon and other utopian thinkers, Geijer was no socialist. Private property was a step forward for civilization. But his defense of equal and individual rights led him, as with women's rights, to adopt a more radical position on labor questions than might have been expected from a sometime conservative professor of history.[45] Like Anatole France decades later, he realized that any freedom that entitled both rich and poor to sleep under a bridge on the Seine was an inadequate freedom. In this regard his personality principle served as a lever. The proletarian, every bit as much as the yeoman peasant, had an individuality that could be developed.

The personality principle did not simply mean that "I" and "you" were equivalent; they ought also to be materially independent of each other because in such a relationship freedom became corrupted: "Selfishness [is] ugly because it is a dependent kind of egotism, highly dependent upon others whose slave it thereby becomes. Selflessness is lovely because it demands and needs nothing. Any love that lives only in the well-being of its object, demanding nothing in return and having no ulterior motive, is supremely beautiful."[46]

In this idea—which, it must be admitted, Geijer more touched on than developed—can be seen the basis for the coming radical attacks on the patriarchal institutions of Swedish society, above all marriage. If love is made ugly and debased by material dependence between partners, then loving partners should be completely free, socially and economically, of each other. But how should individuals be liberated from the harmful ties of obligation and dependence that bind them to each other?

THE STATE CAN EMANCIPATE THE INDIVIDUAL

Before his defection, Geijer regarded the institutions that mediated between the state and the individual—family, the four parliamentary estates, and corporations—as crucial components of the social order. First among them was the family, with its warmth and intimacy.

But even the guild system, the municipal bodies, and the four estates made vital contributions to the living organism that was the Swedish state. The idea that the people—considered as an aggregate of individual citizens with rights—should exercise sovereignty was quite foreign to him.

Even here, however, we see a tiny glimmer of the democratic conversion that lay ahead. As far back as his first book, a prize-winning study of the fifteenth-century regent Sten Sture the Elder, Geijer displayed what John Landquist calls "an aversion to every kind of 'mediating power' between king and people."[47] A theme to which Geijer would repeatedly return in his poetry and historical writings was first articulated here.

In the past, Swedish peasants had been free citizens with the right to participate in forming laws in consultation with the king. During the Middle Ages, however, the people and their king had moved apart. The social distance between the four estates had increased, individual families had gained far more power, the peasants had been excluded from the parliament, and the privileges of the nobility had been strengthened. The result was a weakening of popular sovereignty and the establishment of rule by an aristocratic elite, primarily through the Royal Council. The famous maxim "Sweden's history is that of its kings" is thus more normative than empirical: it was through kings that the people were supposed to rule.

In our time, this historical perspective—what the eighteenth-century historian Anders Fryxell once dismissed as an expression of "anti-aristocratic feeling"—is a favorite topic for historiographers.[48] Yet Geijer's critique of aristocracy was actually part of a far more thoughtful sociology. He tried to find a balance in the relationship between individual, society, and state. In the personality principle, he had developed a reasonably clear understanding of the individual's position, whose alpha and omega were personal rights. But what role should the state and society play? At this point, Swedish history came to his aid. Just as the king had once allied himself with free men against the nobility, so too would state and citizens now make common cause against the feudal institutions that curtailed personal freedom.

Geijer's support for individual freedoms and rights was a principled, if belated, act of affiliation with the ideals of the European Enlightenment. His firm emphasis on positive freedom and the right to independence and personal development came from his own convictions. He drew a connection to this notion by defining the state as the force that would emancipate the individual while also serving as guarantor of its citizens' independence and sovereignty:

> Consider the smaller organizations in society upon which so much importance is placed: the families and corporations of every kind, from the local council to the estate.
> All began with great injustices. . . . What else could have reformed the family but recognition of the rights of the private person?
> —Likewise with the corporation. While it might increasingly be recognizing the principle of mutual rights, it is still very far from being able to extend this recognition beyond itself. Have not corporations always, and even now, fought with each other about their exclusive rights? Who can resolve these contradictions if not the state? And how can they be solved except through a more precise definition of personal rights?[49]

What Geijer said here is that the state will liberate individuals from the obligation and dependence that linger on in the communities that have hitherto constituted society: the family, the four estates, the guild. The formulation is cautious, of course. The intermediary organizations are to be reformed, not dissolved. Still, this was 1840. Quite apart from the constraints of its immediate historical moment, what Geijer set out here was the kernel of a radical social project that would lead, in the short term, to the dissolution of the four estates and the guild system and, in the long term, to gender-equal marriage laws and state-funded childcare for all. But did Geijer really mean that the state was *the only* force able to unite the social atoms that democracy would set free?

Like Tocqueville, who also saw individualism as predestined but worried about the power that would accrue to the state if all "secondary institutions" were destroyed, Geijer could dimly see a future alternative or, perhaps more accurately, a complement. A succession of commentators have underscored Geijer's hopes that independent associations might serve as an alternative to the old corporations— "all these companies, associations, societies for personal and public ends"—not least, that they might offer protection to the workers now threatened by the new power of capital. The new liberal society would be held together by voluntary associations, the grassroots movements of the future, rather than a strong state: this, at least, seems to be Geijer's thinking about what he called, in a revealing turn of phrase, the "adaptable corporation." At the same time, there is good reason to avoid too strongly contrasting his idea about associations with the strengthening of state power. The free associations were, rather, "the serried auxiliaries of the new state."[50] Geijer was uncertain as to what significance to accord these new federations. Political rights—which is to say, the relation between the private citizen and the state— remained paramount.

Such uncertainty about the future relationship between the state and the voluntary movements in civil society is also part of Geijer's legacy. His theories have left their mark on both the right and the left. The philosopher C. J. Boström would use the personality principle to formulate a conservative doctrine in which the state represents its highest personality. And grassroots movements would take up the image of the free yeoman peasant who joined forces with his peers in the assembly in order to assert his rights in the struggle against autocracy.

The question remains, however, as to whether the modern welfare state—in which the state is the ultimate guarantor of the individual's independence while grassroots movements play the part of "arrayed auxiliaries"—truly corresponds to Geijer's vision of society.

REALIZATION OF INDIVIDUAL FREEDOM IS A NATIONAL PROJECT

Recent decades have seen an effort to take the Swedishness out of Geijer. Per Meurling has highlighted the connections between Geijer and Marx.[51] Anders Ehnmark has dismissed all the poems celebrating Swedishness that were drummed into him at school, situating Geijer instead within the broader framework of the history of ideas as "a European intellectual rather than the bard of Swedishness."[52]

In many respects such antiprovincialism is sound. Geijer is without doubt one of the few genuinely great social philosophers that Sweden has produced. He was part of a vital European conversation about the conditions of freedom that began in the eighteenth century. His natural points of reference were Hobbes, Rousseau, Johann Gottlieb Fichte, Hegel, Kant, and Montesquieu. He read the work of his like-minded contemporary Tocqueville and saw at once his greatness. He met Hegel—to his great disappointment, despite the German philosopher's influence on the Swedish historian's development. As he sat in the German holiday resort of Kreuznach, Marx made excerpts from Geijer's 1843 history of Sweden (approximately eighty-five, according to Meurling). Geijer discussed classical history and honed his ideas about a supra-European state. As almost all commentators agree, he was a startlingly modern thinker.

But as Geijer saw it, his ideals could only be realized if he clothed them in national costume. His Gothic verses can seem hopelessly jejune. But in them he outlined the fundamental ideas about individual freedom and its significance for citizenship that would be a leitmotif throughout his writings. The freeholding peasant appears continually in his version of Swedish history, a modern person whose dignity stems from untrammeled authority over his own person and property—a poetic ideal of peasant freedom, to be sure, but not an ideal plucked from the air, either. There was sufficient truth in it for Geijer to be able to develop a narrative whose effects would be felt for a long time. As he himself cautiously put it: "All I know is that Sweden is one of the few countries where the mass of people happens to own land more often than elsewhere."⁵³

With that, we can leave the Viking era and Gothicism. Although they are part of Geijer's legacy, of course, they are more decorative than substantial. Regarding the key features of Swedish history—the alliance between king and peasants against the aristocracy, the degree of individual ownership in agriculture, and the political influence of the peasant estate—Geijer's account still warrants serious attention. The early dominance of *skattebönder*—peasants who owned their own land and paid tax directly to the state but had no feudal obligations—had no equivalent on the European continent, with the exception of certain areas in Switzerland. Similarly unique was their early and stable representation in the Swedish Parliament.

The idea of ancient peasant freedoms was, to be sure, as hackneyed a rhetorical device in nineteenth-century Sweden as the French and American revolutions were in the respective political cultures of their countries. Geijer's friend Almqvist, for example, felt obliged to register serious reservations when, writing in *Aftonbladet* newspaper in 1844, he invoked the Swedish yeoman peasants in support of his demands for a new system of representation: "The yeoman peasants were heads of families. Admittedly, the constitution did not describe a democracy in any pure or abstract sense, insofar as neither woman (free women no more than unfree), nor servant, nor poor person (without land of his own) had a voice in matters of state. Nevertheless, it was a democracy in the sense that all heads of families who were yeoman peasants jointly participated in the organizations of society, decided upon laws, levies, and military expeditions, and chose for themselves their judges and kings."⁵⁴

But for that matter, it is hardly the case that those other oft-cited historical models—the Greek city-states, the Roman republic, France's Declaration of the Rights of Man of 1789, or the early-nineteenth-century American republic—would count as true democracies without substantial qualifications.

Geijer's theories about peasant democracy elicited a powerful political response. Liberalism's classic supporters, the bourgeoisie, were still weak in Sweden. In virtually all Scandinavia, freeholding peasants would form part of the political base for the liberal movements of the nineteenth century. Admittedly, their liberalism was pragmatic and not particularly stringent theoretically. But on a number of issues—above all, that of representational reform—they played a decisive role. The Farmers' Party (Lantmannapartiet), an alliance of larger landowners and well-to-do peasants, continued to dominate the upper chamber of Parliament (which was an indirectly elected senate) long after 1865, while in the final years of the century, the more grassroots variety of liberalism established a strong base among ordinary people living in the countryside.[55]

Geijer's analysis of the political significance of the Swedish peasant class did not extend to his views on the family and women, however. He was similarly indifferent to the social aspects of Sweden's peasant culture. He was more interested in yeoman peasants and masters than in their wives and children. But even though this culture was firmly defined by a patriarchal order, there was also a tradition of individualism and independence in Swedish peasant households that benefitted women and children. Almqvist would build on this version of peasant freedom in his attacks on the bourgeois family culture that was beginning to emerge in nineteenth-century Sweden.

CHAPTER 5

Love and Independence

Erik Gustaf Geijer's ship—fragile or otherwise—was not the only ideological vessel that put to sea in Sweden in 1838. That same year, the steamer *Yngve Frey* leaves the pier at Riddarhuskajen in Stockholm. Among the watchful fathers and giggly daughters are two other travelers, Sara Videbeck, a glass manufacturer's daughter, and a noncommissioned officer named Albert, surname unknown but sporting a dapper curled mustache.

Romance blossoms during the voyage and at an inn among the wooded hills of Tiveden the couple consummate their affair. When Sara wakes the following morning, she feels "agitated like never before in her life." Her eyes, which had "flashed with intensity when she saw Albert, now bore the traces of a mostly sleepless night."[1] She was now a fallen woman.

Sara Videbeck would enter literary posterity, first as "a trollop who challenged the foundations of the existing order" and later, for Swedish high-school students in the latter part of the twentieth century, as a femininist ideal. Yet her most provocative quality was not her erotic impulsiveness. "Steamboat novels" were in vogue in the 1830s. The novelty of steamships, the speed of travel, and the mixing of social classes formed an appealing backdrop for novellas about flirtations and dalliances.[2] But *Det går an (Sara Videbeck)* is more than just a love story. Almqvist's novel is a radically individualist program for women's emancipation and the dissolution of the traditional family.

Sara wants complete independence as a woman, to be able to manage her life. She does not want to marry nor even to make any vows in secret. However, her lover, Albert, can rent a room in her house. They will maintain completely separate households and visit each other only when they genuinely want to meet. They hold their love in common, but all property separately. No wonder that the feminist Ellen Key, writing half a century later, dubbed Almqvist "Sweden's most modern poet."[3]

Almqvist was in his early forties when he wrote *Sara Videbeck*. He came from an established family of priests, government officials, and well-to-do peasants. In the 1810s he studied at Uppsala University, where the future professor Geijer was cutting his teeth as a reader or *docent*, an untenured position. Almqvist enjoyed his studies but had difficulty with his "surroundings"—it is unclear whether he was referring to the intellectual or the natural landscape.[4] His more middle-class progress began with a few years as a government official, followed by a happy time as a teacher, and subsequently principal, at Nya Elementarskolan, an experimental teacher training college in Stockholm. His literary career began quietly enough with philosophical and religious meditations, which were followed by a prolific outpouring of widely acclaimed poems, romantic novels, and more realistic tales such as *Sara Videbeck*. By the late 1830s, he was regarded as a radical writer with a clear political agenda.

Although Almqvist, unlike Geijer, had never been a champion of conservatism, his increasingly outspoken radicalism was also a kind of "defection"—one, moreover, with greater personal consequences. He wrote numerous newspaper articles on questions of the day—mainly in Lars Johan Hierta's *Aftonbladet*—and essays in which he set forth an increasingly sharp critique of society. A mysterious romantic aura surrounds his private life, from his failed effort to become a smallholder in the province of Värmland in the 1820s to his scandalous flight from Sweden to the United States in 1851 following accusations of attempted murder by poisoning. He died tragically in the German city of Bremen, in 1866, pining for his family and homeland.[5]

ALMQVIST AND GEIJER

Almqvist's individualism was more far-reaching than Geijer could ever have imagined. But the similarities between Geijer and Almqvist, who had a tense acquaintance, are nevertheless striking. They were both part of the same liberal awakening. Both held up individual personality as the fundamental building block of society. They were advocates of representational reform and equal rights. Both drew inspiration from a romanticized Viking-era view of Swedes as bearers of particular national virtues. Both Almqvist and Geijer were suspicious of abstract political philosophy. People in society had to be represented concretely, in poetry, novels, or historical accounts. Lastly, both men struggled to see how Christianity's message of love should be transformed into everyday political reality.

In many respects, this was a case of temperamentally different versions of the same cluster of ideas. Geijer was a builder of systems who strove for clarity and harmony. He calmly sorted through principles to find suitable materials for constructing a social order grounded in historical knowledge. He presented Swedes plainly and simply: contented and strong free peasants and Vikings. Geijer's subtlety lay in the sociological composition, a careful reconstruction of society on the basis of the private individual.

Almqvist's writings contain all the key elements of liberal nationalism in nineteenth-century Sweden: the primacy of the individual, the independence from other people, the emancipatory role of the state, and the national foundations of equality. But his temperament was very different, including elements of mysticism and the picaresque, religious ecstasy, and an undercurrent of eroticism that was often plainly visible. Novels such as *Amorina* (1822) and *Drottningens juvelsmycke* (*The Queen's Tiara*; 1834) are bewildering, anarchic, and unpredictable. Almqvist had a talent for description, a lyricism, and a feeling for the fundamental tragedy of existence that far surpass Geijer's.

In Geijer's writings, the alienation that follows in the footsteps of freedom is more of a hypothetical menace, something to think over beside the tiled stove in the cozy lodgings of the Uppsala professor. Almqvist, however, felt it in his bones. His marriage was unhappy, his finances failed, and he regarded his friends as disloyal. Society was, in his words, "an Arctic sea," the individual a castaway who must summon all his strength in order to survive. To be Swedish was "to be poor" and utterly reliant on oneself, not sitting comfortably in a farmhouse surrounded by family and servants.[6]

Almqvist's more curious, artistic nature has led some commentators to question his status as an interpreter of Swedishness. Henry Olsson argued that *The Significance of Poverty in Sweden* exhibits features that are more idiosyncratic of Almqvist than of Swedishness, particularly "a restless feeling of not belonging and a lofty, mischievous attitude toward his surroundings."[7] Yet Almqvist's ideas about feeling alienated from other people and about Lutheran dutifulness as also harboring a kind of irresponsibility were to strike many readers as an apt description of Swedish national traits. Indifference to other people, emotional reserve, lack of psychological insight and empathy—such were the headings under which future discussions would repeatedly return to the question of why Swedes seemed constitutionally incapable of being at ease in their surroundings. They might likewise have found support in Geijer's more genial portrayal of Swedish solitude. His irrational but sublimely unafraid Vikings, like his fear that society could degenerate into a "war of all against all," offers an insight into existential loneliness. And yet in the gloom it was Almqvist who saw even further.

THE EUROPEAN MARRIAGE PATTERN

Matters of temperament and style aside, there is a more substantial difference between the two leading lights of Swedish liberalism. In Almqvist's account, Geijer's upbeat patriarchal view of the family is replaced by a questioning of preassigned gender roles and the traditional marriage order. For the most part, Geijer saw the family as beyond politics and his philosophical system. He was ambivalent about how his defection to liberalism might affect his understanding of intimate relations. In contrast, the family and love between a man and a woman formed the bedrock of Almqvist's philosophy—he would have echoed the maxim of 1970s feminists that "the personal is the political."

Like a great many female thinkers and writers who emerged in the first half of the nineteenth century—Mary Wollstonecraft in England, for example, or Swedish novelist and advocater of women's rights Fredrika Bremer—Almqvist struggled with the question of how individual freedom might be reconciled with the laws and moral regulations that surrounded traditional marriage—although the phrase "traditional marriage" is, in fact, misleading in this context. The more troubled and volatile the world, the more people tend to designate customs and institutions as "ancient traditions."

It is sometimes claimed that the bourgeoisie was responsible for introducing a new ideal of the nuclear family in the nineteenth century, one that differed from the multigenerational and more open familial configuration that had been a feature of the peasant household. This is both true and false. The family structure that dominated peasant societies in Northern and Western Europe after the fourteenth century—the Western European family model—was characterized by clearly delineated single-family households, a relatively high age of marriage, and the placement of children as servants in other households. Compared to the family system that prevailed around the Mediterranean and in Eastern Europe, it was more egalitarian and less patriarchal, and it promoted greater independence and individualism.

In Southern and Eastern Europe, several generations cohabited within a stronger family hierarchy: the older father had authority over the family of his lodger son, brothers had power over their sisters, the age of marriage was low, and service in other families was considered dishonorable. Couples usually married after an agreement was reached between their families, while women were monitored more strictly by the norms of the honor culture and could not work beyond the home. One significant difference related to the age of marriage. In northwestern Europe, the long period that elapsed between sexual maturity and marriage as the partners reached their mid- or late twenties resulted in an extended and more independent period of youth. The night courting rituals of the sexually mature village youth and the intergenerational conflicts between fathers and sons over who was to be the head of the household are both also part of this pattern.[8]

The new middle class in Western Europe, then, did not introduce the ideal of the closed family unit—it was already in place in the nineteenth century. What they did do was to reconfigure family relations inward. Children in more affluent families were not sent away to service as maids and field hands but remained at home with their parents for the greater part of their upbringing. The role of women was thereby also transformed, from a more active partner in the family's farm holdings to the principal caregiver of her own children and supervisor of the domestic servants. Scandinavian peasant culture had not enforced a strict "natural" division between men's and women's work—there were huge regional and local variations.[9] Nor had the peasant household been a closed, tight-knit community. The husband was often away from home transporting goods, stopping at staging posts, or working in another district. In his absence, a community of women formed around childcare and the tasks of productive labor, something that had no equivalent in the new and more intimate middle-class family.

There is no reason to idealize the Northern European peasant culture in relation to gender equality. Yet the rise of a middle-class family culture brought with it a change in paternal authority that in some areas represented a reinforcement. The family was elevated to a "sacred" institution of society, a moral space to be protected from incursion by worldly forces, a view that was quite alien to Sweden's peasantry. Traditionally, Swedish peasants used the archaic Lutheran term "house" to describe their reproductive unit; "family" continued to be regarded, well into the nineteenth century, as a concern of masters.[10]

The dependence of women and children on their husband and father increased, while the tighter family structure made the patriarch more dominant in everyday life. The new paternal role was well captured by ethnologist Orvar Löfgren: "He represents power, but he is also the link to the outside world. Not only is it through him that the family gazes upon the world, it is he who conveys and filters much of their knowledge about that exotic and exciting place, the wider world."[11]

Unsurprisingly, some middle-class women began to mutiny against this new family order. They were typically better educated and had higher material expectations and a broader perspective than women in peasant society—even as they often had a smaller window of time in which to act. "Embroidering an endless grey border . . . is sapping my will to live," wrote Fredrika Bremer, who was to break free from the stifling femininity of middle-class drawing rooms.[12] Emotions and individual love played a greater ideological role in the middle-class family community even as the day-to-day control of fathers and husbands increased, above all via increasingly convoluted and complicated rituals of courtship, proposals, and social intercourse. This conflict is a dominant theme in the burgeoning nineteenth-century novel, from Jane Austen's unmarried daughters living at home to Gustave Flaubert's Madame Bovary.

In a study of Fredrika Bremer, Ulrika Kärnborg highlighted a revealing scene in her 1856 novel *Hertha*. The protagonist returns home rather late, asks to be forgiven for having forgotten the hour, and receives by way of reply the following outburst from her father: "Forgotten! One of these fine days you will also forget that you have a father to whom you have some obligations. Forgotten?—and you say it to me in that saucy manner, as if you have the right to insist upon anything. But as long as I am master in my own house, none but I shall insist upon anything. I shall be master in my own house. I shall have obedience in it, and subordination."[13]

It is, as Kärnborg observed, a chilling scene. But it also describes an increasingly hollow patriarchal order that finds itself having to resort to blunt orders. In Swedish peasant society, the father's power rested on a crass and deep-rooted chain of command that had been instituted for the purpose of meeting the most basic needs of the household. In middle-class culture, the father was an ideological project—a figure of power whose status was no longer self-evident but must be asserted in an aggressive and, as in Bremer's novel, almost hysterical manner.

Almqvist offered few, if any, realistic depictions of middle-class marriage. He instead moved between the utopian world of *Sara Videbeck* and idealized portrayals of the lives of common people. What makes the latter interesting is that they show how clearly Almqvist based his social critique on Sweden's peasant culture. Stories such as *Grimstahamns nybygge* (*The Gristahamn Settlement*; 1839) and *Ladugårdsarrendet* (*The Farm Lease*; 1840) are essentially idealized depictions of the attributes that latter-day family historians have emphasized as characteristic of the Western European model of marriage.[14] The protagonist in *The Gristahamn Settlement* is a widow named Kvast-Lisa—"a curious old dame" who supports herself by making brushes and brooms that she sells every day on Hötorget square in Stockholm. Her twenty-year-old son Johan serves as a field hand on a large farm nearby. With Katrina, the girl next door—"shapely, light-haired, blue-eyed, and beautiful"—Johan becomes a smallholder and starts a family.[15]

Almqvist here portrayed a peasant—more precisely, smallholder—culture whose central driving force is the desire to be independent. Johan's situation as a field hand is not a bad one. His master and mistress are fair, but having his own freedom as a settler is more important. He also refuses an offer to take over his mother's holdings. He wishes neither that his mother should "live like a servant lodger" or that his wife should have to share her home with a stepmother, "something that is always very difficult." Katrina proves herself an enterprising housewife, feeding the cows by herself and selling homespun cloth to pay for a hireling after Johan injures himself. No one is trapped in debt, everyone does their share, and love flows between the principals without any ulterior motives, dependence, or subordination.

A critical reader might naturally wonder whether Johan's urge to be independent borders on inhumanity when he leaves his aging mother to fend for herself on the parental farm. But here, too, Almqvist found a solution that does not compromise the underlying moral of his story. Mother Lisa happens to fall sick when visiting her daughter-in-law and grandchildren at Gristahamn, and by good fortune Katrina has a nook where Grandma can lie. There she remains until her death, surrounded by loving relatives but without causing any mother-in-law unpleasantness.[16]

The Gristahamn Settlement was published in 1839 together with several other similar narratives by Almqvist in a bound series titled *Folkskrifter* (*Writings on the People*). The idea was probably to compete with popular educational works of a more explicitly religious and morally instructive nature.[17] The series appeared at around the same time as *Sara Videbeck*, and it is easy to see the parallel in their moral economies: the importance of love being based on independence between partners. At the same time, this realism, which sometimes drifts into sententiousness, gives a misleading impression of Almqvist's fundamental motives and can make him seem like one of those popular educators who, pencil in hand, are continually translating human relations into material costs. But something far greater was at stake.

WHAT IS LOVE?

The all-pervading theme in Almqvist's lifework is that *true love requires that people be entirely independent of each other*. It is visible as far back as an essay titled "What Is Love?" that he wrote in 1816 at the age of twenty. Almqvist's mother was a great admirer of Rousseau, and her son aimed his polemic, in the spirit of the French philosopher, at the false view of love that prevails in the capital, where disillusioned men and women stick together merely for the sake of appearances. Yet the city in question was now Stockholm, not Paris.[18]

The author contrasted the corrupting influence of civilization with a simple country girl in Värmland, who would laugh if her husband asked her what love was but whose entire being contains the answer. Almqvist likewise followed Rousseau in reminding readers of the natural boundaries between men and women. A man should concern himself with the "good of the whole" and the woman with that of the "domestic sphere." This is, in other words, the traditional conservative understanding of the complementary attributes of gender. We are a long way from the radicalism of *Sara Videbeck*. But Rousseau's teachings are never unambiguous, even on questions of gender. His demands for authenticity, that relationships between people should be transparent and not based on selfishness or exploitation, can easily lead to a radical reappraisal of marriage. At the same time that young Almqvist prescribed domesticity for women, he raged against conventional morality, which he regarded as "one of the strongest bulwarks of egoism." Those who live their lives in accordance with hypocritical principles are condemned to "eternal discontent, indifference, diseased emotions, and disordered thinking." But as yet he could only moralize against a marriage held together by mutual dependence. Somewhat feebly, he held up not social reform but true religious feeling—"pure" love—as the alternative: if women and men followed their God-given natures, things would sort themselves out for the best.[19]

But it was the Rousseau-inspired demand for authenticity in human relations, not ideas about the eternal feminine, that came to permeate Almqvist's lifework. Indeed, it is highly doubtful whether Rousseau's ideas about gender complementarity had as profound an impact in Sweden as is often claimed. In an interesting essay titled "Rousseau—Invoked in His Absence," Inger Hammar argued that there is scant evidence that nineteenth-century debate in Sweden was particularly influenced by Rousseau on gender issues. The notion of a gendered soul ran contrary to the Lutheran understanding of men and woman as spiritually equal. Hammar discerned the outlines of a Protestant peasant gender order whose core ideology assigned women a central role in the household even as it restricted her opportunities for participating in public life.[20]

We cannot know to what extent Almqvist was influenced by the world as prescribed in Martin Luther's Small Catechism, but Almqvist's view of women was negotiable to the utmost degree. He took from Rousseau the ideal of equality and the demand for authentic feelings, yet quickly abandoned the notions of masculine and feminine that strongly influenced the gender debate in France, Britain, and other Western countries. He strikingly combined an erotic view of women with total flexibility about their "true" nature. This holds even for his more phantasmagorical writings in which the boundaries of gender are blurred in quite bewildering ways.

The clearest example is *The Queen's Tiara*, published in 1834. The story, set in Stockholm and its surroundings, centers on the murder of Gustav III in 1793. Its intrigue includes nocturnal love trysts, secret conspiracies, duels, jealousy, madness, and executions. At the heart of it all is the mysterious Tintomara, a young pupil at the Opera Ballet and half sister of Gustav IV Adolf. However, she is not really "she" but an androgyne, both man and woman, or possibly "neither," as another protagonist puts it. She is irresistibly alluring and attracts both men and women but is also rejected from society and ultimately executed.

The spirit of Rousseau hovers over much of *The Queen's Tiara*. When people conceal their true feelings, the result is misunderstanding, duplicity, and betrayal. Civilization is a never-ending theatrical performance in which even the actors can no longer tell the difference between appearance and reality. At a masquerade at the opera, everyone wavers in uncertainty about who they are really mixing with behind the masks. Friend or foe, lover or rival—everything can be exposed, nothing can be known with certainty.

But the opposing pole here is not, as in Rousseau, the simple and the natural, some preassigned masculinity or femininity. Nature, too, is in chaos. Is Tintomara a man or a woman, an animal or a human being? The question is unanswered. Almqvist used the Neoplatonic concept of *animal coeleste*—a "heavenly animal"—to describe her indeterminate, erotically fascinating nature. There is a dream here about emancipation, not only from the rigid order of a society of estates but also from the prevailing sexual contract. As Aristotle put it, to live outside of society one must be either a beast or a god. Tintomara is both.[21]

It was no coincidence that Almqvist chose to make Tintomara so ethereal and unreal. As yet he could see no way to reconcile human freedom—not least, human sexuality—with the bonds of obligation that regulated relationships between individuals. His own personal experiences were a likely factor in this.

In the mid-1820s, Almqvist had married a simple farm girl and moved to a smallholding in Värmland county. It was part of an attempt to realize a utopia of the simple life, far from half-educated Stockholmers and moral decadence. The project did not end well. Friends who had promised to join the colony let him down, and marriage fell short of his high expectations. As Geijer remarked acidly, it is one thing to love the people in principle, another to live with them. A year and half later, Almqvist was back in Stockholm.[22]

But he did not abandon the question of how men and women might live together in harmony. *Sara Videbeck* was an attempt to unite Tintomara with society, to organize marriage and customs in accordance with an androgyne who is both masculine and feminine. Sara Videbeck may seem like a charmless, practical young woman, a caricature of the chilly Swedish woman in sensible shoes who saves receipts in her handbag and never flutters her eyelashes. But Sara, too, is an *animal coeleste*, an androgynous being who crosses the gender barrier and creates the conditions for her own freedom.

This carries its own erotic charge. Sara Videbeck forms part of a feminine ideal that stretches from the nineteenth century's independent Valkyries to Swedish rock star Ulf Lundell's plea to be spared the hassle of teary foreign girlfriends.[23] As art historian Carl G. Laurin explained just prior to the First World War, "Swedish women are sensible, almost impartial, not prudes, and mostly disinclined toward jewelery."[24]

The first thing that readers learn about Sara is that she is hard to define, a cross between two things. After their first meeting, Albert muses over a steak in the steamboat's saloon: "A glazier's daughter from Lidköping—that's a small town, far, far away from Stockholm. Yes, she is what I took her for—a daughter of the middle class, yet not of the lowest grade. A charming and remarkable intermediate! Not a country girl, not at all peasant girl—nor yet entirely of the better class. What is the real status of such an individual? How shall I address her? There is something puzzling about this intermediate state."[25]

As in *The Queen's Tiara*, Almqvist here used ambiguity to create an erotic suggestiveness. But something new was added. Sara's inscrutability is primarily a class question: where does she fit it? She is neither master nor servant. She stands outside the existing social order.

But Sara herself chooses to stand outside. Despite being an unmarried woman and thus technically a minor, she wants to be her own woman. Because of guild restrictions, she cannot take over her father's glazing business but she can make putty and cut glass. The path to independence lies in entrepreneurship: she will open her own business and sell glazing products. We here encounter the same individualistic ethos that Almqvist advocated in essays such as *The Significance of Poverty in Sweden* and *Arbetets ära (The Nobility of Work)* and in his depictions of popular life.[26] As Karin Westman-Berg observed, "Sara Videbeck has important traits in common with the ideal type of person in *The Significance of Poverty in Sweden*."[27] It is, moreover, highly significant that she is presented as coming from the province of Västergötland, in whose name the ancient Norse word *göt* (the name of the inhabitants in southern Sweden during the Viking and medieval era) serves to associate Sara with the very essence of Swedishness.[28]

The goal of Swedes—and of all people—is independence, to be free, Almqvist declared in *The Significance of Poverty in Sweden*. Scarcity and poverty were not good in themselves, to be sure, but they taught people to trust themselves, to look within themselves, and to use their own abilities in order to avoid being dependent on their surroundings. The road to independence lay in hard work and ingenuity. At times Almqvist can sound like an American self-help philosopher as he celebrated the value of hard work and the good fortune of starting out empty-handed: "The greatest honor and good fortune for a person lie in being able to stand on their own two feet, independent of anyone else but God, and to find in themselves all the help they need in life."[29]

We see here the usual liberal promotion of economic freedom against guild organizations. But the goal is not wealth and prosperity—perhaps not even survival in the purely physical sense of the word—but, rather, individual freedom. And Almqvist also included women in his vision of economic independence as both a right and a duty. By now he had left his youthful conservative ideals about feminine domesticity far behind. "It is," he explained, "shameful for a woman to be a burden to her husband." She needed vocational training in order to support herself. In this way she would not be forced to marry a man she did not love in order to have food, clothes, and a house. But even if she did marry, both husband and wife should work and not live off the other, for "in this way they will be able to love each other."[30]

Almqvist's youthful ideal was essentially unchanged. The relationship between a man and a woman must be built on true love. The means, however, had changed. Instead of religious moralizing, Almqvist had now found an effective lever with which to save true love: complete economic independence between man and woman. Or, stated another way, a federation of two equal and socially androgynous beings.

One key point to note is that Almqvist—like Geijer—can hardly be described as a socialist in the modern sense. He was a typical nineteenth-century radical in that he was suspicious of wealth and excessive property. But he argued for small-scale enterprise, entrepreneurialism, and economic independence, not nationalization of the means of production. The task of the state was not to provide for or administer people's lives but to remove all barriers to the individual's self-realization. Yet to this end he was prepared to give far-reaching powers to the public authorities.

THE MAN WITH NO (SUR)NAME

During her journey to Lidköping, Sara Videbeck explains her revolutionary philosophy to the bewildered Albert. She sketches her parents' painful marriage, bound to one another against their wills, and explains how catastrophic it would be if she and Albert married:

> Since it is true that you are fond of me and I of you, we have that in common. That is a great deal, Albert. It is more than a good many others have. But if we set about to have a mass of other, unnecessary things in common, then I will tell you what would happen. If you should take my little house, my means of sustenance, my property and money [. . .] why then I cannot deny that I might begin to be cross, because you might not know how to manage such affairs. I imagine that you hardly know yourself whether you do, since you have had no experience in looking after a house and trade. . . .
> You would find me irritable, at first only occasionally, afterwards more often. Then you would become bitter yourself. . . . No doubt, we should have to begin to take the cure at Lund watering-place, or perhaps squander our money on mud-baths. . . . My complexion would soon begin to fade, my eyes would grow dull, and I should be more homely than I am now. . . . And you would grow tired of it, too, I am sure, because, after all, you are but a human being like myself.[31]

Albert is staggered by the bleakness of this vision. He tries to object: the example is ill-chosen—husband and wife normally share their troubles and woes. But finally he capitulates and looks on her and the matter in a new light: "All the rough, pert, tomboyish air which had often been visible before had disappeared. She now bore the marks of a womanly citizen: the same common sense in everything as before, but a sense that was subdued in the aroma of the deepest devotion, the purest loveliness. The most wonderful thing was that, despite all, the absolute freedom she granted him to leave her if he would and when he would, instead of tempting him to desertion, made her a thousand times more amiable, gay, and delightful in his eyes."[32]

Almqvist was willing to sacrifice love as a social contract, then, precisely in order to save it as a gift. It was a bold move, not least as he lived in an unequal society where the woman was legally a minor, unable to vote, and unable to provide for herself.

But he also seems to have made it easy for himself. The family is not only a relationship between a man and a woman; children are no less important: they are what married people usually have in common besides a varying degree of mutual love. And it is on this issue that the scope of Almqvist's radicalism revealed itself. He may have tiptoed around the question in *Sara Videbeck*, but he made his case forcefully in *Europeiska missnöjets grunder* (*On the Causes of Europe's Discontent*; 1838).[33]

In it, he outlined a new marriage legislation whose basis is matrilineal: Children inherit from their mothers. Until they reach their majority, children are required to obey their mother, and vice versa—she has a responsibility to provide for them. For his part, the man has no duties toward his children. His paternity—like Albert's surname—need not even be known. However, he is welcome to be a loving and faithful "counselor" to his children.[34]

But how could an unmarried woman take care of her children if there were no requirement for the man to support them? "The burden of maintaining the child, the cost of its care and upbringing, cannot be laid upon the mother alone," Almqvist observed. Once again, as with Geijer, the state appears as a savior in order to "purify" the family: "Every mother shall receive from the Child Insurance Authority . . . a yearly income for each child sufficient to meet the cost of its maintenance and upbringing, until it reaches its majority."[35]

The Child Insurance Authority should not be considered poor relief. It should be financed using men's inheritances—a kind of masculine socialization, in contrast to the utopian socialists who wished to nationalize women. Almqvist was quite clear that this involved a massive intervention on the part of society. But he defended it on the now classic grounds that children represent the future and that caring for them was one of society's central tasks. His proposal did not seek to "interfere in the slightest with the right of individuals to manage and use their own property (it is therefore not an example of the so-called phalanstery movement, a variety of communism whose dissolution of individualism by economic means would result in the worst kind of slavery)."[36]

The proposal closely accords with Almqvist's fundamentally antipatriarchal starting point. In a marriage, the husband's power derived from the fact of his having a parent's authority over both his wife and his children and from masculine inheritance laws. For women to be emancipated, they would have to be liberated from men, not only financially but reproductively. They would need to gain full control of their children—or, at least, the husband would need to be stripped of his ability to rule over his wife through their children. This dismantling of the ties between reproduction and marital duties was to lead to Almqvist being accused of advocating polygamy—perhaps not without reason, either.

In his stories Almqvist was continually in search of "double love," and he later tried to show that it was quite possible to love two people at the same time. Given what we know about his unhappy marriage, it is not difficult to see this dream of polygamy as the author's own private utopia. But the ramifications of the question go much further. Did Almqvist really aim to liberate only *women*?

There are two sides to the patriarchal coin. The superior's power is matched by an obligation toward the subordinate. When Almqvist liberated women from the bonds of marriage, he also freed men—not only to seek a multiplicity of partners, but also from economic and emotional responsibility for the children. Albert's eureka moment in *Sara Videbeck* hinged on his realization that he could both eat his cake and have it. In other words, he could enjoy the pleasures of romantic or erotic love—whichever it is called—without giving up his freedom and property. Almqvist defended himself against accusations of recommending promiscuity by referring to Sara's "constancy." But what about Albert's faithfulness? In striking but not untypical fashion, the debate over *Sara Videbeck* came to focus solely on the ideal woman.

In contrast to Sara, whose life and opinions are set out in detail, we learn very little about Albert. He smokes cigars, has dashing mustaches, and is a noncommissioned officer in the army. He has relatively good prospects, thanks to family connections that are only dimly alluded to. To judge from his speedy and brazen courtship of Sara, he has the potential if not yet the inclination to become an accomplished steamboat Casanova. But he feels passionately about Sara and is manifestly fond of children—something Almqvist demonstrated by inserting, for safety's sake, a somewhat needless scene involving two infants.

Albert is surprisingly anonymous, a good-natured but dull young man. He is hardly a worthy representative of Swedish virtues, as Almqvist saw it. He is not particularly self-reliant, intellectually or financially. There is nothing of the self-made man about him; instead, he relies on good family connections. He is, in fact, a masculine bathing beauty, attractive and good-humored, a person who can be imagined settling down in the margins of Sara's planned-out life.

If Sara is a herald of the modern liberated woman, then Albert represents one possible future for masculinity. Almqvist outlined a sketch of men's emancipation from their gender-defined social obligations. Their economic responsibility as parents had been assumed by the state. Their work in child rearing was carried out by women. Fatherhood had ceased to exist, even as a point of view, but was now merely one of several possible diversions if the mood takes one.

Without any doubt there is something subversively and irresponsibly appealing about this new role for men. It is only logical that Almqvist's pliable view of the traditional gender order should have influenced his portrait of Albert, and it cemented his more recent installation as a nineteenth-century precursor of modern queer theory. According to literary historian Johan Staberg, attempts to break out of the prescribed masculine ideal were a feature of two of the literary and political associations in which Almqvist was active in the 1810s and 1820s: the Mannhem League and the Men's Association.

The second of these promoted an intense and romantic dream of masculine community that both reflected contemporary gender norms and rebelled against them. It fused Gothicism with idealization of the yeoman peasant and hopes for religious renewal. But it also encouraged a strongly individualistic questioning of prevailing norms and conventions. Its literary young men asserted their autonomy from the middle-class worlds in which they had grown up, seeking to become, in Staberg's words, "free individuals without ties who would undo these rigid forms and use their own creative processes to refashion them." Few of them, however, would keep their fears and dreams as close to their hearts as Almqvist did. With time, most of these youthful romantics would step into respectable positions in society as government ministers, generals, and professors.[37]

But dismantling the gender order also seemed to run up against Almqvist's liberal doctrine of Swedishness, at least with regard to Albert's life of thoughtless idling. What happened to the ideal of personality, each person's duty to develop their capacities and independence? Where did the citizenry go, those free yeoman peasants who made their way to the assembly? And what about the nobility of work, the source of all human dignity?

Albert has little in common with the hardworking smallholders in Almqvist's sketches of life for ordinary people. Rather, he seems to match the satirical portrait that opponents of individual freedom painted of the emancipated person: a selfish, indolent, and entirely gratified individual who lacked any sense of responsibility as a citizen. The contrast between the energetic Sara and the passive Albert, an inversion of gender roles, makes *Sara Videbeck* a far more provocative and subtle book than it can seem at first glance. But Albert's subversive masculinity also reveals the tension between aesthetics and politics and between romantic utopia and effective realism.

AN ENLIGHTENED MIDDLE CLASS OF FIRM CHARACTER

The nebulous depiction of Albert points to an unstated opposition between Almqvist's individualism and Geijer's. They shared a conviction that society had to undergo a peaceful but radical transformation that would give the individual as much freedom as possible. Increased state powers would shatter the old patriarchal communities. Both men counted on—or at least placed their hopes in—the innate virtues of the Swedish people to protect society from fragmentation and collapse.

These good qualities were particularly evident in the peasantry and the lower middle class: independence, a sense of civic duty, industriousness. The good thing about democracy, Almqvist argued, was that power in society would be vested in the hands of "an enlightened middle class of firm character." From it, a new society would arise, defined by true Christianity and love.[38]

Neither Geijer nor Almqvist was prepared in the slightest for the possibility that the liberated individualist might become a materialist who sought only to maximize pleasure—even though Albert in *Sara Videbeck* suggests that Almqvist's erotic ideal was not readily compatible with a philosophy of poverty. Even if Almqvist and Geijer may have seemed modern in their social attitudes, both were influenced by a comforting Christian worldview that held that human beings had been created in the image of a benign deity. They were perceptive enough to recognize that the flip side of freedom was unsociability and alienation. But they had faith that the boundary between personal self-realization and thoughtless egoism was being guarded by higher powers.

Their confidence was not shared by everyone. *Sara Videbeck* gave rise to a huge debate during which Almqvist was criticized on literary grounds but also ridiculed for his radical ideas. Much of this was a conservative knee-jerk response. But many of his adversaries were also women, not necessarily because they opposed the emancipation of women or took pleasure in moralizing generally but because they mistrusted Almqvist's utopian program. The Child Insurance Authority was a theoretical construct; the possibility of being abandoned with a child was a very tangible reality. In Stockholm, thanks to rural flight and reduced social controls, it was becoming increasingly common for men and women to live together without getting married. From this perspective, Albert was perhaps not an entirely reassuring figure. Though unequal, marriage offered women protection.

Nevertheless, the 1840s were bumper years for liberal reform. Admittedly, the democratic program of universal and equal suffrage, which both Geijer and Almqvist had embraced, was not realized—nor was the marriage law reform that Almqvist had so provocatively advocated. Even so, the old conservative society of estates and guilds was beginning to be dismantled, albeit carefully.

Reformers seized the initiative in the 1841 Parliament. The following decade witnessed the introduction of public and compulsory elementary schools, equal inheritance rights for sons and daughters, poor relief, and a law on stock companies as well as the abolition of obligatory guild membership and the gradual deregulation of business activity. The final days of the four estates Parliament also saw the abolition of the master's right to physically punish servants and their children, the definition of unmarried women as legal adults from the age of twenty-five, the removal of a ban on prayer meetings outside of churches, and the introduction of unrestricted freedom of trade in 1864, just prior to the great parliamentary reforms of the following year. By this time, however, Geijer had died and Almqvist was in Texas gazing at the marvelous night sky and feeling homesick for Sweden.

This slow process of democratization, free of revolutionary drama, has perhaps given us a false picture of the ideological forces at work in Geijer's and Almqvist's thinking. Their ideas were not shaped under intense political pressures. In an era that saw barricades raised in the streets of many of Europe's capital cities, the emergence of Jacksonian democracy in the United States, and the Chartist movement in Britain, Swedish democracy moved slowly forward with a mixture of peasant caution and civil servant prudence.

Beneath the surface, however, a radical transformation was under way. Many of the ideas that drove the pragmatic Geijer and the utopian Almqvist are also visible in the work of other contemporary European intellectuals, from Tocqueville and Marx to Saint-Simon and Charles Fourier. But in Sweden, with its increasingly antiquated political institutions, its weak capital-owning class, and its strong peasant traditions, Almqvist and Geijer found it relatively easy to shake off the individualism defined by an aristocracy that had grown strong in the countries where capitalism was more advanced. Almqvist and Geijer did not turn to the burgeoning class of owners of capital, who aspired to become the gentlemen of a new era; instead, they established a direct connection between the exacting ideals of Lutheran peasant society and a more universal philosophy of equality.

It was hardly a good fit. In many respects, peasants were conservative figures, concerned mainly with protecting their own property and freedom from interference by others. Yet their very crassness, their anxious safeguarding of their own independence, also contained an idea that was egalitarian and subversive when applied to the new structures of gender and class that were emerging in the nineteenth century. Just imagine if everyone—workers, women, children—claimed to know what was theirs.

CHAPTER 6

Supermen and Other People

When he described his own upbringing, the playwright and novelist August Strindberg, who was born two years after Geijer's death in 1847, reserved particular vitriol for the Christian personality principle: "Christian individualism, with its endlessly delving into the self and its flaws, rendered him a thoroughgoing egoist."[1] This was part of Strindberg's settling of accounts with the relatively affluent middle-class Stockholm family in which he grew up, which at least superficially fulfilled contemporary notions of social propriety and gendered domestic harmony.

Yet the young Strindberg's revolt was not aimed at the individual's right to self-realization. Rather, he was reacting to Christianity's idealized version of this concept. He disliked the self-scrutiny, the cringing humility, and the moral demands that the self-righteous middle classes imposed on the emancipated personality.

His critique came from the left, a desire to go further in freeing the individual from Geijer-style moralism and the collective superego of Sweden at the end of the nineteenth century. The allure of community was a threat to truth and to personal self-realization. Conflict is a leitmotif of Strindberg's early literary writings: his Master Olof wishes to be "alone with God." Arvid Falk, the protagonist of *Röda rummet* (*The Red Room*) detests society, "for it is built not upon free accords but a tissue of lies," and gladly flees from it.[2]

This was a revolt that all Europe would hear about. For two decades at the end of the nineteenth century, Scandinavia was a hotbed of intellectual controversy, a place where writers and artists described the conflict between individual and community in more uncompromising and unvarnished terms than anywhere else. Never before or since has Scandinavia occupied so central a position on the intellectual stage of Europe, with Henrik Ibsen, Strindberg, and the Danish critic and scholar Georg Brandes its acknowledged stars and numerous satellites orbiting these fixed points.[3]

"The strongest man in the world is he who stands most alone," declares Ibsen's Dr. Stockmann in *An Enemy of the People*, a provocative idea that can be heard throughout Scandinavian literature at the turn of the twentieth century.[4] It involved a liberation of the subject that transformed society into the background for a drama featuring a single protagonist. As literary historian Thure Stenström has observed, during this period virtually every middle-class convention—and collective community in particular—was felt to be stifling, akin to living a lie, while individual self-realization was regarded as an urgent duty that must be fulfilled at almost any cost.[5]

Comparing Scandinavian literature's breakthrough with another contemporary form of literary avant-gardism, French Naturalism, Stenström discovered a crucial difference. In the former, he argued, "isolation is positive, autism a value." Solitude is voluntary, a way to free oneself from the masses, society, and the various forms of community. In French Naturalism, however, community and the collective are positive values, while solitude is a tragic destiny that is forced on the unwilling individual. In one of his final notes, Émile Zola unequivocally distanced himself from Ibsen: "'The strong person' is not, whatever Ibsen may say, 'the most alone,' but someone who is connected, mind and heart, with other people and within whom all of humanity has its abode."[6]

Perhaps the Scandinavian breakthrough was merely further evidence of the periphery's importance for the advance of modernity. The struggle between the self-realizing subject and the established social order was a central theme in all Western art and literature of the late nineteenth century. Under certain circumstances, however, ideas and conflicts appear with greater clarity the further away from the center one goes.

But why this backward northern corner of Europe? The likely reason was not that its middle-class culture was stronger than in the rest of Europe. The Scandinavian bourgeoisie had arrived late in the day and constituted a thin layer near the apex of a society that was still strikingly rural. In 1880, around 80 percent of the Swedish population still worked the land; only 15 percent lived in cities, almost all the rest in the countryside. In the same year, there were only around 2,500 students at the country's universities and institutions of tertiary education; they were taught by just over 200 professors and other teachers.[7]

Admittedly, economic development had accelerated considerably after midcentury, particularly after a series of barriers to commercial enterprise were relaxed. The late 1800s saw the founding of companies that led Sweden's innovation industries: ASEA (electronics), L. M. Ericsson (telephones), and Alfa-Laval (pumps). In 1885, Stockholm had probably the highest concentration of telephones of any city in the world.[8] But this rapid economic development was taking place in a society that in many ways continued to be defined by premodern institutions.

In the old kingdom, officials still shuffled around in the kind of government departments that August Strindberg would satirize as the "Board of Administration of Employés' Pensions" in his 1879 novel *The Red Room*. Attitudes toward politics were apathetic. In the early 1890s, Stockholm's leading newspapers had limited distribution and circulations of around 10,000.[9] Only a fifth of Sweden's eligible 200,000 voters cast their vote in the 1872 election, which meant that Sweden's Parliament was chosen by around 40,000 individuals—this in a country whose population exceeded four million.[10]

The powerful middle classes that existed in Germany, Britain, and France, with historically deep roots in an urban culture, had no equivalent in Scandinavia. There were few bourgeois dynasties such as the Forsytes and Buddenbrooks portrayed in John Galsworthy's and Thomas Mann's famous novels. The Swedish bourgeoisie consisted more of new arrivals with roots in the clergy and well-to-do peasant class. The urban middle class was weak politically, too, and outflanked by parties representing landowners. Insecurity made the advance parties of the middle class a tempting target for radical intellectuals (known in Scandinavia as *kulturradikaler*); as one literary historian put it, "The writers of the new era hated the people of the new era."[11] The middle class's numerical inferiority likely produced a greater degree of standardization and social control than in the larger European countries and elicited claustrophobic reactions from its young people.

When compared with a centuries-old peasant culture, that of Sweden's middle class seemed affected, false, and lacking in authority. Middle-class claims to religious sincerity and familial community presented a glaring contrast to the independence and self-reliance under reduced and trying circumstances that the older liberalism had ascribed to Sweden's peasant class. Strindberg often compared the wholesome appetite for life exhibited by country folk to the suffocating institutions of the middle class, particularly with regard to the position of women: "Among the peasants, the woman question is resolved.... If the man takes care of what little money comes in, the woman has the key to the flour crates and larder. She can keep what she earns from spinning during the winter evenings as a kitty with which to buy coffee and sugar.... The stronger party is always in charge, whether a man or a woman.... Cultured women are spoiled, by contrast, just like their men."[12]

In his version of romanticized peasant life, Strindberg built on the social ideals that Geijer and Almqvist had portrayed in their writings: individualism, independence, and the importance of poverty in Sweden. Sweden's cultural radicals based their social critique on the same platform of solid timber, figuratively speaking, that they used to build their houses in the country. Perhaps the Swedish middle class had not had enough time to develop ingrained habits and a cultural dominance comparable to its French, German, and British counterparts. Rapid economic development in a traditional peasant culture produced conditions favorable for Ibsen's and Strindberg's attacks on the middle-class family. But their radical subjectivity also went much further.

SO WHO SHOULD WE FIGHT?

The national self-image held up by Strindberg drew extensively on Geijer and Almqvist. Indeed, he basically recycled their ideas in his 1884 essay on the subject, "Nationality and Swedishness." The same goes for Montesquieu's theories about the effect of the northern climate on the human temperament. The influence of Almqvist is immediately apparent: Swedes had been assigned a "harsh reality" in comparison with Mediterranean Europe, where the sun shone and the wine flowed. After subsisting for a while on rye bread and moonshine, they had woken up and "taken world history by the hand."[13]

Geijer is there, too, but, for safety's sake, via a detour through Germany. Strindberg repeated Geijer's verdict on Swedish national character but attributed it to a travel book from 1882, *Schweden—Land und Volk* (*Sweden—Land and People*): "a strong sense of independence and a deeply rooted feeling of personality, combined with a healthy measure of practical common sense."[14] There is even a reappearance of Almqvist's old idea that Swedes are always too easily impressed by things foreign and appreciate their own culture less than it deserves: "Swedes want so very much to be Swedish but at the same time refuse to acknowledge anything that is Swedish until it has been acknowledged by foreigners."[15]

Yet Strindberg's contribution to the doctrine of Swedishness went beyond this mishmash of modernized Gothicism. In his 1886 work *Svenska öden och äventyr* (*Swedish Destinies and Adventures*), he offered a lively interpretation of Geijer's view of Swedish history as a struggle between ancient freedoms and the unjustly gained privileges of the elite—even if he did not admit Geijer's influence on him.[16] For Strindberg, Geijer the Uppsala professor was simply a dyed-in-the-wool royalist who had made the Swedish people into subordinates. He also found Geijer's writing "dull."[17]

Strindberg offered no overarching philosophy of history, no dialectical movement. The alliance between king and people is noticeably absent. In Jacobin fashion, everything is bipolar: people versus masters, freedom versus oppression, progress versus reaction. Instead, Strindberg created a series of powerful tableaux with an underlying theme: the individual's struggle against an oppressive society.

The opening story in *Swedish Destinies and Adventures* concerns a young nobleman who is forced to give up all his worldly possessions. He is weak—a man of the pen, not the sword. In brutally direct fashion, Strindberg's protagonist observes that those without money, who do not belong to any class and whose profession cannot sustain them, are defenseless. Unequipped to make his way in this world and repeatedly humiliated, the young man throws himself into the waters just off Stockholm. The next story concerns an unwanted child whose fierce vitality enables him to survive as a hunter in the forest. The child returns to his village as a rich man in order to exact a bitter revenge on the family who cast him out: "I was taught to lie, and the agents of the law made me a thief. I was honorable, but was not allowed to be so. . . . I do not seek the respect of people who suspect me of being a crook but forgive me because I possess a fine stove and drink wine."[18]

In the third story, we meet a happily married young priest who, against his own conscience, refuses to grant a divorce to an unhappily married couple, solely in order to uphold the Seventh Commandment prohibiting adultery. Yet he himself is affected by a new ban on marriage for clergymen. The archbishop offers to make it up to him: he can have a mistress, of course, just not his former wife. Incensed, the young priest abandons the church and takes up a smallholding: "All right, then, I shall have nothing more to do with the church! Ban me, and I will think it a privilege to be excluded from the church's delightful community."[19]

And so it continues. Every one of society's patriarchal institutions—monarchy, nobility, church, guilds, marriage—receives a lashing. Against them are ranged the strong individuals who are mentally and physically capable of fighting for their survival. All around them are the soft, the malleable, those who can see that the authorities are unjust but who choose to close their eyes or flee.

Strindberg's heroes are cut from the same cloth as Geijer's, but Strindberg's settings are evoked in bleaker terms. This world is deeply social Darwinist. The weak succumb. Inequality is a fact of life and leaves scant room for Christianity's love for others. One of his characters remarks discontentedly, "It is impossible to overcome the strong and wrong to beat the poor, so whom should we fight?"[20] Unlike in Geijer's work, there is no possibility here that a benign monarch or the state will come to their subject's rescue. Rulers always stick together; society is a permanent conspiracy, a tissue of lies.

The underlying reasoning is as simple as it is classic: Man is born free, and everywhere he is in chains. Civilization is false and corrupt; only in nature—in the forest, on lakes, on a lonely plot of land—can people live in freedom. Echoing Rousseau, Strindberg complained that behind its deceitful veil, society contains only "suspicions, mistrust, fear, indifference, wariness, hatred, and treachery."[21] But where Almqvist had given the doctrine of Swedishness a generous dose of anticivilization critique, Strindberg prescribed a kill-or-cure remedy.

All societies, said Strindberg, are by nature evil and corrupt. Only in an infinitely generous state of nature can people avoid the mutual dependence that gives rise to laws, states, and authorities. Here, we are getting close to one of Strindberg's fundamental ideas: nature as a haven from society. The Swedish love of nature, which is made so much of in the literature on national character, is not quite as innocent as it seems. More is at stake than picking mushrooms and taking pleasure in forests and fields. Geijer's writings, and above all Almqvist's, contain the idea that nature is a symbol of freedom. Strindberg, who is justly famous for his groundbreaking depictions of nature, ratcheted this connection up a couple of notches:

> When a man has discovered society to be an institution based on error and injustice, when he perceives that, in exchange for petty advantages society suppresses too forcibly every natural impulse and desire, when he has seen through the illusion that he is a demi-god and a child of God, and regards himself more as a kind of animal—then he flees from society, which is built on the assumption of the divine origin of man, and takes refuge with nature.
>
> Here he feels in his proper environment as an animal, sees himself as a detail in the picture, and beholds his origin—the earth and the meadow. He sees the interdependence of all creation as if in a summary.... He feels at home. And in our time, when all things are seen from the scientific point of view, a lonely hour with nature, where we can see the whole evolution-history in living pictures, can be the only substitute for divine worship.[22]

No self-reliant peasants here, sitting in their lonely farms too far away even to wave to each other, no "I" and "you," just a solitary subject at one with nature. We are also very far from Almqvist's heavenly creature, *animal coeleste*, as a union of nature and the divine in the human. In fact, we have also strayed from Rousseau, who sought to create a new social contract between people. In his most unforgiving moments, Strindberg recast the Swedish relationship to nature as a flight from human community.

STAND BY YOUR CHILDREN

However, on one other point Strindberg—unlike Almqvist—remained true to Rousseau. He had little or no interest in androgyny and the dissolution of gender roles. The ideal of the modern woman was for him "a ghastly hermaphrodite with more than a whiff of ancient Greece."[23] Even Geijer, after his defection to liberalism, had realized that there was no justifiable principle on which to refuse women the same individual rights as men. But his unwavering Lutheran belief that women had a domestic vocation led him to assume that instead of exercising their political rights, they would choose not to become involved in public life. Divinely inspired love and the personality principle's respect for the other would create happy and harmonious families.

Almqvist's view of the matter was less sanguine. Like Strindberg, he regarded existing legislation and moral conventions as an obstacle to free love between a man and a woman. His solution was new laws and a new moral code: matriarchy and state responsibility for children—a politically unrealistic proposal in nineteenth-century Sweden, but an undeniably original scheme of social engineering.

Alternatives of this kind were unthinkable for the young Strindberg. His radical individualism prompted him to proclaim a revolt against both God and the conservative state. Human beings were alone and would have to solve the issue by themselves. They would not receive any substantial help from the church, the authorities, or the legislative bodies. This meant that the conflict between people's need for community and their longing for freedom would inevitably come back to the only place in society where they were played out every single moment of every single day: the family. In Strindberg's work, people's relentless struggle for liberation is fought out in the home and the marital bed. And it was a zero-sum game. Freedom gained by one was lost by the other: "when two powerful minds meet, they realize that there is no possible basis for compromise aside from one of them conceding defeat."[24]

Strindberg's point of departure was simple: All people—men as well as women—were to be free and equal. Women had the same right to individual self-realization as men. This was a staple feature of how cultural radicals imagined a "free love" beyond the constraints of middle-class marriage with its life-effacing property requirements and moral double standard. He advocated votes for women, their right to stand for office, coeducational schools, civil marriages, women's rights over their own bodies, and male and female children raised in the same way.

So what was the problem? Children, of course—reproduction. To try to liberate women from nature was criminal, Strindberg explained in *Giftas* (*Married*). Above all, he reacted fiercely to the fact that Nora, the protagonist in Ibsen's *A Doll's House*, chooses to abandon her children: "She longs for freedom, the personal, egotistical, pleasurable, Ibsenesque freedom to put the furniture where she wants, to not have to apologize when she has done something foolish, freedom to brood over her own thoughts, to work them like clay into small images of the divine, freedom to be wet-nurse and mother—in a word, freedom from the laws of nature."[25]

For all the contempt he directed toward Christianity, Strindberg, like Geijer, drew a distinction between higher and lower forms of individualism. The loftier variety of self-realization did not lie in citizenship, however. It required the fulfilment of an artistic vocation, of disciplined research. One had to serve the good of humanity, to "live for the whole family." Such an end justified ruthlessness and the avoidance of obligations to those nearby. Under these circumstances, as Strindberg explicitly acknowledged in the passage above, it was acceptable even for a woman to abandon her children, who would, as he unsympathetically put it, have to "fend for themselves."[26]

In contrast, Strindberg found unacceptable a purely egotistical freedom that sought merely frivolous personal pleasure, material gain, or a gratuitous indulgence of one's impulses. Nor did the prohibition of a lower kind of individual self-realization affect only Nora. Strindberg also condemned greedy capitalists and petit-bourgeois egoists. Because they served a higher purpose, the artist, the scientist, and—frequently— the exploited proletarian were always justified in putting themselves above convention, moral rules, and consideration for others more generally.

Once we start dividing people into exceptional individuals and the herd, Friedrich Nietzsche is never far off. Around the same time that Brandes was giving his lectures on Nietzsche in 1888, Strindberg came into contact with the German philosopher's work. Nietzsche's writings contained, he explained enthusiastically to his (for the moment) friend, the poet Verner von Heidenstam, "everything you could ask for." He identified with Nietzsche's claims to have an unusually powerful and independent spirit.[27]

In his biography of Strindberg, Olof Lagercrantz described how Strindberg experienced a need both for company and for solitude that was more acute than most people's. On the one hand, he loved family life and the happy social gatherings with friends around the dinner table. He always had one or two male "best friends" with whom he forged intimate, sometimes almost erotic, ties. Strindberg spent a considerable portion of his life in bars and restaurants, and his surprisingly tough constitution managed to endure years of hard living. His colleague Ola Hansson once scornfully accused him of being unable ever to be on his own.[28]

On the other hand, Strindberg felt that continual proximity to other people posed a danger to his own integrity. He was endlessly ditching wives, children, friends, and places. And the danger of emotional ties is a recurrent theme in his work: "One's inner growth is stunted and elements foreign to the soul force their way in, such that one is prevented from arranging one's own mental diet." As Lagercrantz observed, Strindberg genuinely needed other people; he was no unsociable bohemian. Having a family life gave him protection against the complete artistic alienation in which invented reality threatens to become the only reality. But precisely because of this dependence, he also felt that those closest to him presented a dangerous threat to his authenticity and freedom. They could influence him and tie him down with loyalty and personal considerations.[29]

This unsolved conflict between freedom and community lends depth and power to both Strindberg's celebrations of solitude and his depictions of an almost animalistic longing for the company of his kind. Unable to reconcile the two states, he fluctuated between them. Self-consuming loners such as Johan in *Tjänstekvinnans son* (*The Son of a Servant*) and Axel Borg in *I Havsbandet* (*By the Open Sea*) and *Mäster Olof* (*Master Olof*) are matched by a succession of portraits of communities that are, if not idyllic, at least happy and appealing. In them Strindberg followed Zola in offering a Naturalist affirmation of the simple, undemanding community that exists between people: we are bound to each other by our natural need to be with other people, whether to procreate or merely eat, drink, and play together. One's need for independence is far outweighed by the loneliness and social isolation that are the flip side of freedom.

Strindberg's short story "Must," about the confirmed bachelor Blom, is emblematic. A teacher in his early thirties, he is a loner by choice: he lodges with a genteel old lady in Gärdet, an outlying district of Stockholm, and has no social life beyond the few motley individuals whom he regularly meets in the bar.

But one midsummer's eve, the teacher's well-ordered but unsociable existence is shattered. Blom leaves his shabby bachelor's room to go to his local bar. The city is full of simple people who have taken possession of even the more elegant districts. In Berzelii Park he sees a mother breast-feeding her child with "a large, rich breast, which the infant grasped with his chubby hand." He turns away in disgust. But when he comes to the restaurant, he finds it closed. Terribly disappointed, he decides to call on his acquaintances at their homes. Yet he barely knows where they live, and the only one whose address he does know has gone out. Blom wanders around Stockholm, feeling increasingly bitter and alone. All around him, he sees happy families of workers, children playing, young people courting. The experience is a turning point for Blom. Before long he has become married and dissociated himself from his previous life. No longer a regular at the bar, he now thinks that there should be laws against bachelors and has become a firm fixture on jolly family excursions with a baby carriage to the countryside.[30]

As a political ideologist, Strindberg was strikingly un-Swedish, not because of his individualism but in his antipathy toward the state as the agent of conformist thinking. In contrast, he lived up to the national stereotype in his depictions of alienated solitude. Readers were doubtless particularly fascinated by the way that Strindberg's own reason and happiness seemed to be at stake in his portrayal of the conflict between individual and community. The result was provocative and often subversive.

Yet this fundamental conflict was extremely familiar in the national perspective: how to reconcile society's—or the family's—survival with the universal right to self-realization? For all his lack of Swedishness, Strindberg is nonetheless as clearly part of the national cultural heritage as, to borrow a phrase from Björn Meidal, "eating pea soup on Thursdays and dancing around the maypole at midsummer."[31] After the so-called Strindberg Feud, when the author locked horns with Heidenstam over Sweden's eighteenth-century warrior-king Karl XII, he became a people's poet, a tribune of the people.[32] Not for the labor movement, nor for socialism but, rather, for a nation that prized collectivity but wanted individuality.

NIETZSCHE'S SWEDISH PROPHETESS

In Strindberg's works, the conflict between freedom and community primarily takes place in a man's world. The right to break away from the community, to realize oneself with no thought for anyone else, is not defensible if it involves women abandoning their children. In theory, it is true, Strindberg made no biological distinction between men's and women's responsibility to their offspring. Rather, the crucial factor was a weighing-up of the magnitude of the artistic or scientific achievement against one's obligations toward the care of the family and the community at large. To abandon one's children merely out of a vague personal desire for freedom, as Nora does in *A Doll's House*, was reprehensible. And yet such betrayal could be a compelling necessity for people whose freedom and autonomy benefitted the development of all humanity.

In practice, this meant that a man's right to seek self-realization at the price of his family was inviolable, while a woman's right to leave her husband and children was highly circumscribed. This doubleness, to fiercely defend a man's right to rebel while at the same time denying a woman the same freedom, led to conflict with Sweden's burgeoning women's movement around the turn of the twentieth century. After all, wasn't the goal human freedom, rather than men's freedom at the price of women's? Instead Strindberg launched a violent polemic against the women's movement's critique of traditional marriage and made a sharp distinction along gender lines. Yet the intensity of the relationship between Strindberg and the women's movement involved more than their mutual disappointment.

However unfair and spiteful Strindberg could be in his worst moments, he had undeniably put his finger on the weakest point in the alliance between the women's movement and the radical intelligentsia. It was one thing to advocate complete equality and independence among adults, quite another to fail in one's responsibility to one's children.

Feminists had good grounds for claiming that men liked to use children as an excuse for defending a traditional gender hierarchy in which women were subordinate to men. But even if this was true, the underlying problem remained. Individuals can, even if they suffer agonies doing it, cut all ties to their parents, relatives, and friends in order to fulfil their desire for freedom and independence. Yet shirking responsibility for children one has brought into the world runs contrary to a deep moral conviction that seems to be existentially rather than culturally conditioned—a universal taboo akin to those against incest and cannibalism. And in the case of children, women were left holding the penalty card. As a result of their biology and an intricate web of legal, social, and cultural bonds, it was far more difficult for women to follow their personal destinies, their self-realization as human beings.

Thoughtful feminists and radical individualists at the turn of the twentieth century were therefore forced to find an alternative solution to the problems of marriage and reproduction than Strindberg's call for a return to the well-defined gender roles of peasant society. No one devoted themselves to this task with greater energy, perseverance, and ambitiousness than Ellen Key. In influential works such as *Livslinjer 1: Kärleken och äktenskapet I-II* (*Lifelines 1: Love and Marriage I–II*) and *Barnets århundrade* (*The Century of the Child*) and in countless lectures, newspaper articles, and essays, she sketched out a new societal order that corresponded with her understanding of what true individual freedom would mean for women.

Like Strindberg, Key was born in the middle of the nineteenth century. Her father, Emil Key, was an idealistic landowner and an ardent advocate of liberalism, Scandinavian identity, and—by the standards of the time—feminism. But he was also an inept businessman, which resulted in Ellen, while still a young girl, being forced to leave the family's idyllic estate in Småland county and take up a teaching position at Whitlockska secondary school in Stockholm. During the 1880s, her involvement in pedagogy, philosophy, and social questions brought her into the public sphere, initially as a popular educator and lecturer and later as an author. She became one of the most important cultural figures of her day. Stockholm's intellectual elite flocked to her famous Sunday breakfasts at her home on Valhallavägen, while her radical stance on social questions made her the darling of young working-class political activists.[33]

Her death in 1926 at the age of seventy-five was front-page news in the Swedish press and a major story in the international press.[34] Her most important books had been translated into the main European languages. One explanation for her enormous popularity is that she struggled more obviously than most with the conflict between individual and community on the issue of love and sexuality from a woman's perspective. Yet critics on both the right and the left have highlighted her lack of rigor, her breathless style, and the airiness of her contradictory mixture of conservatism and liberalism. Like Strindberg, she found herself in conflict with large swaths of the contemporary women's movement because of her strong emphasis on the differences between men and women.[35]

Not that this brought Strindberg and Key together. In his novel *Svarta fanor* (*Black Banners*), Strindberg included a malicious portrait of Key in the figure of Hanna Paj, a closeted lesbian who takes young women under her wing in order to turn them against their husbands.[36] For her part, Key, who was more inclined to try to embrace oppositions, offered milder criticism of Strindberg. She faulted him for his misogyny and unhealthy suspiciousness: "He has portrayed woman's nature, not with the perspicacity that comes from kindness and understanding, but with the shortsightedness that comes from suffering and mistrust." Even so, she admitted that there was some justification for his "old-fashioned manly demands," which women of today could not simply ignore.[37]

Despite these differences, their views on the question of gender concurred to a far greater degree than the received wisdom would have us believe. They had a common point of departure: the dream of a society in which individuals could freely realize their innate potential. Thereafter their paths separated.

THE RIGHT KIND OF EGOISM

Key defined the core of Swedishness as being entirely a matter of independence and individualism. In an open letter about patriotism that she addressed to Verner von Heidenstam, she wrote, "We must recover the self-respect which manifests itself in consistent fidelity to one's own personality in both public and private life. We need once again to burn with passion for our integrity, that passion which under extraordinary circumstances leads us to stake our life for a conviction, and under other circumstances expresses itself in the courage to . . . take a different path from others."[38]

Key's entire lifework is informed by this radical intellectual advocacy of a private individual in the face of every kind of social convention, official regulation, petit bourgeois hypocrisy, and small-mindedness. She was a believer in great individuals, the exceptional ones, those who had the courage to refuse the demands made by those around them. Like Strindberg, she celebrated the power of egoism, its capacity to both destroy and to create.

The actions of the strong personality, she wrote in her essay "Freedom of Personality" ("Personlighetens frihet"), have the sole purpose of achieving happiness and often cause suffering to others: "Lovers, who seek their union in a form that is called lawless or criminal, often thereby give their families a hale and capable member. The impulse to dominate, which has sacrificed hundreds of thousands for its ends, has indirectly produced results which have benefitted humanity for generations."[39]

And even when the egoism of such exceptional individuals has not benefitted humanity, she added, it can have pedagogical importance as a "revelation of the colossal dimensions which human nature—for both good and evil—can attain."[40] She wanted nothing to do with Kant's moral imperative—that a person should always act in a way that could be made mandatory for all people—since it goes against the credo of individualism. Or, more precisely: societal constraints can be required for "adults who never got to be children properly, scrupulous moral people who lack an individual conscience, or [the] impulse-governed who lack a social conscience," but not for the liberated individual.[41]

With good reason, Key was pronounced to be "Nietzsche's Swedish prophetess" in the debate.[42] She connected his idea of the superman with contemporary debate over Darwinism, eugenics, and racial hygiene: "No other contemporary has shown greater certainty than Nietzsche about the idea that individuals, such as they are today, are merely a 'bridge,' no more than an intermediate stage between animals and supermen. In connection with this certainty, Nietzsche follows [founder of eugenics] Francis Galton in gravely emphasizing the obligations that people have with regard to the improvement of the human race."[43]

How far Key was prepared to take racial improvement is an open question. She referred to the need to manage marriage by means of science rather than religious commandments: "Living in sin" was a union that created deficient offspring or poor conditions for raising them. She cited as a good example the requirement in Germany and the United States that couples provide a doctor's certificate prior to their marriage. But the methods she referred to relate primarily to voluntary racial hygiene. She offered short instructive accounts of men who discover that they bear undesirable hereditary traits and thereafter renounce all romantic relationships—and in one instance even choose the drastic solution of committing suicide.

These stories may seem simply bizarre, but they also indicate the gravity of the question. If people with unhealthy hereditary traits are unwilling to sacrifice their own happiness for the collective good, should the state not intervene to protect future generations?[44]

Like many other social progressives around the turn of the twentieth century, Key was also inspired by Nietzsche's notion of an impending cultural revolution in the development of humanity. In her insightful dissertation on Key, Claudia Lindén observed that it is not very strange that women were drawn to Nietzsche's attacks on Christian and rationalistic value systems, since the latter so obviously assigned women a subordinate position. The same can be said about Nietzsche's attraction to young workers who hungered for knowledge: he was a philosopher of the marginalized.[45]

Key was attracted to Nietzsche's aphoristic formulations about a new kind of human, one more adapted for life and liberated from nineteenth-century Christianity and its slave morality, tedious aversion to knowledge, and bourgeois materialism. But like many of Nietzsche's followers in Scandinavia, she brushed off the overly elitist implications of his philosophy: the superman was a fine ideal, but the principle of equality ought to make it within reach for everyone. Key was also influenced by Nietzsche's radical individualism: his questioning of traditional authorities and his promise to reassess all values. However, she was far more ambivalent in her feelings about that part of Nietzsche's philosophy that emphasized "the will to power" and made spiritual struggle between people into the defining aspect of existence.

The qualified welcome that Key gave to Nietzsche's ideas is illuminating in the context of the discourse on of Swedishness. His philosophy was received enthusiastically in Sweden (as in the rest of Scandinavia). Georg Brandes's famous lectures in Copenhagen in 1888 paved the way, and among Swedish intellectuals his announcement of the German poet-philosopher's arrival reached Strindberg.[46] Later, Nietzsche's ideas would move into public debates, leaving a particular impression on young socialists.[47] His ideas about the strong individual and the superman became an effective tool with which to attack, in particular, Geijer's philosophy of the benevolent personality and the tired liberalism that prevailed at the end of the nineteenth century.[48]

In a sense, Nietzsche's reception had a double effect. On the one hand, Geijer's and Almqvist's ideal of Swedish self-reliance had created a certain receptiveness toward radical individualism; on the other, Nietzsche's cult of the will challenged the moral limits that nineteenth-century liberalism had drawn up around individual freedom. Freedom and independence for Geijer's sturdy peasant and Almqvist's smallholder had been ultimately guaranteed by a powerful judicial tradition in which the relationship between citizens and authorities was clearly regulated by the law. Individual freedom was above all a question of freedom from interference, of knowing "what else there is, is mine," as Geijer put it.[49] For Nietzsche, there existed no such contract, no laws or regulations, only a promise that victory would go to those whose spirit was most powerful.

It is precisely their attraction toward Nietzschean lawlessness—albeit with reservations—that differentiated Strindberg and Key from their precursors Almqvist and Geijer. Turn-of-the-twentieth-century radical individualism and belief in the superman made individual self-realization entirely a matter of how autonomy was experienced subjectively. It was morally right to remove all obstacles to the development of exceptional individuals.

But since this extreme theory of sovereignty was completely divorced from reality, both Strindberg and Key were forced to engage in an elitist process of selection: the freedom of some individuals was more valuable than that of others. Women who wished only to decorate their apartment, or men who wanted to get drunk and go to the brothel, did not share the superman's right to set themselves above existing conventions. According to Key, socialism meant not "rule of the masses" but, rather, a new "social aristocracy": "Even in the new society there will undoubtedly be a superior and an inferior class. But individual virtues, intelligence, and character qualities will eventually come to shape it."[50]

It may seem paradoxical that Key—who in so many areas looked ahead to the equality and solidarity of Sweden's welfare state in the twentieth century—should have had such reverence for Nietzsche. Yet it is no stranger than the Swedish left's making an icon of Strindberg while celebrating Nietzsche and unprincipled free egoism. This apparent contradiction is the subject of this book: that modern Sweden, far from being a collectivist project that merged from a passionate sense of solidarity, is the fusion of an individualistic view of people with a powerful tradition of equality.

ALMQVIST REDUX: LOVE AND INDEPENDENCE

In her attacks on the bourgeois marriage of convenience, Key made reference—among much else—to Strindberg's family tragedies. His great contribution was exposing the shameful secrets within marriage, the falsity of a relationship whose partners "pass judgement on each other's opinions and ideas and thereby give each other a satanic power to cause hurt, to let merits be made into faults."[51]

However, Key did not really need to invoke Strindberg as an authority. In the first part of *Livslinjer* (*Lifelines*), she developed a comprehensive and historically grounded critique of what she called the "neo-Protestant marriage." For her, this term described a semimodernized form of marriage that, though in theory founded on mutual love rather than duty to God, did not recognize the partners' right to divorce once their feelings had turned to ash. This demand for morality was itself deeply immoral, she argued, since it made a loveless marriage into a form of religiously sanctioned prostitution. What Key advocated, however, was more "the freedom of love" than "free love," with its connotations of immorality and bohemianism. Like Almqvist, she wanted to rescue marriage from the lack of authenticity that resulted from the social and economic bonds of obligation. It was dependence and inequality that did harm. Love must be given freely, every day, as a gift: "Application of the personality concept to love has now led us to recognize that property is theft; that the only true gifts are those given freely; that the notions of marital 'rights' and 'obligations' have been replaced with a groundbreaking idea—that fidelity can never be promised but should be earned every day."[52]

Key came very close to arguing for the freedom of love on economic grounds: Contemporary marriage rested on faulty incentive structures. Monopolies were poison to entrepreneurialism, or, as Key put it, "just as it does in all areas of life, the necessity of acquiring will here concentrate the energy."[53]

It is the same freedom and lack of stability that Almqvist argued for in *Sara Videbeck*: Security is an anesthetic that fosters exploitation and oppression. The freedom to break up with someone spurs both partners to not only preserve their love but also to strive for authenticity in their feelings. The only loyalty that matters is that directed toward the needs of one's own personality. Echoes of Almqvist once again: the romantic view of love saved by means of a seemingly bloodless cost-benefit analysis.

Key also took the same path as Almqvist (whom she greatly admired): in order to make her belief in free love between two sovereign individuals into a reality, she had to resort to calculating utility and allowing far-reaching state intervention. Key knew that in doing so she was compromising her fundamental belief in the primacy of the individual, but she excused herself on the grounds that the great majority of people "were not yet ready for complete freedom." Modern marriage law, she explained, needed to build on an awareness of individuals' current erotic needs and drives, not abstract theories or considerations about legal history. Unblinking realism was needed in order for idealism, the "wide and lovely realm of unforced giving" and "the worthy altruism of mutual aid," to operate without constraint.[54]

The wide-ranging and detailed proposal for a new marriage law that Key presented in *Lifelines* was radical, almost utopian by the standards of the time. But although it would not happen until the end of the twentieth century, her program was eventually enacted, bit by bit, in its entirety by Swedish legislators. Much of it now seems self-evident. Its core tenets were that women should have full legal authority over themselves and their property, that divorce should be unrestricted, and that marriage should be a civil union. All this has come to pass, even if religious organizations still have the right to perform weddings. Key also advocated a clear definition of "separate property" so that married people would be treated as individuals "acting together with the freedom of brother and sister or two friends"—a proposal that anticipated the abolition of joint taxation for married couples in the 1960s.[55]

It is not too fanciful to discern in Key's writings an inclusive politics of the family that largely resembles today's: the social organization of childcare, economic support from the state during the child's earliest years, a one-year allowance for mothers, and training and expert support for mothers. She also unflinchingly described the social consequences of radical marriage reform: married couples who did not cohabit, and accumulations of siblings by different fathers and mothers all living in the same home. This perspicuity derived in large part from her recognition, despite her own critique, that marriage and the family were the only reasonable basis for people to live together. She rejected the idea that the state might take responsibility for child rearing. She was a liberal at heart, not a socialist: she wanted to save the family and the loving home, not relegate it to history.

Yet Key's program aimed at more than just creating equality. In seeking to give mothers more power over their children and the home, it also exhibited a strongly matriarchal tendency. Women had suffered more for their children; they understood and loved them better. It was therefore only fair that the current provisions be changed "so that the highest authority is instead vested in the mother."[56] Overall, Key argued that mothers should have priority over fathers. The guiding principle in divorces should be that children should not be separated from their mothers or from each other. And in the case of children born out of wedlock, the woman should retain all rights while the father's only obligation should be to provide maintenance. Key conceded that women sometimes falsely identify men as the father of their children, but, she argued, even in such cases the paternal obligation applies. Only in this way, she added laconically, can their conscience be educated.

As with Almqvist, her proposal had a matriarchal bent. And, like him, she implied that there would also be benefits for men under such a regime. State intervention and women's superior status with regard to children would free men from both the duties of conscience and the heavy burden of providing for a family, a burden that hitherto had fallen on men alone. As in Almqvist's vision, the father is transformed from a mighty patriarch into a supplementary helping hand around the home: "The home will become more synonymous with the mother, something that—far from excluding fathers—contains the seeds of new and superior 'family rights.'"[57]

From a feminist perspective, the marriage form in the nineteenth century was a double-edged sword. On the one hand, it subordinated women and stripped them of citizenship; on the other hand, it was the main source of social and economic security for middle-class women. Attacking marriage as an institution made women defenseless, but defending its current incarnation only made the bars of the cage stronger. Key's solution was to change the power relations within marriage. If women were to become truly free as individuals, they would have to have complete freedom of choice with respect to marriage as an institution. Those who wished to marry and become mothers and caregivers would need more than having an option; their position would have to be reinforced so that they gained dominance within the home that mirrored that of men in society. And those who declined marriage and motherhood must be able to do so without their femininity being called into question.

By making subjective love the overriding factor, Key empowered women to define themselves as individuals. Neither men nor the state nor society, but love alone would set limits to their freedom—something each individual woman could attain only through introspection. This was the "New Woman," a feminist version of radical individualism—in contrast to Strindberg's men fighting to secure their artistic, scientific, or political independence from an oppressive world.

However, in their shared antipathy toward legal principles grounded in history and formal limits to individual freedom, Strindberg and Key moved away from Geijer's view of the law as the basis for individual independence. In Strindberg's case, this was an entirely deliberate and consistent decision: he had no time for Geijer's efforts to preserve the social body by reconciling the rights of the individual with societal solidarity. In Key's case, it was a more ambivalent and hesitant drift away from Geijer, whom she held in far greater respect than Strindberg did. To a large extent, she shared Geijer's impulse to try to reach agreement and concurred with his critique of the raw and egotistical variety of individualism. But the individual whom she held up was not some sullen peasant but a loving, feeling, and motherly subject. For this reason, she put love above the law; Nietzsche trumped Geijer: a woman's self-realization was more important than equality between men and women.

Key's contention that women should become matriarchs and her lukewarm support for the struggle for women's right to vote have damaged her standing among many feminists today. The latter see her as endorsing a view of gender differences as fixed and, at worst, biological determinism. But the question is whether her thinking was, as Lindén argued, actually influenced more by a Nietzsche-inspired dream of a new kind of human being than by the idea of a predetermined feminine biology that is the subject of such lively debate today.[58]

Key went beyond the demands for equality and nondiscriminatory treatment made by liberalism and the social contract. Women were "superhumans," a new elite who would lead humanity into a new and better era. This view fit comfortably with her underlying faith in a sovereign individual whose own self-realization was more important than society's norms and rules. But it took her a long way from Geijer's legalistic view that the only legitimate form of authority and subordination was one that had been arrived at jointly or that was inscribed in tradition.

A SCIENTIFIC EDUCATION

Yet Key's lasting contribution to posterity did not relate to women's issues in any direct sense. Her most influential work is without question *Barnets århundrade* (*The Century of the Child*), in which she outlined a liberal and emancipatory pedagogy for the twentieth century. Though not alone in this undertaking, she was one of its leading lights. *The Century of the Child* was translated into thirteen languages. It had an enormous impact in Germany, and in Sweden it had been issued in three editions by the end of the 1920s.

Key's engagement with child rearing followed from her efforts to emancipate women. For Strindberg and the antifeminists, children were a trump card: how could women abandon the delightful responsibility with which nature had charged her? This was not a trivial question for Key, who had grown up on a country estate in strong relationships with both her father and mother. In her eyes, to be young meant spiritual growth, living in a state of as yet undeveloped and unforeseeable potential—which was also her ideal of the free individual. The fundamental principle of child rearing should be to approach children on their own terms, with knowledge and understanding. However, this demands real expertise in the form of insight and patience: "Only after the child's upbringing has been founded upon . . .

gradual adaptation to the world around them will child rearing become a field of disciplined knowledge—an art."[59]

Children were individuals in their own right. Current child-rearing practices were worse than having none at all. It was better to refrain from intervening than to do violence to children's essential nature. "I have yet to see a person who has been properly brought up," Key explained, only "a few raised in love, more than a few made to grow up, and many disciplined into adulthood." She opposed corporal punishment and rejected all forms of manipulation and deceit in dealings with children. Only by being a good example, she argued, can one influence a child.[60]

Of course, it was no coincidence that this straightforward pedagogy, which emphasizes both the caregiver's role as an expert and the autonomy of the subject being raised, fit well with Key's radically individualistic feminism: As primary caregiver, the mother has an almost professional status; this was a matter of precise knowledge, a real art. Child rearing is an important task that deserves society's respect and support. To claim that children were not simply empty vessels waiting to be filled but unique personalities whose nurturing and guidance required knowledge and engagement also meant an upgrading of the caregiver's own role. In Key's system, the path to greater power and freedom for women lay in strengthening the position of children and young adults in society. Or perhaps it was the other way around: a sound pedagogy for raising children and young adults required the liberation of women. If this was so, it meant that women and children belonged together and represented a joint entity in society with regard to men.

Although this elevation of children and young adults to the status of free and independent individuals would make child rearing more morally and emotionally demanding, it would also give women greater freedom. No longer would their duty be to watch constantly, to punish and to reward, to always be available. Instead, they would set a good example and serve as role models by actively participating in other areas of social life and by demonstrating the value of being a strong and self-fulfilled individual.

It is revealing that Key advocated withdrawing love over physical punishment: the caregiver's displeasure would fall like a shadow in an otherwise sunny domestic atmosphere. Admittedly, this requires the home to be warm and loving in the first place, which is in itself a major undertaking, but it is also a considerably less labor-intensive form of child rearing than that required by the disciplinary monitoring of children. Humanist idealism here meets utilitarian maximization.[61]

Such thinking left a lasting impact on twentieth-century Sweden. Key is often cited in connection with modern Swedish interior design and decoration, as an advocate of a domestic environment that is aesthetic, functional, and free of petit bourgeois ornament. But in this regard, her ideas were no more groundbreaking than those of her inspirations, William Morris and John Ruskin.[62] What made her truly original was her promotion of the idea of children's autonomy from their parents and those around them, as well as her insistence that children's need for independence and individuality be respected. But this emancipatory idea could—and indeed would—be used to legitimize far-reaching state interventions in the family and private life. Key often gave reassurances that, far from trying to expand the powers of the state, she placed her hopes in people's voluntary transformation. It is, however, notoriously difficult to put the genie back in the bottle. When a new, beautiful, good society is within reach, why not use the powers of the state?

THE LIMITS OF RADICAL INDIVIDUALISM

Within her own lifetime, in the year 1921, Key bore witness to the passing of the world's most liberal marriage laws in Sweden and the other Scandinavian countries. And the bourgeois middle-class culture that Strindberg loved to hate did not perish in a revolution but instead slowly faded away as the century wore on.

Even so, Key's and Stringberg's understandings of the relationship between individual and community lay further away from ours than did those of Geijer and Almqvist. They were, in a sense, less modern than their nineteenth-century precursors—but not because their ideas about the individual's right to self-realization have become dated. On the contrary, they were extremely forward-looking when they wrote, from their differing perspectives, about the relationship between men and women and about children and the family. Broadly speaking, Strindberg's *Getting Married* and Key's *Love and Marriage* covered most of the issues relating to these subjects that we are still debating.

The problem lies on a more political level. Both Key and Strindberg justified the individual's sovereignty on the grounds that such freedom would refine human beings and make them strive for loftier scientific, artistic, or political goals. This was absolutely not about fighting for people's right to do whatever they felt like. Strindberg rejected women's right to leave their husband and children in order to be free to decorate their apartment on their own. And Key held that people who remained slaves to their animal promptings must remain subject to simple conventions and rules. Their views were fundamentally elitist: only those capable of using freedom in the right way deserved to have it.

Key and Strindberg had lost contact with one of the core values that had defined Geijer's thinking: respect for the law. For Geijer, freedom was fundamentally a regulated relationship, a demarcation of what one owed to the community and what one was entitled to do oneself, in one's own sphere, on one's own terms. It is true that he worried about the consequences of freedom, what people might get up to if they were allowed to decide how they wanted to live. But this was because he took the law very seriously: it applied to everyone on the same terms. No one could claim that freedom should be arbitrarily granted according to how it might be used.

Key's and Strindberg's exceptional people, on the other hand, made their own laws; what mattered was subjective experience, not external, formal regulations. This was an idea that could be formulated in literature or philosophy, but it was not translatable into a concrete program of political reform. As Norwegian historian Frances Sejersted observed in a major study of Swedish and Norwegian social democracy, "It is . . . remarkable that cultural radicalism had such a striking impact in Scandinavia at the end of the nineteenth century. It is an attitude that hardly leads to socialism. Like the latter, cultural radicalism adopts a critical stance toward established social authority, but on individualistic and antitotalitarian grounds."[63]

The dream of far-reaching individual self-realization was an inspiring prospect. In practice, however, Swedish self-perception was to take another path in the twentieth century.

CHAPTER 7

A Bounded Community

"There is another, more powerful motive force in history," wrote the Swedish political scientist Rudolf Kjellén in 1898, "a personality in the world mightier than individuals, and that is *the nation* of which they are a part."[1]

The nationalistic individualism that had inspired Geijer and Almqvist as well as Strindberg and Key no longer reigned supreme in Sweden and Europe at the turn of the twentieth century. It was being challenged by movements that viewed independence as a threat to solidarity and that put collectivity above the interests of the individual. The conservative variant took the form of a Swedish nationalism that vehemently opposed nineteenth-century liberalism and the burgeoning internationalism of the labor movement.

Kjellén was one of the most intelligent and articulate exponents of this new and more aggressive form of nationalism. As a political scientist, he was part of a group of far-right intellectual radicals who were dissatisfied with what they saw as the anemic and paralyzed state of Swedish conservatism. Having a mixture of authoritarianism and mysticism, his conception of the state heralded National Socialism[2], but his talk of a future *folkhem* or welfare state also had rhetorical similarities to the societal model that Per Albin Hansson would present in the late 1920s.[3]

Kjellén was born in 1864 in a vicarage in the province of Västergötland. He became a professor of political science at Gothenburg University at the turn of the twentieth century, and in 1916 he was appointed to the prestigious Johan Skytte Professorship in Political Science at

Uppsala University. He coined the concept of geopolitics, "the theory of states as geographical organisms," in an 1899 essay, and his theories had a considerable impact in Germany. To what extent he should be seen as a source of inspiration for national-socialist ideas is an open question. His theoretical universe is not thought to have included any ideas about race, nor did he celebrate myths or acts of violence. But Kjellén was also a member of Parliament and his political speeches and pamphlets do contain racist ideas.[4]

Such right-wing nationalism was not an exclusively Swedish phenomenon. Quite the contrary, in fact: it was weaker in Sweden than in most other places. By the turn of the twentieth century, the national rhetoric formerly used by liberals and radicals had gained different overtones. In part, this was a question of the old elite having adapted itself to the new times. Whereas previously they had resisted the idea of a popular community, now government officials, captains of industry, and members of the armed forces engaged the rhetoric of nationalism in the service of the state. With a growing newspaper press, rising literacy rates, and improved communications, it was now possible to mobilize "the people" under the banner of colonialism, national honor, and military aggression—while steering clear of unpleasant ideas such as socialism and wealth redistribution within one's own country.[5]

MASTER RACES AND DEMOCRATIC CITIZENS

The year 1898—when Kjellén formulated his idea of the nation as a supraindividual entity—was a turning point for nationalist movements, from right to left, which were eventually to plunge the world into all-out war in 1914. In France, Zola wrote his famous article "J'Accuse . . . !" in response to the efforts of both army and government to try to save their honor in the trial of Alfred Dreyfus by fomenting antisemitism and appealing to citizens' loyalty to their country's institutions. Within twelve months, Britain declared war on the Boer Republics in South Africa—an affair that, though initially bungled, prompted a wave of popular imperialism and jingoistic flag-waving.

In 1898, the United States also went to war with Spain on highly dubious grounds, managing to subjugate Cuba, Puerto Rico, and the Philippines—for which newspaper magnate William Randolph Hearst claimed the credit on the grounds that inflammatory reports in his newspapers had urged on the American people.[6] The American occupation of the Philippines also put an end to Kaiser Wilhelm II's plans to seize the archipelago for Germany as part of a larger effort to establish his country on the world scene and acquire colonial spheres of influence.[7] And in Scandinavia, the crisis between Sweden and Norway intensified as a result of the Norwegian Parliament's decision to remove the Swedish-Norwegian Union symbol from the corner of its merchant and state flags, the so-called *kravet på det rene flagg* (demand for a clean flag).[8]

Yet this final example also shows the complexity of nationalist rhetoric. Although the liberal and democratic elements of nationalism during the nineteenth century had been weakened, they lived on—above all, in Norway's demands for the dissolution of the Union. In practice, it is difficult to differentiate clearly between right-wing and left-wing nationalism on some higher ideological plane.

The idea of a strong national community is Janus-faced: on the one hand, it looks toward equal rights and popular participation in the political decision-making process within the nation state; on the other, it looks toward competitiveness and antagonism with regard to other national communities. If former liberals had discovered that democratic reforms could be justified on the basis of ethnic solidarity, conservatives at the turn of the twentieth century realized that they could not advance their traditional policy concerns without popular, albeit not always democratic, approval. What decided the nature of developments within different countries was therefore more a question of historical peculiarities: exactly which common values and civic ideals were being invoked?

The drumbeat of nationalism across the West at the turn of the twentieth century sounded in different tones. The influential Pan-German League explained what the stakes were for Germany in the 1890s: "We are ready to stand behind the Kaiser whenever he calls on us ... but in exchange we ask for a fitting reward that will make the sacrifices meaningful: to belong to a master race that takes its share of the world and does not bow and scrape to other nations. Germany, awake!"[9]

Strong industrial and economic growth and an uncertain national identity defined by a history of defeat, failure, and division would prove to be a poisonous cocktail. Like Germany, the United States in the 1890s was a country whose military and political influence in the world did not match its economic and industrial strength. It was no coincidence that the two powers almost clashed over the Philippines. Bolstered by the Monroe Doctrine, the United States was more aggressively asserting its interests in Latin America and the Pacific. The United States, President Theodore Roosevelt explained in a message to Congress in December 1905, would be forced "in flagrant cases of ... wrongdoing or impotence, to the exercise of an international police power."[10]

Although American notions of the United States as having a manifest destiny were shaped by a religious impulse, there was an intrinsic tension between its ambitions for global dominance and its ideals of democratic citizenship. American nationalism was directed inward—at times even isolationist—and had its roots in a repudiation of the feudal institutions and colonial ambitions of the Old World. When needed, Americans could mobilize for daring foreign adventures—from war with Spain to intervention in the First World War—but fundamentally they saw their national role as to protect the United States as a special place where every individual had the right to life, liberty, and the pursuit of happiness as promised by the Declaration of Independence.

In Sweden, too, it proved difficult to rally citizens around aggressive nationalism and a more glorious foreign policy. Admittedly, the conflict with Norway created a window. The Union was the last symbolic relic of the era of the Swedish Empire of the seventeenth century that had held large domains around the Baltic and in northern Germany.[11] The increasingly vocal campaign in Norway for the dissolution of the Union created a countermovement in Sweden that conjured up past glories such as the misty battlefield at Lützen, where Swedish forces had won victory in 1632, and Karl XII's famous attempt to escape Ottoman forces on foot while wearing spurs.[12]

This was a reading of Swedish history that gave precedence to military glory and dreams of empire over Engelbrekt Engelbrektsson, Sweden's fifteenth-century peasant leader, and his invoking of ancient freedoms. Gustaf Fröding described the bombastic rhetoric of this Swedish nationalism as "patridiocy," a verdict that has largely been echoed by posterity—and with good reason, perhaps, when one recalls the dairy firm that in 1894 advertised a more than two-pound bust of Gustav II Adolf in butter, intended for dining-room buffets, to honor the tercentenary of the king's birth.[13]

But Rudolf Kjellén and the Young Sweden movement that he inspired represented more than just unthinking nationalism. His position in the conflict with Norway went beyond the garden variety of jingoism: the Norwegians had injured Swedish honor, it was true, but dissolution of the Union on proper terms was nevertheless for the best in order to prevent the Norwegians' radically democratic stance from destabilizing the political order in Sweden.[14] Kjellén evoked a vision of Sweden as a new economic and great industrial power in which workers and capitalists joined forces in a national coalition. In general, Kjellén's relationship to the emergent social-democratic movement was characterized by deep ambivalence.

In diary entries for 1889, written when he was twenty-five, Kjellén described socialism as undoubtedly a destructive force but nonetheless also a phenomenon that would bring about a new and better order. "Can I not believe," he asked himself, "that socialism ... is a necessary rupture in order to prepare the ground for a new idea—now that the idea of Christianity has lost its power?"[15] According to his daughter's biography, Kjellén suffered from acute feelings of loneliness and detested the ideology of individualism to the point of feeling greater sympathy with socialists than with liberals. The key thing was to find something beyond oneself in which to believe, to have someone to whom one can be a loyal subordinate.[16]

Some of Kjellén's ideas were ahead of their time and would be realized by the social-democratic labor movement, not right-wing nationalists. But Kjellén and his like-minded contemporaries faced a more immediate problem: while they might love their native country in principle, they were deeply disappointed with their compatriots.[17]

MY COUNTRY, RIGHT OR WRONG

Kjellén's starting-point was the Christian personality principle that Geijer had celebrated. There was, he conceded, a personal sphere in which the individual was sovereign. He criticized the city-states of antiquity for having asserted authority over every aspect of their citizens' lives: "The state interfered in family life and tore the child from its mother's arms so as to rear it itself, it persecuted the individual with a conscience, and it handed the freethinker a cup of hemlock." But beyond the constraints to this extremely private freedom, the public had "absolute dominion" over citizens' property, work, and ultimately even their lives. And if any readers were wondering exactly where the line went between individual freedom and state sovereignty, the professor had a ready answer: if anyone hesitated about drawing the boundary, if the individual's interests happened to clash with the good of the state, the latter always had a "natural and indisputable prerogative."[18]

This was a different stripe of conservatism than the one from which Geijer had defected in 1838. It was built on respect for the traditional and hierarchical institutions whose ultimate authority was God: the king, the nobility, the four estates, the church. The new conservatism had replaced God with the state. For Kjellén, the nation was a higher being, a mystical, living entity that was greater than the sum of its parts. One's native country, he explained, "is the nation, in whose unity we private individuals, alongside our own being, form a part and merge into each other, as cells merge in our own body."[19]

Kjellén's organism theory might seem to be related to Geijer's longing for national community and fears of a "war of all against all" in an excessively atomized society. But actually they are polar opposites. Kjellén was an authoritarian holist who rejected the notion that society's smallest component part is the individual. For him, sovereignty was apportioned from above and any private freedom that citizens may happen to have was a conditional holdover, not some historically established right. Kjellén's view of the nation was also anything but liberal. As Staffan Björck noted, for Kjellén what was national was always right: my country, right or wrong.[20]

For Geijer, in contrast, Sweden's national well-being lay in the fact that its historical development embodied certain fundamental principles such as freedom, justice, and equality. Geijer can be accused of being a nationalist in the sense that he twisted Swedish history in order to make it fit his liberal beliefs, but he did not claim that Swedishness was an absolute, irrational value.

The same goes for Key's patriotism. For her, love for one's country came with conditions; in the case of the Swedish nation, some were good, others less so. Kjellén was dismissive of this kind of love for one's native land. When Key dwelt on her delightful memories of childhood, "the rooted feeling of being home among the fragrant woods," Kjellén denounced them as "nature-worship in a temporary abode." True nationalism was an unmediated blood-union that superseded all sensory and empirical experience: "A nation is an individual with merits and defects just like all people. But love does not seek to attach itself to merits only. The son loves his mother, not because she is objectively good or great, but because she is his mother, who bore him in her womb."[21]

Kjellén's problem was that one thing a nation clearly is not, in any immediately observable sense, is an individual or single personality—rather, it is many different individuals and personalities. Even if one accepts Kjellen's idea that the nation is a mother, that does not mean that all siblings are alike or want the same thing.

But, according to Kjellén we are bound together by something. There is an aspect of every citizen's being that is turned toward the nation: a shared set of qualities, the national temperament. "The nation," he wrote, "is the personality that possesses all of those traits—and only those traits—that are shared by its children."[22] It is in the national character, therefore, that we can identify and analyze the supraindividual and empirically elusive entity that is the nation. Conservative nationalism thereby moves its focus away from the land, its physical nature and conditions, to the inner landscape of its inhabitants. When drawing up their inventory of unique national characteristics, Geijer and Almqvist began with Sweden's cold, barrenness, and poverty. For Kjellén, too, Swedish collective identity derived from shared historical experiences that had taken place in a geographically precise area. But he also claimed that the nation is not reducible to history or nature: it is a living organism, a mystical fusion of people, country, and the past.

But how can we acquire knowledge about the nation's personality? Not by asking its inhabitants, argued Kjellén. He rejected the right to vote because, in his view, it appeals to the less worthy impulses of the nation—its citizens' desire to raise their degree of material comfort by creating prosperity for everyone: "in the process, one's country is reduced to being a servant, at the beck and call of every passing whim and the baser instincts of the individual." In such situations, those truly devoted to their country must stand up against ideas and impressions "that flatter their generation."[23]

No, for Kjellén true love for one's country lay, rather, in seeking to perfect the natural abilities of the people by continually developing and improving the national character. And this task falls to those who truly love their country, those able to correctly understand this higher attribute of the nation, those who realize what must be done in order to strengthen and refine its best qualities. What Kjellén presented is nationalism with religious overtones, complete with a mystique of sacrifice and a caste of high priests who relay the demands of the new divinity. Nineteenth-century nationalism, with its positive view of the people and demands for reform of the state, now faced a kind of patriotism that exalted the nation even as it fretted about the quality of its citizens. It is against this backdrop that the intense debates over Swedish national character at the turn of the twentieth century must be understood.

THE EMBARRASSMENT OF RICHES

Early twentieth-century discourse on Swedish national character still recycled tropes found in Geijer and Almqvist: barren North and fertile South, feelings of self-reliance and practical common sense, respect for the law, and excessive deference to all things foreign. Many of the prominent cultural figures of the day—including poets Verner von Heidenstam and Oscar Levertin, historian Harald Hjärne, art historian Carl G. Laurin, religious activist Manfred Björkquist, and statistican Gustaf Sundbärg—in various ways wove these themes into ingenious nets with which to capture the Swedish national character.[24]

And yet a tone of bitterness and dissatisfaction with their own people often crept into their writings. These writers may not have harbored imperialistic fantasies, as Rudolf Kjellén did, but they measured their compatriots against an imagined archetype of Swedishness and found them wanting.

Such dissatisfaction took two distinct forms. The first was that Swedes did not enjoy each other's company—they were unsociable, materialistic, and individualistic. The second was that Swedes lacked any real sense of affection for their native land—they were ignorant of its own history, uninterested in its future, and deficient in the national pride instinctively felt by other civilized peoples. The independence that Geijer and Almqvist had praised as a positive attribute was now a problem.

The most influential among this group was Gustaf Sundbärg, the statistician whom we met in chapter 1. Born in Leksand in central Sweden in 1857, Sundbärg held a professorial chair in statistics, but he conducted most of his professional activities at the Central Office of Statistics, a governmental body. He is best known today for his association with a major governmental investigation into the causes of Swedish emigration.[25] His 1911 study *Det svenska folklynnet* (*The Swedish National Character*) was widely praised for its insightful analysis. Another self-appointed specialist in national character, Carl G. Laurin, held that "one does not have to search for ideas and impulses as if they were peas in a watery soup; rather, one feels that everything has been written by someone whose deepest convictions have for decades been met with indifferent shrugs or outright mockery; having held his tongue the entire time, he now wishes to speak his mind."[26]

Sundbärg's slim volume was an appendix to the investigation into emigration to the United States. There was a logic in this: no phenomenon was more troublesome for nationalism than the fact that hundreds of thousands of Swedes had voted with their feet and moved to the United States. In relation to its population size, Sweden's rate of emigration ranked third in Europe. Despite the hardships of the Atlantic crossing and the notorious dangers awaiting them in North America, many Swedes had chosen to leave their homeland. Their preference for the unrelenting competitiveness of the United States over the warm solidarity of Sweden stemmed from more than just crop failures and economic recessions; it could also be interpreted as a vigorous protest against social injustice, lack of opportunity, and an arrogant ruling class.

Such at least was how many liberals and social democrats viewed emigration. But in conservative circles—despite a reluctant recognition that social and even political discontent lay behind much emigration—the prevailing explanation was that there was something wrong with the Swedish people. The descendants of Geijer's Vikings and freeholding peasants had become too independent and had severed their already fragile ties to their home districts, neighbors, and the national community.[27]

Sundbärg presented his explanations for the discontent among Swedes in the form of anecdotal remarks and aphorisms, mixing pregnant observations with tenuous generalizations. Moreover, he had an unusually hostile attitude toward Denmark and never missed an opportunity to knock Danes under the pretext of lambasting Swedes. The book caused an outcry on the other side of the Öresund Strait and prompted angry polemics from Danish writers. Apart from being anti-Danish and formally strained, the book contained two clear themes.

The first was Swedes' well-known lack of interest in other people. In general—in social interactions, at work, in literature and science—Swedes manifested a psychological inability to understand other people's behavior. Sundbärg painted a picture of an awkward, alienated personality type that bordered on autistic. To be sure, he also indicated hidden depths behind Swedes' stony facade: a willingness to go to the heart of problems when they did actually notice them, a dormant imaginativeness, and a hopeful confidence in dealings with strangers. Even so, the overall impression is predominantly negative—the Swede as a boring and disagreeable sort of person whom one would readily cross the street to avoid.

Geijer's and Almqvist's independent Swedes can nonetheless be discerned behind this critique. Sundbärg had inverted the values that democratic nationalism saw in the people—ruggedness, self-sufficiency, inventiveness, independence, reticence—and had given them negative valuations. It was no longer Sweden's barrenness and poverty that produced good citizens. On the contrary, claimed Sundbärg, with Almqvist in mind, "Our people are poor, but our land is rich."[28] It is hard not to hear in Sundbärg's words a strain of middle-class irritation that the Swedish people were still far too rustic: practical, technical, and interested in nature but lacking any facility for the more subtle satisfactions offered by the life of the mind.

THE EMPTY HEART

The second of Sundbärg's themes is Swedes' lack of national feeling. Swedes, he argued, had slept through the nineteenth century. While other European peoples had been affected by a powerful need "to give expression to their own inner being in every aspect of life," the Swedish sense of national identity had remained dormant.[29] The educated classes had flirted with Scandinavism and cosmopolitanism. Swedes had shown solidarity with Danes and Norwegians by helping them generously, and the latter had shown their gratitude by exploiting Swedes' gullibility and lack of national pride.[30]

Among the masses, agitation by young socialists and correspondence with emigrants to America had given rise to expressly antinational sentiments. "The most wretched Polish field hand in Skåne [in southern Sweden]," explained Sundbärg, "is animated by a national feeling that is lacking in Skåne's own masters and peasants, not to mention its workers."[31] True patriots, Sundbärg claimed, always experience an unconscious but vital sense of well-being when breathing the air of their native land.

But, he continued, Swedes are perpetually dissatisfied with everything that makes them and their country different. If Swedes, unlike other people, spend their free time outdoors as much as possible during the short summer months, it is a fault—even though it is actually good for the health. If Swedish, unlike French, allows compound words, it is a sign of its inferiority—even though it actually makes Swedish more flexible and varied than French. Swedes are incapable of asserting their own preferences, instead treating their finest qualities as faults and lacks in comparison to other cultures.

Yet Swedes are friendly and helpful to foreigners and applaud the efforts of other peoples to attain nationhood. In sharp contrast to how they view their own, "Swedes have nothing against Sweden receiving distinctions and respect—only it must happen without any individual Swede, particularly any of their acquaintance, from acquiring fame and respect. And Swedes are happy to see Sweden becoming rich—if it could only happen without any individual Swede becoming rich."[32]

To Sundbärg, Swedes' hearts are empty, they dislike each other, and they feel no natural solidarity. And underneath this lies the lack of psychological insight mentioned earlier, a "peculiar lack of interest in the purely human, a distinct indifference toward contact with people."[33] This produced the profound unhappiness that, according to Sundbärg, was a strong contributing factor behind the numbers of people choosing to emigrate to North America. Swedes were a restless breed, lacking in judgement, who thought the grass was greener elsewhere. For them, it was a case of "the terrible old saying," according to Sundbärg: they want always to leave.

Of course, there is nothing strange in a patriot accusing his countrymen of lacking in affection for their native land. As shown earlier in this chapter, Kjellén pointed out that fierce love of one's country does not necessarily mean that one is satisfied with everything about that country. On the contrary, it could lead one to urge those same countrymen to aspire to higher goals, to realize the slumbering ideals of the nation. The nation could become braver, stronger, nobler, more generous, and more self-sacrificing.

Yet the picture Sundbärg painted of Swedes as asocial and alienated is so bleak that it leads the reader to conclude that it might be best to entirely abandon the idea of a national community. If the fault had lain primarily in the political system, the upper class, or the intellectual elite, some remedy might have been possible. But Swedes' fundamental inability to feel happiness was deeply rooted in the popular mind and formed a constitutive element of their national character. As a doctor, Sundbärg's prescribed cure seems to have been as affected by the disease as his patient. At no point does he seem to have considered the possibility that the very lack of uncritical patriotism that he regarded as Swedes' biggest flaw might in fact be considered a virtue—and this despite Swedes' tendency, as he put it, to instantly and unquestioningly accept all unfavorable appraisals of Sweden: "In such cases no scrutiny is ever needed; the charge is true, of that there can be no doubt."[34]

JOURNEY TO THE HEART OF DARKNESS

After reading *The Swedish National Character*, the famous poet Verner von Heidenstam wrote angrily to his friend Fredrik Böök, "Yes, it certainly feels strange to sit here reading Sundbärg's big book about opinions that one has oneself championed and made into one's cause, and to find oneself completely eliminated, denied even the courtesy of being included on the list of other living writers whom he regards as promoting the same views."[35]

Heidenstam's complaint was entirely justified. Criticism of Swedes' lack of patriotism was one of the issues he had vigorously promoted in public since well before the turn of the twentieth century. He had anticipated many of Sundbärg's ideas in an essay titled "On the Swedish Temperament" that appeared in the magazine *Ord och bild* in 1896. Moreover, Heidenstam had devoted most of his writing career to the complex questions of alienation and community that Sundbärg lightly touched upon in his aphorisms.

Heidenstam's ambivalent view of the relationship between individual and community made its appearance as early as his first novel, *Hans Alienus* (1892). Hans Alienus (from the Latin *alieno*, "to make strange"), who was originally called Hans Alenius, is the son of a Swedish professor who married a woman from Rome. The marriage is unhappy, and the father leaves his wife, taking his son with him to Scandinavia. Hans grows up into a restless and inquiring youth, clashes with his father, and returns to Rome, where he has the most fantastic adventures in time and space. These are the episodes usually discussed in analyses of Heidenstam's aesthetic vision.

And yet the most interesting part of the novel from the perspective of Swedish self-perception is its final section, "Homecoming." In it, Hans Alienus returns to Sweden and settles down on his father's farm in Tiveden, in central-southern Sweden. No dramatic reckoning takes place, merely a calm and melancholy reconciliation between "the two loners, father and son, who had spent their entire lives apart without ever communicating with the other." What finally brings them together is not love but a feeling of kinship. Together they go through all the family documents and "in this way connecting threads were spun between the dead and their descendants and between father and son, who became more open and intimate." But then the father dies. Hans Alienus leaves the parental farm and once again stands quite alone in the world. It is a bleak story, lacking in any real faith in reconciliation and community: People are on their own and can only be united by the realization that they are part of an ultimate existential community. We are born, we die, and in between there is little warmth.[36]

Heidenstam's biographer and friend Böök described him as a "faux country gentleman," not because there was anything dubious about his aristocratic roots, which, though not ancient, were genuine enough. But during his youth he lived mostly in Stockholm, despite having strong emotional ties to his mother's family farm, Olshammar, on the northern side of Lake Vättern—something he foregrounds in his writing. According to those who knew him, he was, like Hans Alienus, journeying through life alone, "dully silent, poor in friends."[37] Whereas Strindberg, as he put it in a letter to Heidenstam, loved people but felt that they were out to get him, his friend had a more reserved attitude.[38] Instead of alternating, as Strindberg did, between praise for the solitary individual and enthusiasm for the simple, animalistic community, Heidenstam chose to coolly observe the whole game.

Around 1900, Heidenstam increasingly—and not particularly reluctantly—played the part of a figure of national unity whose appeal crossed party lines, a Swedish equivalent to the Norwegian writer Bjørnstjerne Bjørnson. But his advocacy of a collective ideal became more difficult to sustain as the opposing political positions became more entrenched. After being thoroughly castigated by his lifelong friend Strindberg in 1910, Heidenstam came to be associated more and more with the nationalist right wing, even if he was uncomfortable in such company.[39]

ARISTOCRATIC INDIVIDUALISM

Heidenstam's writings contain a measure—scholars argue over how much—of Nietzschean faith in the superman. As Harold Borland observed, it is hardly surprising that Heidenstam's childhood and early adulthood resulted in his becoming an arrogant individualist.[40] When he came into contact with Nietzsche's ideas (via Strindberg) in the late 1880s, he felt an immediate affinity between the ideal of the superman in *Thus Spake Zarathustra* and his own thinking, above all in *Hans*

Alienus. Like Nietzsche, he regarded a people as the raw material from which nature extracted great individuals.

Admittedly, Heidenstam felt direct sympathy for people's existential suffering. But his individualism went far beyond liberal theories of education and Geijer's philosophy of personality. It was also about a fixed relationship between the sovereign individual and the great mass of people. It is an interesting phenomenon that this aristocratic individualist became—if only briefly—the main ideologue of national consciousness in Sweden.

In 1896, Heidenstam published his famous essay "On the Swedish Temperament" ("Om svenskarnas lynne"), after which he unleashed his national fervor in a rapid succession of articles, speeches, and poems. In 1898, he published his verse cycle *Ett folk* (*A People*) in the national newspaper *Svenska Dagbladet*, a work that made its author the undisputed mouthpiece of a democratic-nationalistic Swedishness that was to establish itself in palaces and hovels alike. *A People* combined patriotism and the demand for universal suffrage with rare cogency:

> It is true we own a fatherland
> Which came down to us all,
> An equal right and equal bond
> For rich and poor alike.[41]

Heidenstam here harks back to Geijer. It is the people who "own" the fatherland, a right based in history, and there is a clear connection to a yeoman peasant community of equals. The poem made Heidenstam a unifying figure for a large if motley grouping who hoped for Sweden's national rebirth under the sign of democracy: cultural radicals, freethinkers, temperance advocates, social democrats—in effect, all of Sweden's emerging grassroots movements.

This is how Yngve Hugo, a popular educator and future principal of the left-leaning adult education college Brunnsvik, described Heidenstam's address to students at the Nässla Stone Circle in Östergötland county in 1908: "Tall and stately, he stood there among the stones like the ruler in a solemn ancient drama. Yet his audience felt powerfully that this was no theater. It was much more than that, it was reality. And this was a true prophet and bard, who had emerged to speak to his people."[42] The only real opposition to Heidenstam's national project came from the right, which was throwing up barriers against the demand for universal suffrage, and the relatively marginal syndicalist and anarchist wings of the labor movement.

From the turn of the twentieth century until the Great Strike of 1909, Heidenstam's patriotism lay above and beyond the struggle between left and right.[43] He had countless followers in both camps and made frequent appearances in which he called for national unity and reconciliation across class lines, above all under the banner of the youth movement that emerged in the years following the dissolution of the union with Norway. Like Heidenstam, this movement both waved the flag and demanded votes for all.

Heidenstam cut a paradoxical figure in his role as people's tribune and expositor of the fundamental essence of Swedishness. His thinking was marked by a pervasive skepticism toward people as groups. Even so, it makes sense that the standard-bearer of Swedishness should try to urge modern, cosmopolitan, and materialistic Swedes to form themselves into a nation and a collectivity. Heidenstam regarded the Swedes of 1900 not as a ready-made people but as merely the raw materials of a great nation. "A people, that is what we want to be," as he writes in *A People*, a poem dominated by the future tense. There is even a faintly Hegelian ring to how actual states coexist with potential states: "We are and become what we want."[44]

However, Heidenstam was not entirely comfortable with the idea that Swedes should be welded together into a proud and vital people:

> A people! I tremble at the word,
> So filled with song and sorrow,
> With divine judgement and doom.
> I shiver at the word,
> As at a towering giant
> Whose foot bears down on my breast
> As though I were a mussel upon the sand.[45]

Here, at his most patriotic moment, Heidenstam cannot conceal his aversion to collectivism and mass politics.

While these lines express a fearful admiration for the relentless power that a united people can summon, the poem also makes clear that this power ultimately poses a threat to the independent self and the free individual whom Heidenstam holds in such high regard. If Strindberg was a Swedish champion of Rousseau's theories of independence and equality, Heidenstam gave voice to Tocqueville's aristocratic fear of an impending social order in which the private individual risked being crushed between state and people. There is none of Kjellén's reluctant attraction to the burgeoning power of socialism here. Heidenstam disliked the powerful state outright.

The other side of this coin is a deep ambivalence about the popular. Heidenstam had little sympathy with the efforts made by romanticizers of rural life to find the true Sweden among the common people. Nor did he set much store by their depictions of the life and manners of the masses. To look for national characteristics solely in the peasant class was superficial, he explained in "On the National" ("Det nationella"). In fact, much in peasant life crossed the boundaries of culture: "Work on the land and all that pertains to it permeate not only our customs but even the way we imagine a particular color, as can be observed even in an Egyptian *fellah* village." Genuinely national characteristics, Heidenstam argued, were also to be found in the nobility of other countries.[46]

Key, a close friend of Heidenstam's, regarded his national program as far too aristocratic. She argued that he was mistaken in putting his faith in the educated classes' desire for reform and social responsibility.[47] But in claiming that Sweden's true national character was an aristocratic individualism, Heidenstam hoped to disarm the new collectivist doctrines. It was far-seeing in its unambiguous rejection of the traditional conservative national chauvinism that lacked popular appeal. Instead, Heidenstam offered his countrymen a sublime individualism that only in moments of need could be transformed into a fearsome collective force, a giant, a Hobbesian Leviathan, driven onward by the scourge and capable of crushing a single individual like a mussel on the sand. An impressive image, to be sure, but hardly something around which to rally the nation.

THE PEOPLE THAT FAILED

At the turn of the twentieth century, a struggle was being fought out across the entire Western world over who had the right to speak for a nation. Democratic nationalism was being squeezed in a vice: on one side by an aggressive and chauvinistic conservatism; on the other by socialist internationalism. Fear of being expropriated by the destitute led many in the upper classes to put their hopes in nationalism as an alternative form of collectivism that might save society from turmoil. Resentment at the inequities of class society fueled the working class's suspicion of calls for patriotic unity. In various countries, developments were ultimately determined more by political, economic, and social conditions than by the quality of the national rhetoric.

It should be noted, at the risk of sounding wise after the fact, that circumstances were not favorable for either Kjellén's and Sundbärg's self-critical brand of nationalism or Heidenstam's patriotic individualism. They were all a little too candid. It was almost as if they had conceded defeat in advance by portraying the Swedish people as eternally incapable of feeling national solidarity. It was not the country that had failed but its inhabitants.

The freedom that Geijer and Almqvist accorded the individual was more closely bound up with Christian notions of equality. They would have been deeply offended by the idea that there might exist supermen or that the state might constitute some kind of superior personality comparable to God in Christianity. In their eyes, society was made up of a collection of separate and equal citizens whose mutual relationships could be regulated only by means of laws and rights, either in the form of equal and reciprocal agreements or through traditionally inherited duties and entitlements. Geijer's and Almqvist's liberalism would also turn out to be more appealing to national sentiments than Strindberg's and Key's revolutionary utopianism as well as Heidenstam's lawless aristocrats and Kjellén's mystical state godhead.

Yet Heidenstam's and Kjellen's nationalistic vision of Swedishness left its mark. Some of Kjellén's ideas about the strong state and cooperation between capital and labor were to find a home in social democracy after it established itself as the dominant political party. Sundbärg's informal observations would turn out to have remarkable longevity outside of politics. The issue of Swedes' unsociableness and their sheer lack of interest in people was to be a recurrent motif in the writings of domestic commentators and foreign observers, literary depictions, and sociocultural analyses throughout the twentieth century. Even now it makes regular appearances in gloomy cultural appraisals of the welfare state's inhumanity. And Heidenstam continues to strike a chord in the collective Swedish consciousness with his descriptions of the impoverishment and alienation of family life and his warnings about the powerful state that speaks on behalf of the people when dealing with the individual.

Even so, Heidenstam's ominous admonitions are only a backhanded acknowledgement of the impact of Geijer's paradigm and its emphasis on individual independence. The attacks on "Swedishness" have made clear both the price that citizens have had to pay for their independence and the strong alliance between state and individual that created the welfare state: an unwillingness to get too close to other people and thereby risk the human dependence that creates masters and servants. Heidenstam's ambivalent patriotism nicely captured the intrinsic contradiction within the social-democratic welfare state of the future: the power of the state to give individuals autonomy could also, paradoxically, be turned against them as individuals. In order to explain this development, we now turn our attention to the other end of the political spectrum—Swedish social democracy.

CHAPTER 8

Sweden for the Swedes!

When Sweden's Prime Minster Per Albin Hansson gave a speech on the Day of the Peasant in Stockholm's Skansen Park on July 1935, he read a poem in honor of the legendary national hero Engelbrekt Engelbrektsson, written by Sten Selander:

> When the foreigners' empire lay in muddy ruin
> And the masters' kingdom fell to pieces,
> Then, like the sun atop the earth,
> Appeared the people's just realm
> To Engelbrekt and his peasants true.

In his speech, Hansson praised the Swedish peasants who throughout history had carried their masters' burden but also defended the people's freedoms and civic rights "even when it was not only a matter of taking, but also of giving." Five hundred years ago, Hansson declared, Sweden's first parliament had been "a peasants' day" that united for the first time national consciousness and the will of the people.[1] Winding up, he made an appeal to the Swedish people's common interest: "I, you, all of us have but one cause—to protect our native land and the well-being of the people."[2]

Politicians adapt their speeches to the audience and the occasion. But the prime minister's words were not ad hoc flattery that he hoped would escape the notice of his party comrades. By the mid-1930s, Swedish social democracy had appropriated many of the nineteenth century's national myths and symbols. The blue and yellow flag, noted the talented young social democrat Gunnar Lundberg in 1934 in the pamphlet *Folkstyre eller fogdevälde* (*Popular Rule or Despotism*), was as dear to the labor movement as the red flag—the former a symbol of Swedish people's freedom, the latter of international solidarity.³ Social-democratic leaders of the thirties portrayed themselves as heirs to the freeholding peasants who had brazenly marched with Engelbrekt and supported Gustav Vasa in his fight for independence from Denmark.

In numerous speeches, articles, and pamphlets, the former antimilitarists and internationalists now portrayed Sweden as a country where democracy, justice, and equality were deeply rooted in the soil itself. In historian Åsa Linderborg's succinct formulation, their intention was "to represent social democracy as a natural continuation of Sweden's historical development."⁴

The national turn was not unique to Sweden. Nationalistic and chauvinistic rhetoric was being declaimed in most European languages in the 1930s. More striking was how the Swedish labor movement came to take control of national symbols and sentiments at a time when in many other countries they were being wielded by radical right-wingers and fascists.

The same year that Hansson came to power under the banner of *folkhemmet*, Hitler seized control over Germany using *Volkgemeinschaft*, a "community of the people," as his slogan. Undoubtedly, it was a result in part of Swedish social democrats' skill and dexterity—their famed capacity to win hegemony. Relatively unburdened with Marxist doctrine, Swedish Social Democrats also found it easier to develop a pragmatic and more independent theoretical analysis of their own. Perhaps, too, Sweden's labor movement had not suffered quite as much pain as Germany's.

Above all, however, the historical legacy available to them was fundamentally different compared to that which confronted their comrades in Germany, Italy, and other continental European countries. It was social democracy's good fortune that Geijer's narrative of Swedishness, with its stress on popular freedom, chimed so well with the movement's own fundamental values and political objectives. The Social Democrats' strength lay in having recognized this opportunity and quickly fused the red flag and the yellow-and-blue flag into a homemade version of national socialism, centered on the independence and freedom of both the individual and the nation. In this chapter, we examine more closely the nineteenth-century legacy that Swedish social democracy benefitted from but also refashioned in key respects:

Geijer's concept of history, nationalism, the ethos of Sweden's popular movements, and the prevailing view of the law.[5]

SCHOOLING FOR THE FUTURE

Like many patriarchs, Hansson was tight-lipped about his own upbringing. There were few newspaper articles in the 1930s about his childhood and adolescence. The most personal he became was in a short passage about his mother that, while doubtless sincere, stuck closely to Almqvist's credo about poverty: "helpful to others and proud in not being dependent on alms and charity." Anders Isaksson, author of a magisterial four-volume biography of the political architect of Sweden's "people's home," argues that Hansson saw himself as merely one of "many impoverished working-class boys who ended up joining the labor movement and, through it, making their way into public life."[6]

Whatever the truth about Hansson's background and psychological makeup, he was right about his own background in one respect. His origin in Sweden's impoverished working class at the turn of the nineteenth century was crucial to the policies that he was to carry out under the banner of *folkhem*. Hansson—in company with thousands like him—was shaped by the struggle to transform both his own deprivation and that of others.

Hansson was born in 1885 in Fosie in Malmö, at that time still a fairly rural place. His father was a bricklayer, but the family came from generations of Skåne peasants and farmhands on both his father's and mother's sides. Although there are numerous anecdotes about his time at school and early demonstration of leadership qualities, he mostly played them down. In contrast, his school grades are extensively documented. Although not a straight-A student, as would later be claimed, he got decent grades with plenty of A-minuses.[7] Whatever might be said about the religious and patriotic aspects of his elementary school, it put essential linguistic and mathematical tools in the hands of young people who were ready to try to better themselves and improve society.

What got taught also mattered. Even though history classes fostered deference to authority and respect for tradition, the Swedish history being studied was itself characterized by the democratic and popular perspectives of nineteenth-century liberal and romantic nationalism. The standard textbook in elementary schools was C. T. Odhner's *Lärobok i fäderneslandets historia för folkskolan* (*National History Textbook for Elementary Schools*) from 1877.[8] Odhner, a professor of history at Lund University, was liberal-conservative and pro–free trade in his political sympathies; in his younger days he had been an enthusiastic member of the Scandinavist movement.[9] Odhner's elementary-school textbook broadly followed Geijer in its view of freeholding peasant freedoms: Engelbrekt was celebrated as a champion of the peasantry in their struggle against the lords while aristocratic efforts to introduce feudalism were criticized.[10] According to Odhner, Engelbrekt "gave ordinary Swedish people back their freedom and independence" and united Sweden as a nation.[11]

As historian Erik Lönnroth observed in the 1940s when attacking Geijer's reading of Engelbrekt, "Highly original, Geijer's view of history has entered into the general consciousness of posterity."[12] Or, to quote Hansson himself, "Whatever the deficiencies of official education in what we can call the old days, even though they are not so very distant, it taught us to admire those men who raised the flag of rebellion and led the struggle for freedom against tyrants and oppressors of the people, both foreign and domestic."[13] When, toward the end of the 1920s, Hansson began to turn social democracy in a national direction, Odhner's Swedish history would serve him well.

Of equal importance was Hansson's direct experience of working within various popular movements. When he joined the Social Democratic Party's youth wing in spring 1902, he was already active in the Verdandi Temperance Association and had a job as an assistant in Malmö's Pan Co-operative.[14] He later stated that it was not a commitment to temperance that led him to Verdandi.[15] For Hansson, as for many other working-class youths, being involved in an association was an opportunity for making new friends (not least, of the opposite gender) and for self-development through new skills and contacts. Working in a cooperative, in contrast, was both more concrete and more ideological. Many working-class families were trapped in debt to shopkeepers who gave credit and were defenseless against price hikes and poor selections. Since everything in a cooperative was paid for in cash, members were materially independent yet bound together in voluntary solidarity.

Hansson's job at the Pan Co-operative was to be the start of a long career entirely within the alternative world being created by popular movements. The cooperative embodied a moral logic that emphasized the importance of self-reliance, personal responsibility, and the possibility of realizing oneself as an individual—even as it demonstrated the social and political power that could be mobilized when its individual members chose to subordinate themselves to a shared goal. If history classes in elementary school supplied the ideological superstructure of Sweden's future welfare state (the *folkhem*), the popular movements—*folkrörelserna*—created its practical base.

MY ROOTS AND MY STOCK

Per Albin Hansson was a skilled politician and rhetorician but no bold theorist, in stark contrast to the Social Democratic Party's party secretary in the early 1930s, Rickard Lindström, who was known for his willingness to slaughter sacred cows. During the rise of Nazism, Lindström sent reports from Germany relaying his apprehensions about the sectarian tendencies within German social democracy.[16] This was cause for grave concern: with its vaunted advanced party-run training schools, proletarian cultural associations, heroic martyrs like Rosa Luxemburg and major theorists like Karl Kautsky and Eduard Bernstein, Germany was the homeland of scientific socialism—but now the pragmatic Swedes were making greater progress while their more intellectually accomplished German comrades lost ground to communists and Nazis.[17]

Together with Nils Karleby, a short-lived talent of the post-WWI labor movement, Lindström came to the conclusion that social democracy in Sweden had been shaped not by socialist theory but by the specific historical experiences of the Swedish working class.

Karleby, who died of tuberculosis tragically young in 1926, left behind what is probably Sweden's only original contribution to socialist theory.[18] In it, he rejected classical Marxism's claim to be a field of theoretical knowledge. The only thing we can know about socialism, Karleby argued, was the "living praxis" that exists in the form of workers' subjective values and the experiences gained in political and social struggle. He compared the sterility of German socialism with the pragmatism of its Swedish counterpart: "When the Swedish theory burst from the depths of its workers' hearts, it had a very different dynamism and elemental force. Those who were there will never forget the moment when, at a workers' meeting in Skåne, F. V. Thorsson delivered a paradox whose sheer incorrectness dramatically illustrated how far true socialism prizes the weight of reality above the relative unimportance of outward form: Better roads in Norrland [the northern region] mean more for Sweden than socialism does in its entirety."[19]

Karleby nonetheless provided few concrete analyses of the Swedish labor movement's unique features, devoting his energies instead to a more abstract defense of non-Marxist, reformist socialism. Lindström, who rarely missed an opportunity for polemic, was blunter. The nation was an incontestable fact, he explained in a 1928 pamphlet published by the Social Democratic Youth movement titled *Socialism, nation och stat* (*Socialism, Nation, and State*) pointedly aimed at Marxist internationalism. It was true that the international proletariat had a common interest that gave a "certain uniformity to its political direction," admitted Lindström."[20] But the alliance between British and German workers was weaker than that between British workers and the British bourgeoisie "who both live in the same cities, see the same posters on the walls, read the same newspapers, take part in the same political or sporting events, and at times even talk about each other or about the same people."[21] In a homogeneous nation-state such as Sweden, Lindström argued, the national idea had created a natural seedbed that the labor movement could nurture. Its citizens had been raised in a spirit of collective sensibility and historical solidarity. In essence, it was the same progressive and forward-looking movement that Geijer had seen as embodied in Swedish history.

The problem, as Lindström saw it—and as Geijer clearly foresaw—was not that there was anything wrong with national community in itself, but that the workers had been excluded from it for so long. Lack of patriotism was not to blame. "The working class," he argued, "has anchored all its efforts, consciously or unconsciously, in the nation."[22]

The workers had been excluded by virtue of being denied their rights and their own political agency. Lindström reused Geijer's classic image of the freedom-loving and patriotic farmers who confronted an arrogant and potentially treasonous aristocracy, this time substituting workers for peasants and capitalists for aristocrats. The goal of social democracy, Lindström claimed, was to realize the idea of the nation and make Sweden a true homeland for the working class. Achieving universal suffrage was an important milestone, which would be followed by the next step—an economic leveling that would make citizens socially equal.

Lindström saw no contradiction between internationalism and a "national socialism." He cited the French socialist leader Jean Jaurès: "A little internationalism leads away from one's native country, but a lot leads one back. A little patriotism removes us from the Internationalism; a great patriotism brings us back." He drew the line at national chauvinism, which, in his view, was actually detrimental to the national interest, since it was unable to tolerate any homeland other than its own.[23] Lindström's "national socialism" was basically the same progressive, little-Sweden nationalism that had been created in the first half of the nineteenth century and should not be confused with the better-known national socialism of Hitler's political movement in Germany. Its virtues were to be found in its people, or, more precisely, in its workers: "Nothing has given me the riches that I have drawn from my roots and my stock. Never have I seen greater idealism than that which burns in the eyes of Sweden's socialist workers. Never have I found a greater intelligence, a richer store of wisdom, and a deeper humanity than in the people working in poverty—in the material sense—in Swedish factories and workplaces."[24]

We are hearing Almqvist here: "To be poor means to be thrown upon one's own resources." Or Geijer: "Swedes . . . have mighty resources within themselves that they can call on when needed; there is no other people among whom natural ingenuity is more widespread than the Swedish peasantry." Indeed, if there is any difference in the degree of their reverence for the virtues of the people, it is that Lindström's praise for the workers' humanity and intelligence was even more generous than Geijer's and Almqvist's tribute to ordinary people's ingenuity.

Possibly this was a reaction to Sundbärg's attack on the Swedish people for their lack of humanity. Whatever the case, Lindström's appeal to the image of "decent people versus arrogant masters" proved to be rhetorically highly successful. Far from being foreign imports, the democracy and social justice now being invoked by the working class were time-honored Swedish principles.

In the short term, Lindström's iconoclasm was not particularly effective. Yet within a decade, his national approach had become a given for social democratic politics. In fighting a losing battle in 1920s, the Lindström faction facilitated the changes of course that lay ahead: military rearmament, collaboration with the Peasant's Party (Bondeförbundet), building a *folkhem* instead of class struggle, national consensus in place of unproductive opposition. This was a classic Lindström move. Career-wise, his foresight was a handicap. A successful politician does not run ahead of public opinion but waits until the time is right. In the thirties, Lindström's turn to the nation, which had met with fierce opposition in the mid-twenties, became a reality with minimal resistance under Hansson's fatherly guidance (figure 8.1).

FIGURE 8.1. In 1933 the Social Democrats came to power in Sweden through a historic alliance with Bondeförbundet (Peasant's Party), the agrarian party. In the 1934 municipal elections, the Social Democrats portrayed themselves as part of an almost thousand-year struggle for freedom: from the mythological Torgny Lagman who, in the name of the rule of law forced the Swedish king to make peace with the Norwegians, to peasant leader Engelbrekt, the liberal Hjärta, and the Social Democrat Hjalmar Branting. The poster translates to "The Way of the Swedish People is that of Popular Freedom and Democracy. Vote for the workers' party, the Social Democrats." Arbetarrörelsens arkiv.

By launching the concept of *folkhem*, Hansson managed to fuse the historical legacy of liberal nationalism with the increasingly interventionist state of the thirties. The luster of Geijer's model is immediately apparent in Hansson's oft-quoted 1926 pamphlet *Sverige åt svenskarna—svenskarna åt Sverige (Sweden for Swedes—Swedes for Sweden)*:

> This is why [the middle classes] are unhappy when the workers cheer for their native land. In their ears, these cheers sound like a clarion call. They are not wrong about that. "They may have stolen our land, but we are stealing it back" sing the working-class youth. Political democracy still awaits its social equivalent. Sweden remains a class society in which the great mass of people live in hardship and insecurity. Sweden is not yet that good home for *all* Swedes. For that to happen, it must be entirely taken over by the people as a great mass. Swedish social democracy is leading the way to victory and its watchword is: *Sweden for the Swedes—Swedes for Sweden.*[25]

The first part of the slogan, "Sweden for the Swedes," closely follows Geijer and Almqvist. As individuals, all Swedes have fundamental rights, not from some abstract perspective of natural rights, but simply by virtue of their Swedishness. The second part of the slogan—"The Swedes for Sweden"—is more ambiguous. It implies submission, the idea that individual citizens must also be subordinated to the national community. It can be read innocently, as a statement that what empowers Swedes is their national affiliation.

But it also opens up a more antiliberal perspective, one in which the country's inhabitants are regarded as a natural resource in the service of the state. As Åsa Linderborg noted in her book *Socialdemokratin skriver historia (Social Democracy Makes History)*, sometime between the turn of the twentieth century and the 1930s, a noticeable shift took place in how social democracy viewed history. During its pioneering phase, the emphasis was primarily on rebel leaders. After social democracy became the dominant party of government, it made room for approving descriptions of Sweden's constitutional continuity and kings such as Gustav I Vasa and Karl XI.[26]

In the 1930s, nationalistic ideas about a community of the people were fused with strong state control over the economy in both democratic and repressive regimes around the world. Stronger leaders adroitly exploited the ideas of a national community and a historical destiny in order to rally citizens to their policies. Yet the shared values to which they appealed were not the same. In Germany, Hitler conjured up an expansive and racist figure of ethnic community. In the United States, Roosevelt founded the New Deal on an American tradition of social, almost Christian, solidarity that challenged neither liberal democracy nor the market economy—even if his opponents compared him to Mussolini and Stalin. For its part, the Swedish labor movement discovered a good measure of Swedishness in the Marxist legacy.

GO YOUR OWN WAY

The fusion of socialism and nationalism, of Swedishness and Marxism, was one aspect of social democracy's ability to exploit history and its cultural inheritance. In it, "freedom" was primarily a matter of the nation's independence and the right of its entire people to equal citizenship: no one was subject to another, no one a maidservant or bondsman, master or bailiff. Yet this was only one feature of the emancipatory zeal that permeated the early labor movement. Grassroots activism underscored the importance of another form of independence, an existential freedom: the requirement to be self-reliant, the duty to take personal responsibility, and the right to self-realization.[27]

Hansson's career is also interesting in this respect. In 1884, when Hansson was born, August Palm had just begun to spread social-democratic teachings in Sweden. The first party congress lay five years in the future, and the handful of active socialists were heavily monitored by the authorities and riven by internal conflicts and rivalries.

By the time Hansson joined the Social Democratic Party's youth wing in Malmö at the age of eighteen, social democracy had become an important force, if not yet the mass organization that it would one day grow into. But the movement he entered—above all, its lively youth wing—was firmly convinced that the future belonged to social democracy. Hansson quickly assumed a leading role, although he was neither alone nor unchallenged. He was part of a remarkable generation that included future poets and cabinet ministers, communists and reformers.

Marxist theories and socialist critique of society were only part of the permanent intellectual baggage that a young Social Democrat acquired in the years after 1900. Posterity, and above all the labor movement itself, has often—and not unreasonably—attributed its political successes to an organizational capacity for solidarity work and its ability to mobilize the working classes on the basis of their common economic interests. And yet, in its strong emphasis on collective political action, it also implicitly acknowledged the importance of the promise of individual emancipation.

One of fledgling social democracy's main charges against capitalism and the bourgeoisie was that workers had been stripped of their humanity, the fundamental decency that is the birthright of every citizen. This critique preceded scientific socialism's claim to have laid bare the secret mechanisms of world history. Its origins lay close to the Christian socialism that had inspired the workers on Europe's barricades during the nineteenth century.[28] Ultimately, it was the idea of fraternity, of all people's equal worth. "You should not be your brother's slave, you are as good as he in body and soul" proclaimed an early social-democratic propaganda poster of the 1880s.[29] This fundamentally Christian-humanist demand lives on in the Swedish working-class hymn "Arbetets söner" ("Sons of Labor") with its allusion to *människovärdet vi fordra tillbaka* ("reclaiming our human worth").

Many of the young workers who were drawn to the labor movement had larger agendas than just politics or economics. They were endeavoring to recover their individuality, to be respected as thinking and feeling human beings. The working-class author Karl Östman described this ambition clearly in his novel *Den breda vägen* (*The Broad Road*): "The working class must be rescued from serfdom! We must become human beings in the truest sense of the word and live decently in the world, bodily and spiritually. No longer will that privilege belong to a chosen few. And if helping to achieve that goal does not bring me any personal benefit, well, so be it. I wish to go my own way nonetheless, and I shall not waver. . . . You, too, should choose your own path."[30]

This quotation is found in the intellectual historian Ronny Ambjörnsson's *Den skötsamme arbetaren* (*The Conscientious Worker*), a study of the Swedish temperance and popular education movements. Ambjörnsson also offered an acute reading of Östman's thinking: "What he emphasizes is the importance of choosing one's path independently of others. The protagonist can be influenced by other individuals, but the existential decision is his alone. There is an inner voice that he must learn to heed."[31]

The Social Democratic Party's youth association that Hansson joined as a young man also cultivated a rhetoric of individual heroism that, in places, is more reminiscent of Nietzsche than Marx. The goal of socialism involved creating a new and better kind of human being. The working class would be elevated to a new aristocracy through their heroic struggle; on the cover of the youth wing's magazine *Fram* in 1905, Zeth Höglund wrote these lines:

> Onward you march unhindered
> By the efforts of fools and knaves
> Your strength unmanacled
> By no puny enemies thwarted[32]

The tone is typical of the naively romantic rhetoric that flourished among young social democrats.

August Strindberg and Ellen Key were idolized as models. When the so-called Strindberg Feud, the free-for-all literary brawl over the nationalistic hero-king Charles XII, erupted in 1909, young Social Democrats celebrated wildly: "August Strindberg, the giant, has taken up the flaming sword of his youth."[33] And when Key gave an address at Brunnsvik adult education college, the first of its kind for young workers, she was welcomed at Ludvika railway station by enthusiastic students who unharnessed her sleigh and pulled it to the college themselves.[34] The radical-individualist revolt against middle-class society spoke to young working-class men.

Naturally, this did not preclude a strong feeling of solidarity. Many of the future working-class writers, social-democratic and communist politicians, cooperative organizers, and trade unionists who took part in the social-democratic youth movement around 1900 would later attest to its quasi-revivalist atmosphere. Even the pragmatic Hansson grew faintly nostalgic when recalling his youth in an article from 1938: "I still cherish memories from our association's first congresses—1905 and 1907—of the rapturous mood that characterized the movement. 'It's almost like heaven,' said a man from Dalarna county at the congress. And there was indeed something almost religious about our faith and our work."[35]

There was also more than a dash of yellow and blue in the red. The young socialists' meetings usually began with a song whose text had been composed by K. G. Ossiannilsson to the tune of "Engelbrekt's March." Its drift was that the bailiff's offices should be torn down and the "land of Sweden" liberated—indeed, so fervently did the song appeal to the fatherland that it was adopted by Sweden's Nazi youth movement in the 1930s.[36]

The importance of winning over smaller farmers to socialism was emphasized in the magazine *Fram*, at times in markedly anti-industrial terms: "Shall we henceforth sacrifice our sons to industrialism, to be martyred by the golem of money? No, the Swedish peasant cannot surrender his traditional freedoms for long, cannot abandon his political independence."[37]

Anti-industrialism and agrarian socialism may not have been dominant features of the fledgling social-democratic movement but the tendencies were there. Brunnsvik adult education college—which caused much anxiety among the Swedish middle class, who saw it as a school for agitators—was run by the rural romancer and writer Karl Erik Forsslund, who preferred rough homespun trousers, raged against the nuisance of open-air dance floors, and advocated a return to traditional peasant society.

Much of this rhetoric reflected the campaign for universal suffrage, the great struggle of the day in which socialist workers, middle-class liberals, and small farmers united behind the cause of democracy as an extension of the traditional conflict between "masters" and "the people." The Swedish labor movement did not leap into being from between the lines of a socialist document. It was part of a comprehensive process of self-organization within that vast majority of the Swedish population who lacked the property, education, or social position required in order to take part in politics or make their voice heard in public. This was a matter of economic interest but also of a desire to feel a sense of self-worth, to be respected, and to be treated like an equal citizen.

Popular movements offered something that was historically new: the opportunity to participate in an association's activities on the basis of representative democracy. At a time when the old corporate bodies and trade guilds had been abolished but universal suffrage had yet to be established, free churches, temperance lodges, and worker's associations offered a space where artisans, ambitious workers, and people from the lower middle class could think and act like fully adult, equal citizens. From modest beginnings in the early 1850s—when they were mainly revivalist in nature—these popular movements grew in the twentieth century into a force to be reckoned with. In 1920, they were organizing more than a million people; one in four Swedes above the age of fifteen was part of a labor, temperance, or free church organization.[38] Ideologically fluid and differing in their social composition, these associations had one feature in common as they gathered in dim and drafty halls around the country: they schooled their members in both individual independence and collective action.

It was hardly coincidental that the way had been paved by the revivalist movement itself: the individual Protestant with his God who joins with other solitary beings in Christ. In his 2001 novel *Lewis resa* (*Lewi's Journey*), Per Olov Enquist evokes the importance of pietism for Sweden's popular movements: "It's impossible to understand the development of popular movements in twentieth-century Sweden without Moravianism. . . . We don't want to create any state religions or societies, we don't want to become powerful. Just to permeate. A popular movement is a movement in people's hearts, an idea rather than an organization. . . . The essence of Christianity is not the catechism but an inner union between heart and Savior."[39]

Popular movements, observed Ronny Ambjörnsson, were a gigantic exercise in learning to listen to one's heart, to one's own inner voice. For the most part, that voice was a strict disciplinarian who warned the individual against giving free rein to instinct and instead urged hard work, responsibility, and solidarity. It was the equivalent, in other words, of the Protestant conscience—a puritanism that was directed both inward and outward, at one's ego but also at society. This was an understanding of the individual that derived from a normative conception of what people had in common: a collective individualism, we might say, that in a spirit of communal solidarity recognized the optimal conditions under which people might do justice to their own individuality. Its goal was to elevate the entire collectivity, not elitism but egalitarian individualism.

This utopian perspective nonetheless contains a powerful inner tension. Despite their rhetoric of community and their democratic forms of organization, the popular movements contained a substantial measure of elitism: where does the line go between the individual's right to self-realization and the desire to manage other people's lives? This eternal problem becomes especially apparent in certain associations, perhaps above all in the socialist youth organizations, the educational movements, and in parts of the temperance movement. From the democratic ideal emerges a form of radical individualism bearing many of the hallmarks of the cultural intelligentsia's flirtation with Nietzsche's superman.

The puritanism of the popular movements was intended to create independent individuals, most often in a literal sense, as with the temperance movement's battle against dependency on alcoholism and other stimulants. Alcohol was associated with subjugation, chains, and unfreedom—a lack of self-reliance and autonomy. Shaking off this burden meant taking control over one's life and becoming a complete human being.[40]

But the goal was also to liberate oneself from a humiliating subjugation to employers, poor relief, priests, and other representatives of a class society. The mutual support, the burial associations, and the union solidarity made members less dependent on the charity and whims of a condescending upper class. Popular movements were hardly less strict about respectability and conscientiousness—indeed, if anything, more so—but it was a condition of comradeship among equals, not a disciplining of subordinates.

Independence could also be more metaphorical, as was the case with popular education. This was about freeing oneself from the everyday world of class society—in which members were often subordinated—and, through study and the acquisition of knowledge, reaching a point where one could objectively assess oneself and one's surroundings. As a former student of Brunnsvik adult education college put it, "What, you may ask, did my time at Brunnsvik mean for my personal development? Well, what does it mean for a traveler who knows nothing about where the road he is on leads, when he reaches a vantage point from which he can at least survey the neighboring district?"[41]

But the path to this new individual independence often meant that those who joined popular movements had to submit to their demanding terms of membership. Ronny Ambjörnsson offered a graphic description of joining a temperance lodge: "Initiation into the Word had the trappings of a cultic act in which the pledge of sobriety was seen as introducing applicants to a new life and a new community, unlike that to which they had previously belonged. A pseudoreligious atmosphere accentuated the act's ritual significance."[42]

Similar sect-like practices could be found in the popular education movement whose members' claims to have reached greater heights of knowledge served to provoke other parts of the labor movement. Students at Brunnsvik were told off for having become "educational Philistines" who had renounced their solidarity with the working class. The accusation was that they were seeking knowledge in order to raise their standing with the bourgeoisie or merely for higher pleasures of their own.[43]

Popular movements were founded on an elective community between people who created their own rules of admission and expulsion, established new hierarchies of subordination and authority, and formed powerful ties of reciprocity that equipped members to assert themselves more effectively in a competitive society. While they were democratic because they were open and inclusive, they were in the first instance a means of providing people with better opportunities for surviving or advancing in a class society. That some of these popular movements also aimed to create a particular society—without class, say, or without alcohol—does not change their fundamental character as self-help organizations.

They were, as Geijer put it, the "arrayed auxiliaries" of a new society. Social Democrats raised in this milieu would not have experienced any sense of dislocation in moving from a more class-based rhetoric of struggle to a vision of *folkhem* that advocated greater individual autonomy and a stronger feeling of national community. This much was apparent to the conservative Kjellén even before the turn of the twentieth century: "We live in a Janus-faced era. In one direction, all we can see is the notion of personhood with its demands for universal suffrage and complete equality between people. Looking in the other direction is the association principle, the other's polar opposite, which wants to submerge the individual in voluntary associations and let them plead his cause."[44]

THE LAWS OF THE LAND

In adopting Geijer's concept of Swedishness, social democracy of the 1930s did more than cast itself as heir to the free peasants who had fought for democracy and freedom. Social Democrats also embraced the respect for law and order that Geijer had attributed to Sweden as a nation. When Värner Rydén, a social-democratic educational policy maker, portrayed the Swedish national character in his *Medborgarkunskap för fortsättnings och andra ungdomsskolor* (*Citizenship for Secondary and Other Schools*), first published in 1923 and last reissued in 1959, he emphasized a special reverence for the law in terms that rivaled even Geijer's patriotic fervor:

> *Swedes have a deeply felt sense of justice.* We find in Swedish legislation from earliest times a desire to safeguard the right of the weak and the lowly. As long ago as the early medieval period, Birger Jarl made his name blessed by passing laws and granting women the right to inherit. And his son Magnus earned his fine and illustrious sobriquet *Ladulås* ["locked barn"] for his protection of the rights of the common people against unwelcome guests. In that era of

barbarism and rule by force, there were few rulers with such a disposition. The demand for equality before the law matured far earlier among our people than in the rest of Europe. Sweden's courts were widely respected for their justice and fairness and its officials and officers for their incorruptibility and integrity. Anyone who thinks they have found some trace of class bias in our country's laws or court verdicts can rely on the public's sense of right and wrong to quickly set matters right.[45]

When the State Information Service, a government branch that operated during the Second World War, decided to instruct citizens in the fundamentals of Swedishness, it likewise presented this sense of justice as a key feature of Swedish identity: "There is something which, as it were, provides the framework for everything our institutions do, and, indeed, for all our social life—*the law*."[46]

This emphasis on rights, justice, the law, and obedience to the law was not limited to social-democratic proponents of Swedishness but extended to conservative thinkers and politicians. Liberty and the law were inalienable Swedish values, argued a conservative contributor to the magazine *Svensk Tidskrift* in 1942.[47] Even if the rhetoric was inflected by wartime patriotism, Swedish historians have shown that this was not merely a post hoc romantic construction but had a basis in historical practice.

The key terms in this definition of a Swedish sense of justice were *equality before the law*, *fairness*, *incorruptibility*, and *public sense of justice*—in other words, an understanding of justice that gives primacy to social equality (everyone should be treated alike, be that treatment good or bad) and individual independence (those who administer justice should be independent and protected from outside influence). Yet very little was said about the individual's rights and freedoms, including the right to life, liberty, and happiness. Karleby underscored the fact that the social-democratic view of society ran counter to natural right: "Given what we now know about people's social being—that is, a form of social consciousness that corresponds to the new economic order—we can now abandon the atomistic view of society as being the product of an agreement between individuals and thus a coherent system of individual natural rights and 'natural laws.'"[48]

Swedish social democracy was not founded on a conception of natural rights that regards the individual as having certain inalienable rights that may not be violated. Instead, it was based on a positivistic conception of rights that emphasized the need for justice to be administered in a consistent and egalitarian way. The content of laws is determined by the historical situation, what Karleby called the "form of social conscience."[49]

Acceptance of such legalism and respect for existing institutions had been guiding principles of the reformist tradition in Sweden. Swedish social democrats were quick to abandon Marx's view of the state as the executive committee of the capital-owning class. Instead, they invoked their democratic and Swedish right to take part in political life and demanded that the state remain neutral in the conflict between social classes; the state should be above social struggles and treat all parties equally. More than just a tactical maneuver for seizing power, this move reflected a far deeper commitment to the state as subject to the rule of law.

Much in this view of the state and its laws can be traced back to Geijer. He was skeptical of abstract philosophies of rights, even though after his defection he made individual freedom the fundamental principle of his worldview. Yet this freedom derived its legitimacy not from a higher natural right but from "history's own movement." The free person—for example, the Scandinavian peasant—recognized the authority only of laws "that had been jointly agreed upon or confirmed, or such as those inherited from our forebears"—that is to say, democratically made laws or traditional customs but not the arbitrary exercise of power or the rule of the strong.[50]

At the same time, social democracy partly broke with Geijer's liberalism and clear distinction between individual and state. The peasant was fully aware that he was obliged to give God and king their due but also that the rest belonged to him and could be enjoyed freely. The starting point was that there is a conflict between citizen and state and that there exists a higher justice that sets the terms of their relationship, not that individuals were ideologically bound to sacrifice themselves for the collectivity.

Fundamentally, individual freedom—human beings' divine origin—was legitimated by the notion of personhood, not the nation, the state, or some other collective entity. There was an unstated strain of natural-right thinking in Geijer that limited how much power he was willing to grant the state, even if he formulated it not in terms of inalienable rights but as a devout hope that fear of God and moral purity would protect society.

This notion of individual inviolability can also be found in Swedish social democracy. It was not a given, however. A philosophical tendency called *value nihilism* exerted a powerful influence on social-democratic thought, particularly through a social-democratic jurist named Vilhelm Lundstedt. Value nihilism—which was developed by the Uppsala philosopher Axel Hägerström and partly influenced by Nietzsche and Marx—rejected all ideas about notions about eternal and universal values.[51] There existed no inalienable rights or higher morality that might govern the making of laws and the exercise of power.

On the contrary, Lundstedt argued, the meaning and interpretation of laws should be determined by their value to society—not because society was a higher moral principle but because people's striving for a good life was what shaped their behavior in the real world. From this utilitarian perspective, the notion of individual self-determination was pure hocus-pocus, an unscientific relic from the past. As Hägerström put it in one of his sociophilosophical essays, "The natural individual was treated with the same reverence as social institutions had been in the Middle Ages. Anyone surprised by our own era's unbridled enthusiasm for human rights would do well to remember that behind such reverence lay a deeply ingrained medieval deference to the divine and the supernatural."[52]

One consequence was that the state could be assigned a degree of sovereignty that would have been unthinkable in the nineteenth century. The system of rights was made subordinate to politics, and the law was changed from a governing principle that regulated the relationship between individual and state into the tool of an expansive state authority that could effectively exercise power without limits. This was very far from the Christian notion of personhood that had inspired Geijer.

Geijer had also lived in an era when the personal power of the sovereign still had a historic role, when citizens, as a collectivity, and state power, in the form of the king's own person, were two separate entities. In democratic states like Sweden, where the division of powers does not follow any clear principle, this division can easily disappear. If the secondary authorities that mediate between people and king disappear, there is a large risk that the state and the people will become combined and that the state, because it embodies the collective will of the people, will gain virtually unlimited power and legitimacy.

For the most part, this vulnerability to authoritarianism in social democracy's view of the state was outweighed by the very historical traditions that Geijer praised: the striving for independence, respect for traditions, and citizens' capacity to come together voluntarily in order to protect their own and the public's interests. Swedes may not have been protected by natural rights, but they had individual rights by virtue of being both Swedes and part of the national movement toward liberty to which social democracy had committed itself.

And yet this historical narrative was powerless to protect the individual from certain types of harmful infringements. From a comparative international perspective, the most flagrant example was the program of mass sterilization, mostly of women, under varying degrees of coercion.[53] Perhaps it was allowed to happen because the policy targeted people who did not meet the standards of independence and self-reliance that had become ingrained in the national self-image. Typical justifications for sterilization included illness, poor social adaptation, promiscuous behavior, and mental disability.

In the absence of the Christian faith that had defined the parameters of nineteenth-century individualism, there was no natural recourse when the state turned on vulnerable groups. For all her idealism, Key's ideas about voluntary racial hygiene and new supermen had opened a door that should have remained closed forever.

HAPPY PEOPLE HAVE NO HISTORY

Few Swedes in the 1930s saw any fundamental problem in doctors and state authorities taking control of the reproductive abilities of particular citizens.[54] The searchlight of public debate was trained on other questions than the personal integrity of groups considered marginal: mental defectives, alcoholics, antisocials, and gypsies, as they were designated at the time. More recently, it has been pointed out that draconian methods were relics of the harshness of peasant society and unrepresentative of the new society that Social Democrats wished to build. It had been a perennial concern of parishes and municipal authorities that indigent families with many children—and perhaps no breadwinner—would be a burden on local poor-relief provisions.

While this does not diminish our moral outrage, it tells us something important about a national community that was both old and new. Conservative fears of degeneration and uncontrolled sexuality could be allayed by an extension of the modern and rational welfare state. Far from being a lone exception, this duality comprises one of the most integral mechanisms of *folkhemmet*: the transformation of homespun tradition into gleaming modernity.

As early as 1935, only two years after coming to power, Hansson could proclaim Scandinavia as a model for people in other countries.[55] What he had in mind was not a free peasantry but an embryonic welfare state. A year later, Marquis Child published *Sweden: The Middle Way*, the first in a series of books that painted a picture of Sweden as the prototypically modern country.[56] From having been Engelbrekt's free people, Swedes now became "the people of the future" (figure 8.2). The great symbol of Sweden's love affair with the modern is the 1930 Stockholm Exhibition. More than just an opportunity to showcase functionalist design and architecture, the exhibition came to represent a more general movement toward rational planning and engineering. At stake was more than furniture and houses: all of society was to be subordinated to the same ambition.

But, as the influential Swedish journalist Arne Ruth argued in an insightful essay, the connection between Swedishness and modernity has a longer history.[57] As early as 1916, the journalist and author Ludvig Nordström had written about the splendid Swedish race with its unique talent for engineering and hard work, a progressive people with an ability for organization and rational thought.[58] This theme would come into its own after the Second World War, when social democracy, hitherto backward-looking and preoccupied with history, turned its gaze firmly forward and left history behind. The Social Democratic Party's youth wing was a driving force. If Sweden was the people of the future, then its youth was the vanguard.[59]

Increasingly the past became less a source of strength and pride and more a dreary tale of poverty and suffering. The new mood was well captured in a reading-book for primary schools from 1963. The little girl Greta, who has been given an opportunity to travel back to "the good old days," soon begins to long to return to the modern welfare state: "'I have had enough now,' says Greta. 'I want to go back to our own time. . . . Home to our house with central heating and cooked food and telephones and radio and television and everything, all the other things we have.'"[60]

Many of the explicit references to nineteenth-century nationalist themes will therefore disappear as we turn in part 3 to developments between the 1930s and the present. Paradoxically, the triumph of the

FIGURE 8.2. The Social Democrats didn't just represent themselves as defenders of ancient freedoms. They also aspired to be part of a steel-plated modernity that promised a bright future, as in this 1936 election poster's *"Framtidsfolket röstar med Arbetarpartiet"* ("the people of the future vote for the Worker's Party"). Arbetarrörelsens arkiv.

Geijer paradigm would undermine its rhetorical hold on the Swedish self-image. The yeoman peasant, the Viking, and Engelbrekt would gradually fade away as main protagonists in the national story, to be replaced by the social-democratic worker who stepped out of the darkness and into the light. Swedes would come to view themselves as supremely modern people who had conquered the past and who no longer needed to bolster their self-image with the nineteenth century's folk tales and legends. Other peoples had culture and history; Swedes had rationality and the future.

Attacks by myth-busting historians—including the settling of accounts with Geijer mentioned at the start of this chapter—would rid the country's schoolbooks of heroic kings, peasant chiefs, ancient Nordic sagas, and national self-glorification. "The good old days" became an ironic phrase that emphasized how successful Sweden had become. The purpose of teaching history, as defined in the national curriculum for 1963, was to prevent "complacency and an unwarranted sense of one's own and one's compatriots' superiority"—although there was superiority, of course, but it now came in the form of triumphant modernity.[61]

Although Volvo would replace Engelbrekt as the national symbol par excellence, there is nonetheless a striking continuity between Hansson's romanticizing rhetoric of *folkhemmet* and Erlander's *starka samhälle* (Strong Society). Sweden remained the promised land where democracy and justice held sway in a more natural and firmly rooted way than elsewhere. The Swedish self-image might have been stripped of its historical attributes but it was still informed by the same values: the importance of independence and equality, faith in the state as the guarantor of sovereignty, and suspicion of all relationships that were not transparent.

The general view of popular movements also underwent a similar transformation. Of course, they continue to be celebrated by social democracy as a basis for Swedish democracy. But their most important functions—those that gave meaning to the notions of personal responsibility and solidarity that had been hallmarks of popular movements—were steadily transferred to the state and the market. The expansion of state schooling transformed the popular education movement from an alternative public sphere, in which workers broadened their horizons and prepared themselves to govern the country, into a series of leisure and hobby organizations. Sickness and unemployment associations were gradually absorbed into the state-administered welfare system. Cooperation had been unable to resist the market economy dynamic. State regulation of alcohol replaced the efforts of temperance advocates to combat people's urges.

The voluntary community of people who had joined forces in order to lift themselves into better, more decent lives was permanently sidelined by an alliance of atomized individuals and an impersonal state.

PART 3

Sweden Realized

CHAPTER 9

Nationalizing the Child

In the wake of the French Revolution of 1789, state authority in the West gradually ceased to occupy a position above society, the latter typically characterized by an absolute monarchy, a feudal nobility, and a largely powerless peasant population. In growing numbers of European countries, the state came to be seen as an expression of the national community and as a collective, albeit not entirely democratic, instrument for its citizens. Supreme authority in society was no longer the will of God as embodied in a monarch but popular sovereignty. The end of the nineteenth century and the first decades of the twentieth were a golden age for the nation-state as conservatives, liberals, and socialists united behind nationalism as an overarching ideology.

A core idea in this new perception of the state was that it had a particular responsibility for the young. Whereas children and adolescents had previously been regarded as their parent's property, they were now considered both a collective resource *and* individuals in their own right who needed special protection and care. Conservative nationalists—and often a few socialists—wanted strong, healthy, well-educated citizens in order to build powerful armies, increase production, and enhance the prestige of their native land. But the process of generating children lay in the hands of a population that was often oblivious to the nation's best interest. The French state, for example, had long wrestled with the problem that its inhabitants had developed considerable skill in avoiding having children. The middle classes of many other European countries had shown themselves to be similarly crafty in limiting the size of their families.

Liberals viewed the problem more in terms of individual rights. Progressive doctors, philanthropists, and social reformers discovered the wretchedness of the children of the poor. Ignorant parents living in woefully deficient social environments were arbitrarily limiting the future development of these potentially productive assets to society. While having a night-watchman state and laissez-faire might be defensible in relation to self-sufficient adult citizens, surely there was a communal responsibility toward children and the youth? For both liberals and conservatives, the well-being of its children was a patriotic issue that involved the modern state.[1]

By the 1930s, the reproductive crisis had spread to all of Europe and every social class. Leading politicians and scientists argued over the causes of their citizens' inability to produce and raise enough children. A raft of social problems, often associated with burgeoning urbanization and industrialization, had come to the public's notice.

It was not only that the birth rate was low and population growth slowing. Juvenile crime, infant mortality, overcrowding, unsanitary homes, alcoholic parents, diseases of childhood—everything pointed to the need for more decisive action by the state (figure 9.1). There were calls for better schools, maternity clinics, and correctional facilities for juvenile delinquents, and politicians and social workers debated how best to deal with poor children and orphans. Under the influence of race theories, the eugenics movement, and social-Darwinist fears about the degeneration of the national stock, prominent politicians in most countries, ranging from communists on the left to fascists on the right, came to see intervention in the family as not merely a right but a duty.[2]

In Sweden, the new zeitgeist was captured in the combination of two terms that already had positive connotations: *folk*, meaning "a people," and *hem*, meaning "a home."[3] Part of the strength of the concept of *folkhemmet* lay in its contradictory nature. On the one hand, it echoed *folkstaten* ("the people's state"), a concept from the interwar period that measured the state's legitimacy in terms of the degree of democracy, equality, and popular power in a particular society. On the other hand, it evoked notions of home and its association with warm, organic community, which is also the great appeal of nationalism.

We imagine—and often also experience—the nation as a community that resembles a family. We feel kinship to it. We support its football teams with fierce passion. We are even prepared to fight and die in its defense if necessary. But the nation-state is also a formal system bound by laws and an institutionalized form of government. As citizens

FIGURE 9.1. The well-known economist Gunnar Myrdal (here on his way to the United States to write *An American Dilemma*) and his wife, Alva, a progressive educator who also had an international impact, were the model gender-equal family with three children (Kaj, Jan, and Sissela), which was the right number if Sweden was to avoid demographic decline. Note that the fabric in Alva's dress is the same as in Gunnar's suit. Pressens bild/Scanpix.

and legislators, we can vote and pass laws, but as subjects we are required to obey those laws and regulations. Like the market, the state is imbued with a liberal understanding of individual sovereignty: one person, one vote. In this sense, the nation-state creates the conditions for an individual autonomy that, paradoxically, clashes with the notion of the national community as superior to individual interests.

But the modern nation is comprised not only of the state and the individual but also the family, the only societal institution capable of providing a country with new citizens. The family is closely related to the nation and may even be its original model, an ur-nation. But the development of democracy also made the family the nation-state's greatest rival in the struggle for citizens' loyalties. Nineteenth-century political thinkers had treated state and individual as opposing parties and left the family out of the equation entirely. For Geijer and the other liberals of the time, the family was a political leftover, an institution undoubtedly in need of reform but not of any real significance for the development of democracy.

Things were different in the 1930s. In ways both new and old, the nation-state was making demands for sovereignty based on a democratic popular community. It was no coincidence that Plato had wanted to abolish the family when he outlined his ideal society in *The Republic*. For him, it was a question of allegiance: from a national or state perspective, citizens who put spouses, parents, siblings, or children first are not reliable servants of the community as a whole.[4]

For a democratic state, there are also other reasons to be suspicious of the solidarity between children, parents, and siblings. As an institution, the family is traditionally undemocratic in both its power relationships and decision-making structures. Even in relation to the market, the family is a "fifth column." In the workplace and in economic transactions, love and dependence between family members take the form of nepotism and corruption.

In Sweden and throughout Europe, this complex view of the family found expression in a fierce debate over the so-called population question. In recent years, social engineering, the disciplining hand of the state, and outright violations such as forcible sterilization have understandably been the focus of attention. But the intersection between state and family was even more profound than this. In fact, the welfare state is constructed like a *folkhem*—a large family, warts and all. It is a home the state has built for the nation, as if it were a family, with a steady hand and under the banners of community, solidarity, and security. The essential functions of the family are represented at the level of the nation, as is often summarized, simply but expressively, in the mantra of *"vård, skola, omsorg"* that denotes the state's core responsibility of providing health care, schooling, and care for children and the elderly.

From the vantage point of the present, the expansion of the welfare state in the 1930s seems benign enough: improvement of state pensions (1935), the introduction of maternity payments and other forms of assistance (1937), and entitlement to two weeks' annual vacation (1938). But the idea that the state had an overarching responsibility to ensure the well-being of every citizen, coupled with the authority to intervene in traditional forms of community such as the family, had also been permanently naturalized.

Although a number of groups regarded as weak and vulnerable—the elderly, the sick, and those with disabilities—were the object of more or less respectful sociopolitical interventions, the axis around which the welfare state turned was the alliance between the state and children. A willingness to protect, care and provide for, and educate children—defenseless today but citizens tomorrow and the new society's best hope—became the primary mission of the emerging welfare state. That mission would require a considerable effort. "Society," which is to say the state, would need to intervene and meet its responsibilities with money and expertise. As historian and scholar of childhood Bengt Sandin explained, "As the welfare state became established, the state justified taking a strong position with regard to families on the grounds that children needed protection, among other things from instances of parental incompetence. In this way, state authorities and their associated professionals came to be identified as children's primary protectors."[5]

Besides concerns about parents' fitness to rear the citizens of tomorrow, there were other reasons to be critical of the family. For social democrats, the goal was not only to safeguard the nation's well-being and its inhabitants' security. They also wanted to emancipate citizens by creating an enlightened society of free and independent individuals. In this view, parents seemed not just occasionally incompetent but also far too willing to offer conservative resistance to impending modernity. Like other traditional institutions in society, the family was seen as an antiquated formation, ruled by hierarchical and patriarchal power relationships. For social democrats, the state was the agent that would release the individual of the future from the dead hand of the past. As Alva and Gunnar Myrdal wrote in 1934, "The family's 'right' to let children live in squalor, to neglect their diet and upbringing, to bar them from making a rational choice of profession, and to deny them an appropriate education cannot remain as unlimited as it is currently. But the 'liberation' of the children can only be purchased by society if it assumes an ever greater part of the expense and responsibility."[6]

"Liberating" children—and, later, women—from the family with the help of the state would become a central theme of Swedish social democracy. It was part of a larger effort to liberate people from the unequal and unjust relations of dependency that had characterized the old class society with its authoritarian state. Significantly, the prominence given by this project to the individual's right to freedom strongly recalled the central tenets of liberalism. Accordingly, Swedish legislation in the areas of social and family policy would also be shaped by this tension between liberalism's emphasis on the individual and socialism's striving for equality.

In contrast to the preceding sections, part 3 focuses less on literature and historical accounts and more on specific conflicts over sociopolitical theory and practice. The nineteenth-century notion of Swedishness created the fundamental preconditions for the strong welfare state that was constructed during the latter part of the twentieth century. But it was social, economic, and political developments that created the conditions in which the most radical ideas of the nineteenth century could be made a reality—even as the enormous expansion of the state and the market economy threatened to undermine that originally liberal project.

In this chapter we examine the family policies advocated by Alva Myrdal in the 1930s and their relationship to Almqvist and Key. In Chapter 10, we turn to Eva Moberg, Grupp 222, and the radical-individualist breakthrough of the 1960s. Chapter 11 focuses on the resistance that the new legislation encountered in the 1970s in the form of protests against individual taxation and the debate over the extension of state nursery provisions. In Chapter 12, we analyze the debate over "civil society" of the 1990s, which contrasted different visions of community and the "correct" relationship between individual, family, voluntary associations, and the state. In Chapter 13, we turn to the role of religion in the Swedish social contract, from the establishment of the Lutheran state church to its disestablishment and a new era of religious pluralism after the year 2000.

A FAMILY LIKE ANY OTHER

Probably the most iconic Swedish photograph of the twentieth century was taken at Stockholm Central Station on a day in late summer 1938 (figure 9.1). It shows the Myrdal family just prior to their journey to America, where economist Gunnar Myrdal was going to study the American race problem, a project that in 1944 would result in his classic book, *An American Dilemma*. A large crowd had gathered to see them off. The headline in Stockholm's main newspaper the following day read "Long live the Myrdals! Huge farewell party at Central Station!"[7]

Two claims are typically made about this now classic image. The most obvious of these—and one that was self-evident at the time—was the progressive and patriotic reproductiveness which the Myrdal parents were demonstrating in having three healthy and well-nourished children. They lived in accordance with the argument presented in their controversial book *Kris i befolkningsfrågan* (*The Crisis in the Population Question*). Citizens needed to have more children: one or two were not enough to sustain the rate of population growth.

Closer scrutiny is needed to spot the photo's other message—although it would certainly have been grasped indirectly by contemporary newspaper readers. As Elsy Wennström has noted, beneath Alva Myrdal's unbuttoned jacket it is possible to make out a dress made from the same cloth as Gunnar's suit. The choice of material underscores the closeness and equality in their marriage, and signaled that the spouses jointly shared responsibility for their children while both being important public figures in their own right.[8]

But the image is about more than just the internal relationships of the Myrdal family. It also symbolizes a time when marriage as a mode of shared life reached its most democratic extension. The years in which Alva and Gunnar Myrdal were most publicly active also marked the zenith of the family as an institution in Western Europe. Never before or since that period has a larger proportion of the Swedish population been married.

"The second third of the twentieth century constitutes the 'Marriage Age' in modern Western European history," wrote Cambridge sociologist Göran Therborn in his global study of the twentieth-century family. Going back to the nineteenth century and the start of the twentieth, one finds large populations that, for various reasons—often lack of economic resources—did not marry. By the mid-twentieth century, an overwhelming majority of citizens were getting married even as the number of children born outside of wedlock decreased steadily. Moreover, people were marrying younger, often in their early twenties instead of their late twenties as had hitherto been the pattern in Europe. Divorces were still relatively rare and most women had not entered the labor market—this was also the historical zenith of the housewife.[9]

Nor was this just a middle-class ideal. The nuclear family and the clear division of responsibilities between men and women had become firmly established in the Swedish working class. As Sten O. Karlsson, who has studied family culture in Gothenburg in the 1920s and 1930s, argued, "In Gothenburg, the overwhelming majority of the working-class population had chosen the nuclear family as their model. Women had been given economic and moral responsibility for the children's health and upbringing and for managing the home and the housekeeping. Men's resistance to marriage had been overcome and they now accepted their duties as the family's main breadwinner."[10]

This was more a question of joint survival strategy than adjustment to middle-class values. While men focused on selling their labor on the open market, it fell to women to maintain the collective norms that were needed to provide children with a good home environment and upbringing. Men and women lived in different spheres but they shared strongly felt moral ideals, notably those of *skötsamhet* (sobriety, reliability) and reciprocal solidarity.[11]

Solidarity in working-class families differed, of course, from the intellectual companionship that Alva and Gunnar Myrdal enjoyed. In both cases, however, it represented a commitment to marriage as an institutional form of cohabitation between man and woman. As a witty columnist in one Stockholm newspaper declared of the Myrdals' departure, "There on the platform gathered the entire happy family—excuse the cliché, but nothing else will do—the boyish professor in his broad stripe suit, his wife Alva, young Sissela, half-blinking, and well scrubbed behind the ears, Kaj and Jan."[12]

The photograph from Stockholm Central Station in 1938 signals a national—and romantic—vision of familial happiness. In statistical terms, Gunnar and Alva were part of the interwar marriage generation; they were born around the turn of the twentieth century and married in the 1920s. Many men and women in their age group came to identify with this positive and progressive image of the family. Alva was from the lower middle class, Gunnar from a Danish peasant background. They met when he was twenty and she was seventeen, and they married five years later.[13] Despite their ups and downs, they stayed together all their lives. Quoting the Swedish poet Hjalmar Gullberg, Kerstin Vinterhed's biography of the Myrdals described their relationship as "love in the twentieth century."[14]

At the same time, both Alva and Gunnar fought to modernize marriage, to make it equal, and to liberate women from the dependency and subordination of the housewife ideal. Above all, Alva Myrdal recognized the welfare state's emancipatory power and the family ideal's attractive force, both culturally and socially, as defining factors of the day—and which she herself also embraced. Using the population issue and the interests of children as rhetorical tools, she sought to find a solution that both protected children and gave women greater independence and freedom.

AN EFFICIENT INSTRUMENT

Alva Myrdal was thirty-six when the family left for America. A poll by a Stockholm newspaper had just ranked her among the ten most famous Swedish women at the time, putting her in the company of Greta Garbo and Crown Princess Louise.[15] Alva Myrdal had received a first-rate training in psychology and family sociology during her studies in Germany, Britain, and the United States. For several years she had been chairperson of the women's wing of the Social Democratic Party.

In Sweden, however, Alva Myrdal's fame rested on her co-authorship of *Crisis in the Population Question*. In it, she had set out the basis for a detailed and theoretically stringent analysis of the issue, which she would use during the thirties and forties as a platform for urging a comprehensive reshaping of Swedish society. Many of her proposals were never carried out—although this in itself says little since she had opinions on everything from sexuality to classroom design—but the reformist zeal and sociological passion that she brought to public debate was to exert a decisive influence on future developments.

According to Alva Myrdal, conditions in Sweden were uniquely historically suited for the changes she proposed; the image of her as a social engineer who lived in a world of abstract ideas could hardly be further from the truth. In 1941, she presented her ideas in English to an international audience in a book titled *Nation and Family*, which was translated into Swedish as *Folk och familj* in 1944.

Its opening question is, Why Sweden of all places? In other words, what made her think that her own country had a mission to take the lead in social reforms as a means of solving the population question? After dismissing Germany (too undemocratic), the Soviet Union (no population crisis), France (too ineffective), and Britain (too individualistic), she finally declared that only Sweden had exactly the right conditions.[16]

The portrait Alva Myrdal painted of Sweden is by now quite familiar. It was based on the Geijer-Almqvist model of Swedishness in a modified social-democratic form. Swedish democracy, she wrote in the English edition, has its roots in the pre-Christian era: "In the early course of Swedish history the farmers took large political responsibility. At crucial times they drove foreign usurpers out of the country and preserved national liberty. In cooperation with the farmers the king at times overcame the germinating tendencies toward feudalism. Together with Norway and Iceland, Sweden is, in contrast to all the rest of Europe, a country where the farmers have always been free and where feudalism never developed as more than a threat."[17]

It should be noted that in the Swedish version of this text she used the word *bönder* (peasants) instead of *jordbrukare* (the more modern alternative Swedish word that is the equivalent of "farmer" in English) in keeping with the national-romantic tradition in the spirit of Geijer and Per Albin Hansson, underscoring the historical legacy of the peasants' free status. Swedish poverty also makes a fleeting appearance, reminiscent of Almqvist, when she remarks that Sweden's soil, though thin and labor-intensive, can support the population if it is managed carefully and intelligently.

But, for her, the most important factor is Sweden's strong tradition of rule of law, including its independent civil servants and the broad respect for the law. The new social state, she explained, had inherited an "unusually uncorrupt and reasonably efficient instrument for its endeavors to remodel the old society."[18]

For Alva Myrdal, Sweden in the 1930s represented not the end point of Swedish history but a stable platform for realizing an ambitious social policy the like of which had never been seen in any country in the world. She divided the history of social-reform policy into three phases. First, the conservative phase, when those in power contented themselves with solving the most severe problems though charity. Then the liberal phase, when it had been considered sufficient to create a social safety net using a general system of insurance. And finally, the social-democratic phase, when injustices were rooted out by means of protective and cooperative social policies.[19]

In itself, this line of thought contained little or no state socialism. Alva Myrdal thought that capitalism's drawbacks should be addressed not by nationalization of the means of production but by consumer action. Organized by the cooperative movement, well-informed and strong consumers would force a reorganization of production within the free-market economy. On the other hand, Alva Myrdal endorsed the state making far-reaching interventions in the family in the form of both voluntary support and coercive measures. Not factories but children should be socialized.

The interventionist policies had both benevolent and sinister aspects. On the one hand, much about these policies was uncontroversial from today's perspective: extended prenatal care, child-rearing advice, general training in domestic and technical work, housing collectives, kindergartens, sex education, contraception, children's clothing subsidies, paid family holidays, foster homes, free domestic help for families with children, and subsidies for "necessities" (furniture, utensils, beds). On the other hand, the boundary between social and genetic engineering was blurred. This was most apparent in the sterilization policies that were mainly aimed at women deemed unfit as mothers. But the draconian nature of the welfare state was also evident in the policies adopted in the cases of families that did not live up to the ideals of *skötsamhet* (responsibility and wholesome sobriety).

Alva Myrdal was not alone in thinking that social democracy was poised to make a collective leap forward in its reform of Swedish society. Despite its pragmatic reformism, the Social Democratic Party had inherited a highly utopian legacy. But few others dared to proclaim in such visionary and detailed fashion that today was the past of tomorrow and that the work of social reform had barely begun. By the outbreak of the Second World War, many leading social democrats were simply pleased by how far they had come.

According to Alva Myrdal, a new political way of thinking was needed, one that moved beyond the concepts and categories that had hitherto been used for discussing social issues. Nineteenth-century liberalism's unfortunate focus on the relationship between state and individual had effectively obscured the radical changes that the family had been undergoing during industrialization. The family had been surrounded with taboos and moralizing and had been idealized in literature with a puritanical falseness. Its real problems had not been discussed with the respectful candor necessary for it to become competitive in the new society that was emerging.

In the case of Geijer, Alva Myrdal's critique of the nineteenth century's romantic-moralistic view of the family hits home. His solution—or, more precisely, non-solution—to the issue was to make women equal with men and effectively grant them full civic rights while expecting them, because of their roles as mothers and childrearers, to voluntarily abstain from exercising them.

Neither Almqvist nor Key would have been satisfied with this relegation of love and reproduction to the private sphere. They made similar proposals for new marriage laws that would release the individual from the patriarchal straitjacket of the middle-class family. Their underlying idea was that real love—in contrast to subordination and exploitation—was founded on economic and legal independence. Both outlined a proposal for reforms that were relatively utopian for the time—namely, that the state should assume responsibility for providing for children so as to liberate women from dependence on men. And both Almqvist and Key reached the conclusion that, in order to dismantle the old gender order, women should be assigned greater authority over children. Their proposed reforms were more or less matriarchal.

It is hard to say how much Alva Myrdal was directly influenced by her predecessors. What is clear is that in her youth she read Key enthusiastically.[20] Like Almqvist, she had grown up reading Rousseau. Her father, Albert Jansson (later Reimer), was a loyal social democrat, dedicated to the cooperative movement as well as to *folkbildning*, the Scandinavian variety of adult education that combined technical training with studies in national history and culture. Indeed, Jansson preached Rousseau—or "Jean-Jacques," as the family affectionately referred to the French philosopher—to the inhabitants of turn-of-the-twentieth-century Eskilstuna.[21]

In general, Alva Myrdal seems to have been strongly influenced by the nineteenth-century discourse on Swedishness. As a child, she wrote an epic Gothic poem about a Viking who prefers suicide to dying of infirmity in old age. According to her daughter, Sissela, she also remembered having had an unusually strong sense of self at the age of four: "I sat on a tree stump and suddenly understood that I was on my own. . . . From that moment on, I ceased to have an open and trusting relationship with my family."[22] Concepts such as *individual*, *self-reliance*, and *independence* recur repeatedly in her work.

There is an existential, sometimes almost tragic, strain in Alva Myrdal's writing: "The individual is alone in their fate," she explained in an article about the changing family in the magazine *Vi* from the

1960s, and she recommended that individuals be encouraged to develop a greater sense of self-reliance from early childhood in order to counter the effects of creeping alienation.[23] The logic is familiar: make individuals strong, wrote Rousseau, and they will become good.

Like Almqvist and Key, Alva Myrdal clarified the nature of the problem by situating the family analytically within a grid of power relations. All three of them wanted to lay to rest an ideology of the family that made love and familial relations into mystical, sacred bonds that could not be questioned. Like Almqvist (and, for that matter, Strindberg), Myrdal also saw more equality in peasant society than in the middle-class family of the nineteenth century:

> The dissolution of family-based production and the transfer of breadwinning responsibility to the man alone involved an enormous increase of power for the father in the family, which could never be counterbalanced by moralizing formulations about the equal dignity of women's work in the home.... In terms of power, the transitional family of the nineteenth century was far more 'patriarchal' than the openly patriarchal family of antiquity.[24]

Almqvist and Key wanted to show that the interdependence of family members consisted of more than "pure feelings:" the intricate web of mutual relationships was also economic, social, legal, and cultural in nature. Both discussed housekeeping money, property relationships, the economic value and social utility of housework in the same "realistic" way that Alva Myrdal advocated. For Almqvist and Key, this was a means of liberating "love," of cleansing the family of all the forms of dependence that created inauthenticity and dishonesty.

As we will see, Alva Myrdal had a somewhat different agenda. Notions of love and boundary-crossing emotional experiences had no place in her social-scientific vocabulary. But even she viewed the family as a warm place in a cold world, if only people could be made to appreciate its true value: "Little poetry has been produced to depict those values in which a durable marriage relation can excel other sexual relations: the fullness of one's human relations without inhibitions, the unconditional support of loyalty, the exploration of mutual confidences, and the ecstasy of complete sexual intimacy."[25]

Like Sara Videbeck, Alva Myrdal seems like a levelheaded woman in affairs of the heart. The difference is that Almqvist's heroine does not regard "a durable marriage relation" or "unconditional support of loyalty"[26] as ideals but instead imagines a passionate and spontaneous meeting of sovereign individuals. It may well be that Alva Myrdal, for all her social-science matter-of-factness, was actually a greater romantic than either Almqvist or Key.

SARA, ELLEN, AND ALVA

There is a sequential progression in the trio of Almqvist, Key, and Myrdal. All three advocated similar programs of reform with respect to marriage and childcare. But Almqvist's Child Insurance Authority and matrilineal line of inheritance were ultimately intended to salvage the possibility of free love between a man and a woman. He showed no particular interest in the issue of motherhood or the situation of children. Key had a vision of free love as *both* liberating men and women as individuals *and* empowering women as mothers and childrearers. Alva Myrdal completed the movement: the message of love and individual emancipation were suppressed again, this time in favor of the ambition to create favorable conditions for mothers and children.

At this point, Key and Myrdal meet. Both believed in equal rights for women, and both viewed motherhood as being of decisive importance for a good home and strong, healthy children. And both struggled intently to find a way to give traditionally feminine activities—having and rearing children—a higher social status that did not come at the cost of women who, freely or otherwise, had prioritized work outside the home over having a family. How could women's equality and individual freedom be secured without harming the family and children?

Key's solution was to flip the gender hierarchy and make women superior to men with regard to the family and child rearing. She painted an idealized picture of the "New Woman," a kind of Nietzschean superperson who was not forced into motherhood and domestic life but instead chose it freely as a form of self-realization. Love ennobled a woman and provided a political basis on which she could make her demands for a new social order.

For Alva Myrdal, too, it was important that motherhood and childrearing occupied a central place in society without impacting women's opportunities on the job market. In many regards, her proposals regarding prenatal care, childcare, support for families with children, and education are very similar to Key's—except that they are vastly less utopian than Key's mix of radical liberalism and notions of a "third realm." Alva Myrdal was scientific, concrete, and unwavering in her

Nationalizing the Child

conviction that the state offers an unproblematic tool with which to solve these problems.

Like Key, she also had difficulty in situating women's right to paid work within a social-philosophical approach that was primarily directed toward bolstering the position of women and children within the family. Yvonne Hirdman has acutely described her ideal as "the socialist housewife:" a self-assured, well-educated, responsible woman who manages the home and children in the knowledge that it is one of society's most important tasks—not so very different from Key's dream of a "New Woman."[27]

Yet there is a crucial difference between Key and Myrdal. Much has been made of Alva Myrdal's advocacy of "social engineering" and her desire to "arrange life" (*lägga livet tillrätta*) for the citizens. She was a social scientist, a functionalist, and thus supplied a steady stream of statistics: family life, sexuality, and reproduction were transformed into a domain of scientific social planning akin to the labor market or education. At heart, however, both Almqvist and Key were as much "social engineers" as Myrdal. They, too, presented detailed plans for social reforms and state regulation.

What separates Myrdal from Key and Almqvist is not engineering but her overarching perspective, the fundamental reason why family life and child rearing had to be reformed. Almqvist and Key were both utopian and liberal. They wanted to make far-reaching social changes and were prepared to give the state a decisive role in order to realize those visions. Yet the basis for their involvement was a belief in the individual as the alpha and omega of society, a striving to emancipate people from all forms of dependence and subordination—to make them fully adult.

Myrdal's starting point was the Swedish people as a supraindividual community. The reason the state should support families, build houses, and look after children's teeth was the apparent population crisis. It is quite possible, as is sometimes claimed, that Gunnar and Alva Myrdal, deep down, were not as concerned about population growth as they liked to pretend. Historically, population growth has almost invariably been a source of concern for conservative nationalists: to assert itself, militarily and economically, a country must have a healthy, strong, and growing population.

The left—liberals as well as social democrats—have, on the other hand, mostly been concerned about the welfare of citizens as individuals and their opportunity to realize their potential regardless of wealth or social status (even if an individual has been part of a collective, such as the working class) and has justified social reforms based on their intrinsic value for the individual. By marrying leftist welfare ideas to conservative involvement in the population question, Alva and Gunnar Myrdal created a formidable reform program that disarmed their opposition on both the right and the left.

But even if Alva Myrdal did have a secret agenda, the key issue is what she wrote and said. By yoking her social reformist cart to the population question horse, she gave impetus to a tendency within social democracy toward an essentially conservative view of the state. In Alva Myrdal's family policies, middle-class nationalism became social-democratic statism.

Swedish women were to receive support from the Swedish state—but in order that they might have more and better children for the nation. This was not a line of thinking that roused much enthusiasm even among social-democratic women. In an internal survey on population policy conducted by the women's wing of the party in 1941, the criticism was caustic: "As social democrats, we cannot agree with any part of the new way of life here outlined. . . . Society cannot be an end itself, and its members need to lead an existence that is fit for human beings. . . . We maintain that the individual comes first and society second."[28]

A movement as large and heterogeneous as Swedish social democracy cannot be reduced to the Myrdals' social reform program of the 1930s. Nevertheless, the symbolism is hard to miss: *The Crisis in the Population Question* made an enormous international impact even as the labor movement's customary demands for economic democracy and greater power for the working class—in their role as producers—were put on the back burner. In the 1920s, demands for socialism had been buried in a major commission that failed to deliver any significant findings. And the successes of welfare policies removed the urgency of dealing with the question of popular control of the means of production.

Socialism and the nationalization of private property had never been a winning issue for Swedish social democracy. Every time an attempt had been made to initiate a more direct transfer of economic power, the electorate had reacted negatively. In the 1928 election—dubbed the "Cossack" election in reference to the Bolshevik hordes depicted on scaremongering posters—the right successfully punctured any lingering plans for socialization among social democrats.[29]

And the same pattern would repeat itself with the passage of time. After the Second World War, the right again mobilized resistance to economic planning; a quarter of a century later, plans to use employee funds to gain economic control of companies became another millstone around the neck of social democracy.[30] When it comes to questions of ownership, there is a deep continuity in the Swedish electorate that Geijer would have recognized: "I know only what is *mine*."

Things have turned out very differently with regard to the state's role in the matters of family, children, and the relationship between a man and a woman. Here, classic liberalism has been unable to provide any convincing answers. As far back as the midnineteenth century, as shown in Almqvist's writing in chapter 5, it was under siege from an emancipatory critique. Cultural radicals leveled devastating criticism at the middle-class marriage and its suffocating power relations. The rise of feminism brought to the fore the issue of women's place within the paradigm of the independent individual who had emerged from the murky forests of Swedish barbarism.

Key had tried to shift the problems of reproduction and sexual love to the center of social debate. A declining birth rate in the 1930s helped Alva Myrdal to do precisely that.

THE DEPENDENCY QUESTION: "IN CASH OR IN KIND?"

At the same time, the proposals for family policy reforms that were launched in the 1930s were modest in comparison with what was to come. This was partly a result of the fact that Alva and Gunnar Myrdal's penchant for social engineering was not shared by everyone within the Social Democratic Party. Political scientist Bo Rothstein has criticized Hirdman's influential thesis that Swedish family and social policies of this period sought to "arrange life" from above. Rothstein argued that the Myrdals certainly had paternalistic ambitions, as is abundantly evident in their books and articles. But it was the position of Gustav Möller, the minister of social affairs and a powerful member of the Social Democratic Party leadership, that prevailed in the area of family policy. Möller wanted to provide people with the basic resources that they needed to live decent lives without becoming dependent on humiliating poor relief, whether private or public.[31]

This line of thinking leads directly to the logic of universal social rights and investments that has become the hallmark of the modern

Swedish social policy, which stands in sharp contrast to the needs-based and stigmatizing social "welfare" that dominates in, for example, the United States. The central principle of the Swedish social contract is reciprocity rather than charity, and it is based on the notion that all citizens are expected to work and pay taxes so as to be able to legitimately claim what is their due. After the Second World War, Möller fought hard—particularly against his social-democratic colleagues in government—to exclude various forms of means testing (which were introduced at the end of the 1940s) from increases in pensions and child benefits. As Rothstein noted pithily, using a quotation from Karl Höjer in 1952, the new reforms "gave cash payments and left people in peace."[32]

In comparison to Alva Myrdal's respectable background, Gustav Möller virtually hailed from the lumpen proletariat. He had grown up fatherless in Malmö, and his mother had died when he was fourteen. He felt strongly the vulnerability and subordination that came with poverty, especially after spending several alienating years working (as Rousseau had) as a private secretary (albeit not to a nobleman but an industrial magnate from Skåne). In his diary, Möller describes explaining to his bewildered benefactor why a poor single mother from the working class would refuse a place in the workhouse, even though her children would get decent and regular meals: "I told him that the best way to help a poor woman with children was to give them rent money and let them work and look after themselves."[33]

This resistance to dependence on charity and sanctimonious bureaucrats also struck a strong chord in Swedish society. Besides their expectations of a better material future, large swaths of the Swedish working class shared a key conviction: to be labeled poor and to accept gifts and charity, whether from the state or well-intentioned members of the upper class, was a stigma, one that ran counter to the entire Protestant philosophy of self-help that had defined Swedish popular movements since their emergence in the nineteenth century. Not for nothing has Strindberg's famous depiction of charitable upper-class ladies visiting Vita Bergen, a poor district in Stockholm, echoed through the twentieth century: "'Is the woman offering salvation?' asked the carpenter, pausing in his work. 'Where did she get it from? Perhaps she has charity, too, and humiliation, and conceit? Eh?'"[34]

In 1913, Sweden's Parliament was one of the first in the world to approve—almost unanimously—a universal state pension, albeit with extremely low benefit payments. Steady movement away from means testing and conditional social rights is, as many scholars have noted, a constitutive feature of the development of the Swedish welfare regime. Even so, as historian Klas Åmark has observed, this shift toward universalism was less self-evident at the time than it can seem in retrospect to those in a position to see the final result.[35] Needs and income testing would linger on alongside the universal—and therefore nonstigmatizing—system of general rights.

It was far from given that all systems of social support would be made into fundamental social rights common to all citizens. From the start, Gustav Möller's social-policy goals had restrictions: the social rights being guaranteed were those of responsible masculine family breadwinners, not women or children. On the eve of the 1928 election, Möller wrote, "Civilization will be reached only when every decent and hard-working citizen can, without unreasonable difficulty and intervals of literal distress, support himself and his family and give his children a proper civic upbringing."[36] To a large extent, the decency and independence prized so highly by Möller and others belonged to the proud male worker.

Alva Myrdal undoubtedly made a fatal political miscalculation when she advocated payment in kind rather than cash subsidies. But her argumentation on this question—which takes up an entire chapter of *Nation and Family*—did not reflect opposition to general social rights on the part of the public. In fact, she tried to turn the question around precisely by using the 1913 state pension as a model: "Sweden has successfully resisted the temptation of artificial limitation of social problems to the labor market, developing its insurance schemes for all the people and not for wage workers only. It is thus not extraordinary that Sweden should try to construct its family income scheme on some other basis than wage reforms."[37] It should be stressed that this is not in itself an argument for payment in kind—Möller began with the same thought and nonetheless advocated direct payment in cash—but it shows her approach to the problem.

Social policy looked different when viewed from the position of children and women. They were often dependent on that same universal male citizen-worker, who was not always sober, hardworking, or even physically present. To the argument that payment in kind circumscribed "free choice in consumption," Alva Myrdal replied tartly that "children hardly have much of a say in how a family chooses to spend its free income."[38] She was advocating neither "charity" nor moral interventions in general terms but targeted measures by the state that would guarantee children as decent an upbringing as possible, what she called a "socialization of children's neglected needs."[39]

Although Myrdal lost the battle over benefits paid in kind, her view of the relationship between state, individual, and family would ultimately prevail. She promoted the principle that the state had a direct relationship to family members as individuals, not to the family unit collectively. It is doubtful whether much is gained by portraying Alva Myrdal and Möller as the representatives of two different paths taken by Swedish social policy. Rather, the relationship might be postulated in terms of a slightly simplistic formula: *Myrdal + Möller = the modern Swedish welfare state*. Möller contributed a passionate critique of anything that suggested poor relief and dependence, while Alva Myrdal broadened the way citizenship was understood so as to include women and children.

This is not to say that the criticism of Alva Myrdal is unjustified. The idea of individual emancipation led to its opposite: unpleasant notions about people being malleable putty, a population mass that the state both was responsible for and had access to. She thought paternalistically and wanted to manage people's lives. But whatever one thinks of the idea of the state as being in loco parentis—taking the place of the parents and perhaps especially of the father—it is important not to confuse this position of the state with the kind of conservative paternalism that has historically been a feature of other welfare regimes.

As we noted in chapter 3, Germany's welfare state—despite having introduced measures every bit as far-reaching as Sweden's—is based on an understanding of the family, not the individual, as the fundamental unit of society. The state has acknowledged the man as the family's breadwinner and has legally subordinated women and children as his economic responsibility.

Looking farther west to the United States (a major inspiration to Alva Myrdal), we find a welfare model that is obviously more individualistic than the German while also being less universal than the Swedish. Alva Myrdal failed to introduce in Sweden the kind of means testing and investigative social work that makes people effectively wards of the state, but in the United States such stigmatizing policies have impacted profoundly on poor (and often black) single mothers in ways that are truly paternalistic—the state literally wielding the power of a father.[40]

Welfare systems must be understood three-dimensionally as a drama played out between state, individual, and family. Unless we remove one of the components in a spirit of utopianism—as neoliberals or communists are in the habit of doing—the question inevitably raised is: Which two trump the third? The state can ally itself with the individual against the family (Sweden), the family and the state can team up against the individual (Germany), or the family and the individual can join forces to keep a tight rein on the state (USA).

WOMEN'S TWO ROLES

Another reason why reformers in the thirties did not go further is that Möller and the Myrdals ultimately shared a relatively conservative view of the family and the relationship between a man and a woman. The emphasis was on justifying the state's increased power over the family.

On the other hand, both the Myrdals and Möller took for granted the family's continued existence in a form in which women and men would still have different and complementary roles. Alva Myrdal was certainly aware of women posing a "social problem" compared to men.[41] Because of women's dual ambition to be both mother and worker, the state would need to become involved, not just with ready money but also in the form of nurseries. In her 1935 book *Stadsbarn (Urban Children)*, Myrdal paints a vision of the future that resembles child-care provisions today. Day care would be available to children between the ages of two and seven. The aim was not to replace or eliminate the family; rather, the family would be "properly supported and developed through publicly funded day-care centers, so as to give children the opportunities for play, care, and upbringing that not every family is able to provide."[42]

Alva Myrdal was radical for her time, not least in her own life. Her fight for married women's right to work—in 1938, a law was passed prohibiting employers from dismissing women if they married or had children—was hugely important. Her demands that the state and its experts should have a right and an obligation to intervene in citizens' private lives in order to help them organize their lives was groundbreaking and, for many, highly provocative. But by the late 1950s, Myrdal nonetheless seemed far too traditional in the eyes of many feminists.

For more radical feminists, the limits of Myrdal's thinking were made clear by the influential book that she and Viola Klein published in 1956–57, *Kvinnans två roller (Women's Two Roles)*.[43] As the book's title indicates, Myrdal accepted that women, unlike men, had two primary roles, as wife and mother and as worker. Myrdal of course supported women's right to work. But for her it was equally self-evident that women had primary responsibility for the home and children. The solution to this dilemma, which Myrdal had been engaged with since the thirties, was to imagine a woman's life as several phases. First, she would begin a career—or a job, at least—after which she would withdraw to the home in order to look after the children while they were very young (her husband continued to work). In phase three, when the children were old enough, she would resume work outside the home.

This normative vision epitomized Myrdal's pragmatic mode of thinking as a gender-equality policy maker. In the pioneering 1962 anthology *Kvinnors liv och arbete* (*Women's Lives and Work*), Edmund Dahlström identified three factions within the increasingly fraught debate over gender roles: conservative, moderate, and radical. He concluded that Myrdal's was neither the conservative position, which held that a woman's place was in the home as mother and wife, nor the radical position that would come to define public debate in the 1960s and '70s. On the issue of women's position in the family and in the world of work, she was a moderate.[44]

Of course, the reason the once radical Myrdal could now be considered as merely a moderate in her feminist convictions was because, in the early 1960s, new and more radical feminists were beginning to join the public debate. Foremost among them was Eva Moberg. For her, the dual role advocated by Myrdal was a problem rather than a solution.

CHAPTER 10

Asocial, Unnatural, Inhuman

In 1945, the year after Alva Myrdal published *Nation and Family*, there appeared a book whose protagonist came from what Myrdal would have termed a *stympad familj* ("broken family"). A nine-year-old girl who had lost her mother and whose father was a largely absent seasonal worker, the protagonist desperately needed to be taken into the custody of the state. Written by an unknown housewife in Stockholm, the Pippi Longstocking books became one of Swedish literature's greatest successes and are today translated into more than fifty languages.[1]

Like Alva Myrdal, Astrid Lindgren was born in the first decade of the twentieth century and came from a modest background. She grew up on a farm outside Vimmerby in Småland in southern Sweden, a location that was to provide material for her variously idyllic and bleak descriptions of childhood. Lindgren shared Alva Myrdal's and Ellen Key's conviction that children should be brought up to be strong and independent individuals; Ulla Lundqvist's doctoral dissertation on Pippi Longstocking is aptly titled "Århundradets barn" ("The Child of the Century"), a pun on the title of Key's best-seller, *Barnets århundrade (The Century of the Child)*.[2]

As Lindgren recalled, two things made her childhood joyful: security (*trygghet*) and freedom.[3] Although she would consistently side with children, championing their integrity and freedom, she did not in the first instance counterpose this freedom to a family that was necessarily suffocating and patriarchal. Good families such as her own consisted of two adults who loved each other and cared for their children while also respecting their freedom, "who were always there when we needed them but otherwise let us happily flit about unhindered."[4]

Security and freedom are key features of Lindgren's own characters. Occasionally they are combined in the same person, such as Ronja the Robber's Daughter; more typically, her characters embody one or the other. In the Pippi books, happiness and freedom are divided between the two leading female characters: on one hand, the strong, free, and willful Pippi, who lives alone in Villa Villekulla; on the other, the kind and timid Annika, who lives with her affectionate, if excessively orderly, nuclear family in their spick-and-span house next door.

Many of those who have been tickled or appalled by Pippi's cheeky and anarchic manner seem to have missed the fact that, notwithstanding her horse, monkey, and gold coins, she has a tragic side. Without Annika (or Tommy), the Pippi books would be a grim entry in a social worker's casebook. The children next door invite identification: the young reader (or listener) can go in and out of Villa Villekulla, hang out with Pippi and admire her—but then go home to their parents, where they do not have to fall asleep on their own, with or without their feet on the pillow.

This duality—these "two roles," as Alva Myrdal would say—lays bare the contradictions within the nineteenth-century conception of Swedishness. Geijer's order is there: obedience to the law as embodied in the conscientious daughter Annika and the regulated social world of the neighborhood. But also Pippi's rebelliousness and unpredictability: the sovereignty that Strindberg and Key defended. In a letter, Lindgren described Pippi as a "little *Ubermensch* [Superman] in the form of a child."[5] This is, of course, Pippi's secret: she is not just an unruly child, a charming good-for-nothing, but supernaturally strong, wise, and brave. It is a good question whether Pippi would have ruffled so many feathers if she had not had these Nietzschean qualities.[6]

Perhaps Lindgren was unintentionally provocative in other ways, too. Pippi, Tommy, and Annika's carefree existence in Villa Villekulla was a herald of the Swedish *folkhem* after the Second World War. Admittedly, there was no suitcase full of gold that citizens could just help themselves to. But Sweden had escaped the destruction of war: times were good, wages were rising, and there was plenty of work. A series of social reforms in the late 1940s and early 1950s—increased state pensions, universal child benefits, and a national health insurance system—signaled that poverty in Sweden had now been consigned to history. Everyone could enjoy a minimum of security, if not yet prosperity.

Freedom of religion was introduced in 1951 and Herbert Tingsten, Ingemar Hedenius, and other cultural radicals waged a campaign against the church, the monarchy, and other traditional authorities. Although not orphans like Pippi, citizens were increasingly able to live their lives in the present without exaggerated deference to the past. The Swedish self-image came to be defined by modernity rather than inherited tradition: history was taught more critically and came to exclude sagas, myths, and notions of national character, including Geijer's national narrative.[7] Although the fundamental elements did not disappear, they were now couched in terms of modernity rather than Swedishness.

There were limits to this freedom, however. Even if nothing is forbidden in Pippi's garden, the world around it is defined by order and security. Admittedly, there are meddlesome officials, tedious teachers, and annoying police constables sticking their interfering noses into everything. Yet they are not malicious but merely represent—albeit stereotypically—the stability and solicitousness that any decent society requires. Full individual sovereignty is possible only exceptionally, for fleeting moments, in the world of fantasy, in the criminal underworld—and then only in opposition to an essentially benign and conformist society.[8] Asociability, Kant would have said, implies sociability—a social contract.

WOMEN ON PAROLE

Although works of literature are able to reconcile contradictions, in society the balance between different principles and forces is more often temporary. Pippi's demands for individual sovereignty gradually became increasingly vocal even as the Annikas of the world found it harder and harder to defend their subordination and dutifulness.

In the late 1950s, the family model of a husband in gainful employment and a housewife at home began to be called into question. This was partly a result of the increasing demand for labor that was bringing growing numbers of women into the labor market. But it is also unclear whether the model itself had really been as dominant as has sometimes been claimed. Many Swedish women, particularly in the countryside, had always contributed to the family's finances in various ways, by means of part-time jobs or helping with their husband's business.[9] During the era of the housewife in the 1940s and 1950s, around a third of all women whose age made them eligible to work outside the home were doing so.[10]

The principles on which the welfare state was being expanded were also a factor. Gustav Möller may have won the battle for cash benefits payments but he lost the tug-of-war over the design of the new health insurance system in the early 1950s. Instead of benefit payments being uniform, a clause that tied the benefit level to salary was introduced. Presumably unintentionally, this gave women an incentive to enter the labor market.[11]

And besides the economic factors, resentment was growing among many women, particularly those who had gained higher education, at being made to feel like second-class citizens. Between the late 1940s and 1961, the proportion of women among new high-school (*gymnasium*) graduates rose every year, from around 35 percent to 50 percent.[12]

Between the 1930s and the end of the 1950s, the social democratic state had focused on emancipating a particular type of individual—the working man—from dependence on the institutions of shameful charity. Moreover, it had prioritized the care and upbringing of children, who were citizens in embryo with rights but also in need of protection. Yet the concept of the individual had not yet been fully expanded to encompass women.

At this point, a battle took place over granting women the same rights to social, economic, and legal independence that men had won. "A precondition of equality between the sexes is that women have full economic and social independence from men," wrote Eva Moberg, a journalist and editor on the Fredrika Bremer Association's magazine *Herta*, in an article from 1961 titled "Women on Parole."[13] To reach that goal, women would need to enter the labor market, which in turn was conditional on family policy reforms.[14]

"Women on Parole," first published as a pamphlet, then an article in *Herta*, attracted a huge amount of attention and was reviewed and discussed by supporters and opponents alike. The text was republished the following year together with a number of other pieces by Moberg, including her replies to the reactions to the original article. She provocatively titled the book *Kvinnor och människor* (*Women and Human Beings*).

Moberg's point of departure is a respectful but thoroughgoing critique of Alva Myrdal. Myrdal's positive view of women as breadwinners was doubtless challenging for many in Sweden in the late 1950s. However, Moberg argued that her thesis about a woman's two roles rested on traditional notions of "women as having a predetermined main function, namely caring for and rearing children, homemaking, and housekeeping."[15] Underneath all this, according to Moberg, lay a crucial assumption: that women had to subordinate their own interests to the needs of their children.

What made Moberg's text so radical was that she chose to attack precisely this deeply rooted notion. Contra Myrdal, she argued that women would never be emancipated until men abandoned the idea that women had a greater responsibility for the children. This was no easy task. Motherhood is not only a burden imposed on women but also a source of profound gratification for most women and an object of societal respect and admiration. "Motherhood," writes Moberg, "is history's most exploited feeling," and women take a risk in questioning this sacred principle: "To assert women's rights as individuals in relation to the rights of the children is to be seen as asocial, unnatural, unfeminine, inhuman, rabid, et cetera."[16]

It is striking how Moberg equates the concepts of *asocial*, *unfeminine*, and *inhuman* and associates all three with *individualism*. Choosing individual sovereignty implies a fundamental break with the human community and the social contract to which individuals subordinate themselves in the name of society. This break is even more serious for a woman. Her primary task, in contrast to the man's, is to take care of the home, society's primary school for social virtue. She has to save the man from a desire for freedom and independence that comes at the price of children's, women's, and society's well-being—because men, it would seem, are innately attracted to individual autonomy. The fact that they are searching for their own freedom would appear to be something that society simply has to live with—a predictable and natural part of what it means to be a man. But if women also begin to see individualism as a guiding star, then society's future is truly in danger.

Rousseau—together with numerous other famous male philosophers—and many early-twentieth-century feminists had written enthusiastically about women's role as being to raise men. Alva Myrdal and Key argued, albeit on slightly different terms, that women had a special task in society for which their social and maternal qualities uniquely suited them.

Myrdal was less at ease with the notion of fixed gender identities: the female, as she described it, was a problematic gender. Her solution was a pragmatic compromise, one that released women, it is true, but on different terms from men's. Moberg, by contrast, would have nothing to do with such essentialism. As she declared emphatically, "We need to stop banging on about 'women's two roles.'" Instead, she argued, people should accept the idea that "both men and women have one role, that of a human being."[17] It is in this context that the title of Moberg's epoch-making article must be understood. Those who do not recognize this principle—that both men and women both have one, and only one, main role—"must accept that the women's movement will never be more than what it is now: a conditional release."[18]

For some, women's supposed talent for social and maternal tasks and their key role in propping up society held out the promise of self-realization and social martyrdom. Moberg, in contrast, saw the myths of motherhood and femininity as a prison from which she wanted to release women—unconditionally and permanently.

In her article, she sought to present a defense of women's release on the basis first of principles while also showing how it was possible to safeguard children's need for care, instruction, and security. Besides making a negative critique of the principle she wanted to refute—that of women's dual role—Moberg also based her argument on a positive principle derived from her liberal beliefs. "What possible ideological basis is there for demanding women's full release?" she asked, before giving the answer: "The liberal demand that the individual should be given the greatest possible opportunity for development."[19]

It is no coincidence that a liberal should have emerged in this way as the central figure in the 1960s struggle for gender equality (*jämställdhet*, a term that Moberg coined). Within social democracy and the labor movement, in contrast, feminism had long been regarded as a distraction.[20] This was a legacy partly of Geijer's worldview, which took for granted that women would voluntarily give up their political rights, and partly of the Marxist perspective, which prioritized class struggle over women's rights. Feminists were often dismissed as right-wingers for their liberal emphasis on a woman's right to freedom as an individual. Moreover, working-class men (and women) were relatively conservative in their attitude toward gender roles. Insofar as women's liberation can be said to have existed at this time, it was largely confined to the middle classes. It was no accident that Myrdal was more radical in her personal life—an independent and career-oriented middle-class professional with a university training—than as a social-democratic ideologue.

But Moberg did not have just a classically liberal view of the world. Rather, she was typical of a certain type of radical social liberal who, while emphasizing "the liberal demand for individual freedom," was also prepared to give the state an authority over the individual that went far beyond the terms of classical liberalism.[21] In this respect, she was following Almqvist's analysis in *Sara Videbeck*. Like Almqvist, she believed that "true equality of the sexes requires that women become as economically and socially independent of men as men are of women."[22] In order to realize this vision, the liberal principles of putting freedom first and maximally limiting state power would need to cede priority to the central social-democratic idea that the state had a legitimate duty to promote equality. Or, to put it another way, equal freedom of choice for women and men could be achieved only if both women and men had the necessary resources, which, in crass terms, meant income in the form of ready cash. Economic independence would give women the power to make decisions about their own lives—if necessary, against a husband's wishes.

It is clear from Moberg's emphasis on the necessity of "eradicating" marriage as a division of economic roles that she was well aware that she was radically challenging the traditional view of the family. She also made explicit reference to the classic idea of marriage as a form of prostitution, which had been a commonplace for socialists and radical freethinkers since the 1884 appearance of Friedrich Engels's *The Origin of the Family, Private Property and the State*. "It is very strange that we condemn free prostitution," she writes, "while approving of marital prostitution."[23]

Eva Moberg inherited her ability to write expressively and forcefully from her father, Vilhelm Moberg, celebrated author of *Utvandrarna* (*The Emigrants*), a series of epic novels about Swedish emigration to America. But there was also a far deeper congruence in their writings. In both his fiction and his political journalism, Vilhelm Moberg often invoked the freedom of Swedish peasant life and the struggle of its industrious, taciturn, but also fearless yeoman peasants against the powers that be. Johan Norberg was perhaps being slightly anachronistic when, writing in the mid-1990s, he described Vilhelm Moberg as neoliberal, but he was pointing out an important aspect of his writing: a classically Swedish kind of individualism that emphasized the value of independence and self-reliance above all else.[24] Now the novelist's daughter was arguing that women, too, should seize the freedom that Swedish yeoman peasants had fought for down the centuries.

Eva Moberg's declaration of independence for women led to a minor culture war between radical critics and conservative defenders of the family as the "fundamental unit" of society. The debate was heated and wide-ranging.[25] Stina Engström, chairperson of the Association of Housewives, accused Moberg of "rampant individualism"—something she did not intend as a compliment.[26]

Not all of the arguments were between different ideological camps, however. The issue was taken up by the Social Democratic Party, which appointed a series of commissions in the 1960s and 1970s, and the result was a swath of new and proposed laws that revolutionized Swedish family legislation and family policy. These were often drawn up in accordance with the fundamental principles and concrete proposals that Moberg had outlined in her article. Nonetheless, as we will shortly see, reality would not entirely live up to Moberg's vision of the future.

What was Moberg's vision? One of her arguments in *Women and Humans* was that men should do their half of the housework and childcare. Once women had been fully integrated into the world of paid work, the working day would be shortened to six hours in order to allow more time for families. Moberg also pressed for a substantial increase in the number of state-owned nurseries and preschools and the introduction of either a so-called state childcare allocation, to cover either a benefit payment for those who wanted to look after their children at home or a place at a nursery or preschool. As this list of principles and proposed reforms indicates, Moberg was trying to find a solution that would balance children's needs with men's responsibility without compromising the demand for women's unconditional release.

GROUP 222: THE TRUE REBELS OF THE SIXTIES?

What Moberg's pamphlet both heralded and partly made possible was a strange but politically powerful synthesis in which liberal demands for individual freedom, independence, and sovereignty were combined with social democrats' resolute and unsentimental view of the state as an emancipatory instrument in the struggle for greater equality. This instrument had primarily been used for liberating classes—that is to say, the working class—rather than individuals. But this sober view of the state as a handy tool proved appealing to the relatively small and ineffectual group of social-democratic liberals and feminists who embodied a simultaneously new and old kind of radical individualism—an individualism that, against all odds, would one day largely become a reality. Before long, this alliance between radical liberals and gender-equality socialists led to the formation of a loose but potent network called Group 222 (Grupp 222).

Group 222 had its roots in two pioneering texts on what came to be known as the issue of gender roles. One was Moberg's "Women on Parole"; the other was an anthology titled *Kvinnors liv och arbete* (*Women's Lives and Work*), which appeared a year later, in November 1962. As Annika Baude, a founder of Group 222, explained thirty years later, the anthology's appearance was a major media event: "As I recall, the book was reviewed at length the following day in every single daily paper in the country."[27]

Women's Lives and Work further intensified the debate. In sharp contrast to Moberg's short essay, it provided comprehensive factual evidence. Above all, the book's matter-of-fact content and scientific tone lent it authority and made its arguments difficult to dismiss as mere political rhetoric. But *Women's Lives and Work* also operated at the level of principle in a way that made a direct connection to Moberg's text. In particular, it established the concept of gender roles. Edmund Dahlström's analysis of the gender roles debate was cited with particular frequency. As mentioned in chapter 9, Dahlström divided the debate into three ideological camps: conservative, moderate, and radical, with an emphasis on the latter two. As an example of the conservative position, he pointed to the Conservative Party (Högerpartiet). As representative of the moderate position, he named the 1947 parliamentary enquiry *Familjeliv och hemarbete* (*Family Life and Domestic Work*), which had been chaired and principally authored by Brita Åkerman, and *Women's Two Roles* by Alva Myrdal and Viola Klein. And as an embodiment of the radical tendency, which he defined as "founded on liberal political ideology," he held up Eva Moberg as well as Margareta Bonnevie, whose 1955 book *Fra mannssamfunn till menneskesamfunn* (*From a Man's Society to a Human Society*) had also influenced Moberg.[28]

The first edition of *Women's Lives and Work* sold out in five months. The Swedish Trade Union Confederation (Landsorganisationen)—known by its acronym LO—and other organizations and companies showed great interest in its factual data, and immediately after the book's publication, work began on producing an abbreviated version suitable for study circles, a traditional activity for Sweden's *folkrörelser* (popular movements). It was from this milieu of lectures and study circles that Group 222 and other similar groups would emerge.

In February 1963, Baude issued a general invitation to a meeting that would, she wrote, "deepen our knowledge and draw conclusions from *Women's Life and Work*."[29] More organized activity got under way when the first meeting was held a year later, in February 1964, at Baude's house in Stockholm; the group derived its name from her address, Alviksgatan 222. A number of those present would play key roles in the gender roles debate as well as in the group's work on family policy reform.

The group was also politically diverse and included not only Eva Moberg but other liberals such as Gabriel Romanus and Olle Wästberg. Moreover, its Social Democrats represented a broad and possibly crucial range of positions. Predictably, many of them, such as Maj-Britt Sandlund and Siv Thorsell, were deeply involved in women's issues and the question of gender roles. More surprisingly, the group also included members from LO, which, from a feminist perspective, represented the traditionally more conservative wing of the Social Democratic Party. One of them, Gustav Persson, who early on gave a talk to Group 222 about how the preschool issue was "a labor market problem," went on to play an important role in getting LO to agree to policies that promoted gender equality. Even the Communist Party, forerunner of today's Left Party, was represented. There were also a number of people with far looser affiliations to the existing political parties.

The group had no concrete plan for political action. Romanus later described it as a network rather than a group with a definite political identity.[30] Even so, party politics were very much present in the group. There was rivalry between social democrats and liberals. Yet the Liberal Party and the Social Democratic Party represented different perspectives. Liberals put the individual at center stage while social democrats emphasized the principle of equality. Both impulses are clearly discernible in the reforms that were subsequently implemented. Reading the memoirs of Group 222 members, it is clear that the group's activities facilitated the more practical work of reform carried out by Parliament and the various commissions of inquiry. "Our experience in Group 222 was fundamental," wrote Romanus, in helping to ensure that "subsequent interactions were characterized by trust and friendliness, which greatly facilitated finding solutions to the problems that arose."[31] Although the importance of Group 222 ought perhaps not to be overstated—the group has acquired a legendary aura—it seems nonetheless to have played a vital role in forging alliances that facilitated their later work on potentially explosive issues. Group 222 continued until November 1967, when its last meeting took place.

The disbanding of the group has been variously interpreted. Some have argued that it was a victim of its own success in that, as Thorsell put it, the group had "achieved most" of what it set out to do.[32] Others contended that the group grew weary of political pluralism. Barbro Backberger, who was a founding member of the feminist organization Group 8, argued that Group 222 gave up the ghost because its members were "not willing to analyze society's structures and economic relationships."[33] The presence of liberals and representatives of the business world may have irritated Backberger, for whom radical gender ideology implied "a society in which the state has considerably greater economic resources and wider powers."

Most likely is that Backberger and Thorsell are both correct in their explanations for why this radical liberal group disbanded. On the one hand, Group 222 was unable to resist pressure from the more revolutionary and Marxist winds sweeping across Sweden in the late 1960s. On the other hand, it had "won its own defeat," as will become clear in the following account of family policy reforms in the late 1960s and the early 1970s.

THE DISCREET CHARM OF SWEDISH TAX POLICY

The first major question that Group 222 debated, and that it wanted to put high on the political agenda, concerned family taxation. The battle was between those who wanted to retain the existing policy of joint taxation for spouses and those who wanted to introduce separate taxation or—as they preferred to call it—individual taxation.

The reform radically changed the situation for married women who were choosing between paid work and a traditional housewife role. Joint taxation had created a so-called threshold effect by which a woman's salary was taxed heavily when she reentered the labor market after having been at home with children. The family had already benefited from her deductible, which her husband had included in his own tax declaration, and her salary was also subject to a higher marginal tax rate as a result of being assessed together with her husband's salary, in effect as an addition to his salary.

From the family's point of view—rather than the woman's—this could be considered a net loss. Not only did the family lose the woman's unpaid labor in the home, her net earnings were fairly meager. As Romanus explained laconically, "A man who was not particularly keen on his wife getting a job outside the home could easily show that her work would not bring much money into the family."[34] This was compounded by the need to spend money on childcare if the woman worked while the children were still young, since subsidized childcare would not be available until the 1970s.

Individual taxation would do away with this barrier and open the door for women to move into the labor market.[35] The 1960s were boom times for Sweden's economy, and one of the pressing questions was how to get more people into the workforce. Women were seen as an "unexploited labor resource" that government, trade unions, and businesses were all anxious to utilize. Yet this crass perspective cannot be divorced from or given primacy over the more ideological question of equality, both gender and class, and the principle of individual autonomy. Tellingly, Gustav Persson, who early on engaged with the preschool issue from the perspectives of gender equality and the labor market, was a member of Group 222 as well as LO—and he was far from being the only link between LO and gender equality issues.[36]

Another important forum was Conference 65 (Rådslag 65), an advisory group that was jointly organized in January 1965 by LO and the Social Democratic Party as a way to involve more people in the formulation of concrete policy. The deliberations of Conference 65 led to the publication of *Familjen i morgondagens samhälle* (*The Family in Tomorrow's Society*), intended to serve as the basis for further studies and discussions. It also published *Resultat och reformer* (*Results and Reforms*), to be read in tandem with *The Family in Tomorrow's Society*. It offered a vision of the new family as characterized by emotional warmth, gender equality, and democracy between men, women, and children—in contrast to the masculine dictatorship that was sometimes said to be the hallmark of the old family.

The new perspective centered on the individual was also clearly articulated. Emphasis was put on "the right to develop one's personality without any hindrances based on one's sex."[37] In concrete terms, Conference 65 wanted to stimulate discussion of questions such as joint versus individual taxation as well as the feasibility of introducing a system of public support for families—all questions that by this time had already been the subject of intense public debate.

As regards principles, the issue was whether the fundamental taxpaying entity should be the independent individual or the whole family.

In an early article published in 1959, Sonja Lyttkens, a member of Group 222 who took an active part in the debates that preceded the reform, stressed that the underlying rationale for joint taxation was precisely that "the family should be considered as a single entity."[38] This fierce debate would to a large extent hinge on technical questions about the economic effects of various taxation models on individuals and families of different social classes. But, as Lyttkens wrote in *Dagens Nyheter* in February 1962, what gave the debate over joint taxation such intensity was "a growing realization that this in fact represents a demand for women's economic independence."[39]

In *Hög tid för ny familjepolitik* (*About Time for a New Family Policy*), published in 1962 by the youth wing of the Conservative Party, Ingegerd Troedsson responded furiously to Eva Moberg's "Women on Parole." Troedsson was particularly upset to find such arguments being advanced by a liberal. She and her party colleagues wanted to safeguard the family's freedom of choice and the true liberalism that rests on the principle that state interference and regulation are to be avoided as far as humanly possible.

Right-wing commentators sought to counter the radicals' talk of class and gender equality with the concept of "equal worth." They stressed children's need for their parents, by which they meant their mothers. The aim, they said, should be to "try to help mothers cope with the transition to housework after they have children—economically, psychologically, and environmentally—instead of making the first priority, as is currently the case, to get them out of the home."[40]

Troedsson argued that radical liberals were advocating "a socialistic system in which society assumes primary responsibility for children." The combination of individual taxation and large-scale construction of preschools would eventually result in "children belonging to society rather than to their parents, with everything that would entail."[41]

In an article published in *Svenska Dagbladet* the following year, Troedsson turned her ire on Lyttkens, whose proposal for individual taxation would mean "the complete reversal of all the progress that has been made toward fair taxation for families with children." Lyttkens and other advocates of individual taxation were accused of seeking to "break apart the economic community that the family represents."[42] The primacy of the family would also be invoked by defenders of joint taxation as the fundamental principle of their argument, in much the same way as the individualization of tax liability had been the fundamental principle for advocates of separate taxation.

Unsurprisingly, the first party-political organization to officially support the demand for separate taxation was the Swedish Liberal Students' Association, which adopted the demand in 1963 in a revised version of its pamphlet *Solidarisk familjepolitik* (*Solidarity in Family Policy*), first published in 1962.[43] It was symptomatic of the rivalry between liberals and social democrats mentioned earlier that the first newspaper to argue for individual taxation was *Aftonbladet*, the social-democratic daily whose editor Kurt Samuelsson felt very strongly about the issue. *Aftonbladet*'s first article on the subject appeared on January 31, 1961. Even so, the issue was problematic for the Social Democratic Party.

It was not only men who usually took a conservative line on gender issues who hesitated. As Lyttkens noted, the issue was also "extraordinarily sensitive" for the women's wing of the Social Democratic Party.[44] Many of its members were older housewives who had little to gain and often much to lose from the reform. Many of them, according to Lyttkens, did not share the younger, intellectual women's "radical ideology of gender roles." The labor shortage issue was an important factor in persuading leading social democrats such as Gunnar Sträng of the advantages of separate taxation. In drafting the individual-taxation reform proposal, Sträng also managed to mitigate a number of immediate effects that threatened to impact lower-income families in which the wife stayed at home—families that the party regarded as loyal supporters.[45]

According to the economist and political scientist Nils Elvander, individual taxation was so politically sensitive that the party leadership avoided raising the issue even within their own ranks.[46] The principle of individual taxation was adopted in the report that the social democrats and LO's equality group completed in 1968 and published the following year. But it was not until 1970, the year after the commission of inquiry into family taxation had submitted its final report *Individual Taxation* and the government had drafted its annual tax proposal, that the social democratic leadership decided to go on the ideological offensive in support of the tax reform.[47]

In their summary of the objections to the existing regulations, members of the commission of inquiry noted that joint taxation was considered "disadvantageous with regard to population policy and family social policy." They cited the view that neither gender nor civil status should play a role in calculating tax liability. "Complete equality, both legal and civil, between the sexes as well as spouses' joint responsibility for their children" should be "enshrined in the legislation." Commission members also referenced the critique of what they called a "collectivist" view of tax-paying capacity and tax liability. This view was described as antiquated and arbitrary: "In a society that guarantees individuals security in old age, sickness, disability, and unemployment, their economic dependence on relatives decreases. The only tenable principle is therefore to tax private individuals without considering either their status as breadwinners or the composition of the household of which they are a part."[48]

The inquiry even included the labor market perspective as seen by women and Sträng himself. "Given the current availability of adult education courses and employment training, it should as a rule be possible for a housewife without children at home to earn an income if she so wishes," ran the text, which continued, "In recent years, the labor market aspect of this issue has also come to the fore. Investigations into the longer-term development of the labor market have revealed the scarcity of available labor and the consequent importance of those married women who are currently working at home. With this in mind, it has been noted in a number of contexts that married women's inclination to take on paid work ought not to be obstructed."[49]

The principle of the individual's independence from the family was now beginning to be established in both theory and practice. The new law mandating individual taxation was a giant first step, and a succession of other reforms in the 1970s would anchor the precepts of individualization and gender equality even more deeply in state institutions and the law.

A LACK OF QUALIFIED STAFF IN THE HOME

At the ideological level, the ideas that had been formulated in organizations such as Group 222 and Conference 65 were taken up and developed further by the women's wing of the Social Democratic Party, the Social Democratic Women's Association.

The party had initially been skeptical of the new ideas, which had their origins in radical liberal feminism.[50] Since many housewives came from the working class, this was neither a trivial nor an easy question for the Social Democratic party or its women's association. For example, Nancy Eriksson, vice-chairperson of the women's association, wrote in 1964 a book titled *Bara en hemmafru* (*Just a Housewife*), in which she called for housewives to be treated more respectfully.

Housewives, she argued, filled an important function in society: "If we abolish the housewife, we will find that much of what constitutes our living standard disappears with her."[51]

Eriksson naturally refrained from attacking the effects of the new family individualism on children as aggressively as conservative critics had, but she nonetheless spelled out her concerns for children. The result would be "latchkey kids" in search of "human contact" having to "wait until their parents come home." Above all, she gave a voice to the experience of profound condescension felt by many housewives when listening to radical, often university-educated women talk about gender equality and the necessity of doing paid work in order to live a full and meaningful life. They might be "only housewives," Eriksson warned, but "most people only miss the cows when the barn is empty."[52]

However, in publishing *The Family of the Future: A Socialist Family Policy* in 1972, the women's association of Sweden's Social Democratic Party signaled its unambiguous support for the new individualistic ideology. In this pamphlet, a program for the future written just prior to the party's annual congress in 1972, the association announced its aim of "building a society without social and economic inequalities" in which "every person has the opportunity to develop themselves individually."[53] It also cited the party program, in which individual autonomy took center stage (where it relied, ironically enough, on Marxism's utopian promise of individual freedom once the state has withered away):

> Social democracy seeks to let democratic ideals define the entire structure of society and people's mutual relations so as to thereby give every individual the possibility of leading a rich and meaningful life. To this end social democracy seeks to reorganize society by placing the decision-making processes for production and its distribution entirely in the hands of the people, by liberating citizens from dependence on any kind of power grouping outside of their control, and by replacing a social order based on class with a community of people working together on the basis of freedom and equality.[54]

The women's group's pamphlet then went on to list four fundamental demands and goals, all of which were defined by the idea that the foundation of a good society is collaboration in a spirit of solidarity between independent citizens. The first demand was that "all adults should be given the opportunity to develop independently in accordance with their interests and desires, in solidarity with other people." This was the general principle that combined the two complementary ideals: solidarity and independence. The second point addressed the relationship between adult family members more directly: "All adults should be economically independent of their relatives."⁵⁵ This demand looked back to the recently implemented tax reform but also ahead to changes that would be made to the regulations governing loans and grants for students.

The third demand engaged with a line of reasoning developed by the family-law experts who had contributed that same year to an official report on Sweden's marriage statutes. In a clear reference to the privileged status of marriage, it called for "society to adopt a neutral stance with regard to people's domestic arrangements." The final demand focused on children and their need for an alliance with the state: "Children's social, intellectual, and cultural development shall be independent of their parent's economic circumstances."⁵⁶

In affirming the individual's autonomy in this way, the social democratic women explicitly distanced themselves from the "liberal freedom" that gave no consideration to the collectivity. Solidarity had to be secured by a strong and impartial state. With regard to family policy, they noted that "all parties are competing with each other to propose the most far-reaching measures." The women's association emphasized the issue of class and the need for a fundamental change in economic life. Liberal freedom of choice was not enough. On the basis of their first two demands, they invoked an idea that Eva Moberg had articulated a decade earlier—that true independence and freedom of choice become possible only when every individual is economically independent: "A fundamental condition for realizing these goals is that everyone has gainful employment. Earning a living is a precondition for individuals to develop an active and independent personality. Additionally, doing paid work oneself is a condition for being economically independent of other people. This requirement is extraordinarily important, particularly for women."⁵⁷

After discussing the issue, the Social Democratic Party women formally dissociated themselves from the traditional housewife role that more conservative male workers expected of women. With Alva Myrdal in mind, they also rejected the dual role model that reckoned on women spending an interim period of ten to fifteen years without paid work. Instead, they endorsed the six-hour-day as a long-term goal and demanded flexible working hours and the right to paid leave—for men as well as women—around the birth of new children and for taking care of sick children.

This was a radical vision of the future of the family and of marriage. The women's wing of the Social Democratic Party took its point of departure from the family as an economic entity whose members were materially reliant on each other. Their aim was to "reject this view and instead proceed on the assumption that adult family members should live economically independent lives," something that would require "far-reaching changes within different sectors of society acting in tandem." They stressed that this was, needless to say, not about rejecting the family itself. "Marriage," the pamphlet stated, "should naturally continue as a form of shared living even as society seeks to establish its legal parity with other forms of domestic cohabitation in their essential social and economic aspects."[58] It necessarily followed that the existing laws, which accorded marriage a privileged status, would have to be changed: "Current legislation relating to the family should be incorporated into a new body of legislation on domestic cohabitation based on an understanding that the family is a voluntary form of cohabitation by economically independent individuals. The word 'family' therefore describes all forms of cohabitation between two or more individuals."[59]

However, this radical stance was not defined solely in terms of the individual's right to independence. It also invoked community as an ideal. "We believe it is important that the community that exists, and will continue to exist, between people in our society, and that is of fundamental importance for people's harmony, will best be developed if it is based on economic independence."[60] Even the love between a man and a woman was integrated into this way of thinking about community. Once again, we here catch a glimpse of Almqvist and what we have called the Swedish theory of love—namely, that true love can blossom only between people who are economically independent of each other and in relationships where neither party has power over the other.

New laws were needed to deal with questions like the division of property and child custody in cases when the partners were not married, had other domestic arrangements such as extended families and sibling households, were homosexuals, and so forth. The women's association held that "in principle the same conditions should apply to those who are married and those who share a household without being married." Separate taxation was identified as a model for future legislation intended to emancipate the individual. Other aims included "removal of the requirement to make maintenance payments once women's economic independence has increased and the social security system has improved." Children's obligation to support their parents would be abolished as society gradually assumed responsibility for the cost of raising and educating children."[61]

This critique of marriage and the primacy of the family led to the question of raising and looking after children. In legal terms, the women's association was arguing that the legal status of children "should be the same for children regardless of their parents' marital status." Economic independence was described as a fundamental precondition of "equal opportunity for both sexes," not only in the workplace and in education but also "in relation to children." The pamphlet articulated a view that was frequently reiterated by radical critics of the family in the 1960s: the nuclear family was not merely unequal, it was a barrier to children's social and intellectual development. "To prevent their development from being impaired," it was argued, "the nuclear family needs to be supplemented by a collectivity comprised of other children and adults."[62]

The authors did not mince their words, arguing that "today we live in a society hostile to children" in which children are "handicapped" by "a deficiency of stimulus." Dealing with this wretched state of affairs would clearly require vigorous intervention. The association divided children's needs into four categories—material, emotional, social, and intellectual. "Today's family is not enough," it declared, "which is why society must take on a completely different responsibility for the child's development." The authors explained, "As regards emotional support, family and society are both very important and have a shared responsibility. . . . As regards social, intellectual, and material support, society ought to have primary responsibility for ensuring that all children have the opportunity to develop their potential."[63]

What did this mean concretely? Most immediately, obligatory preschooling. Making preschool obligatory was presented as a requirement for achieving equality. All children had to be treated equally. Preschool existed not merely to allow women to achieve self-fulfillment at work but to teach children to manage social situations. "Most researchers now agree that children need contacts from an early age," the text asserted. An accompanying illustration showed how a group of children learned to play and work together, while another depicted the following exchange. The first child says, "I never get to have fun mucking about like this at home. Do you?" "No chance," replies the second child, "I don't have trained staff there, you know." The text directs us to conclude that "today's small family is far too limited and cannot satisfy a child's need for activity."[64]

But the preschooling requirement was just one of many proposals, all with the same purpose. Since three years was seen as the most suitable age at which to "start more systematic collective, social, and intellectual training," preschooling could not address the needs of younger children. For this reason, a program of parental training needed to be rolled out and measures taken to meet the need for childcare from the age of six months. The list of institutions caring for children grew longer and came to include after-school clubs, youth health-care centers, and social service centers. Although special attention was clearly directed toward children, there was a movement to apply similar principles to other vulnerable, weak, and generally needy groups: the unemployed, sick, or elderly and those having and looking after children.

The women's association's list of demands and ideological manifesto was undeniably extreme, both in its criticism of the family and in its demand that society and the state should assume primary responsibility. As such, it became an easy target for critics who saw themselves as defending the family. Nonetheless, the association was representative of a broader social current in its emphasis on the state as having a duty to promote the emancipation of the individual from the family in a spirit of equality and solidarity. This will become clear as we turn our focus to two other commissions of inquiry and the new legislation they helped bring about.

STUDENT GRANTS

The view of adults as economically independent was given currency in the early 1960s by a series of commissions of inquiry appointed to prepare revisions to the framework for calculating student grants and student loans, and it made its way into new laws and regulations. The pioneering work was done by Olof Palme, subsequently Social Democratic prime minister. At that time a young but rising parliamentarian, he headed a commission that had been set up to reform the somewhat arcane system of loans for college students. The commission had not set out to abolish the practice of means-testing loans against the economic resources of the recipient's family. As the commission's work progressed, however, Palme opted for a model that treated all students as autonomous individuals who were eligible to receive the same loans and grants, regardless of their parents' or spouse's economic status. As the report of one of these commissions explained in 1971, "In approving subsidies and grant for students, no consideration is to be given to the parents' financial means.... Students on post-secondary-level courses, even if, as may be the case, they have not yet come of age, are to be treated without exception as independent of their parents' economic status."[65]

At this stage, however, the principle had not yet been definitively established. Students were not infrequently part of two families, one in which they were the child, one in which they were a spouse. The proposed measure addressed only the student's original family. As commission member Staffan Nilsson noted, with regard to the "second" family, "the commission suggests that the policy of means-testing spouses when allocating student grants should remain." Nilsson did not share this view, however, and argued that "assessment of spousal income when allocating student grants should be phased out."[66] How did he make his case?

Nilsson pointed out that the then-current policy of means-testing was based on the idea that "the family's combined means" should be assessed. But, Nilsson objected, "our view of the economic relationship between spouses has changed." Currently, he argued, there was "a clear understanding that even married people should be treated whenever possible as economically independent individuals." In support of this principled position, he cited as evidence *Kungl Majt:s direktiv till familjelagssakkunniga (His Majesty's Instructions to Family Law Experts)*, the commission of inquiry that had been appointed to investigate legislation on the family. To further buttress his claims, he referred to the recent reform of the tax system that had been established on the "principle that spouses were economically independent of each other."[67]

Skipping forward a few years to a commission report on student grants from 1977, we find a supplementary directive from October 1976 in which the government directed its experts to draft proposals intended to "dismantle the connection between spouses' personal finances in a way that mirrors the changes currently being made to tax legislation."[68] In other words, the logic invoked by Staffan Nilsson in his special remarks from 1971 had now become sufficiently established to serve as the basis of a supplementary directive. In an appendix to its findings, the report even briefly summarized the ongoing changes to student financing policy in two other countries.

The 1977 report concluded that there was now a trend in the student grant policies of other countries toward "assessing the student's own income rather than that of parents." The purpose of removing needs testing, it argued, had been "to make students economically independent." This pattern, the authors noted, "is particularly noticeable in the Scandinavian countries."[69]

In most other countries, parents were expected to support their children, even if the latter were adults, during tertiary-level education. In the United States, for example, parental income and assets had to be factored in when applying for needs-based loans and grants, unless applicants could prove that they had already been economically independent of their parents for an extended period of time.

MAINTENANCE OBLIGATIONS WITHIN THE FAMILY

The same logic that connected tax law reform to new regulations for calculating student grants was also evident in a commission of inquiry that ran for several years and became known as *Familjesakkunniga* (loosely translated as "the family experts"). The directive given to the commission by Herman Kling, the minister for justice, was radical. According to Gabriel Romanus, Carl Lidbom had been in charge of its drafting. The directive's point of departure was gender equality and the idea that marriage should be treated as a union between two independent individuals. Romanus, who, as noted earlier in this chapter, was one of Group 222's liberal members, served on the commission himself for almost ten years.[70]

The directive that Kling issued in August 1969 began by reviewing how things had previously stood: "Although spouses were equal according to the letter of the law, it was also clear that legislators assumed a normal state in which roles were divided between spouses, with the husband as the family's primary breadwinner and the wife as occupied with domestic tasks. Spouses were jointly responsible for bringing up their children. In turn, children were in principle required to contribute as needed to supporting their parents in old age."[71]

But the situation had changed—or would do so very shortly. The directive's summary is worth quoting in full:

> It is becoming increasingly common for both married spouses to have gainful employment. Equality between men and women in the labor market is no longer regarded as utopian, even if there is a growing

awareness that it will take determined efforts by politicians and trade unions over a considerable period of time to implement the idea of gender equality fully in the real world. Society has assumed a significant share of the costs involved in having children, and children's educational opportunities are no longer dependent on their parents' means to the same degree as they once were. Social insurance and other measures of social security offer protection against loss of income due to unemployment, sickness, disability, or the death of a family's breadwinner and in old age. Fewer and fewer people are dependent on the economic support of their relatives. The obligation under family law to make maintenance payments now primarily applies to younger children. Inheritance rights are still a significant legal institution, but surviving relatives rarely depend on an inheritance to maintain themselves. From the point of view of the private individual, this reorganization of society represents an ongoing process of liberation and growing security.[72]

The directive emphasized that the process remained incomplete. Large differences, such as access to work, existed between different parts of the country. Likewise, significant differences existed between generations. The options available to a family were also limited by a shortage of nurseries and preschools. Both the directive and its authors tended to take it for granted that society would have to adapt to a particular development. For example, they declared that "the family has declined in importance as a fixed economic entity for the production of resources needed by its members."[73] Yet this seemingly inevitable development was also the result of reforms that were based, in turn, on normative goals. A reform creates conditions that, after a while, are seen as self-evident and natural and that are then used as the basis for new reforms in the same direction.

We saw in the preceding section how the new tax law was used as a justification for further reform of the regulations governing student grants. To a large extent, the family experts shared the same fundamental values with regard to the importance of promoting what they called "the economic independence and equality of spouses."

The family experts also seemed to share the view of marriage that we encountered earlier in this chapter in *The Family of the Future: A Socialist Family Policy*, published by the women's wing of the Social Democratic Party. In their general guidelines for the work of reform, they stressed that new legislation needed to be "neutral with regard to differing shared domestic arrangements and moral precepts." They also claimed that "for married couples, the rules should generally be framed so that spouses can retain a large degree of independence within the marriage." Kling concluded by arguing that marriage should be seen as "a form of voluntary shared living" in a time when education, labor market, and social policies had resulted in "reduced mutual dependence between spouses."[74]

Following this directive, the family experts worked for a decade, during which time they produced a series of reports that in various ways sought to realize the directive's principles, above all as regards the maintenance obligations of family members toward each other. In 1977, the family experts presented an interim report containing a "proposal for legislative changes relating to maintenance obligations in family law" in which they addressed the issues of "maintenance of children, spouses, former spouses, and parents." In it, they proposed that parents' obligation to support their children should "cease" when a child turned eighteen. (The obligation would remain "only if the child has not yet finished school.")[75]

In the case of spouses, the principle should be that "divorced spouses are individually responsible for their own maintenance." The members of the commission nonetheless left some room for special cases in which maintenance might be due. Yet these situations, they wrote, were "exceptional in nature and primarily intended to authorize maintenance payments for a limited time only." On the question of children's obligation to support their parents, the report's authors were blunt and to the point: "We recommend the repeal of current regulations concerning the child's obligation to contribute to the maintenance of a father or a mother who is unable to support themselves because of illness or for some other reason. In light of societal measures with regard to illness, such regulations no longer have practical significance."[76]

These same principles that guided the family experts in the 1970s would later find expression in the abolition of widow's pensions, with some temporary exceptions, in 1990.

CHILDCARE

The individual taxation reform was a necessary, albeit not a sufficient, condition for women to leave the home. Of comparable importance was the extremely rapid extension of childcare provisions after 1970. Once again, Group 222 played a key role by shaping public opinion as well as by providing a forum in which key figures within the Social Democratic Party and the Liberal Party could meet to discuss and work out their ideas. Moreover, Siv Thorsell was the key author on the 1968 commission of inquiry into nurseries, an inquiry that was a key factor in the massive increase in nursery construction after the commission submitted its report in 1972. Thorsell was a member of both Group 222 and Group 8.

Whereas Thorsell represented a feminist perspective on preschools, Gustav Persson, who had worked on the issue for LO, represented a labor market perspective. As we have seen earlier in this chapter, the labor market perspective has often been presented as a driving force behind the sweeping reforms of family policy that brought women into the labor market in large numbers. Persson, a member of Group 222, gave a talk to the group on the topic of his book, *The Pre-school Issue: A Labor Market Problem*, which was issued by LO's publishing house in 1962. Its immediate context was the current shortage of labor.

The book's preface, which was drafted by LO, also noted that "the issue of access to preschools has been considered primarily as a social problem. While this is of course correct, there are good reasons for pointing out that it is also a labor market problem. . . . Women remain a largely untapped source of labor that urgently needs to be exploited. In this context the issue of childcare becomes a key issue."[77] At its annual congress in 1961, LO had already committed itself to a massive extension of preschools and after-school clubs, and the publication formed part of that campaign.[78]

In his book, Persson considered issues such as the number of women in the labor market, the need for more preschools, the importance of more state investment, and even the sensitive question of whether preschools and working mothers could be harmful for children. He pointed to the processes of structural change that had created new opportunities for women as well as a need for their labor and, with it, more preschools. He presented statistics showing that many women were already working outside the home and that the trend was accelerating. There was a huge and growing demand for new preschools, he argued, yet the construction program had stagnated. He offered a cautious estimate of the future need for preschool places—at least 19,000 in the 1960s.

Persson also commented briefly on the "emotional debate" over preschools. He devoted a short chapter to the family day nursery—a facility where parents could accompany their children—as a complement to regular nurseries. He expressed a hope that the opposition to preschools would subside. But this was not to be. On the contrary, the issue of preschools and of children's well-being would be debated again and again. Many radicals believed that preschool was not merely an acceptable alternative but superior to the home environment. Others were more critical. However, the expansion of preschooling was a crucial factor in the ongoing individualization of Swedish society, above all with regard to women's opportunities to choose paid work instead of being a housewife. In 1962, as Thorsell noted, there were only 11,000 available preschool places in all Sweden; thirty years later, the number was 338,000.[79] At the same time, and as Gabriel Romanus lamented, the issue of quantity would be given precedence over the issue of quality. The latter, he argued, became "bureaucratic" and preoccupied with "norms for classroom dimensions, group sizes, and staff-to-children ratios."[80]

REVOLUTIONARY INDIVIDUALISM?

Tax legislation, student grants, preschools, family law—these are hardly questions that have taken center stage in the long debate within social science research regarding different models of welfare provision. Instead, the dominant themes have been the conflict between capital and labor and between needs testing and universal entitlement.

Internationally, however, the greatest difference between welfare regimes lies in their respective views of the relationship between individual and family. The series of reforms outlined above, which were implemented in Sweden between the late 1960s and the mid-1970s, are among the most far-reaching measures to create a socially and politically individualized society that the world has ever seen. If the word *revolution* seems like hyperbole, we might recall historian Christina Florin's description of "something resembling a bloodless revolution."[81]

Welfare states are the norm in Europe—to such an extent that the social responsibility of the state has come to be regarded as what fundamentally differentiates the European market economy from the American. Even so, everyday life differs enormously among European countries. In a number of countries, the point of departure continues to be the family as a communal entity. Wages, taxes, student loans, and other subsidies are based not on the private individual but on the family's collective situation and resources.

Joint taxation remains in effect in many countries—in both Germany and the United States, for example, a breadwinner can make deductions for a partner and children living at home. On an American tax form, the first question is, Are you the head of the household? For the respondent who replies yes, there is a follow-up: How many dependents do you have? These are questions that would raise many eyebrows in Sweden.

In Germany and Italy, patriarchal power remained enshrined in law right up to the 1970s and 1980s: a woman could not go into the labor market without her husband's permission. Although German women are now entering the workplace in increasing numbers—particularly after the introduction of universal part-time childcare in 1996—German social policy is still based on the model of the male breadwinner and the family as primary provider of support for its members. It is socially acceptable for women without children to work outside the home and have a career, but a woman who tries to combine motherhood and self-realization in the labor market can expect to be accused of being a *Rabensmutter*, a "raven-mother" who abandons her chicks before they are ready to fly.[82]

Striking children was long permitted in most European countries, whereas Sweden's early efforts to outlaw the practice were often met with puzzlement. In the United Kingdom and Ireland the state would support, if at a low level, single mothers, who were not expected to participate in the labor market.[83] While there are undeniably large differences between the non-Nordic countries in Europe, nowhere has the welfare state achieved a more individualized relationship to its citizens than in Sweden.

The consequences of these family policy reforms are far-reaching. By guaranteeing education and health care, prohibiting violence toward children, and treating even children and adolescents as individuals with rights of their own, the state has succeeded in liberating these groups from the deep dependency on parents that characterizes many cultures. By providing subsidized childcare, taxing people individually, and encouraging women to seek paid work, the state has helped women to liberate themselves from dependency on a male breadwinner. In detaching women and children from the traditional family, the state may have stripped men of their position of power, but it has also freed them from the responsibilities that came with it.

Swedes have been transformed into social atoms, free to make their own way within the limits imposed by their conscience and respect for collective norms. The state provides everyone with a fundamental security that makes citizens flexible and adaptable. Individuals can get an education, change jobs, move, divorce, and have children without becoming dependent on family, friends, or employers, secure in the knowledge that all they need submit to is the impersonal power of the state. Thus, Swedes have arguably gained greater control over their lives and become more independent—but also become more adaptable as employees and consumers in a continually changing capitalist market.

Why Sweden? asked Alva Myrdal in the 1930s when she presented her ambitious plans to reform the Swedish family. Her answer was that the historical conditions were good. We concur with this explanation—and firmly rebut those who see revolutionary individualism as either a fortuitous or lamentable consequence of the global "1968" movement.

Naturally, this is not to say that the broader radicalization of the time was unimportant. There was nothing particularly Swedish about feminism and the break with traditional authorities. From Paris to Washington, DC, from Berlin to Rome, young people, women, and minorities demanded greater freedom and the abolition of patriarchal guardianship.

But this does not explain why Sweden went so much further than most other countries. As the sexual revolution raged and hypocrisy everywhere was attacked, Swedish bureaucrats and politicians busied themselves introducing individual taxation, preschools, and student grants. This was not *l'imagination au pouvoir*—putting the imagination in power—as the graffiti in Paris proclaimed. With little fanfare and far from the limelight of the student uprisings of 1968, Swedes were replacing the traditional mutual obligations within the family with new institutions and legal frameworks that made its members increasingly independent of each other.

Though controversial, these reforms were consistent with how Swedes had historically valued individual independence while nurturing a suspicion of all forms of subordination. Geijer, Almqvist, Key, Strindberg, Myrdal, Moberg, and Lindgren had all shown the way. Radical feminists played a key role, but their successes had been highly dependent on alliances with men in leading positions within LO and the Social Democratic Party as well as the broader support of other political parties. As we see in the next chapter, there are also reasons to be doubtful about whether radical individualization should be viewed as a victory for feminism or as the extension to other groups in society of a specifically "Swedish form of masculinity."[84]

Sweden is hardly more feminist or socialist than other countries. And yet, in a culture that equates human value with individual autonomy, it is hard to take a principled stance against female citizens—and, as far as possible, children—being allowed the same measure of independence from other people as that enjoyed by adult males.

CHAPTER 11

Just a Housewife

There is a dialectical movement in the history of statist individualism in Sweden: First, a struggle for emancipation, respect, and equality played out against a background of the lived experience of injustice, unfreedom, and humiliating personal dependence. Abandoned, neglected, sick, and wretched children. Women denied their fundamental legal and political rights. Old people left on the edge of the abyss. Poor people unable to get medical care and help on the same terms as wealthy people. And married women having to depend financially on their husbands despite having been legally recognized as full citizens.

By the mid-1970s, this long battle had been essentially won. Yet victory gave rise to a reaction and a new political struggle, fought under different ideological colors. For some people, the dream of solidarity, equality, and respect for individual autonomy became a reality defined by loss and belittlement. For them, the welfare state and its radical family policies—separate taxation, preschools, and individualization at the expense of the family as a community—comprised a system that denied them the right to a life of dignity on their own terms. The freedom of one became the unfreedom of the other. And those who had until recently been on the barricades had turned into defenders of the system.

A book mentioned in chapter 10, Nancy Eriksson's *Just A Housewife* (1964), had sounded an early warning note. The title captured the acrimony that surrounded the housewife's declining status in a new world in which all adults worked and all children went to day care. But Eriksson was using the phrase rhetorically and in a tone of irony.

There were, it is true, commentators even then who could imagine a new world in which all adults worked and all children went to daycare.

For most, however, this seemed an almost utopian—or dystopian—notion of gender equality. In 1962, there were only 11,000 preschool places in all of Sweden. It was hard to imagine that, thirty years later, there would be spots for almost 400,000 children.[1] What is more, Eriksson was herself a Social Democrat and a member of the party's committee convened in 1965 to draft proposals for family tax reform. She was anything but a hapless victim of state manipulation.

Five years later, things looked very different. The position of housewives was increasingly being called into question, and many women felt caught between old and new gender values. Their sense of helplessness and frustration is visible in *Report on Women*, a study by author and journalist Carin Mannheimer that came out in 1969. Mannheimer had conducted in-depth interviews with thirty Swedish women from different backgrounds. Today their voices seem to speak to us from a painful transition phase when people were expected to adopt a new way of living even as they continued to follow their old habits.

In their testimony, Mannheimer's housewives described their acute feeling that women's traditional role, looking after other family members and being responsible for children, had been devalued. Kerstin, thirty, a housewife with three children, described her situation vividly:

> My husband is very successful and greatly respected. And that makes me feel even worse. . . . Because it feels like something negative about me . . . I'm positive all the time. . . . But no one ever appreciates me for it! And everyone wants to feel appreciated. You need it. But being a mother of young children doesn't count in society today. Quite the opposite, it feels like people think you're crazy for choosing it . . . I think people don't like children. If we did, we'd value the people who look after them, whether they're the mothers or the day-care staff. . . .
>
> Women are born to have children, though. But that means you should be valued for it. . . . Or else society should make sure that there are day-care places and that fathers and mothers can job-share. People our age are caught in the middle, I feel. We're in the middle of a transition time. Because society is moving to a place where there won't be any housewives.[2]

Within a decade, Sweden had gone from being a country in which the housewife ideal was firmly established to being a radically experimental workshop. By international standards, the Sweden of the early

1960s had not distinguished itself as being particularly feminist. There were considerably higher numbers of women in the labor market in Denmark, Britain, and Austria. The number of Swedish women in parliament was average for Europe.

The reorganization was rapid. Between the introduction of the contraceptive pill in 1965 and the legalization of abortion in 1974, Sweden adopted individual taxation, undertook a massive preschool building program, and enshrined in law women's right to paid work. In the first half of the 1970s, the divorce rate increased dramatically (reaching a peak of 26,800 in 1974) while the marriage rate declined.[3] Ingmar Bergman's celebrated 1973 television series *Scener ur ett äktenskap* (*Scenes from a Marriage*) not only reached a large audience but captured the contemporary mood of anxiety and longing for freedom.

THE FAMILY CAMPAIGN OF SWEDEN

One of the more well-organized revolts against the new order was the Family Campaign (Familjekampanjen). Indirectly, it was a reaction to a statement made in January 1970 by Gunnar Sträng, the minister of finance, in relation to the new tax legislation. In a reply to critics who claimed that the new law would restrict women's opportunity to choose to stay at home, Sträng said that "we are not forcing women out; they will have the right to choose." He added, provocatively, "If they want to stay home and enjoy a lower standard of living, they can."[4]

According to housewife Brita Nordström, the leading light of the movement against individual taxation, Sträng's "cynical statement" was the spark that ignited the campaign.[5] Sonja Lyttkens, who was a fierce supporter of the reform, agreed. The campaign, she writes, "can be seen in part as a protest against how the political parties dealt with the clash of interests on the issue of individual taxation."[6]

The Social Democrats' new family policies, which were supported by the Liberal Party, were felt to be ungenerous toward families with children and hostile to those with a housewife. The new feminist rhetoric was also viewed with skepticism by influential figures inside the women's wing of the Social Democratic Party. Eriksson's book gave voice to feelings and opinions that, though politically out of step with the times, were far from unusual. And she was only one of several key individuals within social democracy who wanted to slow the pace of change precisely because many of those housewives belonged to the working class.[7]

Lyttkens argued that the Family Campaign should be understood as a "reaction to the radical gender debate in the mass media" and, in particular, to the devaluation of housewives.[8] It is a plausible claim. As Eva Moberg's article showed, public feeling ran high on this issue; on Christmas Eve 1965, *Dagens Nyheter* published a widely read attack on the family by Barbro Backberger under the mocking headline "The Holy Family." Following its early successes, the Family Campaign launched a "Save the Family" appeal that published a series of opinion pieces in which Backberger's article was identified as typifying the "furious and vindictive attacks on the family as an institution for having been, and continuing to be, largely responsible for most of the failings and misery of contemporary society."[9]

A cofounder of Group 8, the even more radical successor to Group 222, Backberger was an obliging bête noire. Her campaign against the family was only getting under way. Nordström quoted the following article on Group 8's ideology that appeared in *Dagens Nyheter* in April 1970: "The idea of earning a living for others can never be accepted in a socialist society. This is why marriage has to be abolished as an institution of economic support, children have to be provided for by the state and brought up collectively, and all adult individuals need to support themselves by their own earnings. We demand preschool and afterschool places for all children between six months and twelve years, and we demand that 25 percent of all new construction be allocated to residential collectives."[10]

This radical feminist rhetoric, Sträng's heavy-handedness, and the uncompromising reality of the new family policies are the collective context in which the Family Campaign must be understood. The Family Campaign did not come to an end after Parliament voted to introduce individual taxation. By June 1970, the campaign had gathered some 63,000 signatures for a letter to the prime minister.[11] This energized Nordström. Moreover, the government had appointed three new commissions to examine family policy and family law: the Preschool Commission (Barnstugeutredningen), the Family Experts (Familjesakkunniga), and the Committee on Family Policy (Familjepolitiska kommittén). Nordström and other defenders of the family responded with a series of appeals and publications between 1971 and 1975 with titles like *Familjekampanjen fortsätter (The Campaign for the Family Continues), Rädda familjen (Save the Family), Skall familjen krossas? (Will the Family Be Destroyed?)*, and *Rätt till familjeliv (The Right to Family Life)*.

What were they against? Under Nordström's leadership, in the period 1970–72, the campaign focused its criticism on the recent changes to tax legislation and the new commissions that would eventually lead to the extension of preschools and the introduction of paid parental leave (*föräldraförsäkringen*). For Nordström, the central issue was the attack on the family as the fundamental unit of society. She and other campaign activists were protesting against what they felt was the coercing of women to seek work outside the home. They saw the tax system as designed to "serve as an effective instrument in the transformation of Swedish society into a socialist people's republic of the all-too-familiar kind."[12]

After systematically reviewing the new laws and commission reports, Nordström came to the conclusion that the fundamental principle uniting these seemingly separate measures was the goal of "freeing the individual." Jon Peter Wieselgren, who worked at the Ministry of Health and Social Affairs and in 1972 co-authored *Rädda familjen* (*Save the Family*) with Brita Nordström, explained it thus:

> Certain leading radicals [aim to] 'liberate' individuals from any family connections that might prevent their personal development. They believe that not being 'tied down' is the best way to achieve this. This faction has also chosen to ignore the fact that in nature there are fewer storm-weathered pines than there are grasses in the meadow. In contrast, the Marxist groups do recognize this fact and accordingly promote the emancipation of individuals from their families, precisely in order to make them more dependent on society and its various institutions.[13]

Nordström's own starting point was what she saw as a devaluation of the family and marriage: the claims that "the nuclear family was the source of a great deal of evil" and that the traditional family with a housewife represented a kind of prostitution. Based on her analysis of the new family policies, she then drew the conclusion that these attitudes were now also insinuating themselves into legislation. If this "family socialization program" were to be fully realized, she feared that "the human and economic community of the family" would be effectively destroyed. "Treating individuals in isolation in every respect makes them entirely dependent on society, which can then use economic laws and regulations to manipulate us according to the wishes of those in power."[14]

Nordström returned to this theme in 1973 in her next book, *Krossa familjen* (*Destroy the Family*). In it, she analyzed family policy in relation to reports by three commissions that had appeared in 1972: *Family and Marriage* (Family Experts), *Family Support* (Family Policy Committee), and *Preschool* (Preschool Commission). She noted that the authors of *Family and Marriage* saw their mission as being to change the roles in the family. Their aim was to "break the old patriarchal family model, in which the man was head of the family and trustee of its concerns, and replace it with a democratic model in which men and women were equal." Moreover, Nordström argued, the commission members sought to "prevent spouses from becoming excessively dependent on each other." She also highlighted their conviction that "only if both the man and the woman are in paid work can their mutual economic dependence cease and their full economic independence become a reality."[15]

After a hundred pages of analysis, Nordström concluded that the three reports put "autonomy before human solidarity": "It is only in our relationship to the state that independence is seen as undesirable. Yes, you will be free—as regards human solidarity. But you will be unfree in your reliance on the state. And this is perhaps not what you understand by freedom."[16] Her finding can be read alongside Rousseau's seemingly identical description of state power and the value of independence: "[E]very citizen [should] be perfectly independent of all the rest, and in absolute dependence on the State. And this is always effectuated by the same means, for it is only the power of the State that secures the freedom of its members."[17]

However, while Rousseau valued individual autonomy and saw the role of the state in this regard as both legitimate and necessary, Nordström detected a more infernal logic. For Nordström, the family was the fundamental unit of society. Marriage and the home were the obvious environments in which to bring up children. She ended by invoking the UN Declaration of Human Rights, whose articles, she argued, had been contravened in Sweden. Her appeal in *Save the Family* ended by expressing a hope "that future family and tax legislation will be designed in such a way that the family as a human, economic, and legal unit is guaranteed conditions that mirror its great importance and accord with human rights as formulated by the Council of Europe, the United Nations, and UNESCO."[18]

After 1972, the campaign was taken over by more marginal Christian associations whose family ideal was even more conservative. For them, the central issues were abortion and the threat of more extensive sex education. In contrast to Nordström, this group, which was led by a Free Church pastor named Tom Hardt, found themselves unable to mobilize the public's interest and subsequently languished on the fringes of Swedish political life. However, as late as 1994—declared the Year of the Family by the UN—they were still working on a "petition against homosexual partnership."[19]

At around this time, John Hammarlund, an artist at the other end of the political spectrum, organized a Front Against Family Fundamentalism (Front mot familjefundamentalismen). Its ranks included "representatives from the left, the women's movement, and homosexual organizations" who felt an increased threat from looming European Union membership. In January 1994, the Front invited the feminist historian Ann-Sofie Ohlander to a meeting in Stockholm at which she reportedly referred to the family as "an old feudal institution" built on the principle of "protection in exchange for obedience." Even in modern times, she argued, "feudal principles to some degree live on within the family." Only the welfare state could redress this lamentable state of affairs. For Ohlander, it was the political drive to "dismantle these social systems of social welfare" that posed the real threat to the good, modern, and gender-equal family. She closed with an exhortation: "Save the family from family fundamentalism."[20]

The Family Campaign and the countermovements it inspired are interesting for several reasons. Closer examination of the Family Campaign and the advocates of the new family policies reveals that the ideology that we are calling statist individualism was central to both supporters and opponents of the 1970s reforms. It is Rousseau versus Tocqueville, positive and negative mirror images of the state as liberator of the individual. It is also striking just how feeble the resistance was to all these reforms.

Even though the Family Campaign marshaled some 63,000 signatories, it quickly became a distant memory. Overall, Swedish resistance to gender equality reform was quite weak.[21] When Sweden's parliament debated proposals for the new tax system during two long sessions on May 14 and 15, 1970—the year in which the Family Campaign was most vocal in its opposition—family taxation generated relatively little attention outside of the Liberal Party. But as Sonja Lyttkens noted: "As usual, the standing committee on taxes and duties recommended the rejection of any attempts to move a resolution, and Parliament followed the committee on all points."[22]

This can be compared to the United States, where in the early 1970s Phyllis Schlafly, a Republican mother of six, built a grassroots movement that successfully blocked the Equal Rights Amendment, which would have enshrined equal rights for men and women in the US Constitution.[23] And yet it would soon become clear that the reforms considered above were in some respects the high-water mark of statist individualism in Sweden. Turning now to another of the great family policy reforms of the 1970s—the introduction of paid parental leave—we see how statist individualism ran up against its own limits and how announcements of the death of the family proved premature.

PARENTAL LEAVE INSURANCE AND THE LIMITS OF STATIST INDIVIDUALISM

The Committee on Family Policy was appointed in 1965 with Ingemar Lindberg as its chairperson.[24] It was active for seven years and delivered its final report in 1972, which resulted in the following year's Parental Leave Bill. In other words, the framework for parental leave was devised during the same historical phase as the other reforms we have been examining. As historian Roger Klinth emphasized in his doctoral study of Swedish policies relating to fathers between 1960 and 1995, it was likewise promoted as a "gender equality reform by virtue of being targeted at men."[25]

Yet paid parental leave deviated in one crucial and fascinating aspect from the principles that had guided the other reforms. Around 1970, social democracy as a whole "distanced itself in the strongest terms from the idea that freedom of choice should be the basis for family and gender equality policies." But, as Klinth noted, this was not the case with parental leave: "Even though the reforms of the tax, healthcare, and social insurance systems had followed the principle that social systems should be tied to the individual, not the family, paid parental leave was designed as a collective benefit."[26]

How did this come about? And what does it say about the nature of statist individualism and its limits? Social democracy had rejected freedom of choice in the late 1960s despite its having been embraced by Tage Erlander in his 1964 manifesto *Kvinnans jämlikhet* (*Women's Equality*). Its immediate context had been the gender equality debate that we have just reviewed. As early as 1967, Birgitta Dahl, writing in *Tiden*, a social-democratic political and cultural magazine, had presented freedom of choice and equality as diametrically opposed. Equality required solutions that applied to everyone; they were not a matter of "choice."[27]

For Dahl as well as Eva Moberg and other feminists at the time, this primarily meant that the labor market needed to make room for women before there could be any talk about freedom of choice, whether in the family or somewhere else. Genuine—that is, social-democratic—freedom of choice had to rest on a foundation of equality. Dahl rejected what she called the bourgeois notion of freedom of choice, which was directed against the state's efforts to increase equality, calling it a "false freedom of choice."[28]

This point of view established itself within the social democratic movement and became a key part of the ideology of statist individualism. In the words of a 1969 report titled *Jämlikhet (Equality)*, which had been commissioned by LO and the Social Democratic Party, equality would now be "asserted on every level." In his speech to the annual party congress in 1972, Olof Palme criticized "careless liberal talk of freedom of choice," which he interpreted as an appeal for "liberation from society." By way of rebuttal, he invoked the idea of "cooperation and solidarity with other people."[29]

The practical upshot of this emphasis on equality for relations between men and women and between spouses can be easily summarized: paid work for women, day care for the kids. A central motif in all this is the idea that equality requires economic independence and that this can only be achieved if women do paid work. But if housewives disappear from the home, the question arises as to who will look after the children. The solution lay in a massive expansion of preschool capacity.

This was also a solution that appealed to those radical critics who saw the family as a narrow and flawed institution. The model of the future would be that parental leave would give parents the opportunity to stay at home during their progeny's first years. Thereafter both men and women could return to work and the children would be offered places at preschool.

In retrospect, this might seem self-evident. But that was not how it looked in the sixties and seventies. Moberg's writings contained the germ of another, more radical solution to the dual challenge of creating gender equality and individual independence within the framework of communal solidarity. This model was based partly on a critique of the primacy of work and partly on the division of roles between men and women, above all as regards labor, whether in the home, with children, or in the workplace. To begin with, Moberg called for a six-hour day, a radical and as yet unfulfilled challenge to the prioritizing of work over home, family, and social life. A shorter working day for everyone would at a stroke have changed the basis of the social contract between men, women, and children. Secondly, Moberg called on men to meet their responsibility for doing half of the childcare and housework. Only after these two main demands did she get to the need for preschools and financial assistance for the parents of young children.

Moberg was not alone in her view. The women's wing of the Social Democratic Party was also pushing for the six-hour day. In relation to the idea of men as more active fathers and working at home, there was also a good deal of talk about their "dual emancipation."[30] Indeed, at times it almost seemed as if it were men who most needed liberation. Men lived stressful, short, and dangerous lives with insufficient contact with their family and friends. On several occasions, both Tage Erlander and Olof Palme referred to the idea that women's emancipation and men's went hand in hand.

Yet, as Klinth wrote, when the Committee on Family Policy presented its findings, "the gender perspective—the logic of dual emancipation—was largely noticeable by its absence."[31] Paid leave was tied not to the individual but to the collective category of "parents," and gender equality policy became a private, internal matter for parents. The very freedom-of-choice approach that Social Democrats had criticized so harshly became a guiding principle of their redesigned system of family benefits.

The shift was striking. How should we explain it? One reason is that gender equality policy in Sweden has been largely premised on the idea that the main arena for female emancipation would be the labor market. In the 1960s, this policy coincided with the national interest because of the widely held view that Sweden needed a larger labor force. Another explanation is that there was no male equivalent to the women's movement, no "men's movement" calling for masculine emancipation. Feminists had long fought for access to traditionally masculine resources and privileges, such as equality before the law, the vote, and the right to work, but men seemed to show no comparable interest in gaining equal gender rights in feminine arenas.

From this perspective, reforms aimed at reducing the fraction of life spent doing (masculine) work became far more problematic on every count. It would be costly to introduce a six-hour day and induce men to (partly) abandon work in order to devote themselves to looking after home, children, and wife. In gender terms, it would involve a direct confrontation between women's identity as "primary caregiver" and men's identity as "primary breadwinner."

Instead of challenging these powerful forces, policy makers chose to use preschool as an ideological buffer. Women could withdraw from childcare duties without men having to give up their position of advantage in the labor market. Women had gained economic independence, in accordance with the logic of statist individualism, with the state's support. They just hadn't gained the same equality as men—that is, they had achieved a form of difference-based equality rather than an absolute sameness equality.

But independence and self-reliance do not have to mean absolute equality. There is a qualitative difference between working and not working. In one instance, the individual is dependent; in the other, not. However, there is only a quantitative difference between a woman who earns less as a part-time public employee and a man in the private sector who earns overtime. In a conflict between the man and the woman, the woman in this situation can still assert her independence and show the man the door—or get up herself and leave. In existential terms, this is of crucial significance.

Paid parental leave was and continues to be a half measure from the point of view of gender equality. This has not prevented it from being viewed from an international perspective as representative of the Swedish welfare state in the same way as the class-leveling reform programs of the 1930s were. It is invoked as evidence of Swedes' fearless modernity and bold progressiveness: no other country in the world has gone as far in creating a child- and parent-friendly society. At the same time, its results underscore the fact that Sweden's willingness to do away with ingrained gender roles is less resolute than it seems at first glance.

If the hallmark of the successful compromise is that it leaves everyone unhappy, then paid parental leave was a perfect compromise. Its gender equality ambition was undermined by men's unwillingness to stay at home with their children. Many women were dissatisfied. Those who would have preferred to be housewives felt a sense of defeat at being forced into the labor market between births in order to keep their benefit levels up. Others, who wanted their half of the power in the workplace, were disappointed to find segregation continuing both at home and work.

Even as paid parental leave served to reinforce ingrained gender roles, the two other reforms—individual taxation and expansion of preschool—had the opposite effect. Women entered the workplace in droves. Children went to preschool. But neither parents nor politicians could ignore the problems that surveys at the time began to reveal: that children were spending many hours in day care and that this was perhaps not for the best. Meanwhile, men voted with their feet and stayed at work.

FROM UTOPIA TO REALITY

Brita Nordström, leader of the Family Campaign, offered a sharp take on the political logic behind statist individualism in Sweden. At a more emotional level, Nordström also experienced the devaluing and questioning of her own life choices. Being "only" a housewife was already well on the way to becoming a social problem.

In defense of the traditional family, Nordström pointed to a series of problems with the new policy, particularly preschooling. She produced facts and statistics showing that children in day care fell ill more easily and more often. She cited research to show that children suffered psychologically when separated from their mothers for long periods while still very young and that they ran a greater risk of becoming delinquent and drifting into a life of crime and unhappiness. Above all, she protested the fact that preschools were so large, often comprising more than fifty children. She reported from other fronts in the battle, in Småland and Dalarna provinces, where single mothers had fought for the right to be exempted from "the public's will" in relation to childcare. Recalling Sweden's history—particularly the uprisings of Småland and Dalarna peasants in the sixteenth and eighteenth centuries—Nordström asked whether it was a defining trait of "people from Småland and Dalarna to refuse to be put in chains? For they have long been famous for their love of freedom and their determination!"[32]

Nordström, a woman who proudly identified herself as a housewife, felt that the basis for her way of life was acutely threatened. She suggested that the campaign on behalf of the family was a latter-day equivalent to the storied Engelbrekt Uprising of 1434. In her 1973 polemical tract *Skall familjen krossas? (Will the Family Be Destroyed?)*, she quoted the famous verses by Bishop Thomas on the rebels' struggle for freedom against German soldiers, Danish kings, and Swedish nobles: "Freedom is the greatest thing." She concluded the pamphlet ominously: "People get the leaders they deserve."[33]

It is tempting to dismiss Nordström, an individual citizen without the support of a party. Admittedly, she managed to gather 63,000 signatures for a petition addressed to Minister of Finance Sträng, but her ability to exert long-term influence was negligible.[34] With her passionate and at times overblown rhetoric, she doubtless seemed to many people like a misguided crusader. Yet in 1971, the same year that Nordström launched her Family Campaign, Eva Moberg—the mother of gender equality ideology—wrote a sharply worded article in *Vi*, a popular monthly magazine. Titled "No to Eleven-Hour Days For Two-Year-Olds!" it was a fierce attack on the new family policy.[35]

This may come as a surprise in view of the fact that much of what had happened since 1961 was visibly in line with Moberg's demands in *Women and Human Beings*. She had argued there for women's right to work, for their economic independence, and that they should not be narrowly defined by a maternal role. But a closer reading of her manifesto from the early sixties reveals that Moberg's vision was also about creating greater balance between work and home as well as between men's and women's contributions in both arenas.

Ten years later, she was warning about the excessive emphasis being placed on work at the expense of home life and, in particular, children's well-being. Moberg's idea had been that introducing a six-hour work day would be key to making the new gender contract a success. Instead, this reform had been detached from the other measures—individual taxation and the massive extension of day care and after-school clubs—with which it should have been integrated. The consequences had been all too predictable. Calculated on the basis that each parent worked eight hours, with another two hours of journey time between home, work, and preschool, this meant that small children would spend up to nine hours at preschool, perhaps more. Preschools, which Moberg had presented as a welcome complement to child minding at home by offering children a larger framework for social contacts, now increasingly looked more like a holding pen than a social and pedagogical supplement to parental primary care. A child, wrote Moberg, "can derive great benefit from being at preschool for six hours, but suffers immediate harm from being there for eleven hours."[36]

Moberg's critique to some extent found a hearing. The Social Democratic Party discussed her proposal at its congress in 1972, and her arguments were also incorporated into the family policy program of the women's wing, *The Family of the Future*, which was discussed in chapter 10. Reducing the working day, particularly for parents of young children, and introducing parental leave quotas for fathers and mothers were likewise debated in the media. However, when all was said and done, both the six-hour day and the quotas were dropped from the agenda. On January 1, 1974, as construction of new preschools proceeded apace, the new provisions for paid parental leave came into effect.

Yet Moberg's misgivings about children and preschool were to be confirmed in statistics submitted by the ongoing Familjestödsutredningen (Family Support Commission). A survey of 8,000 children in daycare institutions and nurseries revealed that more than half of the children were spending at least nine hours a day in these facilities. Among the very youngest, those under three years old, a quarter of the children were spending at least ten hours in day care. These figures offered confirmation of the nightmare scenario that Moberg had outlined in her speculative article four years earlier.[37]

One effect was that the terms of the debate changed. The family, which had been subjected to frequent and scathing criticism in the 1960s, now began to appear in a more positive light. It is possible to see the beginnings of a shift toward a more pragmatic and less ideological attitude toward issues of family and gender equality.[38]

At around the mid-1970s, figures came out showing that during the first year of paid parental leave, only 2.4 percent of fathers (568 out of 24,000) had made use of their entitlement.[39] The consequences of choosing to design paid parental leave around a contract between state and family, rather than state and individual, became immediately apparent. For various reasons—men's hesitation to take on a traditionally feminine role, women's unwillingness to give up what they saw as precious time with their children, and, above all, the negative economic implications for a family, given that the entitlement did not cover 100 percent of the salary if the man, who usually earned more money, took paid parental leave to a greater extent—the gender-equalizing effects of parental leave failed to materialize.

This design flaw in parental leave provisions proved fatal for gender equality not only in the home but also in the workplace. Chosen freely or otherwise, women's decision to stay at home for long periods of time during their children's early years had a negative effect on their ability to compete with men on the same terms. Bizarrely, and despite its good intentions, paid parental leave thus had a negative impact from the point of view of gender equality. Far from creating a level playing field for men and women, as the tax reform had done, it institutionalized gender differences in both the family and the workplace.[40]

Reality, in other words, had begun to cast a dark shadow over the optimistic visions of child-friendly gender equality that had dominated the debate in the 1960s. Unable to ignore the dire statistics, Social Democrats eventually began to accept the idea of introducing, if not systematic leave quotas, then at least a mandatory "father's month." But it was too late. In the following year, 1976, they were voted out of office for the first time since 1933.

Not even the Liberal Party managed to stand up for the principle that paid parental leave should be tied to the individual rather than the family. A rare exception was Olle Wästberg, a prominent Liberal who had been part of Group 222 from its very first meeting, and his reflections on the Liberal Party's national conference in 1975 are worth reviewing here. By this point, the issue was not even proper individualization of parent leave—that ship had already sailed. The question was now whether the party would support the idea of a one-month quota exclusively reserved for fathers.

Wästberg described in an article how the various factions lined up. On one side was a conservative grouping "that championed the rights of housewives and was critical of preschool";[41] on the other side was a radical-liberal grouping in which Wästberg included himself. Between the two positions lay the party leadership, but even they adopted an essentially conservative stance and sought to safeguard the family's freedom of choice. The difference between Wästberg and his allies and the rest of the party was that the latter viewed the family as a collective, while the radicals regarded family members as autonomous individuals.

In his article, Wästberg recalled how liberalism's bedrock principle, that the individual is the fundamental unit of society, had informed many of the legal reforms enacted in recent years: "Changing the laws governing surnames, loosening the divorce laws, and abolishing joint taxation were all steps on the road toward fulfilling the liberal view of the family as comprised of individuals." Wästberg worried that the Liberal Party, by giving primacy to the principle of freedom of choice while abandoning liberalism's model of the family, was now evolving from a progressive party that supported individual emancipation into a force for conservatism. He offered a cogent explanation for his reasoning: "Some people call this a 'quota system' and an intervention in how an individual family chooses to manage its domestic arrangements. But is it really? Isn't it actually the reverse? When parental leave is tied to the individual rather than society, don't people enjoy greater freedom? The Liberal Party once waged a campaign for many years for individual taxation. This is the same principle—individual freedom instead of family ties."[42]

A mandatory "father's month" was eventually adopted with the enthusiastic support of Bengt Westerberg, leader of the Liberal Party (Folkpartiet) and minister of social affairs during the early 1990s, but its impact proved to be limited. Although it might seem to be a step in the direction of individualized parental leave, it has also, paradoxically, had the opposite effect. In emphasizing that taking a month's leave is important for fathers, it effectively signaled that the other months are "normally" taken by mothers. In other words, it is a reform that, if anything, gives legitimacy to the very imbalance it was supposed to redress.[43]

DAY-CARE CENTERS—NO THANKS! A HOUSEWIFE'S REVOLT

Six years after the introduction of paid parental leave, Monica Wiegert published a book titled *Dagis—Nej Tack!* (*Day-care Centers—No Thanks!*). Its dust jacket presented Wiegert as "a mother from Varberg who has small children" alongside the slogan "A child has a right to its mother." In the book Wiegert launched a furious attack not only on day-care centers but on Sweden's entire family policy. The immediate catalyst, she explained, was her own experience.[44]

But she also identified the ideological and legislative roots of the malaise. Phase one of what she dubbed "Operation Destroy the Family" had been the abolition of joint taxation. This was a form of economic blackmail that forced women out to work and removed mothers from their children. Her main criticism, however, was directed at preschools and what she saw as their most important ideological advocate: the women's wing of the Social Democratic Party. Wiegert scrutinized *The Family of the Future*, the program we examined in chapter 10, and pronounced it a macabre document that "laid the foundations for the entire preschool madness." She urged anyone with the slightest interest in their children's and their own future to go through its "readable but indigestible text"—but with this caveat: its authors' astonishing contempt for ordinary people was not for the faint of heart.[45]

For Wiegert, this was more than just a question of abstract principles. She was driven by years spent battling psychologists, social workers and their superiors, lawyers, the Parliamentary Ombudsman (an agency that supervises public authorities), and other authorities and bureaucrats. Using a series of anecdotes, she related experiences that paint a picture of the social pressure that had been created in order to get mothers into the workplace ever since the mid-1970s, when she had had her first child. She described an economic reality that, in crassly monetary terms, left little space for freedom of choice. She felt mistreated by authorities who neither understood nor cared about children's well-being. But what upset her even more was the attitude and condescension of other women toward a woman who had chosen to stay at home with small children.

Wiegert expressed what she saw as a mother's natural desire to be with her children. For her, it was likewise natural for parental roles to be divided, with the man going out to work and the woman looking after the children. She viewed the ideology of gender equality as a degradation, an attempt to refashion women according to masculine norms: "We should begin to value ourselves instead of making ourselves ridiculous by playing at being men. We should be proud of the fact that we are women. It is we who are in fact superior."[46]

Here Wiegert reminds us of Ellen Key in championing what is sometimes referred to as a "radical" or "difference" feminist approach, which celebrates women's gender-specific traits and capacities. This can be contrasted with a liberal or "sameness" feminism that assumes women are more similar than not and that women thus should be granted the same rights and responsibilities as men. This understanding of the detrimental effects of liberal/sameness feminism also characterizes Wiegert's treatment of men and parental leave. "The most dismal parody of all is 'paternity leave.' I can accept it in cases where the mother is so ill that she cannot look after her child. In all other instances, it is utterly unacceptable and humiliating for the child's mother." Small wonder, she argued, that infants get stomachache "when they are being given powdered formula by inept fathers." Preschool was by definition a harmful environment for children. Like Brita Nordström, Wiegert described it as a breeding ground for disease: "Only viruses and lice enjoy day care." Nor, declared Wiegert, did preschools exist "for the child's sake—they are storage facilities."[47]

Wiegert was baffled by women's willingness to leave their children so they could go to work. Many of the women she met spoke readily about how fulfilling their jobs were and how they provided an opportunity for "self-realization." But working-class women had let themselves be duped by the myth of how boring it was to look after children at home: "if only I can get a place at preschool, I won't have to sit at home and listen to a screaming infant." In reality, Wiegert argued, their jobs were deadly dull. Had Swedish women really been so brainwashed during the previous eleven years? She had no doubt about the answer: "Clearly they had. And it was hardly surprising. For more than eleven years, radio, TV, newspapers, gender equality committees, and politicians had joined forces to discriminate against women who wanted to raise their own children, while at the same time glorifying paid work and throwing money at women as a thank-you for abandoning their children."[48]

Put in a slightly longer perspective, however, a rather different picture emerges. The difference-feminist values articulated by Wiegert, in combination with a less brainwashed view of ordinary work, have prompted many women to follow Eva Moberg's precepts when choosing their own paths. By effectively using the instruments available—paid parental leave, including the possibility of taking a large proportion of the time that would have gone to the man in an individualized system; the clause giving higher benefit levels to parents whose second child was born within a specific period of time after their first child; and the possibility of working part-time, particularly in the female-dominated public sector—many women had been able to minimize their time at work while maximizing their time with their own children.

Women would quietly find practical solutions to the dilemma—this impossible choice between children and work, income and poverty, independence and reliance on their husbands. Over time, they would create their own version of the six-hour workday that Moberg had argued was crucial for a healthy balance between home, children, family, work, and self-realization.

These choices made by both men and women came at the price of an extreme segmentation of the Swedish labor market.[49] While Swedish women constitute a highly visible presence in the labor market, from an international perspective Sweden's labor market is also one of the most segregated. Women work in the public sector, are paid less, more often work part-time, and seldom hold senior managerial positions. The statistics also have a partly concealed class dimension. The ideal kind of work, in which individuals can fulfill themselves and find an outlet for their creativity, certainly exists. But it is rare. For the vast majority, the bitter reality is that work is a source not of personal self-realization but of much-needed income. And in a society like Sweden's, where the differences in income between "regular" jobs are relatively small, it matters little what kind of work is being done. If someone can get by on a combination of paid parental leave, income from work, housing subsidy, and child allowance, in which the net gain is "free time" (not leisure time) that can be devoted to children, relatives, and friends—well, why not?

From the perspective of statist individualism, the person retains his or her independence. They are dependent on the state, it is true, but this is a minor problem. In reality, as Rousseau saw, dependence on the state is precisely what makes freedom possible in relation to other people—including husbands and wives.

In what sense can this social contract be considered feminist? Even as the debate continues to rage over the effects of "state feminism"[50] and the degree to which the Swedish welfare state can be thought of as "woman-friendly,"[51] Sweden comes out on top in every international ranking of gender equality.[52] This development is perhaps a reflection more of women's greater access to traditionally masculine arenas than of those arenas having been feminized in any deeper sense. The primacy of paid work is unchanged. As several researchers have pointed out, the classic model of full-time work remains the norm, even for women.[53] Other solutions are possible, but they are second-choice arrangements that entail lower status and salary.

Perhaps the new gender order has freed men more than women. Before, when a family's income came from just one person, breadwinners had a responsibility that was legally and morally binding in ways that limited their freedom. They had duty to support their children, spouse, and parents. In the era of statist individualism, the state took over from men as a guarantor of security, allowing them to come and go largely as they wished. Moreover, men were more often employed within the private sector, which offered better pay and working conditions than the welfare state's crisis-racked public sector. These dual effects offered a man a stronger basis on which to assert his individual sovereignty.

Swedish men seem reasonably gender equal by international standards.[54] But when it comes to choosing between home and work, they remain fairly traditional. If there is any sense in which they have been demasculinized, it is primarily in having shaken off their traditional role as primary breadwinner, not in having relieved women of any of their childcare or other familial responsibilities. The conservative hat has given way to the casual cap, and the ponderous paterfamilias of yesteryear has become a more equal member of the family—apart from not being around the house much more than before.

Statist individualism may have *liberated* men from their traditional roles as head of the family, provider, and protector, but it is doubtful whether it has led to the *emancipation* that would have made women and men equal, both within the family and in the marketplace. What we instead see emerging is a new masculine ideal that is detached from paternal responsibilities while retaining most of the privileges enjoyed by the old patriarchy.

Somewhere in heaven, Carl Jonas Love Almqvist must be smiling. Albert—he of the dashing mustaches and no surname—has become the model man of a new era. And Sara Videbeck is struggling to run her own business in between taking their children to day care.

FROM MIDDLE WAY TO NARCISSISM

The year after Wiegert published *Preschool—No Thanks!* the conservative politician Staffan Burenstam Linder brought out a polemical book of his own, titled *Den hjärtlösa välfärdsstaten* (*The Heartless Welfare State*). It portrays Sweden as a country where the state has assumed care responsibilities that ought naturally to be borne by families or through voluntary social work. Burenstam Linder was concerned that the state's growing role would lead to feelings of powerlessness and isolation: "The state cannot transfer ever more of the family's duties to preschools and after-school clubs without diminishing the degree of personal interaction between parents and children." And if this natural intergenerational contact were eroded, it would put both younger and older people at risk. If children learn that "everything should be managed by institutions" and that "the welfare's taxes and systems leave parents without any time to spend with their children," the result would be that "when they grow up, children will feel that they do not have time for their old parents." The result would be a society in which citizens had lost their capacity for compassion. A welfare state "dilutes or removes our sense of the importance of caring for others ourselves and our capacity to be responsible for others." Factor in the economic aspect—namely, that in the long run the state would never be able to afford all of the services needed—and the result would be, as Burenstam Linder concluded grimly, "a state without money and people without conscience—the welfare state's final stage."[55]

The following year, with the fateful date of 1984, Elisabeth Langby, a former lead writer for *Svenska Dagbladet* and rival to Carl Bildt as rising star of the Moderate Party, published a nightmare vision of Sweden's future that provoked widespread debate. In *Vinter i välfärdslandet* (*Winter in the Welfare Society*), she prophesied that Sweden's already overburdened economy would be driven into the ground by overeager social engineers, to be followed shortly after by the collapse of democracy.[56] Langby's prediction has not come to pass. But the process of steady expansion that defined the 1960s and '70s had indeed been checked, and the 1980s and 1990s were characterized by acute anxiety about whether the welfare state could be sustained. Just as statist individualism seemed to run up against a moral-political limit to its continued expansion, Sweden during these decades was increasingly seen less as an exemplary success story than as a cautionary tale with dystopian overtones.

The rest of the world has always viewed Sweden with ambivalence. From the 1930s, when Marquis Childs wrote his legendary account of *Sweden: The Middle Way*, until the 1970s, most foreign observers were impressed by the combination of peace, economic prosperity, social equality, and a democratic political culture that seemed to differentiate Sweden from other countries.[57] But as far back as the Cold War, conservative politicians in the United States began to wonder where Sweden really belonged in their politically black-and-white map of the world.

At the Republican Convention in Chicago during the 1960 presidential campaign, Dwight D. Eisenhower notoriously referred to Sweden as a "fairly friendly European country" whose people suffered from rampant drunkenness, skyrocketing rates of suicide, and a lack of capitalist ambition.[58] This lamentable situation was caused, needless to say, by the moral laxity that "socialism" brought with it. Things did not improve in the sixties, when Olof Palme's support for North Vietnam led the United States to blacklist Sweden.

But Roland Huntford's book *The New Totalitarians* nonetheless came as a shock to most Swedes who read it or heard it discussed. The book was lightweight in many respects. Nuance and shades of gray were not Huntford's forte: "Similarly, equality of the sexes, once it had been adopted as party policy by the Social Democrats, was placed on the school curriculum. . . . At an early age, conventional ideas of male and female roles were broken down. Boys were taught to sew, and girls to wield hammer and chisel. Equality was taken to its logical conclusion . . . to destroy the customary belief that a woman's place is looking after a family and substitute the idea that her proper duty is by the man's side, in office and factory."[59]

Yet his furious criticism of a country whose citizens were unable to differentiate the concepts of "state" and "society" was hardly more superficial than Childs's ardent enthusiasm in the 1930s—just correspondingly less flattering. What Childs saw as a willingness to compromise and a striving for consensus were, for Huntford, evidence of a fundamental personality defect in Swedish people.

In both cases, the author's underlying political agenda affected the way he represented Sweden. Childs was one of the first in a long line of social liberals and democratic socialists who saw in Sweden living proof that it was possible to combine a market economy with policies to promote equality and to create a social security net fine enough to catch all citizens. They would gladly see similar reform programs implemented in their own countries. Sweden was quite simply a model for how the problems of class society could be tackled in a thought-through, democratic, and sensible way. And an equivalent undercurrent likewise informed Huntford's critique. Conservatives and out-and-out market liberals worked hard, if not to smear Sweden then at least to highlight the Swedish model's failings.

But even if Childs's and Huntford's views of Sweden were both ideologically inflected, their analyses nonetheless express important movements of the time. After all, they relied on information and knowledge gleaned from Swedish sources. Childs may have been tendentious, but he likely conveyed much of the pride, confidence, and faith in the future that was felt by many Swedish liberals and social democrats in the mid-1930s.

Swedes may not have been quite as wonderful, wise, and rational as Childs claimed, but he foresaw many of the economic and sociopolitical successes that would come about in the 1950s and 1960s. And no matter how preconceived Huntford's opinions about Sweden and its regimented joyless citizens may have been, he captured the growing feelings of unhappiness and alienation about the statist individualist project that also afflicted some Swedish citizens.

In the wake of Huntford's *The New Totalitarians*, a new and more critical tone began to creep into American reporting on Sweden. It was not just that Swedish family policies caused astonishment and dismay, nor that it was no longer quite as self-evident to left-wing researchers and journalists that Sweden was a model country. Alongside a shift from class politics to family politics, political debate in the most advanced Western countries was entering a new postmodern landscape. Issues of identity, culture, and lifestyle had begun to challenge redistributive issues. People's loyalties and antipathies could no longer be easily located on the classic left-right scale.

In 1989 Alan Wolfe, a sociologist married to a Dane and an admirer of the Nordic model, pointed out in an article titled "The Day-Care Dilemma: A Scandinavian Perspective" that "public day care is provided primarily to serve parents and only secondarily to serve children."[60] Although Wolfe had a balanced view of Swedish preschools, he encouraged American readers not to try to follow Sweden's example but, rather, to turn the backwardness of the American view of the family to their advantage: "A society that loves children will use the state to provide for them, but will also allow parents the time to be with them."[61]

A more ruthless attack on Swedish family policy came from David Popenoe, a conservative American sociologist. In his 1988 book *Disturbing the Nest: Family Change and Decline in Modern Societies*, he painted a dystopian vision of Sweden as a country in which the family was in a state of near collapse.[62] He went on to launch the idea that "there is a strong likelihood that the family has grown weaker there than anywhere else in the world." The reason, as he put it, was that "people's dependence on the state has grown while their reliance on families has weakened." In his analysis of the decline of the family and the rise of the welfare state, Popenoe emphasized how a number of newly implemented institutional changes had resulted in Sweden becoming a place where "individual family members are the most autonomous and least bound by the group."[63]

In particular, he pointed out that parents no longer had authority over their children (this was a reference to the banning of corporal punishment), that children and adolescents were not economically dependent on their parents, that husbands and wives were financially autonomous, and that the elderly were taken care of by the state rather than the family. In his efforts to account for this state of affairs, Popenoe enumerated a number of factors: a culture of narcissism, economic security, gender equality, welfare state ideology, and secularism. Above all, he argued, the dogged struggle to increase equality and strengthen the individual's independence from other family members had resulted in significantly deleterious consequences for the Swedish family's continued existence.

Popenoe's articles and book caused a degree of fuss in Sweden. Several researchers sprang to the Swedish family's defense. Among them were two scholars of youth and childhood, Karin Sandqvist and Bengt-Erik Andersson, who jointly published a riposte to Popenoe.[64] In it, they pointed out that the evidence for a crisis in the Swedish family was thin. The birth rate in Sweden had risen during the 1980s and by 1992 was second only to Ireland and Iceland. Teenage pregnancies were unusual, and educated women were more likely to have children than in other European countries. Overall, Sandqvist and Andersson presented an image of a welfare policy that, if anything, strengthened the family.

Judging from developments in the last few decades, the truth lies somewhere between what Popenoe wrote in 1988 and his Swedish adversaries. The crisis of the family is a general phenomenon in the West, affecting countries with both conservative and liberal family policies. Popenoe had nonetheless put his finger on a sensitive point. Fertility rates and the incidence of teenage pregnancies are one thing, but the issue of children and parents' security and mutual relations is something else entirely. Time and again, public debate in Sweden returns to the question of the quality of family life, the frequency of divorce, the leaving of children in preschool, and the conflict between individual self-realization and community. Is it not possible that Popenoe, like Nordström, Wiegert, Burenstam Linder, and even bitter Neander-Nilsson, despite everything, had a point? Each of them seems to be describing the same statist individualism as their opponents, only in reverse. How exactly are plus and minus related?

The ambivalence about whether Sweden is a model to be emulated or an experiment to be avoided has not been limited to the United States. In Germany, too, Sweden has figured in the political debate as both a source of inspiration and an example of a path not to be taken. The opposition between state and society is less acute in Germany than in the United States, since the former continues to nurture the Hegelian idea that the state is a legitimate instrument for asserting the interests of society. Yet, as we discuss in chapter 3, Germany also differs from Sweden and is more like the United States in how it views the family: individualistic values have historically had to cede priority to a more traditional view of the family, the role of women, and civil society's responsibility for welfare provision. Of course, it is unsurprising that Germans should value the family so highly while remaining reluctant to embrace a dominant role for the central state, given that their state collapsed twice during the twentieth century. When the Federal Republic of Germany (West Germany) was created in 1949, the prevailing gender order was enshrined in the constitution: men were the family breadwinners and women and children were dependent on him. Women's role remained confined by the traditional mantra *Kinder, Küche, Kirche*—children, kitchen, church.

The German social contract remained fundamentally unchanged even by the spread of feminism in the 1970s: as well as doing paid work, women were expected to take care of the children and be at home when their children came home for lunch. Labor participation was conditional: only when it did not interfere with their housewifely duties was it acceptable.

Burenstam Linder argued that Swedish citizens were the victims of a "blind faith in central government, coercion, and devaluation of the individual" that cannot lead to a "humane and vital society."[65] The flaw in this thesis is obvious: in election after election, the Swedish people have voluntarily contributed to this development. Perhaps they are simply the victims of false consciousness, as Marxists used to say when people wanted the wrong thing—or brainwashed, as Wiegert claimed.

But can everything really be blamed on the manipulation of an obedient and gullible population by devious social engineers? Or might it be that the majority of Swedish citizens were in earnest when they chose personal independence—even if it came at the price of central government and alienation? Have what Neander-Nilsson called "the people with ice in their hearts" created Burenstam Linder's "heartless welfare state"—of their own volition and with no real regrets? In the next chapter, we follow this debate into the 1990s in a Sweden where no one could claim to have a monopoly on how fundamental social and political problems should be formulated—or answered.

CHAPTER 12

Competing Visions of Community

Sweden's statist individualism has never been without its opponents. On one hand, it has been argued that its underlying view of people is materialistic and crass. Ever since Per Albin Hansson first formulated the ideal of *folkhemmet*, critics have objected that the good society must be organized around higher, more spiritual or moral aims—whether their starting point has been a close Christian community or a dream of a classless society.

On the other hand, there is also a long history of peaceful resistance to the growing power of the state. From the sulky peasant radicalism of Vilhelm Moberg's emigrant novels in the 1950s to the more recent rediscovery of individual-rights philosophy, there have been frequent warnings about the limitless opportunities for exercising political power that are intrinsic to the ideology of the welfare state.[1] On occasion, the various parties have even met each other halfway by agreeing that there has been too much state and too much individualism.

In 1968, these various strands of dissatisfaction crystalized into outright revolt against the Swedish project. The countercultural movements of the sixties were often able to unite in rejecting the corporative society and atomistic individualism that isolated people and stripped their lives of meaning. Workers went on strike against scientific management and inhuman conditions on the conveyor belt, students occupied university buildings to protest the underfunding and industrialization of higher education, and long-haired youths moved into collectives to create alternative communities in a challenge to the prevailing conformity of *folkhemmet* culture. Yet the sprawling movements of 1968 made so many different critiques of *folkhemmet* that they canceled each other out. Instead, it ended up giving the statist-individualist project new energy.

In other words, the successful establishment of statist individualism as an expression of Swedishness had created a difficult catch-22 for presumptive contenders. To have mass appeal, a rival vision would need to reconcile the tension between autonomy and community in similarly convincing fashion. *Folkhemmet* was built within the framework of a self-image that Sweden had nurtured since the mid-1800s: an easily recognizable community of free, independent individuals. The protagonists in Swedish political culture were well established: a warm national community, a strong but cold state, and an autonomous, genderless, timeless, and equal citizenry. An alternative utopia would have to accommodate a similarly broad array of fundamental conditions for human existence.

At the beginning of the 1990s, just such an alternative vision seemed to be taking shape, one that decisively rejected the traditional Swedish faith in a strong state. It took its point of departure in the social institutions that were not part of the public sector—primarily, popular movements (*folkrörelser*), voluntary associations, and special-interest organizations—what would later be gathered under the heading of "civil society."[2]

Although the factors that lay behind this break with the consensus around *folkhemmet* policy that had existed since the 1950s were varied, they were connected. The depressed state of the Swedish economy following the 1973 global oil crisis steadily eroded the basis for expansive social policies. The Social Democrats abandoned the spirit of collaboration with employers, which had been formalized in the historic Saltsjöbaden Agreement of 1938, and launched so-called "wage earner funds" (*löntagarfonderna*), a revolutionary proposal to gradually transfer full control of Sweden's largest stock-market-listed companies to its trade unions. The resulting conflict served to destroy the bonds of trust that had existed between the Swedish Employers Association and the Social Democratic Party. The former steadily withdrew from participation in central negotiations and turned its back on Sweden's culture of compromise. An important step in this process was the association's founding in 1978 of Timbro, a free-market think tank, whose explicit purpose was to challenge the dominance of leftist ideology in the public debate.[3]

Critiques of social democracy came from the left, too. The patchwork 1968 movement charged the Social Democratic Party with a multitude of sins: forming a corporatist alliance of state and capital at the expense of ordinary citizens; pursuing a Fordist program in which economic security came at the price of alienation; and allowing their socialist vision to be reduced to soulless labor-market policies and overprotective social measures. Left and right were united in their antipathy to the ossification of Swedish life into *betongsamhället*—literally, "concrete society"—and state socialism. They objected to the statism and the autocratic attitudes that, it was argued, left the individual utterly powerless—a view that would find support in the influential Commission on Political Power (Maktutredning) that was active during the second half of the 1980s.[4]

From this negative critique of the welfare state emerged an alternative vision of a society whose individuals would have more space in which to exercise what would come to be called *egenmakt* (empowerment) and thereby form new, voluntary, and authentic forms of organic community. Civil society would become a utopian concept that, like *folkhemmet*, involved both a striving for community and a desire for individual liberation.

And just as the left and right had fought over *folkhemmet* in the early 1900s, so too would their successors compete over civil society in the twentieth century's final decade. The left played up the connection with the grassroots organizations. The right claimed to be reviving an ancient, almost forgotten liberal notion that had begun with classic philosophers such as Adam Ferguson, John Locke, and Adam Smith.

In this chapter, we analyze the civil society debate in Sweden.[5] We begin on the left side of the political spectrum with the leftist popular movements (*folkrörelsevänstern*), for whom the question of voluntary community had far older roots than the relatively recent coinage *civil society*. We examine the powerful movements, particularly within the SSU (Sveriges socialdemokratiska ungdomsförbund), the youth wing of the Social Democratic Party, which during the 1970s and 1980s became increasingly skeptical of creeping centralization. As part of its efforts to revitalize the ideal of a party based on popular movements, the SSU tried out new concepts such as *självförvaltning* ("self-management"), *empowerment*, and finally even *civil society*, despite the latter concept's association with a right-wing, neoliberal critique of the welfare state.

We then move on to Timbro's launching of civil society in the early 1990s as an alternative to the social-democratic welfare state. Much of Timbro's ideological inspiration came from the United States, in whose history and current political debate communitarian thinking figured prominently. The advantages of this were obvious. Before long, Timbro stood out as one of the most ideologically innovative think tanks in Sweden. But how well would this conceptual import be able to coexist with Swedish political practice and the deeply rooted notions on which it rested?

Finally, we discuss the critiques of civil society as an ideal that were formulated by a number of high-profile leftist intellectuals (*vänsterintellektuella*) in the 1990s. Now sailing into a headwind, left-wing advocates of the welfare state lacked a clear and appealing political vision and often found themselves forced into a defensive position. In this political situation, talk of civil society seemed mainly to be a cover for neoliberal attacks on the welfare state.

Much was at stake, it seemed. In the words of one critic, Sweden was standing on the brink of "systemic change second only in magnitude to that of the 1930s."[6]

THE POPULAR MOVEMENTS: A FORGOTTEN HISTORY

Although the concept of *civil society* would become associated in many people's minds with Timbro's right-wing ideological offensive in the early 1990s, it had in fact never belonged exclusively to the right. It had been introduced into Sweden back in 1980 by Håkan Arvidsson and Lennart Berntson, at that time both Marxists. In their book *Makten, socialismen och demokratin* (*Power, Socialism, and Democracy*), they confronted the statist tradition within Marxism. The book gained a certain amount of attention in the 1980s, primarily among SSU members who were pushing for a more critical stance toward the state.[7]

Arvidsson and Berntson's book can be thought of as a Swedish local version of the debate among 1968-era leftists in other countries about the proper relationship between state and society in a democracy. Yet their critique also needs to be understood from a specifically Swedish perspective. As Rolf Alsing, a prominent social-democratic journalist, noted when the debate was at its most intense, there had always been tension within the labor movement between the statist and the popular-movement wings, between those who favored politics from above and those who stressed politics from below.[8] The question of civil society's role inevitably arose in relation to the popular movements: were they a libertarian social-democratic alternative with roots in the cooperative movement, or a liberal "fifth column" that posed a threat to universal social rights? Their amphibious character—now connected to the solid ground of the state, now swimming in an ocean of free and self-organizing individuals—created confusion.

These ambiguities partly stemmed from the fact that the Swedish labor movement had in recent years been cultivating a mythologized image of popular movements. Their original identity as liberal self-help associations, in which people joined forces to support each other as individuals, had been largely obscured by an overemphasis on class-based community and solidarity with the political goals of the labor movement. There was a historical logic to this. As the welfare state increasingly assumed more and more responsibility for education, social insurance, and mutual support, which had previously conferred legitimacy on the popular movements, all that remained were slogans about community and solidarity. Perhaps it was not so strange that many people came to believe that this empty shell was the actual core of the popular movements—and dreamed of an era that had never existed, when people had voluntarily organized themselves in a spirit of pure solidarity and political consciousness-raising. Absent from this view were the dream of individual emancipation and the more straightforwardly material needs that drove people to form cooperative organizations, self-improvement societies, and temperance lodges.

Nineteenth-century liberals emphasized the importance of the new spirit of the free associations that was emerging in the shadow of the older trade-guilds system. These movements were often politically hostile to the predemocratic state, and civic associations and societies were to play a decisive role in the development of the modern public sphere.[9] This was also true for Sweden. According to historian Torkel Jansson's pioneering study *Adertonhundratalets associationer* (*Associations of the Nineteenth Century*), the rapid proliferation of clubs, leagues, and associations of all kinds was crucial for the emergence of the modern Swedish state. Associations—the occasionally bewildering multitude of organizations that at that time represented civil society were in Swedish called *borgerliga associationer*, a translation from Hegel's German *bürgerliche Gesellschaft*, meaning "citizen associations"—were the institutional basis of liberalism's challenge to the predemocratic, authoritarian state.[10]

For a long time, Swedish historians underplayed this fact. The popular movements were instead incorporated into a teleological narrative about social democracy's marvelous destiny in Sweden. In their grand narratives of the emergence of *folkhemmet*, history books tended to offer only a limited and biased treatment of the popular movements and their origins. Particularly revealing was their choice of associations and societies to focus on. In the writings of Sven Lundkvist and other scholars of the popular movements, the central role is given to organizations closely aligned with social democracy, primarily the temperance, labor, and cooperative movements.[11]

For classical liberalism, on the other hand, the free associations were guarantors of diversity, independence, and sober criticism of the state. Their role had been emphasized by Tocqueville in his analysis of the fledgling United States and by Geijer in his arguments for liberalism. It was also a view that permeated the early labor movement. Tellingly, when Childs came to write his famous book on Sweden in the 1930s, what impressed him and other foreign observers most was still its cooperative movement.[12]

But after the Social Democrats took power, the role of the associations as oppositional, independent bodies with respect to the state was gradually sidelined. Liberal ideas now had to compete with a discourse that was almost diametrically opposed. The state would make *folkhemmet* a reality by building a *Folkets Hus* (People's Hall) and a *Folkpark* (People's Park) in every town. Meanwhile, associations and organizations were assumed to exist in a harmonious and symbiotic relationship to the (social-)democratic and, thus, good state. This double perspective is reflected in the contradictory image of Sweden as simultaneously a democracy of popular movements and a state-dominated, corporatist political order.

SSU IN THE 1970S: DIVIDED BY AN IDEA

During the late 1960s, the traditional associations rooted in the popular movement tradition increasingly came under pressure. Their status as champions of democracy and of citizens' rights and freedoms was questioned, as was the closeness of their relationship to the state. The origins of this critique lay in growing unhappiness with the centrist welfare state, which, critics argued, left far too little space for local democracy and private initiative.

Criticism came from many quarters. The Center Party underwent a transformation, evolving from a party for farmers and rural people into a vanguard of decentralization and environmentalism. The Liberal Party urged that democratic processes be decentralized. LO and the Social Democrats demanded more democracy and increased influence over workplaces. In magazines such as *Zenith*, *Pockettidningen R*, and a host of other periodicals, the social-democratic state was attacked from radical socialist, anarchist, anarcho-syndicalist, and Maoist perspectives. Young people turned to new social and political movements to air their political grievances. These included Viet Cong supporters, environmentalists, women's movement activists, and so-called R-associations (*R-förbunden*) representing vulnerable minorities (the disabled, prisoners, the mentally ill, and homosexuals), including advocates of hospital and social services reforms that gave more power to patients and care users.[13]

The exalted status of the traditional, membership-based popular movements was increasingly questioned. By the 1970s, the positive view of their activities had been replaced by a more negative discourse interspersed with epithets such as "petty fiefdom," "bureaucracy," and "passive membership." Both the left-leaning daily *Aftonbladet* and the right-leaning *Expressen* ran campaigns that have since been described as "persecutions of popular movement organizations."[14] People asked whether it was even possible to speak of popular movement organizations in the original sense of the word. In its editorial on December 26, 1973, *Expressen* mused on the question "Where are the real popular movements?" and drew the following conclusion: "A popular movement is characterized by its ability to stand on its own two feet, wage its own campaigns, manage its own activities, follow its own ideals, and proceed under its own steam. But how many popular movement organizations still have the energy to do that in Sweden today?"[15]

In autumn 1974, SSU launched a campaign under the slogan *"tillsammans för en idé"* ("together for an idea"), a manifesto that it followed up with a broad political campaign. Its goal was ideological renewal: "SSU sought to move away from the party's traditionally strong emphasis on the state's role in building socialism. Long-forgotten ideas about guild socialism were dusted off. Popular movements would help build the new society and arrest the slide toward large-scale planning and centralized bureaucracy."[16] *Frihet*, the journal of the SSU, referred to the need to expand democracy. According to SSU, democracy was facing two threats. Not unsurprisingly, the first threat came from the capitalist, commercial parts of society. The other came from unchecked expansion of the state that ultimately restricted people's freedom. From this perspective, as the SSU's chairperson Lars Engqvist pointed out, "popular movements were both the means and the ends of social democracy." What was needed, declared *Frihet*, was a revival of older forms of practices "that emphasize community, solidarity, and comradeship." Like cooperatives, these were organizations that not only realized the vision of political and economic democracy but addressed the need for social community at a more existential level.[17]

SSU's line of thought was not uncontested, as Håkan A. Bengtsson noted, with some understatement, in his intellectual history of the SSU.[18] Particular controversy was caused by the idea that a number of (vaguely defined) responsibilities that now lay with the public sector ought to be transferred back to popular movements. Hans Gustafsson, the minister for municipal affairs, poured fuel on the fire by promising that the government would work more closely with popular movements. The Ministry of Municipal Affairs would create a special section for popular movements that would consult with representatives from different organizations. At times Gustafsson sounded like a continental enthusiast of the subsidiarity principle: "There are many reasons why society should not take over duties that popular movements can manage equally well or even better."[19]

The reaction was violent. Conservative editors and politicians accused the government and the SSU of trying to co-opt popular movements and "fit them into the social-democratic model of society and socialist ideology."[20] The same conservative forces that, less than twenty years later, would see the organizations of civil society as a possible alternative to the state, were implacably opposed to the idea of strengthening the societal role played by popular movements.

A number of liberals, however, not only took a dissenting view but seized the opportunity to argue the case for a liberal understanding of popular movements. The most prominent of these was the future leader of the Liberal Party, Per Ahlmark. ABF (Arbetarnas bildningsförbund, "Workers' Educational Association") is the name of the Swedish labor movement's educational section, and in an article in *Expressen* sardonically titled "Will ABF take over Sweden?" Ahlmark echoed the general concern among conservatives that popular movements would be turned into tools of social-democratic power. Yet he too suggested that popular movements could play a positive role—in which case, Ahlmark argued, liberals should proceed on the basis that "popular movements can continue as guarantors of a pluralistic society only if they avoid becoming pawns of the state apparatus."[21] Ahlmark's critique largely anticipated a position that would reappear in the 1990s in the debate over civil society and the state.

More striking, and considerably more ominous for the modernizers in the SSU, was the no less critical line taken by the social-democratic newspaper *Aftonbladet*. In an editorial in the summer of 1975, *Aftonbladet* asked, "Are the popular movements about to become tools of the state?" The writer began by claiming, somewhat condescendingly, that SSU's campaign was in many respects harmless. The idea of invigorating the popular movements, including the demand that they should be "provided with larger state subsidies and have more women in leadership positions," would doubtless ensure that SSU received "the support of the Swedish Women's Voluntary Defense Organization (Lottakåren) and the country's philatelic societies."[22]

What *Aftonbladet* found disturbing, however, was not merely that the SSU was calling for "close cooperation between the state apparatus and the popular movements" but that it also seemed to think it would be "splendid if a great many municipal responsibilities were handed over to grassroots organizations." Were this to happen, *Aftonbladet* argued, echoing Ahlmark, popular movement organizations would risk becoming "more of an interface between state authority and citizens than a forum for critical and independent debate" and, indeed, even a part of the public administration apparatus.

Aside from these essentially liberal concerns, *Aftonbladet* saw another danger. It framed the problem in terms that were to be a recurrent feature of debates over civil society and the public sector in the 1990s: "Popular movements . . . cannot take on societal functions in which citizens need to be guaranteed equal access and conditions. Childcare, health care, and primary and secondary education are all areas where popular movements cannot be given an administrative role. To argue otherwise is to give a green light to privatization and segregation within these fundamental areas, which is precisely the reason why conservatives are so supportive of this development."[23]

Aftonbladet's attitude throws into sharp relief a key line of demarcation between different normative ideals. Local self-determination versus universal welfare policies, grassroots democracy versus state socialism. The conflict would flare up repeatedly in internal debates in the SSU and the Social Democratic Party. Resistance from state socialists rather than criticism from liberals was the decisive factor behind the modernizers' progress in concrete policy terms. As *Aftonbladet*'s leader-writer and other state socialists saw it, the danger was that SSU's enthusiasm for popular movements and local democracy would be a Trojan horse from which, to the applause of jubilant conservative opponents, privatization and segregation would emerge.

SSU IN THE EIGHTIES: THE SELF-MANAGEMENT BATTLE

The campaign to stress the value of popular movements exposed the conflicts within the left's view of the state in relation to society. In the eighties and nineties, modernizers and traditionalists repeatedly faced off, first in the debates about self-management and then in the clashes over civil society as a potentially leftist intervention and the attempts to launch the concept of empowerment (*egenmakt*) within the SSU.

In several areas, a new market-oriented rhetoric that was critical of the state had begun to establish itself. Much of its inspiration came from Ronald Reagan's United States and Margaret Thatcher's Britain. But growing economic and administrative problems, particularly within the health system and other parts of the public sector, were also creating opportunities for new solutions and perspectives. Freedom of choice and consumer power became cogent arguments in radical demands for systemic change as well as more modest attempts at welfare reform. The hegemony of the left, which had lasted from the 1960s until the late 1970s, was followed in the 1980s by what is now often described as the left's lost decade. By 1983, Lars Engqvist, architect of the popular movement campaign and now chief editor of the social-democratic daily *Arbetet*, was already concluding that "the only utopian vision with any vitality being offered today is about the potential of the free-market economy."[24]

In a similar spirit of self-criticism, the SSU's new debate magazine *Tvärdrag* ran a special issue on "Socialism Faces Reality" whose title echoed a classic tract from the 1920s by Nils Karleby. It asked the question "Is Social Democracy Able to Appeal to the Youth of Today?" The headline appeared above a photograph of two fashionably made up young teenage girls dancing in a nightclub and possibly high on more than just the atmosphere (figure 12.1). The article focuses on the era's new kind of individual, a narcissist whose main attributes are

FIGURE 12.1. The 1980s brought an identity crisis for Swedish Social Democracy. This article from a magazine published by the party's youth movement wondered if the members were ready to deal with the new generation: "preoccupied with themselves, living for the moment, and intent on personal self-realization." Photo by Jonas Hallqvist.

"self-centeredness, a fixation on living for the moment, and a conviction that personal self-realization is what matters."[25]

Faced with this reality, the modernizers within the SSU and the Social Democratic Party made a fresh attempt to criticize the party from within. In *Det nödvändiga uppbrottet (The Necessary Break)*, a critical anthology that appeared in 1980, ten Social Democrats sought to identify a number of areas "where social democracy needs to reevaluate its postwar tradition."[26] The overarching idea was self-management, which became a key theme of social democracy in the early 1980s. Exactly what self-management meant was unclear. But the first goal, according to Håkan A. Bengtsson, the leader of the left-leaning think tank *Arena*, was "to change existing structures within the public sector, to gain influence over decisions without taking over ownership."

In the background loomed the fact that surveys of public opinion taken since the Social Democrats fell from power in 1976 showed a growing antipathy toward bureaucracy among voters. This was no trivial matter for a party that was heavily identified with the public sector and its management. When the Social Democrats regained power in 1982, the question of public-sector modernization therefore acquired particular urgency. Freedom of choice would be increased to satisfy the ever more demanding 1980s individuals—but only within the existing public sector. And citizens would be given greater opportunities for involvement in issues that affected them directly. In its more radical incarnation, self-management would come to represent the classic variety of utopian socialism in which people working at a local level would create, in the words of Widar Andersson, a leading proponent of self-management, "a living and unbureaucratic democracy."[27]

It was at this juncture that the SSU, taking their cue from Arvidsson and Berntson's book *Makten, socialismen och demokratin* (*Power, Socialism, and Democracy*), introduced *civil society* as a useful concept in the modernization project. In an interview given to the magazine *Tvärdrag*, the authors discussed the institutions of civil society in terms of self-management. Berntson highlighted the criticisms of the state-socialist left: "The problem today is that the left persists in claiming that the solution to the problems of the market is an extension of the state. This is a fallacy." Instead, he argued, the task was to keep centralism in check: "But the only force able to do this is a strong civil society. The question is whether it can still resist centralism, given how much civil society has been weakened. We can formulate it like this: liberal civil society has been weakened and the labor movement has failed to create an alternative civil society that can replace the liberal one. To find a historical alternative to the market and the state remains the task of socialism."[28]

As with the popular-movement campaign of the seventies, talk of self-management and civil society encountered strong resistance within the SSU and the Social Democratic Party. Bengtsson notes that the party program titled "Facing the 1990s" ("Inför 90-talet") discusses strengthening civil society and popular movements, which some believed could take over at least some activities from the public sector.[29] Yet these ideas, Bengtsson continued, "met with resistance at the party congress." During the debates, many speakers "argued that transferring public functions to popular movements and civil society was the wrong way to go." It was a line of argument that echoed the one used by *Aftonbladet* against the SSU in 1975:

> What is civil society? Is it a nonstate society, a nonmunicipal society, or a liberal, bourgeois society? The concept of civil society was used by conservatives in the late nineteenth century as a designation for something that the bourgeoisie should defend. It was to be a social order based on the efforts of individuals. We have instead built up a public sector, which in the 1980s has faltered and had its problems. What is being offered as an alternative is civil society, which has several features that I feel will increase segregation, including the kind of cooperative solutions that I suspect some speakers are pushing for.[30]

The modernizers within the SSU and the Social Democratic Party lost this battle too, but they did not give up. In 1992 they relaunched their ideas in *En ny socialdemokrati* (*A New Social Democracy*), a book that included the slogan "from the 'strong society' to civil society."[31] The reference to "strong society" was a critical gesture toward Tage Erlander, the Social Democrat who served as prime minister of Sweden from 1946 to 1969 and who launched this notion as a modernized version of his predecessor Per Albin Hansson's idea of *folkhemmet*. The book argued for reforms to allow greater individualism (called "social individualism"), emphasized the importance of diversity as opposed to homogeneity, and spoke warmly about local democracy and the European project. But the terms of the debate had already changed, and on the right Timbro was poised to resume the battle over who got to define civil society and on what terms. Moreover, this time around the initiative would be taken not by leftist modernizers in sympathy with popular movements but by advocates of a liberal concept of civil society that was more friendly to the market.

ON A VISIT TO THE LITTLE WORLD

During the 1970s, the almost ritual attacks on high taxes and socialist tendencies under social democratic rule had brought together a significant but largely unchanging number of voters. Even so, focusing on tax fatigue and ownership rights proved to be a relatively ineffective strategy for prying loose the Social Democrats' iron grip on Swedish society. Socialism and the employee funds were easier targets—chinks in the social-democratic armor.

Breaking social democracy's hegemony required an alternative analysis of social democracy's true strength: statist individualism.

Timbro discovered that the most useful critique came not from the economic liberals but from the so-called *communitarian* thinkers, who drew attention to more existential aspects of all-encompassing state power—namely, alienation and lack of community. In effect, the right picked up the baton dropped by the 1968 left.

An early example of a Timbro publication that used this ideological tactic was Staffan Burenstam Linder's 1983 *Den hjärtlösa välfärdsstaten* (*The Heartless Welfare State*), discussed in chapter 11. Admittedly, Burenstam Linder did not use the actual concept *civil society*, but in his analysis he presented welfare *state* and welfare *society* as opposing terms. The distinction, he argued, was crucial: "Anyone who mixes—deliberately or otherwise—the terms *state* and *society* will be unable to see the key difference between a welfare state and a welfare society."[32] Burenstam Linder was critiquing the state while also celebrating private individuals and their voluntary organizations.

Five years later, Timbro published another volume—P. J. Anders Linder's *Demokratins små plattformar: Om nätverk och gruppsamverkan* (*The Little Platoons of Democracy: Notes on Networks and Group Cooperation*). The book's conceptual apparatus was taken from Peter Berger and Richard John Neuhaus's 1977 book *To Empower People*, particularly their idea of *mediating structures*.[33]

Berger and Neuhaus represented the start of a wave of conservative American thinkers whose ideas gradually came to permeate the intellectual climate at Timbro. Linder also drew on Rousseau in order to explain the inner logic of Sweden's welfare state. The philosopher, Linder claimed, had sought to "replace the old order based on reciprocal relations with a new community of feelings." This had changed the meaning of the word *community*: "It was no longer understood as denoting friendship with responsibilities but as atomistic egalitarianism." The consequences had been fatal: "In trying to find the perfect community, Rousseau succeeded in conjuring up totalitarian power." Linder was neither the first nor the last to see Rousseau's critique of the feudal political order as containing the seeds of totalitarianism. His efforts to show a connection between Rousseau, totalitarian power, and the Swedish welfare state would be repeated by later commentators.[34]

In his book Linder used the concept of civil society as one of several alternative formulations that included *free society*, *networks*, and *autonomous groups*. Another two years would pass before the concept became a key fixture in Timbro's emerging ideological discourse.

Ironically, the same commentators who had launched the concept on the left ten years earlier were now staging a comeback with the opposing team. Arvidsson and Berntson, both now ex-Marxists, were given the opportunity to reintroduce the concept in two essays that appeared in the 1990 Timbro anthology *Civil Society*.[35] This time they ignored the debate within Marxism over the meaning of the term, which they instead connected to Ferdinand Tönnies's analysis of community (*Gemeinschaft*) versus society (*Gesellschaft*) as well as to Tocqueville's liberal ideas about the role of associations in democracy. And they explicitly identified "the modern welfare state as the antithesis of civil society."[36]

The conceptual importance of civil society for Timbro and the Moderate Party was further strengthened by sociology professor Hans Zetterberg, head of the opinion polling firm Sifo and former chief editor of the conservative daily *Svenska Dagbladet*. He contributed to the drafting of the 1990 Moderate Party program Ideas for Our Future (Idéer för vår framtid) and between 1992 and 1997 led the Social State Project at City University, a privately owned university in Stockholm with ties to Timbro.[37]

In many respects, Zetterberg was a perfect link between American and Swedish communitarian traditions. In his youth, he had been actively involved in various associations and Free Church organizations in Sweden. But he had also spent long periods living and working in the United States, where he had become familiar with the lively world of American voluntary organizations and societies, both as a feature of everyday life and as an academic subject.

So what did Zetterberg mean by civil society? This is how he formulated it in *Ideas for Our Future*: "For one, we have chosen to state that in the future the main burden of responsibility will fall on civil society, which is to say the little world (family, neighborhood, district, network, associations), and on areas of the larger world not under the control of politicians: churches, universities, companies, cultural institutions, ethical committees, artistic activities, independent contractors, and tradespeople, et cetera. We are not arguing, as neoliberals do, that companies and the free market should take over everything; we are saying that civil society should take over wherever feasible."[38]

Timbro and City University used the concept of civil society in different ways. Defining civil society in opposition to the state made it possible to point to bureaucracy and planned economies in the public sector while implicitly associating Swedish social democracy with communist totalitarianism in Eastern Europe. For the neoliberal free-marketeers at Timbro, civil society was another concept to be mobilized in the political struggle against the state. But in Zetterberg's account, the concept *civil society* became elided with a substantially different idea—namely, the notion of the *little world*, the organic society on one's doorstep whose watchword is *community*.

Zetterberg picked up the notion of the *little world* from the well-known film *Fanny and Alexander*, by Ingmar Bergman, in which the patriarch of the family, in a speech at Christmas, uses the term as a contrast to the larger world of politics and business. In this spirit, the writings of Zetterberg and other communitarians exhibit a socially conservative longing for an organic community that is not merely less expensive but also more human. They wished to (re)create a society with warmer and more authentic human relations, in which people take care of each other lovingly, unconditionally, and without payment. This was not primarily a critique of the economic implications of a "social state" regime but an expression of anxiety about the social consequences of impersonal, institutionalized social care.

The right's utopian privileging of civil society thus faced in two directions. One was a hypermodern liberal world populated by empowered and independent individualists, in which private forces (which almost always meant governed by the free market) were the primary agents. The other was a very different, almost antimodern world, defined by social community and Christian ethics.

This tension within right-wing intellectual circles would eventual resolve itself by Timbro and City University moving away from the market-oriented neoliberalism that dominated discussion of these issues in the 1980s (figure 12.2). An index of this shift was the theme chosen for Timbro's annual conference in 1994—the New Reformation. According to the program, this rubric referred to a proactive agenda for limiting the public sector and replacing it with a synthesis of market, individual empowerment, and community. Welfare-state collectivism was counterposed to civil society and its so-called communities.

For the classic liberals among the right, the emphasis on community was not entirely unproblematic. Liberals and communitarians might be united in their hostility to the large state, but the latter were equally skeptical of the market and its corrosive effects on civil society. As Zetterberg put it, "We . . . need to take care that the market does not behave like a cuckoo and drive the rest of civil society from

FIGURE 12.2. In the 1986 parliamentary election, the Social Democrats tried to style themselves as an attractive option for young urban professionals. In this poster, the message from the man in the sports car is that he is voting for the Social Democrats because he wants the country to have a stable economy. Arbetarrörelsens arkiv.

the nest."[39] If, as is often pointed out, while free-market liberals most easily make common cause with economistic social democrats, communitarians tend to lean toward classic social conservatism and Christian democracy in their prioritizing of ethics and the primacy of the *little world*.

This new image was remarkable, given that Timbro was viewed by most people as a mouthpiece for the Swedish Employers Association by virtue of its long battle with the left over *problemformulerings-privilegiet*—the power to define the political issues and problems of the day. Timbro's original purpose had been to free the market from the state, rather than to develop (to simplify somewhat) a borderline antiliberal perspective. But thanks to the ambitious design of Zetterberg's Social State Project, Timbro and City University became for a while the most important haven for communitarian ideas in Sweden. Rather than one-sidedly putting the market above the state, Zetterberg postulated that society was sustained by three pillars: the market, the state, and civil society.[40]

As political scientist Mats Dahlkvist has observed, the three-spheres thesis represented an innovation in the theory of civil society. The older model of two spheres—state and civil society—was reimagined as a tripartite division that separated the market from civil society.[41] According to Zetterberg, civil society thus referred to institutions whose guiding precept was "love thy neighbor": the family and voluntary associations are spaces in which we live by other rules, where we find the real love and community that can never be replaced by the heartless care of the welfare state. The problem, Zetterberg argued, is that the state and the market have invaded the sphere of civil society. Zetterberg's and Timbro's thesis might be summarized rather crudely as follows: we have created a system—the welfare state—that, despite having been built in the name of solidarity, is now preventing us from loving each other.

Of course, this thesis presumed that a desire for strong community actually existed among Sweden's citizens. It was on precisely this point that the conservative vision at the end of the nineteenth century of a Swedish nation-state built on an organic sense of affinity had failed—almost exactly a hundred years before Timbro launched the vision of the close-knit communities of civil society as an alternative to the strong welfare state. In the late nineteenth century, the Swedish people had left no doubt that they preferred a liberal and democratic state guaranteeing individual rights and social opportunities to an authoritarian national community.

To be sure, Zetterberg was not an antidemocratic nationalist. On the contrary, the civil society utopia that he and Timbro so keenly supported formed part of a vision of European integration that went beyond the nation-state. But like Kjellén and Heidenstam, who had sensed that socialism would be in the ascendant during the twentieth century, Zetterberg tried to formulate a vision of community that could represent an alternative to the strong social-democratic state. Much water has passed under conservatism's bridge since the nineteenth century. Even so, the right continues to wrestle with the same problems: the Swedish people's unwillingness to abandon the alliance between individual and nation-state. Perhaps it is not so strange, then, that Zetterberg—despite being in broad agreement with left-wing communitarians on many points—nevertheless emphasized that civil society was a utopia of the right. But he worried that civil society would be lost to the left, as had happened with the notion of *folkhemmet* between the early years of the twentieth century, when it was primarily used by conservatives like Kjellén, and 1928, when it was appropriated and redefined by the Social Democrat Per Albin Hansson.

LEFTIST RESISTANCE TO THE CONCEPT OF CIVIL SOCIETY

From early on, Timbro's capacity for seizing the initiative in debates relied to a great extent on the fact that leading left-wing commentators, notably the influential poet and cultural journalist Göran Greider, accepted the right's diagnosis of the political situation. But there was also a historical and cultural explanation for the knee-jerk hostility toward market forces and civic associations among many on the left.

The Swedish left differs in one crucial respect from the American and German left traditions that produced thinkers such as Andrew Arato, Jean Cohen, and the new left Telos group in the United States or Jürgen Habermas and Claus Offe in Germany.[42] The American left had fought for civil rights and free speech in the shadow of McCarthyism and the Vietnam War, while its Germany counterpart had criticized a conservative state for failing to deal with its Nazi past. In both cases, the state was the main threat. Notwithstanding the radical voices within its popular movements, the Swedish left has instead tended to regard the (social-democratic) state as an ally. In the early 1990s, demonization of the market, coupled with glorification of the state and the public sector, made it difficult for many Swedish leftists to accept that civil society might be a sphere in which power could be concentrated, social experiments organized, and democracy extended.

Peter Antman, a Swedish intellectual historian who was active in the civil society debates during the early 1990s, argued that associations were the preserve of the well-to-do middle class where those with resources could further enhance their position by creating new social capital. "Associations," he claimed," are strongly elitist in nature," and the working class is underrepresented in them. Moreover, they were no longer political movements in any real sense but, rather, "clubs offering outlets for people's individual life projects, such as sport, outdoor pursuits, and hobbyist organizations." Citing data from the Commission on Political Power (*Maktutredningen*), Antman pointed out that the so-called new social movements—the environmental, women's, and peace movements—were exceedingly small. Only 2 percent of respondents claimed to have been actively involved. From a left-wing perspective, the idealization of such "movements" was downright dangerous; instead, it should be recognized that the basis for equality and devolved power in Sweden had been reinforced by the creation of the "corporatist state," as political scientist Bo Rothstein described the Swedish model in one of his books.[43] "The myth of a civil society run by popular movements is a dead end," argued Antman, because it undermined the vital role of the labor movement as partner in a contract with state and employers.[44]

Why? Because it was precisely the weak who had most to gain from centralization. According to Antman and Greider, the advocates of civil society were romanticizing local self-governance. Decentralization led to inequality and arbitrariness. As for the myth of civil society itself being a grassroots movement, the facts showed that "public investment reduces inequalities in society, while investment by private actors or associations increases or confirms the inequalities that already exist."[45]

Yet the battle lines were drawn not only between Timbro rightists and *folkhem* leftists. There were obvious tensions within the left, a continuation of the struggle between state socialists and grassroots democrats that had continued through the 1970s and 1980s. Not everyone shared the view of Antman and Greider when they warned of the "dangerous associations" and a reduction in welfare that would mean a "farewell to equality."[46]

The reaction to Antman's attack on social-democratic grassroots idealists was predictably swift. Modernizers in the Social Democratic Party viewed the new interest in associations as promising, a chance to get away from the excessive fixation on the state. Civil society might serve as new bottles for that fine old wine, the Swedish popular movements. Leif Linde, for example, insisted that these latter had a key role: "We in the ABF [Workers' Educational Association] are now developing our role with new initiatives." "Society" (i.e., the state) had unfortunately taken over many of the functions of the popular-movement associations in the 1960s and 1970s, but Linde now felt that he could see a road to renewal by "building a loose, action-oriented structure comprised of study circles, cultural groups, clubs, and the like."[47] He lamented Antman's passivity and called instead for a continued struggle for an active democracy based on membership of popular movements. To simply demand that social democracy expand and protect Erlander's "strong society" was to ignore the "urgent and positive" criticism that had been directed at a system in which "there is always someone else who can 'do the caring.'"[48]

Linde was not alone in this view. He represented a group of social democrats with deep ties to the grassroots left that had argued for self-management in the 1980s. These were people who worried that "strong society was being pushed too far," to the extent that "citizens were becoming clients instead of responsible adults," as the SSU's chairperson Karl-Petter Thorwaldsson put it.[49]

For these critics of the "super-strong society," the main purpose of empowerment, community, social economy, and other allied concepts was to stimulate what they variously called the "shared sector" or civil society.[50] This would, in turn, remedy the powerlessness felt by increasing numbers of people with regard to the political system. These critics took seriously the reports by the Commission on Political Power, which described citizens' experiences and sense of powerlessness when dealing with public-sector institutions—school, day care, health care—as well as surveys showing that involvement in popular movements was low even though membership levels remained high.

THE PECULIARITIES OF SWEDISH CIVIL SOCIETY

As the polemics flew and the political debate raged in the early 1990s, a number of researchers began to realize how little was really known about civil society in contemporary Sweden. Research on the public sector had long predominated. However, after 1992 scholars began more systematically to carry out empirical investigations of Swedish civic engagement and associational life in both quantitative and qualitative terms.

Revealingly, much of the initiative behind this research came from within Swedish civil society rather than from state authorities or the traditional academia in state universities.

Thus the Swedish Red Cross played a crucial role by financing research being carried out by Lars Svedberg and his colleagues at the Sköndal Institute in Stockholm and Filip Wijkström at the Stockholm School of Economics. This resulted in several large-scale surveys providing more solid data with respect to the size and makeup of Swedish associational life and civic engagement.

When they came in, the results completely contradicted the notion that Swedish civil society had been rendered moribund by the pressure of a continually growing public sector.[51] Swedish civil society might differ in some ways from those of, say, the United States or Britain, but its reach was no less extensive. On the contrary, one comparative study after another showed that Sweden and the other Nordic countries led the way with regard to social capital and membership in associations. Not least, it revealed that Nordic civil society is predominantly comprised of democratic member organizations rather than charities, foundations, or nonprofit organizations structured along a more top-down and hierarchical model. These results have since been confirmed by a succession of international and comparative studies.[52]

Political scientist Bo Rothstein had been skeptical from early on about the claim that Swedish civil society was in decline. He argued that those who presented the public sector and civil society as opposing forces were ideologically blinkered. No such opposition existed, he insisted. In fact, civil society in Western Europe had begun to flower "precisely because of the emergence of a *state*."[53] This was especially true in the case of Sweden's welfare state, since its social policies were intended to minimize the kind of dependence and coercion that characterizes the relationship between individual and state in countries where needs-based social programs predominated. Universal programs, Rothstein wrote, "reinforce the autonomy of citizens and thus represent no threat to the civility of civil society."[54]

Against this backdrop of similar empirical data and theoretical analyses, a picture begins to emerge of the culturally specific character of Swedish civil society. This peculiarity becomes clear once we compare

Sweden to the United States. In Sweden, as we note above and in chapter 2, relations between the state and civil-society organizations are close and intertwined. It can be viewed as an interplay between special interests expressed in civil society and the attempts by the state to represent the common good.

In Anglo-American political culture, the normative ideal is that civil society should have an independent and occasionally antagonistic relationship to the state. One source of inspiration is Alexis de Tocqueville's influential book *Democracy in America*, in which the plethora of voluntary associations is celebrated as the very foundation of democracy. This is a conception that has become part of what the American sociologist Margaret Somers calls the "metanarrative of Anglo-American citizenship theory." In this account, civil society is prior to and superior to the state, which in turn is viewed with suspicion, as always "on the brink of being a source of tyranny," as Somers puts it.[55]

Furthermore, the role of civil society is not limited to safeguarding a pluralist liberal democracy but also involves the provision of social services. In the United States, a legion of religious communities and charitable organizations work to meet a wide range of social and economic needs in the populace, from schools and day care to crisis management and care for the homeless.[56] In Sweden, this type of organized nonprofit social work has been far less represented in civil society, which has instead been dominated by membership-based organizations, including trade unions, political movements, and cultural and sporting associations.

Another way of putting this would be to say that civil society in Sweden seems to comprise organizations whose primary moral logic is reciprocity rather than charity and political voice rather than social service. Yet this generalization should not be exaggerated. Civic engagement in the form of volunteering, informal help, and giving is strong in Sweden and throughout Scandinavia.[57] Additionally, Sweden has since the 1990s been conducting what the economists Mårten Blix and Henrik Jordahl describe as a "Swedish experiment": a series of reforms that have allowed for both for-profit and nonprofit actors to establish schools, hospitals, and elder-care institutions in competition with public-sector providers.[58] Furthermore, one can observe a revival of philanthropy influenced by the American tradition.[59]

Still, it remains more difficult in Sweden to talk in the same way that Americans do about the "obvious" role of religious communities and charitable organizations in the sociopolitical sector. Anyone who does can expect to be immediately quizzed about universal access to resources, respect for the independence and dignity of the individual, and public democracy versus private hierarchy.

THE STRONG STATE AND ITS COMMUNITARIAN OTHER

In the impassioned debate that took place in the early 1990s, three ideals of community were counterposed to each other: First, *the utopia of civil society*, as championed by Zetterberg and the communitarian right, a vision that included a critique of the big state and the excessive politicization of society. Second, *the popular movements of the left*, which to some extent shared with the communitarian right a skepticism toward the colonization of civil society by the state. Third, *the defenders of folkhemmet*, consisting of commentators who, like Greider and Rothstein, stepped forward to defend statist individualism.

In attempting to assess the practical result of this debate, it appears that three decades later the jury is still out. The public sector remains the main provider of education, care, and health care: profit-making companies, while growing, are a distant second, and the gap increases still further when it comes to nonprofit organizations. In part, this is the result of unfavorable legislation that makes it difficult for smaller nonprofit actors to assert themselves on the market.[60] But laws and regulations also reflect political preferences. Although the utopia of civil society ostensibly represented the same miraculous synthesis of community and self-empowerment as *folkhemmet*, it was also felt to be far too collectivist. In contrast to the classic individualism of the liberal market or the statist individualism of social democracy, it left relatively little space for individual autonomy.

Our view is that those who advocated for a greater role for civil society both underestimated the appeal of the welfare state and overestimated their own visions of close-knit community and civic engagement. Critics of the big state were often blind to the strength of statist individualism: the way in which it liberated the individual from precisely the kind of personal responsibility that they were applauding. To take personal responsibility was in many respects an attractive ideal, no question. But quietly and in private—in voting booths, for instance—people were choosing individual autonomy over personal responsibility, no matter how attractively advocates of civil society presented their vision of intimate and caring community.

Nonetheless, we see reasons to stress two long-term trends dating back to the late 1980s that favor the challenge of statist individualism. One the one hand, there is the neoliberal legacy favoring privatization and choice. While there is little evidence so far suggesting substantial growth of a nonprofit sector, the argument is stronger for the emergence of a for-profit sector supported by the center-right parties and tolerated by the Social Democrats. On the other hand, we can observe an increase of "community-talk" on the left, linked to the rise of an identity politics suspicious of civic universalism since it is viewed as insufficiently sensitive to minority and group rights.

Both these trends hark back to the breakthrough of the concept of civil society, which carries with it a strong antistatist thrust useful to both those on the right who prefer a smaller state and to those on the left who envision diversity from below rather than state-dominated universalism from above. In the latter case, such aspirations and ideals also tend to be wedded to another concept—human rights—that came into vogue during the early 1990s.[61] Like civil society, human rights is inherently a concept that questions the primacy of the nation-state and the exclusionary logic of citizenship. Taken together, these two trends have weakened the political consensus in support of the *folkhem*, both in terms of the community of the nation and the institutional structure of the state.[62]

As we see it, there are arguments both for seeing a weakening of statist individualism and for imagining a revival of strong statism predicated on a desire to protect equality and individual autonomy. In the coda to this book, we will return to how we view these trends stretching into the future. But for now, let us note that the Swedish state has already been weakened, not least with respect to the institutions for national integration that used to be the glue of the alliance between state and individual.

The standardized national primary and secondary school, which once upon a time was created in order to break down class segregation in the education system, is probably the best example of how a once-cohesive institution has been fragmented in the name of family and community choice. In the next chapter, we look more closely at a central institution that has played a key role in the historical emergence of the alliance between state and individual but that has now been detached from the Swedish state: the Church of Sweden.

CHAPTER 13

A Lutheran Modernity?

The single greatest change in the relationship between state and civil society in Sweden's entire history took place in the year 2000. After almost five hundred years as the state church, Evangelical Lutheranism was reduced to the same status as other religions and rival denominations within Christianity.[1] Yet the decision provoked no significant debate. Almost behind the scenes, the Swedish Parliament had changed the constitution in order to pave the way for the separation of church and state. The following year, Church of Sweden laws were reduced to church ordinances, and by the turn of the millennium the postseparation redistribution of assets had been satisfactorily completed. Newspapers dutifully published a few articles, but overall the public was far less concerned by the consequences of the disestablishment of Sweden's state church than it was by the prospect of a computer bug bringing the digital world to a standstill on New Year's Eve.

Why in the 1990s did it suddenly seem more or less self-evident that religious matters should be divorced from the state and moved into civil society? The idea that the state was responsible for both general welfare and spiritual community had long been generally accepted, even under social-democratic rule. But now the questions had become separate. On the one hand, debate swirled over whether civil society or state should be given priority in relation to the economic and social freedom of the individual. On the other, the state church had come to be seen as posing so grave a threat to individual freedom that it had to be abolished. This would seem to be a rather belated insight, given that principled liberals and religious dissidents had been complaining about the Church of Sweden's monopoly since the eighteenth century.[2] Perhaps the drops of water had finally worn the stone down—decades of liberal arguments for freedom of religion finally bearing fruit.

But there is much to suggest that other forces were at work. The separation of state and church was, after all, only one of a number of similar reductions in the Swedish state's control of national institutions in the 1990s and 2000s. The most striking examples are primary schools, the Post Office, radio and television, and obligatory military service, historically the most important instruments of integration in the modern nation-state.[3] No one claimed, of course, that a separation of church and state would make the nation's spiritual life more efficient in the same way that privatization was supposed to make the postal service more productive. But there was a common denominator: a broad understanding that integrative national institutions that partly relied on state coercion of citizens had become obsolete and were no longer needed in a postnational globalized world.

Whether this really is the case is a question we will return to in the coda. For now, the separation between state and church raises a more retrospective question: to what extent has Sweden's Lutheran state church influenced the alliance of state and individual that characterizes the Swedish social contract? The existence of a historical connection between statist individualism and Protestantism feels plausible on an intuitive level: in the former, citizens have a direct relationship to the state without intermediary institutions, and in the latter, believers communicate with God directly and without the involvement of ecclesiastical authorities. But the connection immediately becomes more complicated when Sweden is compared to the United States and Germany. Both these countries have also been profoundly influenced by Protestantism—the United States has been called the most Protestant country in the world—but neither has a state church. This in turn has both a political and a religious explanation.

The United States, as we remarked in chapter 2, was founded by dissidents who fought for the communitarian freedom to create a form of social life that accorded with their religious convictions and without interference by the state. Moreover, many Anglo-Saxon, Dutch and French immigrants to the Americas had been influenced by the French theologian John Calvin, who, unlike Luther, did not accept that believers should submit to the authority of the state. The Lutheran Protestants from Germany, in contrast, had a more positive view of the state; after the Peace of Westphalia in 1648, two organizations resembling state churches, *Landeskirchen*, were formed in territories controlled by Protestant dukes. But the unified German state that emerged in the nineteenth century was far too divided by religion—primarily between Catholics and Protestants but also between different Protestant denominations—for a centralized state church to be viable. The fact is that the institution most resembling a state church in Germany's history was the Protestant Deutsche Evangelische Kirche, the Nazi Reich Church that existed during the Hitler years.

As these comparisons with the United States and Germany suggest, the connection between Protestantism and statist individualism is more complicated than at first appears. The idea that the individual is alone with God does not necessarily lead to a conception of the state as a protector of individual freedom. It can just as easily result in believers cutting themselves off so as to collectively guard against state interference in the practice of their religion. The issue is not simply the teachings themselves but the historical moment in which they circulate.

In what follows, we argue that the alliance between state and individual in Sweden has its roots in an interplay between a local interpretation of Lutheran theology, the development of the Swedish state since 1500, and the challenge posed to the state church by nineteenth-century revivalist movements. In the twentieth century, these tensions would give rise to efforts to transform the state church into a Folkkyrka (People's Church), a campaign that paralleled the transformation of Sweden's state administration into a *folkhem*. We conclude this chapter by considering the problematic legacy of the Lutheran state church in a society that aspires to diversity and pluralism.

SWEDEN RUNS ON LUTHER

In secular Sweden today, "Luther" has become a cliché. The rebellious sixteenth-century monk is seen as responsible for a catalog of features of Swedish culture, positive as well as negative: a strict work ethic that borders on workaholism, an adherence to the law that tends toward subservience, a feeling of joyless obligation, a patriarchal idealization of the nuclear family, and, above all, a sense of individual responsibility that can lead to loneliness and social isolation. When Swedes drag themselves to work despite having a bad cold or find themselves at a particularly tedious and formal social event, they sometimes curse their supposedly Lutheran heritage that crushes all joie de vivre and denies their longings for pleasure and frivolity.[4]

In this popular tradition, Luther is typically blamed, as cartoonist Staffan Lindén put it, "for giving us a sense of guilt."[5] At other times, Swedes and other Scandinavians pride themselves on their Lutheran birthright and emphasize its merits: this Luther has given us the Nordic "supermodel" whose work ethic, lack of corruption, and high degree of social trust are amply documented in indexes of almost everything, from economic prosperity and social security coverage to citizens' well-being and internet connectivity levels. Luther's teachings, wrote theologian Gustaf Wingren, are the basis for "the work ethic in Sweden, Finland, Norway, Denmark, and Iceland, relatively barren countries but with extraordinarily effective social structures. People here learned, firstly, to 'read books' and, secondly, to work with the worldly things for which God has given them a vocation. The result is that Nordic prosperity is respected the world over. Sweden runs on Luther. Wherever our five flags, all with the same cross, are raised, the people of the world view us with respect."[6]

This Lutheran inheritance is both political and existential. Its mainstay is the Church of Sweden, which down the ages has legitimized its religious monopoly by portraying Luther as especially "Swedish" and Swedes as especially "Lutheran." From this perspective, Luther has given us not only guilt, joylessness, and a bad conscience but also our fundamental political institutions: the Church of Sweden, of course, but also democracy and equality. It is impossible to imagine Sweden without Luther, advocates of the Church of Sweden argued in the early twentieth century; what characterizes Sweden is precisely this powerful combination of the worldly and the spiritual, of state and church, of the Lutheran and the Swedish—how Sweden's cause was also that of the Reformation.[7]

A SWEDISH MOSES

A revealing instance of the nationalist Lutheran tradition in Sweden is offered by Olle Hjortzberg's fresco in the Uppenbarelsekyrkan (Church of the Epiphany) in Saltsjöbaden, just southeast of Stockholm. In it, Luther stands beside King Gustav II Adolf, the "Lion of the North" who came to the rescue of German Protestants in the Thirty Years' War and in the process acquired sizable chunks of real estate on the continent for the Swedish Crown. Both have halos, and Sweden's hero-king is receiving a sword from heaven. The image evokes Old Testament prophets and the Jewish people's long journey to the Promised

Land. According to Archbishop Nathan Söderblom, whose instructions for the church decoration inspired Hjortzberg, the idea was that the fresco would connect the Christian gospel with the Swedish people's struggle for freedom and national identity down the ages. The other candidates for inclusion were Bishop Thomas who in the fifteenth century sided with Engelbrekt in the struggle against the king, the sixteenth-century Lutheran reformer Olaus Petri, the nineteenth-century archbishop J. O. Wallin, and Erik Gustav Geijer.[8]

Nationalists usually have God on their side, of course. But the ties between church and nation have been uncommonly close in Sweden's history because the Reformation happened to coincide with Gustav Vasa's separatist revolt against the Danish king, who was the head of the union between Denmark, Sweden, and Norway that had been forged in 1397 in the Swedish city of Kalmar. This meant that the rebellion against the Union of Kalmar and the formation of a separate Swedish state came to be regarded as ideologically inseparable from the break with the Roman Catholic Church. Nationalistic Swedish historiography transformed Luther from a modernizing Christian theologian to a Moses figure who led Sweden's suffering people from Danish serfdom and papist backwardness into the light.

As far back as the seventeenth century, Sweden's celebration of Luther differed from other countries'. In the evangelical world, Luther's centenary was usually calculated from 1617—which is to say, a hundred years after Luther presented his Ninety-Five Theses in Wittenberg. But not in Sweden, which celebrated it in 1621 and 1721. Not until 1817 did Sweden fall into line with other countries. A common misconception, which was circulated during the jubilee celebrations of 1817, including by Archbishop Jacob Axelsson Lindblom, was that the previous date had been linked to Luther's appearance before the Diet of Worms in 1521.[9]

The real reason is given in an edict issued by Gustav II Adolf, which determined that the jubilee should be celebrated in 1621 on the twenty-first day of January, February, and March. The date of the celebration had been chosen because it was then that Gustav Vasa had become leader of the men of Dalarna.[10] The edict reads, "In that fateful hour, the Almighty prompted our ancestor, whose memory shall remain sacred, Gustav I, King of Sweden, to boldly and successfully assume the great task, and on January 21, 1521, he began the liberation of our oppressed native land by driving out the [Danish] tyrant Christian II. God used our great ancestor as an instrument for dispelling the papist

A Lutheran Modernity?

darkness from our land and opening the eyes of all those who love their country to the light of the gospel."[11]

At the celebrations themselves, the oration was *Suecia gnothi se auton*—Sweden, know thyself—and Gustav I Vasa was extolled as "peacemaker and savior." Theologian Carl Axel Aurelius hardly understated the case when he noted that "the first jubilee celebrations of the Reformation in Sweden were highly nationalistic."[12] Yet Lutheranism played a key role not only during Sweden's imperial era but also in the political conflicts and compromises that made modern welfare policies possible. When the labor movement changed its approach to nationalism in the 1930s, it became, as pointed out in chapter 8, more supportive of the military, flew the Swedish flag alongside the red flag in May Day parades, and held up Gustav Vasa and Engelbrekt as historical precursor. Claiming Gustav Vasa as the first state socialist was, however, easier than turning Martin Luther into a party member. Yet the Social Democrats managed not only to make peace with the Church but also incorporate it into their welfare-state project.

The Swedish working class had no love for the state church, preferring militant atheism or revivalist Christianity. Admittedly, Hjalmar Branting, the leader of the Social Democrats between 1907 and 1925, had early on addressed the general hostility to Christianity in the labor movement by declaring that religious belief was a private matter. But this position did not solve the problem of religion's hold on the Swedish state, particularly in education. Mandatory reading of the Catechism was abolished in primary schools in 1919 as part of a larger push for curriculum reform by liberals and social democrats. Värner Rydén, the social-democratic minister of education, became a scapegoat for discontent. During the interwar years, primary-school teacher trainees were taught to sing "Rydén the red fox, he took our Catechism and he'll take the Bible if the gets the chance." Rydén instead wrote *Medborgarkunskap (Civic Education)*, a secular catechism for schoolchildren of the new secular era that was first published in 1923 and reissued fifteen times, the last in 1959.[13]

When the Social Democrats returned to power in 1932 and took the state apparatus in a firmer grip, the problem presented itself again, this time on a larger scale: How should social democracy deal with the state church? The labor movement's initial idea had been to abolish the state church. A subtler approach would be to neutralize the church by turning it into a governmental department. The latter view was embodied by Arthur Engberg, who succeeded Rydén as minister of education. But during the 1930s, more church-friendly attitudes gained ground within the party: social democracy, it was felt, should create a popular, democratic, and independent lay church as a complement to the *folkhem* state.

This vision of a popular church with social-democratic trappings had long been championed by a social-democratic politician and priest named Harald Hallén. It was an uphill battle. As a young student, Hallén had attended a church synod in Huskvarna in 1907 that focused on the crisis in the Church of Sweden. The church had lost ground in the 1890s, and many young people were turning to the burgeoning grassroots movements: free churches, temperance associations, and organized labor. The idea of a People's Church was the main item on the agenda at the Huskvarna Synod, which is often described as the starting point for the so-called Ungkyrkorörelsen (Young Church Movement). Its founders included Einar Billing, Nathan Söderblom, J. A. Eklund, and a young Manfred Björkquist. According to church historian Urban Claesson, Hallén left Huskvarna "full of enthusiasm."[14] It was the start of a long career that by the 1920s had brought Hallén into the upper echelons of the party, where he joined those advocating *folkhemmet* in opposition to the class-struggle approach that had hitherto dominated party strategy. He also promoted the idea that a democratized church would allow Christian ideas to permeate *folkhemmet*.

FOLKHEMMET AND THE YOUNG CHURCH MOVEMENT

Prior to the First World War, predictably few Social Democrats shared Hallén's enthusiasm for the Young Church Movement. The nationalism of the latter ran directly counter to the labor movement's international outlook at that time. The tone of its glorification of Gustav II Adolf and Sweden's imperial era was also highly unappealing. Moreover, leading figures in the Young Church Movement such as Manfred Björkquist had launched a major fund-raising initiative on behalf of Sweden's military as part of a wider campaign against the liberal Prime Minister Karl Staaff, which led to the famous Bondetåget (Peasant March) of 1914 in support of armament. This was one meaning of Björkquist's famous slogan "Sweden's people—God's people": Swedes had been chosen.[15]

Björkquist's more militant nationalism contrasts with that of his friend Nathan Söderblom, who went on to become archbishop of Uppsala and primate of the Church of Sweden. Though undoubtedly patriotic, Söderblom saw the Church of Sweden as part of a universal and ecumenical Christianity centered on the individual rather than the nation. As Söderblom explained in his 1918 book *Religionen och staten* (*Religion and the State*), "Christianity's universalism is not bound up with one nation or another but lies in its very nature. The eternal value of the individual soul that this refers to, which is to say Christianity's individualism, takes the form of a universalism in which there is no Jew or Greek, no serf or free man, no man or woman, but where all are one in Jesus Christ."[16]

This perspective mirrors the more forward-looking side of the Young Church Movement: a radical attempt to renew the state church and make it more attractive for the working class. Björkquist was among the first to use the term *folkhem*, long before it came to be associated with Per Albin Hansson. Björkquist was probably inspired by his father-in-law Rudolf Kjellén, the nationalistic political scientist presented in chapter 7, who is generally regarded as having coined the term *folkhemmet*. For Björkquist, *folkhemmet* was virtually synonymous with *folkkyrkan*, the church as a home for the people. As he saw it, this was a battle-cry. This was the other meaning of the claim that Swedes were "God's people."[17]

Björkquist criticized the official church for being stale and hidebound; it was, he wrote, "a People's Church that does not struggle, whose being lies not in struggle, is like an idea that never becomes more than idea, or like a skeleton whose rattling vertebrae proclaim its death."[18] The Young Church Movement was thus about struggle, revitalization, and modernization of the state church. For Björkquist, the individual should be center stage: "I need hardly point out that the Swedish nation means people, first and foremost, and that the Church's most important duty is to ensure that everyone comes to Christ and gives an account of themselves. Our primary goal is always salvation of the individual soul."[19]

"The people" should, of course, be understood as an association of free individuals who have voluntarily chosen to take part in a joint project. Björkquist distanced himself from the obligation that had been a feature of the old state church: "Our People's Church will be a Lutheran church of the spirit, where every individual can live their own religious life while also living that of the people. A church should not constrain the individual with laws and forced teachings. Rather, individuals should find each other in free community. 'Where the spirit of the Lord is, there too is freedom.'"[20]

The church should be moved, in the words of Björquist biographer Torbjörn Aronson, away from "government officialdom and being tied to the state" to "civil society, voluntary society."[21] At the same time, Björkquist warned against restrictive claims to narrow community and adherence to dogma that were occasionally made by both free churches and the free associations that remained within the church, which he saw as a threat to individual freedom. As he saw it, the strength of a broad, nondoctrinal People's Church lay in the fact that, far from being a sect-like church, it provided space for a wide range of confessional approaches. In his view, this was something that separatist movements were not fully capable of: "The Church should have room for the individualist type who is made nauseous by stuffy meeting-houses. For this is what makes the service held under the lofty vaults so beautiful, that those sitting there can be alone with their God while also being supported by a congregation. This is why individualists, too, have felt at home in the services of the Church."[22]

For Björkquist, the issue was renewal of the church as it engaged with a changing society. He wanted to use the energy that he saw in the popular movements to transform the old authoritarian church. The People's Church, he argued, would be inspired by voluntarism and the adult education and temperance movements. Above all, it would transcend barriers of class: "Any church that styles itself as the People's Church has a formidable scope—the Swedish people.... This means that it cannot have its basis in class or party.... All classes should feel equally at home in the Church. Employers and employees should speak with equal enthusiasm about 'our Church.' In the Church, the servant girl and the mistress sit beside each other; the factory owner and the worker genuflect at the same altar. Thus it has been throughout the ages."[23]

It could reasonably be objected that masters and hands had not exactly sat side by side in Swedish churches throughout the ages. Even so, there were undeniable similarities between Hansson's talk of *folkhem*, with its famous formulation that a good home makes no distinction between privileged and neglected, favorite child and stepchild. In both instances, an emphasis on individual freedom was fused with a notion of community, albeit somewhat aloof and far from the speaking in tongues and sect mentality found in the free churches. Moreover, this ideal of community was tied up with a conception of a historically defined national identity.

As with *folkhemmet*, there were different versions of the People's Church: liberal (Söderblom), social-democratic (Hallén), and conservative

(Björkquist). As Lars Gunnarsson explained, "The idea of a People's Church was politically ambiguous. It had both national and democratic aspects. It fitted with both conservative and liberal understandings of the Church. For High Church adherents, the People's Church overlapped with a conservative view of the state. The Low Church position foregrounded the democratic role of a People's Church. This accorded with the liberal view of the state. The People's Church was seen as an associative body."[24]

The conservative nationalist aspect of the People's Church idea would prove troublesome for its advocates when the Nazis took power in Germany and adopted the idea of the *Volkskirche*. Theology professor Einar Billing, one of the advocates for a People's Church (more on this below), wrote in 1942 that he "winced as if struck with a whip" when the Nazis appropriated the concept of a People's Church. He was particularly discomforted by Björkquist's slogan "Sweden's people—God's people."

Billing argued that the idea of the People's Church had never for a moment implied that "our nation was somehow superior to others."[25] For his part, Björkquist continued to assert his nationalist views, although in 1934 he published an article in the magazine *Vår Lösen* in which he distanced himself from Nazi theories of a racial national community; he condemned the idea of a homogeneous culture under such a secularized and racist state.[26]

LUTHER AS A NATIONAL ROLE MODEL

What, then, did Martin Luther have to do with *folkhemmet*? For the Young Church Movement, it was important to secure religious legitimacy for its neonationalist ecclesiastical program. This meant showing that the spirit of Luther was hovering benignly over Sweden's state church. No one responded to this challenge with greater zeal than Einar Billing, the bishop and theology professor mentioned earlier in this chapter as one of the founders of the Young Church Movement. For most of his life, he sought to disprove the claims of more radical Protestant free churches that a state church was un-Lutheran. Billing, the son of Gottfrid Billing, a prominent conservative churchman, sought to form links with the new popular movements rather than resisting them as his father had.

In his 1927 book *Sveriges ställning i den evangeliska kristenheten* (*Sweden's Place in Evangelical Christianity*), Einar Billing offered a thorough description of the strong ties between Luther and Sweden. When first presented in German as a lecture at the University of Königsberg, it opened as follows: "Sweden's position in evangelical Christianity is entirely defined by a unique feature, namely that Lutheran faith and creed have been taken up by the entire nation." In support of this thesis, Billing began by discussing what he saw as three high-water marks in the history of the Swedish nation.

The first was the parliament of Västerås in 1527 whose subject, according to Billing, was less Luther than a breach with the Roman Catholic Church and its deeply entrenched hierarchy within Sweden. There could no longer be two sovereigns, the Parliament declared. Billing underscored that these proceedings obviously had a crasser aspect—Gustav I Vasa's avarice for the church's property—but also that Vasa, unlike England's Henry VIII, was not an absolute monarch acting primarily in his own interests but a leader who "traveled from district to district in order to rouse the people to fight for Sweden's freedom from its alien oppressors."[27] The country's poverty weighed heavily on Billing, and it was in this context that the Crown's confiscation of the Church's excess wealth should be understood.

And in this fusion of temporal and spiritual, the state and the church had found a common cause: "Two liberation movements, one national and the other religious, met in the persons of Gustav Vasa and Olaus Petri. Lutheran and Swedish, the cause of the Reformation and the cause of the new free Swedish kingdom—that is what we wish here to emphasize—were banded together from the beginning."[28] This union was then confirmed at the Uppsala Synod of 1593. King Johan III was dead and his Catholic son Sigismund, who was already King of Poland, was expected shortly in Sweden. At that critical moment, Sweden's clergy—a deeply unimpressive body that, according to Billing, comprised "rustic peasant types lacking any trace of cultivation"—came together to safeguard the Lutheran faith.[29] These simple but courageous men succeeded in holding out against not only Sigismund but also his Calvinism-besotted uncle, Duke Karl, who was made livid by the news of the priests' decision. In them, Billing argued, the spirit of Luther at Worms in 1521 lived on.

Summarizing the significance of the Uppsala Synod, Billing quoted the words supposedly shouted by its presider: "Now Sweden is worthy of a man and we all have one God." He was entirely correct, observed Billing: "At that moment, Sweden definitively secured not only its religious unity but also its national unity." Billing then turned to consider

Gustav II Adolf and the Battle of Lützen in 1632, Sweden's world-historic contribution to saving the Reformation from the papist hordes. Billing asked whether the king's motives were political or religious. Yet that question was wrongly formulated, he explained. Rather, one could "safely take him at his word" when he said "Sweden's Sovereign and God's Church, which rests thereon, are well worth our submitting to pain and even to death itself." This, Billing argued, was a declaration of the old Germanic idea of the state as "the collective responsibility of everyone before God and under the law, with the king as its head, as supreme regulator of the affairs of the kingdom. Thanks primarily to the fact that Sweden's peasant class, never yielding to serfdom, had always had its say in matters of state, this idea had always been kept alive in Sweden. Now, the unheard-of determination of Karl IX and Gustaf Adolf, coupled with the Reformation, had given it new life."[30]

At this point Billing's real purpose becomes apparent: to anchor the idea of the Church of Sweden as primarily a People's Church rather than a state church. His principal objection to the idea of a state church is that it is associated with coercion, not that it is national or subordinated to temporal authority. He traces this back—once again—to the "old Germanic idea of the state," putting the emphasis firmly on "autonomy." Here we glimpse Billing's own historical moment in the idea of equal and universal suffrage, something that was felt to set Sweden's Lutheran tradition apart from those of other, especially Catholic, countries: the parish's autonomy and its right to choose its own priest. This democratic feature, Billing argued, embodied a Swedish tradition "unlike that of any other country" and had remained unbroken since the Middle Ages. The right of the congregation to elect its own vicar was in conflict with the demands of canon law, something that Billing saw as one of the factors that "as early as the medieval period made Sweden a problem child in Rome's eyes—and although Rome managed to partially restrict it, abolishing it outright proved impossible."[31]

The Church of Sweden was thus more than a state institution, for the simple reason that the relationship between people and priests was "far more personal than with any other official." These historical roots preceded the Reformation, and in several key aspects the Church of Sweden was more conservative than other evangelical churches—for example, as regards the office of bishop, which, in remaining unchanged since the Middle Ages, had preserved the apostolic succession. This continuity in the religious tradition, Billing argued, had enabled the Church of Sweden to put down deep roots. And yet, he continued, the Reformation had lent new force to this project of national liberation: "If the Church of Sweden has always been a People's Church, then it has and continues to be, to an even greater degree, a strictly Lutheran People's Church." Billing emphasized how "deeply the Lutheran and the Swedish have permeated one another," indeed, to such a degree that "Luther himself and his personality have gained a place in Sweden's national consciousness."[32]

Such was the completeness of this process that Billing felt able to conclude that "truly Luther has become Swedish, in the sense that it is quite unthinkable for us to imagine Sweden without him."[33] For Billing, then, the Reformation was closely tied to the struggle for national liberation, in much the same way as Lutheran theology was thought to have an intrinsic affinity with Swedish ideals and practices of freedom and democracy. And so it needs to be asked whether the ideas of the Young Church Movement drew their force from a seductive and self-flattering fantasy of the past or from how that past had actually been.

LUTHER AND THE SWEDISH STATE

What Luther would actually have thought of the Swedish state church is unclear. It is, of course, quite anachronistic to ascribe to him more or less modern notions of the state; he lived and wrote in a time before John Locke, Thomas Hobbes, and other social-contract theorists. He had no fixed opinions about the state, whether Swedish or any other—which was one of the reasons why some Nonconformist denominations argued that a state church was "un-Lutheran."[34] As Luther saw it, the church's power had a corrupting influence in the temporal world. Its proper domain was the inner life of the spirit, which should be entirely free so that people could become true Christians. At the same time, Luther was not necessarily trying to abolish the church as a universal organization so as to be able to replace it with national or local churches. Although he wavered between advocating confessional and territorial church organizations, his goals were unquestionably to put an end to the sale of indulgences for the redemption of sins, to convince people that the path to salvation lay in faith and not good works, and to replace the religious authority of the Catholic Church with the word of the Bible.[35]

The church had a duty to concern itself with the salvation of the individual and not to involve itself in worldly struggles for power. Luther wanted to distinguish between spiritual and temporal kingdoms, between the realm of faith, in which a Christian enjoyed complete inner freedom in accordance with the word of the Bible, and the prevailing political order and its laws. As he saw it, the boundary between these two realms had been muddied by the church's historical development into a hierarchical institution that prescribed how the Bible should be interpreted. And if the church neglected its primary duty as spiritual guide, the temporal power would be forced to intervene and rectify matters. Yet *temporal power* referred not to a state or an institution but to the people and laws that governed society. Unlike the church and canon law, these temporal laws constituted an authority appointed by God to which all Christians were bound to submit—not because they represented some higher political principle, however, but because they were sustaining the divinely ordained order and stability that was required in order for Christians to practice their faith in peace and quiet: Saint Paul's statement that "authority does not bear the sword in vain" was one of Luther's favorite Bible verses.

Luther expressed this view with particular clarity in his attack on the impoverished German peasants who launched a desperate uprising under the leadership of the radical Protestant preacher Thomas Müntzer. In 1524–1525, this revolt swept across Swabia, Thuringia, and Franconia before being brutally crushed by the nobles. The peasants presented their demands in Die Zwölf Artikel (the Twelve Articles), which included the people's right to choose their own priests, a reduction in the tithe, the abolition of serfdom, less day work, more reasonable rents, and the restitution of common lands.[36] At first, Luther was relatively favorably inclined toward the peasants' demands and urged both sides to show restraint. But after the peasants advanced violently, burning monasteries and manor houses and causing people to flee, he sided with the masters and exhorted them to crush the uprising. In May 1525, he penned the tract "Against the Murderous, Thieving Hordes of Peasants" in which he wrote these notorious words: "Whosoever can, should smite, strangle, and stab, secretly or publicly, and should remember that there is nothing more poisonous, pernicious, and devilish than a rebellious man. Just as one must slay a mad dog, so, if you do not fight the rebels, they will fight you, and the whole country with you."[37]

According to some estimates, around 100,000 peasants were killed.[38] Even so, Luther's response to the German peasants' revolt provides some support for Billing's larger thesis that Luther's two-kingdoms doctrine worked well in Sweden for sociopolitical reasons. The division into temporal and spiritual powers took on a very different meaning in Sweden than it did in Germany. In Sweden, there was no conflict between feudal princes who invoked ancient Roman laws in support of serfdom and the landless peasants who had been radicalized by Luther and other reformers' ideas about spiritual equality. Instead, Luther's ideological attack on the Catholic Church was exploited by the newly formed and centralized nation-state. For Gustav I Vasa, preserving the supremacy of temporal authority meant, first and foremost, confiscating the church's property.[39]

And the Swedish peasants were not serfs but free men who owned their own land, were accustomed to local autonomy, and had their own estate in Parliament; the German peasants' Twelve Articles had in key respects already been fulfilled in Sweden. While this of course did not prevent Gustav I from both deceiving and brutalizing the peasantry, the situation in Sweden in the sixteenth century is hardly comparable to the bloody Peasants' War in Germany. Instead, the guiding principle was summarized in the slogan "a country must be built on laws," even though both kings and nobles had a tendency to stretch the precept.[40] From a Lutheran perspective, this was important: Luther had condemned the German peasants because of their violent lawlessness, not because he was opposed in principle to their calls for fairer treatment.

This did not mean that that Sweden's peasantry was particularly receptive to Luther's ideas.[41] On the contrary, there is near-consensus among scholars that Sweden's peasant population clung to the old Catholic customs and rituals for as long as they could. Sweden's was a top-down Reformation. Luther offered an excellent weapon in the struggle between elites in Scandinavia, particularly for Gustav Vasa's separatist project. Although political power in the Union of Kalmar was fairly decentralized—the court in Copenhagen found it difficult to manage the local rulers in Sweden and Norway—the Scandinavian Church as the extended arm of Rome was a reasonably effective and centralized institution. This did not mean that all bishops supported the Union—rather, that some of Gustav Vasa's main opponents were Swedish bishops who had the Danish king to thank for their appointments. And in this instance, the temporal authority claimed by the Catholic Church had played a crucial political role. In 1520, when Gustav Vasa just had taken up arms against the Danish king, a hundred or so presumed rebels against the Union of Kalmar had been executed, the so-called Stockholm Bloodbath. They were not executed as rebels against the crown, however, but as "heretics" according to canon law. While the Swedish bishop Gustaf Trolle was a driving force, the Danish King Christian II presumably had nothing against being rid of his opponents, including Gustav Vasa's father.[42]

For Gustav Vasa, whom Billing describes as indifferent to doctrinal questions, the appeal of Luther's teachings was that they conferred legitimacy on his efforts to break the power of the church. In the early 1500s, the church owned about a fifth of all cultivated land in Sweden, roughly as much as the nobility, which made the bishops important political players.[43] The state was weak by comparison, with only 5 percent of the cultivatable land; the rest, around half, was owned by free peasants. Moreover, the king was massively in debt to the Hanseatic city of Lübeck, which had sponsored his uprising. Confiscating the church's property was thus an attractive policy on several counts: in the short run it would allow Gustav Vasa to pay off the debt to Lübeck, and in the long run it would strengthen the power of the sovereign. The confiscated property could also be used to buy support among another elite group that might present problems: the nobility.[44]

The effects of Gustav Vasa's reinforcing of temporal power at the expense of the church were felt in several directions. On the one hand, the Reformation meant that the church's spiritual authority was transferred to the state. This had been decreed by God, and so no other authority—the Pope, for instance—was able to countermand decisions or actions taken by the king. This meant that the state could claim authority over practically every aspect of their subjects' lives. Relatively poor but heavily militarized and doctrinally homogeneous, Sweden's unitary state proved to be a formidable instrument of war in the service of king and nobility.

For Sweden's peasant class, however, the rise of an ambitious unitary state was at times a human catastrophe that bore little resemblance to the Germanic community evoked by Billing. During Sweden's imperial period, in the seventeenth and eighteenth centuries, Swedish peasants were subjected to ferocious pressure from above in the form of heavy taxes and conscription, which had received the blessing of preachers in their parish churches. Everyday life was also strictly regulated by religion. Karl XI's Church Law of 1686 set down detailed prescriptions for religious practices such as baptism, holy communion, weddings, funerals, and the ceremony known as churching of women.[45] From this perspective, the Lutheran unitary state that evolved in Sweden in the seventeenth and eighteenth centuries was a frighteningly conformist society in which the state controlled its subjects both spiritually and materially.

On the other hand, the weakening of church power had benefits for local communities and the peasantry in Sweden. Since not all power could be transferred to the fairly primitive state apparatus, the surplus often ended up in the hands of the local peasantry and parish council. More than just tools of state authority, these local forums were, as Eva Österberg put it, "organs for solving local problems but also a political stage on which local communities could formulate collective protests against their rulers."[46] We are arguably dealing with a Lutheran version of Catholicism's subsidiarity principle.

What is more, as Billing pointed out, Sweden had a long tradition of popular influence over the choice of parish priest, which the Catholic Church had never managed to break and which had now been sanctioned by Luther's stance on the issue. This freedom to choose might often have been curtailed by local nobles or state interference, but it did represent a limit on the church's power in the local community: priests were required to do the king's bidding, but they also had to remain on friendly terms with at least the most influential parishioners. These power relations were not static, of course: the struggle between king, peasantry, and nobles ebbed and flowed. In the long run, however, Sweden's peasants held their own relatively successfully. After the nobility's advances during the first phase of Sweden's imperial era—particularly under Gustav II Adolf and Queen Christina—came Karl XI's Great Reduction, which in one blow curtailed the power of the nobility and restored both the power of the crown and the position of the peasantry.[47]

FREEDOM AND SUBJUGATION

Even so, there is perhaps some truth to Billing's claim that Luther had become Swedish—but in another sense than the bishop intended. At a deeper level, what makes Sweden Lutheran is not the good relations between priest and congregation or the popular basis of the state church but the fertile soil that Sweden offered for some of Luther's ideas about the position of the individual in relation to community, the importance of reading, and family relationships between men, women, and children.

Devout Christians are in direct contact with God, claimed Luther; they answer to no higher temporal or spiritual authority on the issue of salvation. This was the fundamental idea behind the Protestant Reformation and also a main thread in Luther's own life. He was born in 1483 into a relatively affluent family in the Thuringian town of Eisleben. His father was a successful mine owner and his mother came from a burgher family; the idea was that Martin would train to become a lawyer. However, at the age of twenty-two, shortly after having earned a degree in philosophy and begun his legal studies, he rebelled against his father's plans and became a monk. Although his father was furious, Martin had the approval of a higher power: after his father was almost killed by lightning, Martin had a vision that he should enter a monastery. Backed by his own readings of the Bible, he then took on the church.[48]

From one perspective, Luther was truly a rebel. This was the view taken by Hegel, who, always inclined to see grand narratives of development through history, argued that Luther paved the way for the modern conception of the free individual.[49] Luther's position on individual freedom of conscience marked a break with an older Christian tradition of torturing, burning, and executing those who offered interpretations of the Bible that contradicted church teachings. In this regard, Luther was very different from other Protestant reformers, notably John Calvin, who ordered the execution of Spaniard Michael Servetus as a heretic during his rule of Geneva. From another perspective, however, this inner freedom can be considered a form of discipline. The individual freely submits to higher authorities—fathers, priests, rulers, societies—on the understanding that their commands are the voice of the individual's own Christian conscience. Instead of asserting their own irrepressible will and challenging the collectivity and its instruments of power, pious Lutherans internalized society's norms, making it both easier and cheaper for rulers to govern them.

This strand of criticism of Luther began with Nietzsche's attack on the Reformation. Nietzsche's principal objection to Luther was that he had successfully revitalized Christianity; had Luther failed in this, what Nietzsche called the slave religion would have died out, making room for the aristocratic sovereignty that Nietzsche wished to see in the individual. But Nietzsche, who never did anything by halves, hated

Luther on every level, from the personal to the philosophical: Luther was weak willed and invented the idea of salvation by faith alone only because he was unable to perform the good works that the church expected from him. In doing so, he created a hateful conscience, that troublesome inner voice that prevented people from realizing themselves.[50] This critique would find an echo, across the twentieth century, in Michel Foucault's famous condemnation of Western modernity: the soul has become the body's prison.[51]

Even though Luther attacked the Roman Catholic Church's claim to have a monopoly on interpreting the Bible, he also insisted that professional clerics had special privileges with regard to the interpretation of God's word. Protestant priests had authority over their congregations and directed their reading of the Bible by means of sermons, pedagogical simplifications, prefaces, and several other more or less subtle exercises of power. This was not merely an issue of doctrinal control; it was a pedagogical measure made necessary by widespread illiteracy. The Lutheran project presupposed a major educational initiative by which the people would be taught both to read (but not necessarily to write) and to correctly understand the sacred texts. The most important tools were the catechisms, which hammered the message home in a series of questions and answers:

What does such baptizing with water signify?

Answer: It signifies that the old Adam in us is to be drowned and destroyed by daily sorrow and repentance, together with all sins and evil lusts; and that again, the new man should daily come forth and rise, that shall live in the presence of God in righteousness and purity forever.

Where is it so written?

Answer: Saint Paul, in the Epistle to the Romans, chapter 6, verse 4.[52]

The indoctrination aspect of Lutheranism has been noted by many historians. Hilding Pleijel, a prominent Swedish church historian, coined the phrase "a world of Household Codes" to describe the intellectual horizon of the Lutheran unitary state. Part of the Lutheran Catechism, the Household Codes comprised a series of Bible verses that prescribed how various members of society should undertake their duties in accordance with the so-called Three Estates Doctrine, a functional division of people into the domestic estate (economics), the spiritual estate (religion), and the temporal estate (politics). Pleijel explained it thus:

It is unquestionably difficult for people today, who have grown up in the wake of nineteenth-century individualism, to form a clear understanding of the commanding position that the Household Codes occupied as social norms in the old Sweden. They were, in effect, the very foundation of how people thought and acted with regard to social issues. In sermons and expositions of the Catechism, in the statements of the church leadership and in biographical accounts, in the rituals of the Mass and in the visual arts, indeed, even in parliamentary and committee records—everywhere we see the pervasive influence of this fundamentally Lutheran approach to things.[53]

At the same time, since its publication in 1970, Pleijel's book *Hustavlans värld* (*A World of Household Codes*) has been challenged by scholars who argue that it overstates both the public status of the Household Codes and the ease with which rulers controlled their subjects' thoughts. For instance, several historians of the seventeenth century have pointed out that free peasants occupied a relatively strong position in local society and that priests functioned more as administrators at parish committees than as agents of the central authority.[54] The real change brought about by the Reformation concerned perhaps less the content of the religion than the forms in which it was communicated. Ideological persuasion now took the place of commands.

For all its conservatism, the Lutheran Catechism was subversive in form: the congregation asked questions ("what does this mean?") and the person in authority replied by referring to the relevant Bible verses ("it is written"). In her 2013 doctoral dissertation, historian Kajsa Brilkman argued that the Lutheran unitary state's ideal object was a subject who not merely obeyed but who understood the reason for obedience. Studies of church records show that the Reformation failed in one of its central ambitions: a large number of people still had only a very hazy understanding of Christianity's fundamental tenets. This was nonetheless, as Brilkman put it, discursive progress: the idea that people could be defined on the basis of their relationship to knowledge of the Bible had now been established.[55] Reading, too, came to assume a central role in this context.

Although in practice priests expected congregations merely to rattle off the catechism by rote, the ability to read was an ideological precondition of Lutheranism. From an early stage, Luther had argued for the establishing of *Volkschule* (schools for the people) in Germany, while in Sweden the pressure to learn to read grew after the church introduced *husförhör* ("house interviews"), annual tests of its members' literacy and knowledge of Luther's Small Catechism. In the Church

Law of 1686, congregations were instructed to make arrangements for some school teaching, which eventually led to the National School Act of 1842 (Folkskolelagen). Other factors that helped spread literacy in Sweden included the structure of the book market. While books in major European languages could count on a relatively large aristocratic audience across national boundaries, Scandinavian publishers had to contend with far more limited national markets. As a result, they were forced to publish books that appealed to people with more modest means, such as works on practical subjects like farming and other business activities.[56]

Rising literacy rates did not, of course, change the fundamentally repressive and collectivist features of the Lutheran unitary state. On the contrary, the primacy accorded to reading rested on the existence of a privileged text that, though open to private interpretation, was not allowed to give rise to public divisions that might affect the collective solidarity. At the same time, increased literacy also led to a profound shift within contemporary Swedish society. More Swedes than ever before were now able to acquire knowledge about worldly matters such as agriculture, law, medicine, and other practical subjects. Moreover, the state had weakened the church's power on the local level, where growing numbers of well-to-do peasants had learned to read, argue, and quote from the Bible—abilities that they could also use when negotiating with state authorities.[57] In public life, there were virtually no opportunities for imagining a world without rulers, but as private individuals, those at the bottom were now far better equipped to meet those in power.

FROM CONVENT TO GIRLS' SCHOOL

Interestingly, Billing entirely omitted to mention a central aspect of the Lutheran heritage that bears heavily on the historical development of social relations in Sweden: its view of the family. When Luther explained the Fourth Commandment in his Large Catechism, he offered the following clarification: "For all authority flows and is propagated from the authority of parents"; because the authority of parents comes directly from God, so, too, does all other power. This is a deeply patriarchal notion, of course, particularly if one follows Luther's subsequent reasoning, which is concerned solely with the legitimacy of paternal authority. "On the inside, we are all alike, and there is no difference between man and wife; but on the outside, in society, God has decided that the husband shall rule and that the wife should be subservient to him."⁵⁸

However patriarchal it may be, this emphasis on the family's importance differs suggestively from the Catholic view of everyday life. For the latter, celibacy was one of the good works through which a person might achieve salvation; the slogan was "marriage populates the earth, virginity populates heaven."⁵⁹ Luther, in contrast, regarded sexuality as one of God's gifts to humanity. For this reason, Germanist and Luther scholar Birgit Stolt has tried to correct the image of Luther as a killjoy by drawing attention to his almost frivolous view of "wine, women, and song."⁶⁰ In his table talk, Luther, wondering aloud about how to keep the devil and despair at bay, had himself famously declared "then you should eat, drink, and seek company" and fly with your soul "to other thoughts, dance, or pretty girls."⁶¹ The good Christian environment was no longer the chaste life of a monk or a nun but the good home, which acquired an almost sacred status in Protestantism.

While Luther's veneration of the family and the home might now seem deeply conservative and misogynist, it involved a reassessment of prevailing gender relations and bolstered the position of women and children in important respects. As with his view of freedom, its pedagogical goal was complex: Luther wanted to "bring children up to be outwardly submissive to parents and other authorities while being inwardly independent of them."⁶² This perspective may not have been full-throated liberal individualism, but it deviated from the patriarchal orthodoxy and, if anything, seems to have anticipated Ellen Key's idea that children should be raised to have inner self-reliance.

Luther also led by example. In the summer of 1525, he married Katharina von Bora, one of several nuns whom he helped to escape from their convent by hiding them in a cart that delivered food. Their long and happy marriage resulted in six children, of whom four survived. Luther and Katharina also fostered a number of nephews and nieces, which swelled their household considerably. Luther liked to portray himself as being firmly under his wife's thumb when at home and presented Käthe, as she was known, as head of their house. While this may have been an exaggeration, she was evidently an energetic and resourceful woman. She turned their home, a former convent, into a small family business comprising a guesthouse, brewery, piggery, and large fruit orchards and vegetable gardens.⁶³

Luther's theological valorization of the family served to increase the respect and esteem in which women were held. Marriage ceased to be about intercourse with a woman—"anyone could do that," Luther argued—but about running a household and rearing children. Luther could not imagine life without women: "Homes, cities, businesses, and governments would disappear. Men could not cope without women. Even if men were able to conceive and give birth to children, they would still not be able to cope without women."[64]

Luther's view of the family must be seen in this light: not as reinforcing the patriarchal order but as shifting its locus from the religious spaces of churches and convents to the peasant household. For women, this meant a loss of empowerment: as an institution, the convent had been a space of freedom for women who wished to devote themselves to cultural and intellectual activities. But it also meant that women and children became visible in society in a new way—still subordinated but now seen and included. Paradoxically, this strengthening of family culture can be thought of as increased individualism: assertion of the family's role in socializing children points to the growing importance of teaching, child raising, and personal development.[65] People should be shaped in ways that better prepared them to deal with a changing world and perhaps even to improve their position in society.

Luther's recommendation of primary schooling for all was crucial in this respect. As early as 1520 he had published *An den christlichen Adel deutscher Nation von des christlichen Standes Besserung* (*To the Christian Nobility of the German Nation*), a tract in which he encouraged every city to establish schools for boys and girls.[66] The consequences of Luther's appeal became clear when other reformers followed him by starting schools for girls and writing schoolbooks specifically for girls. When the Reformation was officially put into effect in Brandenburg, the heart of what would later become Prussia, there were four schools for girls and fifty-five for boys. By the end of the sixteenth century, the number of girls' schools had increased to forty-five, compared with one hundred for boys.[67]

In this regard, there was a convergence between the Reformation and the marriage patterns of northwestern Europe that we examined in chapter 3. This region included Catholic countries, of course, but for the most part the geography of Protestantism coincided with countries where nuclear families, late marriages, and few children were the norm. This pattern is also evident regarding schools and education for girls. It is particularly interesting to consider Germany in this light, which offers a perfect case study by virtue of having both Catholic and Protestant regions. When women were first admitted into universities in Prussia in 1908, their number included eight times as many Protestants as Catholics, even though Catholics made up a third of the population. Although today the gap is greatly diminished, even now there is a significant difference in educational level between Catholic and Protestant women in Germany.[68]

Whether Luther in fact argued for women to be subordinate to men is thus debatable. As Inger Hammar has observed, his view of the family and his assertion of men and women's equality before God would subsequently be used by women seeking greater gender equality.[69] When religious feminists in nineteenth-century Sweden demanded better education and a stronger position for women within marriage, they did not attack the Household Codes but instead invoked Luther's ideas about Christian freedoms. Among those who shared the Lutheran worldview, this conflict ebbed and flowed. In the early nineteenth century, the text of the marriage vows was changed so that women promised not to submit to their husbands but simply to be devoted wives—a reform that conservative priests in the 1870s sought to reverse.

REVIVALISM AND DIVERSITY

The launch of a Lutheran "People's Church" in the early 1900s was a way to counter the challenge presented by the revivalist movement; it was hardly a coincidence that the Young Church Movement arose at around the same time as Pentecostalism began to establish itself in Sweden. This does not mean that the conflict between pluralism and uniformity was entirely new. This issue had kept the Swedish authorities busy since the eighteenth century, when the first signs of discontent with state church orthodoxy began to appear.[70]

As could have been predicted, the first threat came from within the Lutheran tradition in the form of *pietism*, a movement that, far from breaking with Lutheran logic, followed it to its logical conclusion. As its name suggests, pietism strongly emphasized the role of piety and private spirituality in religious life; adherents viewed the regulation of worship in churches as austere and emotionless. Instead, they organized more spontaneous meetings, in private homes and without the presence of a priest, at which the focus was on personal transformation and the individual's relationship to God. The movement originated in Germany—its spiritual home was the city of Halle—and spread to Sweden in the early 1700s. Although the Swedish authorities sought to suppress pietism, issuing strict edicts against it in 1684 and 1706, it was an uphill battle. The movement was given a further boost by the soldiers of Karl XII who returned to Sweden in 1720 from Russian prisons where they had been influenced by pietist ideas.[71]

Pietism, at least in its less radical form, made significant inroads into the Swedish state church, thanks in part to the publication of the hymnal *Mose och Lambsens visor* (*Songs of Moses and the Lamb*) in 1717. But it was also firmly suppressed by the adoption of the Conventicle Act of 1726, which outlawed religious meetings held outside of the Church of Sweden. This tug-of-war set the pattern for relations between the Swedish state church and its critics: alternating phases of repression and conflict followed by co-optation from above and infiltration from below. It neatly illustrates the dual position of a state church: the church's monopoly gave it a tremendous advantage over rival religious groups but at the price of deference to a state authority that had plenty of other concerns besides doctrinal orthodoxy. Between the early 1800s and early 1900s, the state pushed for greater tolerance for Catholics and Jews even as the more orthodox positions were eased by growing interest in scientific discovery and education. The Swedish clergy's close integration into peasant society played a key role in this process. As Nina Witoszek noted in an essay on the so-called Nordic Enlightenment, Scandinavia was characterized by a more practically oriented Enlightenment philosophy that relied on rural priests rather than nobles.[72] The real challenge to the unitary state church came from the nineteenth-century revivalist movements to the west, principally the United States and Britain.

Radical new ideas put pressure on the state church. The struggle over doctrinal authority once again moved center stage. "Where is it written?" revivalist preacher Paul Peter Waldenström used to ask, contrasting independent reading of the Bible with the church's own interpretation.[73] We see here the radical implications of the Lutheran idea that everyone should be able to read the Bible in their own language: this ability could be used to challenge the existing authorities, be they in Rome or Uppsala.

As Mark Daniel Säfström asked in his doctoral study of Waldenström, "How was it possible that Sweden went from being a society in which national solidarity rested on identification with a unitary Lutheran state church, to being a society that permitted religious diversity and freedom of conscience?"[74] The key word here is *national*: the Swedish state church had invested almost its entire ideological capital in the notion that there was complete agreement between the nation and its variety of Protestantism. But if this was not the case—if one could be Methodist, Baptist, or something else, and still be a good Swede—then what remained of the state church apart from an empty shell? And, vice versa, were those who left the Church of Sweden not in danger of being relegated to membership of a marginal sect that had no connection to Sweden's central political institutions? When Archbishop J. O. Wallin wrote a fiery speech attacking the Methodist George Scott, whose friend and disciple Carl Olof Rosenius would become a leading figure in the revivalist movement within the Church of Sweden, he criticized him for putting excessive emphasis on "inner feelings." He contrasted such "enthusiasm" with a Swedish tradition anchored in the state church: "Our nation . . . is fundamentally godfearing, honest, open-minded, law-abiding, both earnest and life-affirming, loving, and brave. . . . We are still the nation of Gustaf II Adolf who rose from prayer to win victory. Such a people cannot become *Methodist* without first ceasing to be *Swedish*."[75]

The solution was an ambiguous compromise. After the relatively severe suppression of revivalist movements in the first half of the nineteenth century, the state church's religious monopoly was gradually dismantled in a series of measures, among them the Conventicle Act of 1858 and the Dissenter Laws of 1860, that made it possible for Swedish citizens to be members of certain religious groups such as the Catholic Church and the Methodist Church; in a somewhat ambivalent concession to pluralism, the state church's official name henceforth would be the Church of Sweden. Other stages in this process included the municipal reforms of the 1860s, which changed parishes into political entities, and the parliamentary reforms of 1865, which abolished the four-estates parliament.[76]

Sweden's leading intellectuals and priests were strikingly open and pragmatic in their attitudes toward revivalist reading and religious fervor. Geijer, for example, saw in the crisis of Christianity an upward movement of mighty social forces. In a letter to Fredrika Bremer in 1841, he wrote punningly that in "the present chrisis of Christian faith" he expected more from the laity than from the clergy, "who speak on behalf of their office and style themselves lawyers for our Lord." This was especially true of women: "These may think that their cause needs no advocacy. I wish to add a conviction of my own. I believe that *women* will play a decisive role in this crisis."[77] Geijer also connected the struggle for religious freedom, "particularly Anabaptists and

Methodists," with another social movement: "Dissenters have earned everlasting glory since it is chiefly due to their tireless exertions that the Slavery Abolition Act has been passed by the British Parliament.... It is thanks to the truly Christian zeal of these sects in our time that the state churches have been awoken from their long slumber."[78]

Perhaps it is unsurprising that Geijer, who by this point in his career had left his old conservative views far behind, should have taken this view. But his old comrade from the Gothic League, Esaias Tegnér, would also adopt a pragmatic approach to the revivalist movement that was emerging in the figure of the charismatic Emilie Petersen—known as "the grandmother of Herrestad" in reference to her farm in Tegnér's own parish of Växjö. Petersen held prayer meetings, started one of Sweden's first Sunday schools, and founded a private school for local children—all this in the 1830s. When the harvest failed in 1838, she created a women's association that trained poor women for work, and at the end of her life she founded an institution for rehabilitating prisoners on the model of Charles Fourier's phalansteries.[79] As Tegnér wrote of her, "She is famous as an educated if somewhat excitable woman, deeply religious and devout, though very possibly guilty of extravagant 'readery' and pietism, but since her behavior is otherwise exemplary and she, like other readers, would rather serve than condemn her fellows, she is welcome to fear God in whatever way her conscience and convictions dictate.... This arrangement has undoubtedly done much good in the congregation."[80]

But the new revivalist movements also took a more ambivalent stance. Pietists and Moravians had a tradition of being active within other churches. Here is P. O. Enquist's depiction of Swedish revivalism in his novel *Lewis resa* (*Lewi's Journey*): "The core of Christianity is not dogma but an inner union of the heart with our Savior. Not a state-building religion, this is something private, a thought; we provide an idea, if other congregations take it up then all is well, and we then disappear like morning mist after sunrise."[81]

Plenty of Nonconformists remained in the Church of Sweden. The Dissenter Laws, for example, were a deterrent for many Baptists, who did not regard themselves as "apostates"; they were simply including the "evangelical doctrine."[82] For its part, the Swedish Evangelical Mission (Evangeliska fosterlandsstiftelsen) saw proximity to the state church as an aid to the work of expanding the kingdom of Christ since people trusted the Church of Sweden more than they did so-called separatist movements. Other denominations, such as the Methodist Church and the Salvation Army, never considered themselves part of the state church. The ambivalence was neatly summarized by Waldenström when he explained at an ecumenical meeting that the state church was "from a Christian point of view contrary to the Bible, from a church point of view contrary to principle, and from the perspective of Lutheranism contrary to Luther." Even so, he continued, it did not "negatively" follow from this that the state church should be abolished; it was needed to prevent Sweden from becoming a nation without religion.[83]

THE LUTHERAN SYNTHESIS

The free churches were modern Sweden's first popular social movement. Historian Gunnar Hallingberg describes the Nonconformist revolt as a "liberation movement," a struggle targeted at both the temporal scheme of things and the spiritual.[84] But in the Swedish context, it must also be understood in terms of Lutheranism as a state church. The Free Church movement developed and radicalized the emancipatory ideals immanent in the Lutheran tradition; the result was a dialectical process with unexpected and occasionally even undesirable consequences.

One example is what was known in the nineteenth century as *reading*. While there is fierce disagreement over whether Luther should be seen as a liberator or an authoritarian, almost all commentators agree that his insistence on being able to read the Bible in one's own language was historically crucial. Many historians have underscored the fact that most Swedish adults, despite their country's poverty, were literate by the start of the nineteenth century. Luther may not have anticipated the political and economic consequences of widespread literacy, but they are hardly the less important for that. In the same way as Luther's Reformation unintentionally paved the way for much that we now associate with national democracy—nation-states, an independent middle class, national languages, state schools—so too did this learning, as Elisabeth Gerle put it, "perhaps unintentionally . . . advance the progress toward democracy."[85]

However, the religious concept of reading is a more complicated question than it seems. Within the framework of the state church, reading meant studying the Catechism. It was more about giving people training than giving them freedom. And it was here that the world of the Household Codes anticipated the directives of twentieth-century social engineers. The free churches turned Lutheran orthodoxy on its head: reading should be critical and active; people should interpret and analyze texts, not just learn them by rote. The free churches also put a very different emphasis on writing. As Ronny Ambjörnsson explains, "The goal was not to learn about Martin Luther or Carl Olof Rosenius, it was to become a Martin Luther oneself."[86] The free churches' view of active reading was to influence the emerging labor movement, which put egalitarian education at the heart of its political vision.

In taking inspiration from the United States, Sweden's popular movements also absorbed Calvinist ideas, which, in contrast to the Lutheran tradition's emphasis on faith, assigned a prominent role to action. Sweden's free church, temperance, and labor movements likewise helped to disseminate relatively strict notions of industriousness and hard work centered on individual responsibility. As Per Svensson remarked, there is something slightly suspect about the supposedly "Lutheran" aspect of the Swedish work ethic.[87]

Luther's most fundamental idea, the idea that defines his revolt against the Catholic Church, is that faith, and faith alone, leads to salvation. No matter how many good deeds you do, God's grace is given only to those who are willing to receive it. For this reason, Sweden's state church has historically been regarded as doctrinally uninterested in virtuous living, from the fictive wayward priest in Selma Lagerlöf's *Gösta Berling's Saga* to the very real Anton Sundberg, the late-nineteenth-century archbishop who proverbially is supposed to have declared that "after religion and morality, what I hate most are small *snaps* glasses."[88] By "religion and morality," he meant the culture of virtuous living then being promoted by the temperance and free church movements. Nevertheless, both the free churches and the other grassroots movements were to make heavy demands not only on individual virtue but on how voluntary associations and congregations organized themselves as communities.

All of this brings us back to Björkquist's reflections on how a People's Church differed from free churches. For many people, the free churches' promises of more radical freedom and more genuine community were, at least initially, hard to resist. But the People's Church held two trump cards. For the large and growing number of people who were not particularly attracted by the prospect of joining a tight-knit, demanding, and at times even suffocating community, a state church or a People's Church presented an appealing alternative—a relaxed and diverse community with room for everyone and no burdensome demands on the individual.

Sweden, as Urban Claesson noted, is therefore defined by a unique synthesis: on the one hand, a Lutheran tradition that enjoins faith and subordination to the state; on the other, an Anglo-Saxon-inspired strand of thought that prizes personal responsibility, stubborn independence, and communitarian solidarity. Luther has both been preserved and marginalized in this process. As Claesson wrote, "Whatever of Luther still survives in Sweden today, it is not his strictures on morality. Sweden's legacy of personal virtue has its roots in another Protestant tradition, one in which we can distantly make out the figure of Calvin."[89]

Despite Hallén's untiring efforts to establish a People's Church in which the word *people* would stand for democratic ideals rather than an organic national community, he was ultimately defeated, even if he temporarily succeeded in recruiting Per Albin Hansson and Tage Erlander. Religion had already lost its grip on large swaths of the population by the time Social Democrats abandoned the antinational, class-based rhetoric of Marxism and threw themselves behind the idea of the "people" in the 1930s.[90] The ideals of nation, people, and democracy would instead be realized in *folkhemmet*, the secular twin of the People's Church.

Yet this tension between Luther and Calvin, far from going away, was translated into secular forms. Even today, there is a visible strain within social democracy between state socialists and grassroots leftists, which to a large extent hinges on different views of the state, the individual, and what we now call civil society. The state socialists combine a tendency toward Lutheran-style popular instruction that emphasizes faith (in the state) and affirms a form of individualism, while the grassroots left clings to a more demanding and communitarian view of individual responsibility that takes a critical view of the state and embraces self-management and empowerment in the associations and cooperatives of civil society.

At their best, these traditions form a productive, if sometimes unstable, amalgam. Even so, there is much at stake. The fact that the statist-individualist social contract includes an anticommunitarian element makes it difficult for those who wish to live in more independent communities, in a more autonomous civil society, and in accordance with values that quite possibly express a profoundly radical otherness in relation to the values of the unitary state and the customs and habits of the majority culture.

The question then arises whether Sweden can accommodate a deeper diversity without jeopardizing the social contract. Can citizens cope with a more pluralistic civil society without undermining generalized social trust and confidence in common institutions of universal reach? Setting aside their shared interest in the principle of live and let live, are Swedes actually capable of living alongside people whose values and practices they dislike? Contrarily, if the price for continued trust and solidarity is exclusion of the other, is that a price worth paying? Might it be the case that Sweden's high degree of social trust and public confidence in public institutions, despite being widely praised, are actually signs of an overly homogeneous society that has too much faith in the good and all-powerful state?

Pluralism is often celebrated in Sweden so long as its scope is limited to things that are essentially superficial. Diversity in the form of a wider range of food, music, and clothes is fine, but objections quickly arise when the issue is religion, gender relations, or the role of the family vis-à-vis care institutions and schooling. These objections are usually conveyed in terms of "quality assurance" and "evidence," which lead, in turn, to the values of standardization and uniformity implied in the Swedish social contract and the trump cards of its shared value-system: gender equality, children's rights, social equality, universalism, and individualism.

As the sociologist of religion Linnea Lundgren has shown, state policy with respect to religious minorities have for long been ambivalent. On the one hand, she described a celebration of minority religious communities and religious pluralism as a "resource." On the other hand, she noted a constant worry that these groups constitute a "risk," potentially undermining social cohesion and constituting a threat to national security. In an earlier period, such hopes and anxieties were directed at Catholics and evangelical Protestants; today Muslims are their focus.[91]

In countries such as the United States and Germany, churches have long played a key role in the areas of health, education, care services, and universities. Many leading universities in the United States have religious origins, and its pluralistic civil society is entirely based on a tradition that has not merely upheld religious freedoms but assigned a major role to churches and religious associations in the provision of welfare, care services, education, intellectual pluralism, and social community at large. In Germany and the Netherlands, religious diversity is also reflected in a different moral and institutional logic with regard to the organization of welfare and the influence of civil society on the (welfare) state.

A Lutheran Modernity? 293

In Sweden, in contrast, the Church of Sweden early on took the view that its duties were more moral and pedagogical in nature and that the state was responsible for citizens' physical well-being. In his 1916 tract *The Social Mission of Our Church*, a parish priest named Per Pehrsson noted that the church had a social role to play. But, he argued, its work with *diakonia* (a concept, imported from Germany, meaning service to the poor and oppressed) did not involve providing health care and care services as such but of encouraging a sense of shared responsibility that could then be fulfilled by the temporal authorities: "The view of our Church is that it properly falls to the state and the municipalities to provide care services for those in need, while the Church should work to strengthen our sense of responsibility to them."[92] As clarification, he pointed warningly to the Catholic Church and the Anglo-Saxon traditions of philanthropy, both of which were unsuited to Sweden.

But the warning gesture has been pointed in the other direction as well. Catholic theologian William Cavanaugh formulated a strong critique of the nation-state's claim to represent the "public good."[93] He described a historical process in which the size of the state increases in parallel to the accelerating individualization of society, as the medieval social order built on *societates* in the plural is steadily replaced by a modern society in the singular. Cavanaugh connected this development to the disintegration of natural communities and invoked Scottish philosopher Alasdair MacIntyre's suggestive portrait of the modern state: "The modern nation-state, in whatever guise, is a dangerous and unmanageable institution, presenting itself on the one hand as a bureaucratic supplier of goods and services, which is always about to, but never actually does, give its clients value for money, and on the other as a repository of sacred values, which from time to time invites one to lay down one's life on its behalf. . . . It is like being asked to die for the telephone company."[94]

The Catholic Church's mission, Cavanaugh argued, is to demystify the nation-state, to expose its similarity to the telephone company, and to restore the church's role as a set of core values, a community, and a care institution. In contrast to the Swedish theory of love, with its emphasis on state, individual, and universalism, Cavanaugh offered what he calls a "Christian theory of love" that brings together the church, the communion, and pluralism under the precept of *love thy neighbor*.[95] Although this critique reflects a synthesis of Catholic and American views on the relationship between state and civil society and is not specifically aimed at Lutheran nations, it is nonetheless an accurate enough description of the Swedish state, which has historically demanded enormous sacrifices from its subjects and managed their welfare in a bureaucratic fashion. In contrast to both Catholicism and Calvinism—which often prize community above loyalty to the state—Lutheran thinking seems to be open to the modern, effective, bureaucratic state (the telephone company) to a quite different degree than other denominations.

The consequences of this approach are not only that the church loses some of its social importance for its members—for whom a loss of faith is perhaps outweighed by a need for medical and other care services—but also that the ecclesiastical community becomes largely a transaction between an individual and a sermonizing priest on the one hand and between an individual and a distanced God on the other.

We find ourselves back where we started with Ingmar Bergman's and Paul Britten Austin's "vast Swedish theme" of painful, inescapable isolation and loneliness: in Bergman's case, in the shadow of a still-present Lutheran Church; in Austin's case, against a Swedish background of socialist equality and solidarity that is nonetheless impersonal—a secularized Lutheranism. In this book we seek to revise this dystopian vision by showing that loneliness and isolation are also about independence and freedom—these are two sides of the same coin and, for most Swedes, have been sources of both pleasure and suffering. In our coda, we accordingly turn to the future in order to offer our reflections on the possibilities and the limitations of this, perhaps the strangest of social contracts, in a time when the Lutheran unitary state is steadily retreating in the face of a more open but also more turbulent social order.

CODA

Prospects for Swedish Love

Freedom or Alienation?

"It is not necessary that God himself should speak in order to disclose to us the unquestionable signs of His will; we can discern them in the habitual course of nature, and in the invariable tendency of events," declares Alexis de Tocqueville in *Democracy in America*. His overall thesis is that history moves inexorably toward democracy, equality, and the kind of alienated individualism that he associates with equality.[1]

The authors of this book do not believe in God. Nor do we believe that changes in how people live are the result of iron laws of history. Even so, we are unable to disagree with Tocqueville. *If* history has a direction, it is surely moving toward a future in which more and more people see themselves as separate, independent individuals who consider their own lives, ambitions, and dreams as equal in value to anyone else's. This assumption is also supported by the World Values Survey (WVS). Since it began in 1981, WVS has shown a steady rise in the proportion of people identifying with what German political scientist Christian Welzel calls *emancipative values*, including freedom of expression, participation in decision-making, political activism, gender equality, and tolerance of ethnic minorities, foreigners, and homosexuals. According to Welzel, WVS is an index of a growing desire for freedom in the world, something he claims to have proven in a study pointedly titled *Freedom Rising* that draws on WVS data.[2]

This is not to say that people do not want community. Love, consideration, and empathy are every bit as natural as the desire for self-realization and freedom. It will always be gratifying to join with other people—indeed, even to submit to their will—to be rid of the painful obligation of being alone and become part of a larger context. Close-knit religious, social, or ideological movements will always return. It would be the height of liberal naivety to think that religion, nationalism, communism, and similar phenomena will ever be consigned to the dustbin of history. On the contrary, the desire for social community and a meaning in life beyond merely satisfying one's immediate needs will always be there, promising as they do to fill the existential vacuums created by capitalist alienation and social-democratic utilitarianism.

Yet no single ideology of community will endure for long. Over time, the close-knit community will always end up imposing a barrier on the individual's desire for autonomy. People like to talk about community but then act individually. The choice between freedom and subordination in a close-knit community is existentially rigged. Whoever chooses to leave the farm, the village, or the church can always tell themselves that they are free to return—that it is possible to have your cake and eat it too, to combine freedom and community. But this choice is possible only from a position of individual autonomy. Those subject to a closed hierarchy have no freedom of choice—whereas the autonomous individual is at least theoretically free to choose to return to the community.

This is why we replace our original bonds of community with increasingly provisional ones based on interests, feelings, and convictions that are immediate but also less socially coercive. The new communities that emerge to replace those vanishing traditional institutions are often ersatz temporary associations that lack real cohesive force.[3] Associations that prevent their members from leaving are unlikely to last long: the price for exit cannot be too high. Nation-states that confine their citizens are becoming rarer. Marriage can only survive if divorces are allowed. The future of the family depends on women having the same opportunities for self-realization as men—either through shared responsibility or external childcare.

There is no guarantee that this movement toward greater individualism will end happily. For Kant, the solution to people's asocial sociability was a global bill of rights that in a structured fashion could give the world's citizens freedom and equality, a vision he outlined in his book *Perpetual Peace*, published in 1795. But during the intervening two hundred years, we have seen time and again—from the French Revolution to the Arab Spring—how a desire for freedom slides into war and anarchy, which in turn paves the way for authoritarian, dysfunctional, or totalitarian states. While this in no way negates Kant's dream of a global bill of rights, it highlights the difficulty of balancing relations between state, family, civil society, and individual.

It is from this perspective that the prospects for Swedish statist individualism should be understood. The current social contract in Sweden is obviously under pressure. The modest and uniform national entity that was established in the first half of the eighteenth century today seems increasingly inadequate. Swedish society has become far more heterogeneous and pluralistic. The romanticism of Geijer's "Vikingen" ("The Viking") and "Odalbonden" ("The Yeoman") feels not only hopelessly inadequate but tainted by Nazism's worship of all things Nordic. In surveys, Swedes stand out in their rejection, by a huge margin, of an ethnic understanding of national identity in favor of one stressing rule of law and citizenship—and this notwithstanding the rise of the right-wing nationalistic Sweden Democrats (Sverigedemokraterna).

It would be premature, however, to announce the death of statist individualism. This book examines a historical legacy that has not only drawn its strength from the past but acted as midwife to modernity in Sweden. Geijer's vision of Swedes as independent and self-sufficient individuals, bound to their fellow citizens in a voluntary community guided by the rule of law under the protection of the state, has shown a remarkable ability to evolve in tandem with the changing needs and processes of the time.

One can be critical of the ideals and values implicit in Swedish political culture, but they have had tremendous historical impact. Far from petering out into naive utopianism, they have been fulfilled within the framework of politics as the art of the possible—for better and for worse. In this coda, we offer some reflections on three central issues relating to the tension between normative community and the inexorable march of history: First, what are the downsides and paradoxes of statist individualism? And second, is there an underlying and perhaps even self-destructive logic to the historical dynamic of statist individualism? Finally, we ponder the future prospects for this social contract: what is the prognosis for statist individualism in a future that is unfolding under the banner of globalization?

ON SERVILITY AND POWERLESSNESS

The Swedish social contract, as we argue, has been part of a movement toward individual freedom. But this liberation has always come with conditions. Its rhetoric has emphasized social equality and national solidarity. The Swedish social contract may in practice have served to promote the individual's emancipation from traditional social constraints, but it has come at the price of subordinating the individual to the state. This at times unholy alliance with the state has, at least potentially, left the individual vulnerable in relation to the state authorities. People's desire to escape from the social imperatives of membership in a community that creates dependency has been given recognition within the rigid framework of the welfare state. Greater individual autonomy *through* the state has not been accompanied by greater individual rights *in relation to* the state. Freedom and equality, autonomy and community have not always coexisted peacefully in *folkhemmet*.

Sweden's statist individualism is not unique in this regard. All societies are built on some kind of subordination of the individual vis-à-vis the collective. Social virtues are imprinted during childhood and formally institutionalized in laws and regulations. Modern sociology since pioneers Émile Durkheim and Marcel Mauss has its origins in the idea of social conformity and subordination in much the same way as modern political theory starts with contract theory in Hobbes and Locke.[4] Humanity's evolution from a state of nature to one of culture, it is argued, presupposes that individuals waive their claim to natural sovereignty. In this view, being an individual without compromising in the slightest would mean having to break the social contract and become a criminal.

According to the French philosopher Georges Bataille, the modern individual therefore confronts a fundamental choice between social obedience and individual revolt. Bataille aimed to show the absurdity of a system in which everyone and everything is a subject and no one is sovereign. He contrasted the purposelessness of eroticism with the servile functionality of utilitarianism. Drawing on Durkheim and Mauss, Bataille counterposed the sovereign "man himself" to what he called "*servile* man." The latter is trapped in a world of utilitarian thinking, order, productive labor, obedience to the law; servile man is confined within the social contract. "Man himself" is the *sovereign* man that has breached the social contract and lives in a world beyond usefulness, a world of disorder, destruction, crime, laziness, eroticism, and unlimited and meaningless consumption.[5]

These ideas had been developed by Michel Foucault, probably Bataille's most prominent disciple. There is a suggestive link to Sweden here: the French philosopher spent three unhappy years as a researcher in Uppsala in the late fifties. At Uppsala University, he worked on early drafts of his famous history of madness, the first in a series of studies of the diabolical nature of institutionalized power in the modern democratic state. In Foucault's analysis, the modern welfare state is portrayed as a decentralized system of insidious, subtle, all-seeing, and normalizing acts of power within which the individual scarcely exists except as the locus of isolated and futile moments of eroticized rebellion.[6]

It is hard to avoid the thought that Foucault's youthful experiences of Sweden, the well-meaning but cold welfare state par excellence, played a part in his intellectual and political development. In a 1968 interview he gave a decade after leaving Uppsala, where his dissertation had been savagely critiqued, Foucault made this reflection on Sweden: "It is perhaps the mutism of the Swedes, their silence and their habit of talking with elliptical sobriety, that prompted me to start writing and develop this endless chatter that I believe can only irritate a Swede.... [In Sweden] a human is but a moving dot, obeying laws, patterns and forms.... In its calmness, Sweden reveals a brave new world where we discover that the human is no longer necessary."[7]

Whatever the case, Foucault's analysis is clearly highly relevant for any deeper understanding of modern Sweden, a society in which obedience to the law and social control are so deeply imprinted in its citizens' souls that the authorities are seldom called on to take more concrete measures. Put more positively: Swedes always come out on top in international rankings for trust in both the state and fellow citizens and at the bottom for corruption and lawlessness (see the next section).

This voluntary subordination has been a source of provocation for both domestic rebels and foreign observers. The roots of discontent with Swedish conformism go deeper than the social-democratic welfare state. Even before the turn of the twentieth century, Ellen Key and August Strindberg—inspired, above all, by Nietzsche—were asserting the right to be egotistical; individual self-realization took precedence over the requirements of civic conformity. They may have directed their critique at a predemocratic Swedish society, but much of it was echoed by later critics of *folkhemmet*. One example is Roland Huntford, cited in chapters 2 and 11, who denounced Sweden as totalitarian.

Huntford's and Foucault's reactions attest, above all, to their painful encounter with the mentality that is locally known as *jantelagen*—a term derived from the conformist "laws" imposed by the fictional town of Jante in a 1930s novel by Danish-Norwegian author Aksel

Sandemose. Sandemose's intention was to describe how the ordinary townspeople had internalized their own subordination in the most brutal fashion, but *jantelagen* has taken on a life of its own in modern Sweden. Sometimes is invoked to describe how social-democratic egalitarianism stigmatizes talented and successful citizens.[8] At other times, it is used to describe an inner moral compulsion that makes Swedes obey rules and norms scrupulously, even in everyday situations when other countries' citizens typically behave in a more anarchic fashion.

Yet the state and social power are not always so subtle when it comes to traffic rules and numbered tickets for customer assistance. In some cases, the interventions are on the whole trivial. As British-American historian Tony Judt put it, if a certain measure of joyless conformism were the worst that could be said about the successful welfare-state model, then the Social Democrats could be forgiven for laughing all the way to the bank.[9]

At other times, however, the power of the Swedish state has manifested itself in an uglier fashion. The clearest example is perhaps the program of sterilization to which poor and vulnerable women were subjected in Sweden between 1934 and 1975. Formally, the law may not have authorized operations against the patient's will, but in many instances this was what happened in practice. The sterilizations were also part of a larger cluster of laws, regulations, and directives that impelled the state authorities and their administrators to act in various ways in the service of public health and public education. In this spirit, they assumed primary responsibility for "vicious" children, "immoral" women, and "degenerate" men.[10]

In many cases, this approach involved methods that in hindsight seem relatively unproblematic: child health-care centers, foster-care homes, schools, nursing homes—in other words, the entire battery of sociopolitical measures that are collectively termed the *welfare state*. Of course, there is no logical connection between creating favorable conditions for citizens and forcibly sterilizing people—but we cannot entirely get away from the fact that these two activities were not seen as contradictory by most people at the time.

Nor did Sweden's sterilization policy take place in a historical vacuum. American historian Peter Baldwin, who researched the ways that Western democracies handle deadly epidemics, argued that Sweden has a strong tradition of encroaching on the rights of the individual in the name of public health. As far back as the cholera epidemics of the nineteenth century, the Swedish state was an international outlier. Long after other countries adopted milder measures, it continued to physically inspect travelers, put the sick in quarantine, fumigate houses, and disinfect trade goods.

This pattern was repeated when the AIDS epidemic broke out in the 1980s. New laws were passed that extended the terms of existing legislation. General testing became the norm, doctors were authorized to instruct patients as to acceptable sexual behavior, and anyone who did not follow their instructions was liable to be taken into custody and put in quarantine. By the mid-1990s, this law had been invoked more than sixty times. Those taken into custody usually stayed there for around a year. Among other democracies, only the German state of Bavaria came close to Sweden in the use of coercive measures to combat the spread of the disease. As Baldwin noted, these draconian methods represented a continuation of a puritanical tendency that had long characterized Swedish society, particularly its grassroots movements. The fight against AIDS was bound up with the relentless war on drugs, prostitution, and alcoholism. Dionysus had to toe the line when public health was at stake.[11]

Sterilizations and measures to combat epidemics show that two mutually related phenomena have weakened the position of the private individual in the Swedish tradition. First, there is no counterweight to the state in either the political system or civil society. Sweden was and remains a kind of parliamentary autocracy. Unlike the United States or Germany, Sweden has no supreme court that can be asked to uphold or strike down laws that conflict with fundamental principles—for example, as inscribed in a constitution. The professions and trade guilds that might have offered some moral opposition were not independent either. Priests, doctors, and others working in health care and social services all were servants of the state.

Second, then as now, Sweden lacks a clear and legally binding rights legislation that would enable its citizens to make an effective case against the state. Of course, this is not to say that Swedes lack rights. On the contrary, the Swedish social contract is constructed as a network of rights to all kinds of social goods, from cradle to grave.[12] But the rights enjoyed by Swedish citizens are of the kind that are usually termed *social rights*, rights that attach to the population as a whole, often legally formulated in terms of relatively vague "obligations" that relate to the state's responsibility rather than recognizing the individual's inalienable rights that can be invoked in a court of law.

Paradoxically, for this reason Swedes have more concrete power in their relationships in the private market than in their dealings with their "own" democratic state.[13] If, for example, your child is injured at day care, the odds of your securing damages from the municipality are considerably less than those of your successfully suing your car mechanic. This has been called the silent powerlessness of Swedes with regard to the welfare state.[14] The individual's only means of exerting power is via political parties and membership in associations that have a consultative role. But these avenues are very indirect and limited.

It is true that the rules of the political game are changing. The old corporatist order dominated by the state, large companies, and a centralized trade union movement has been undermined. More demanding and self-confident than ever before, individuals and minority groups are today arguing for greater opportunities to assert themselves in the sphere of political power. Rights policies lend this discussion an ideological basis as it relates both to the state and to regional and municipal entities. With respect to the handling of epidemics and navigating the balance between state power and individual rights, between concern over collective security, national health, and personal responsibility, the global COVID-19 pandemic is one example of this shift. Following Baldwin, one might have expected Sweden to follow a more draconian policy, but instead a more liberal, even libertarian, approach came to dominate, at least during the first phase in the spring of 2020.

And yet the fundamental tensions between different normative ideals remain. Individual rights often have to take a backseat, partly to the principle of municipal autonomy and partly to welfare policy in general. Local democracy and national quality are trump cards compared to the claims and demands made by individuals and minorities.

In other words, the statist individualist contract, by which the state guarantees the individual certain resources (social rights), within the framework of the principle of universal welfare and social equality at a national level, tends also to undermine individual claims to power and real rights that can be asserted in law.

ON ALIENATION AND ANOMIE

Thus far we have considered the problem of the overly powerful state, but there is also reason to be concerned about how far individualization might go. Writers, intellectuals, and politicians have been grappling with this question ever since modern market society began its triumphal procession in the late eighteenth century. The state's iron grip on the individual may have threatened the legitimacy of the social contract, but leading philosophers and intellectuals have been no less exercised by the troubling possibility that individualism might dissolve the social glue that binds society together.

Some of these thinkers have claimed to discern an inherent and self-destructive logic whereby our ever-growing preoccupation with our own egos will lead inevitably to the dissolution of community and our deeper alienation from each other. Others, taking a more hopeful view, have tried to encourage political leaders and people in general to seek a moral reawakening or higher goals. Whatever their opinion on this issue, commentators are in agreement that market society, in tandem with the modern state, has fatally detached people from the social ties that are a precondition for social virtues. From this perspective, the affirmation of individual autonomy within the framework of a welfare state defined by statist individualism necessarily leads, sooner or later, to the collapse of the social contract.

Classical sociology and its neighboring disciplines in the social sciences have thus analyzed, from a range of perspectives, the dark sides of modernity—namely, the narcissism, social indifference, distrust, and suspicion that undermine community and society. Within all of these fields of intellectual enquiry, concern at the decline of social trust and the potential collapse of society has become a key issue. Ferdinand Tönnies's thesis that modern society is characterized by a movement from "community" (*Gemeinschaft*) to "society" (*Gesellschaft*) remains the most original and influential of the explanations offered. According to Tönnies, these concepts describe an ongoing transition from the premodern to the modern, from "warm" small communities to "cold" urban mass societies with their atomized and isolated individuals. Above all, Tönnies associated *Gesellschaft* with an emergent market society. But the market was not the only villain of the drama. He also identified the modern state, with its bureaucratic formalism and bloodless legal apparatus, as a conspirator in *Gesellschaft*'s creeping domination over *Gemeinschaft* in modern Western countries.[15]

But Tönnies was far from alone in this view. We find many names for those we love, and if we look more closely at Émile Durkheim's discussion of anomie, Max Weber's analysis of the iron cage, or Karl

Marx's thesis that alienation inevitably follows capitalism, we find—albeit from divergent scientific perspectives and essentially different political universes—a similar view of modernity's downsides.[16]

Indeed, this topic has become an object of renewed interest for sociologists and political scientists, who have recycled Tönnies's conceptual pairing, though with changed terminology. In *The Lonely Crowd* (1950), David Riesman and others analyzed contemporary American society in the spirit of Tönnies. Writing in the 1970s, Christopher Lasch worried about the emergence of a new kind of narcissistic individual. At around that time, Jürgen Habermas also wrote about the state's colonization of what he called "lifeworld," and Zygmunt Bauman followed Weber in examining the consequences of bureaucratic society and its formalization and instrumental regulation of human relations. During the 1990s, this same underlying anxiety about the nature of modern society found expression in the launch of the term *civil society* in a new, communitarian sense. And since 2000, research into social cohesion has been influenced by Robert Putnam's theory of social capital as a fragile and dwindling resource in Western societies where asocial TV-watching has replaced bowling and other kinds of social activities and gatherings.[17]

In this book, we argue that *folkhemmet* can be understood historically as a refined mixture of *Gemeinschaft* and *Gesellschaft*. Yet we can only speculate about the future. If the critics are right, the balance will irreversibly tip in favor of an increasingly impersonal *Gesellschaft*. A society driven by genuine empathy and concrete solidarity will have been transformed into a "social state" in which individuals look to their own interests first, a society in which talk of solidarity sounds increasingly hollow as individuals consistently seek to maximize the advantages that can be extracted from the system.

This kind of moralizing critique may well be justified; the ethical values that define a society affect not only the nature of personal interactions but also the institutional solutions for which people strive. As Bauman put it, the challenge to "love thy neighbor as thyself" (which of course presumes that people really do love themselves) is the cornerstone of every civilized society.[18]

In this respect, there may be something to learn from Sweden and the other Nordic countries. In the last few decades, social scientists have developed a comprehensive empirical apparatus for measuring and comparing social cohesion in almost every country in the world, data that presents considerable challenges to theoretical assertions

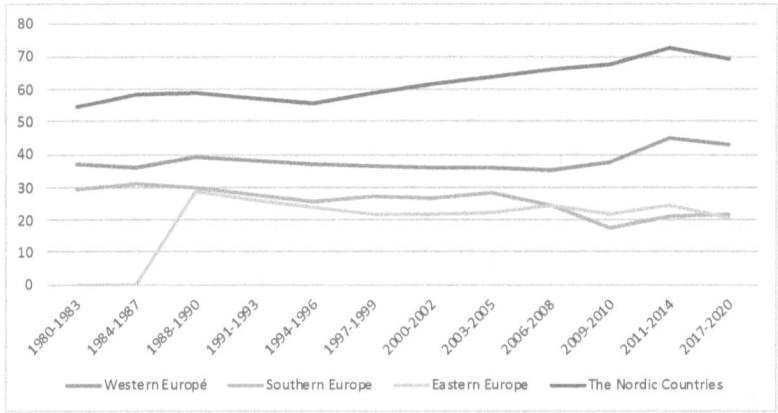

FIGURE C.1. General levels of trust in various parts of Europe: the table and graph show trends by region from 1980 to 2020, data that presents considerable challenges to theoretical assertions about the links between increased individualism and reduced trust. Source: www.mchs.se/arkiv/projekt/ccf/tillits barometern.html.

about the links between increased individualization and reduced trust.[19]

First, trust varies dramatically from country to country, as the graph in Figure C.1 shows. Second, there is no general or universal trend of declining trust. Sweden and the other Nordic countries have considerably higher levels of trust, which, moreover, have actually been stable or even grown in the last ten to twenty years. Third, comparative data suggests that individualism tends to be correlated with higher social trust, not lower.[20] And fourth, while there is a long-standing trope lamenting the supposed loneliness of individualistic Swedes, the evidence in fact suggests Nordic citizens, including the elderly, are more satisfied with their social networks than those in more communitarian and family-based societies.[21]

All four of the above points means that even if we restrict our focus to the relatively rich and modern countries in the West, it is clear that modernity in itself cannot account for the large differences between, say, Sweden and other countries such as the United States and Germany. What is more, this variation is distributed in an intriguing way. The defining feature of the few countries in which a steady majority claims to trust other people is that they are modern, not traditional. In other words, it is far from self-evident that the individualization of society necessarily results in the collapse often evoked by critics.

Even so, it should be stressed that the high levels of trust in Nordic countries are a special type. They are not the "hot" bonds of trust that typically characterize traditional families, clans, and close-knit associations, including religious congregations. Rather, they exemplify the broader but "cooler" bonds of trust that arise when blood ties and honor-based relationships give way to a social order based on the law—a trust radius that extends to all society and not merely those within one's own in-group.[22]

STATIST INDIVIDUALISM AS THE FUTURE

A hundred years ago, most observers had already realized that there was a connection between rising individualism and the growing dominance of international capitalism. In part, the modern nation-state functioned as a counterweight to this development and was regarded as a guardian of the national interest and social solidarity in general. In this spirit, Swedish statist individualism has always clearly recognized the destructive force of modern market society, its capacity to sever all ties and redefine all values. Confronted by this implacable and devastating revolutionary force, the modern Swedish welfare state has so far managed to offer vulnerable individuals *both* freedom *and* security, social mobility for individuals as well as social trust and solidarity for society.

One way to make sense of this seeming paradox is via a concept that has become fashionable in the last few decades: *social capital*. In concrete terms, social capital is a measurement that combines data on social trust and civic engagement. In social science scholarship, it has two main strands. The first is associated with Putnam, who argued that social capital is primarily a societal resource. The other, which derives from Pierre Bourdieu, argues that social capital is actually an individual resource, just like regular money and cultural capital (such as education).[23] In the former, it is possible to discern a conservative angle; this is an issue of social control and integration. The latter views social capital more dynamically, as an issue of freedom, and emphasizes social mobility and individuals' capacity to realize their goals and expectations.

Both perspectives are relevant in Sweden's case, and together they offer a key to understanding modern Sweden, where social capital exists as a collective societal asset and also as an individual resource that is fairly equally distributed among citizens. All in all, this social capital has mitigated capitalism's destructive tendencies while also creating favorable conditions for the market economy in the form of a mobile and well-educated labor force.

But how long can the nation-statist compromise continue without imploding under the strain of its internal contradictions? Indeed, a persistent theme in the public conversations during the recent decade has been a worry that globalization will inexorably undermine the nation-state's ability to maintain the social contract. This brings us to several critical questions for Sweden and its welfare state: If we are facing the imminent dissolution of the national community and the collapse of a social contract based on the state, does the future look bleak for Sweden's statist individualism? Can the twentieth-century social order, which is based on a fusion of state, nation, and society, really survive in the era of globalization?

Despite everything, we believe that there are several reasons to answer in the affirmative. The first is that reports of the demise of the nation-state are greatly exaggerated—not only in the negative sense of there being no viable international or supranational alternative for securing democracy and human rights, but also in a more positive sense. The nation-state still has considerable powers in most areas of society, from schools and health care to taxation and defense. It is true that the economic conditions for any individual nation-state are to a large degree determined by the vicissitudes of the global economy, but this is hardly a historical novelty.

Global capitalism may be vastly stronger in the 2020s than during the zenith of the nation-state between the 1930s and 1970s, but national governments are still able to influence, fend off, and compensate for the consequences of economic crises. While the mobility of modern capital has undeniably weakened the negotiating position of national governments with regard to transnational corporations and global finance markets, to portray the modern nation-state as powerless is a distortion. Most people neither wish to nor can leave their home country, and they represent both a powerful tax base and an enormous social and economic resource so long as they have access to education, health care, and other social investments.

Sociologist and political scientist Joakim Palme has drawn up with his colleagues a new paradigm based not on the Anglo-Saxon notion of "welfare," suggesting handouts and benefits, but on the notion of the "social investment state."[24] In this view, what defines the Nordic countries above all is their investment in all individuals—in the form of schooling, education, health care, and care services—so as to give everyone a better chance of successfully navigating the modern global market society. Whereas the older paradigm was about protecting individuals from global capitalism by "decommodifying" key resources, the new is more in step with global market society. It treats welfare as a productive investment rather than a net outlay within the framework of an economic zero-sum game. Yet there is also continuity: the nation-state's responsibility for ensuring social equality and equal opportunities for all citizens to share in economic and technological development.

The second reason why the statist-individualist contract has a better prognosis than people often assume is its enduring popularity. There are very few signs that significant numbers of Swedes are keen to dismantle the welfare state. At this point, however, we need to offer a caveat. The fact that no serious party in Sweden says it wants to dismantle the welfare state does not mean that the future of the welfare state is secure. As we point out at the end of chapter 12, the Swedish welfare state has witnessed huge changes during the last three decades in how it is managed, ranging from profit-making free schools to New Public Management in the public sector. In some areas, these changes have weakened the state in such a way that they might well threaten its ability to uphold its end of the state-individual alliance. Privatization, outsourcing, and deinstutionalization have undermined not only the effectiveness of the state but also the traditional ethos of professional civil servants. But we would argue that, in spite of these neoliberal experiments, the social contract between state and individual still remains fundamentally intact and attractive to most people.

This becomes even clearer if we take a broader comparative view. Sweden and the other Nordic countries are still international models for how an effective market economy and a strong civil society can be combined with high taxes and a large public sector in order to enhance citizens' equality and social security. The "Swedish model" or, indeed, "Nordic supermodel" (as *The Economist* termed it in 2013) is presented as an alternative to the existing social contracts, whether statist-authoritarian or rampantly neoliberal.[25] While this may well change, for now we would like to underscore the fact most people in Sweden and in many other countries seem to want both the state and the market—security as well as freedom.

The third reason why we believe that statist individualism still has a future relates to global changes in the situation for women. Across large swaths of the world, rates for both marriage and birth are falling at the same time as the model of the family based on a male breadwinner is losing ground. Outside the West, tremendous changes are also under way, particularly as a consequence of rapidly rising levels of education among women. The result is not always an improvement in women's situation; on the contrary, pressure on existing gender relations—even on the very idea of fixed genders—can lead to a backlash marked by greater misogyny and oppression both of women and of sexual minorities. Whether the result is greater or less gender equality, however, the issue of how women can combine having children with doing paid work has now moved to the fore.

The pattern may be uneven and difficult to analyze, but the evidence suggests that Sweden's welfare policies have managed to weather this development better than many other Western countries. The question is whether statist-individualist family policies—if this is not a completely self-contradictory concept—have saved parenthood at the price of marriage.[26] The fact that women are able to work and have children has protected the family's most fundamental functions: reproducing itself and rearing children. This does not mean that relationships within the family have not experienced a qualitative decline: it is quite possible that in the 1950s the family was a warmer and better place. Yet the evidence points strongly to the opposite conclusion: that the state makes possible a functioning community despite increased individual autonomy—particularly for women, children, and the elderly—by supporting its citizens both within the family and in the market.

In light of this trend, American sociologist David Popenoe has modified his criticism of Swedish family policy that we considered in chapter 11. Thus, while he still argues that Sweden "certainly fall[s] short on the enduring two-biological-parent ideal," when it comes to the key value of enabling "structured and consistent contact time between parents and their children in a family-friendly environment, they are well ahead of us."[27] From this perspective, American political culture is contradictory. Suspicion of state intervention in the family sphere makes it difficult to implement key sociopolitical measures that would support and help citizens, particularly children, in a postpatriarchal society with high divorce rates. Market liberalism affirms individual (feminine) liberation from the patriarchal family but offers no solution to the human and social problems that divorce creates, above all for children. Meanwhile, communitarian critics of the unholy alliance of market individualism and social liberalism can only reply that individuals—parents—must give up their own freedom and return voluntarily, for the children's sake, to an empty marriage.

In Germany, low fertility rates have forced politicians and researchers to question the vitality of the German family and the wisdom of traditional, conservative family policies. Germany's family policy has become a confusing object of debate and is now crisscrossed by many different policy directions: extension of day care, childcare allowance, and paid parental leave. The only policy that is proving difficult to put on the agenda is individual rather than joint taxation: "A 200-Billion-Euro Mistake" was how *Der Spiegel* characterized Germany's family policy in 2013. This has led to a renewed interest in Scandinavia, in particular the more individualistic family policies of the Nordic countries that are also more in line with the liberal and market-friendly policies characteristic of German political culture. To some extent, this turn toward the Nordic model may be spurred by the fact that today's unified Germany is to a large degree led by women from the old Deutsche Demokratische Republik (DDR) of East Germany. They have brought with them their experiences of a social experiment that in certain respects resembled the family and gender policies of the Swedish model.

In the United States, as noted earlier, there is visible concern that the collapse of the family will lead to greater social isolation, with all its attendant psychological problems. While it is naturally difficult to quantify the existential significance of changing and disintegrating family structures, the American sociologist Eric Klinenberg has cogently argued that there is no empirical support for the claim that increased individualism causes exclusion and social problems. On the contrary, people who have chosen to live in a one-person household are happier, healthier, and more active in associations and society at large than their peers. Rather, it seems to be a class issue: people with education, money, and contacts more often choose to live alone than those with fewer resources.

In this context, Klinenberg also pointed to the fact that Sweden, Stockholm in particular, holds the world record for the proportion of one-person households—around 60 percent in Stockholm—without having experienced greater individual unhappiness or social collapse. What differentiates the United States and Sweden, Klinenberg noted, is the role of the state; the equation between freedom and security is very different.[28] The radical antistatism in the United States—not to

Coda

mention the abhorrence of anything redolent of "socialism"—makes any reference to Sweden and Scandinavia fraught and risky for a politician. The example of Bernie Sanders is interesting, both for his ability to mobilize and play the Scandinavian card and for the backlash that in the wake of the 2020 presidential election led some Democrats to call for an agreement that the word *socialism* would never again be used in Democratic political rhetoric. As this book makes clear, Sweden is far from socialist in the sense that the word is usually understood. Indeed, Sweden and the Nordic countries are among the winners in the global market society. But as a potent meme, the specter of Swedish socialism lives on.

STATIST INDIVIDUALISM EXHAUSTED?

There are also reasons to be skeptical about statist individualism's prospects. The most common objection to an overly optimistic view of the Swedish welfare state's chances of survival is that it is unable to cope with pluralism and more profound cultural differences. The alliance between individual and state has a strongly universalistic component: not only laws but the very spirit of the social contract is based on individuals having the same duties and obligations toward both the state and other citizens. There is limited space for strongly collective communities that deviate from the general norm, and its members cannot request special treatment on the basis of some particular status or cultural identity. The values of the unitary state and the norms and habits of the majority culture have the final say.

If increased global competition has created doubt about national sovereignty on the economic level, then increased migration has dislodged the national homogeneity that, at least historically, has been a precondition for the successful alliance between state and individual. Today, roughly one in five Swedes was born abroad, most in a non-Nordic country. If we are to believe the results of the World Values Survey mentioned in this chapter's introduction, there are large differences between how most major immigrant groups and native Swedes view religion, the family, and traditional values. Native Swedes are very far from the global median as regards acceptance of divorce, gender equality, homosexual rights, religiousness, views on children's obedience and autonomy, and other moral questions.[29]

A pessimistic reading of these studies would be that there is a real risk of serious conflict between a strongly secular, individualistic, emancipatory majority culture on the one hand and, on the other, religious minorities, primarily Muslim, holding conservative views of the family. This theory also finds support in surveys of social trust, which appear to show a negative correlation with the degree of immigration-related diversity.[30] Since the millennium, political developments in Europe have shown with the utmost clarity that the dominant national-statist approach, which emphasizes a narrow, demanding, and exclusive definition of national identity and citizenship, is under severe pressure.

Yet this does not mean that the American version is the obvious alternative. It is true that the United States has created a liberal notion of citizenship that tends toward a cosmopolitan understanding of human rights, which in practice makes people more open-minded about immigration. But the deeply rooted libertarian suspicion of the state has also led to American society, despite its impressive economic growth, becoming increasingly unequal, with large groups now living on the margins of a productive but heartless market society. Furthermore, the United States is far more communitarian than Sweden and also far less individualistic. Indeed, while there is a rhetoric that celebrates American rugged individualism, "individualism" is more often than not a code word for "antistatism." In everyday life, generalized individualism takes a backseat to family values and communitarian demands. This politics of recognition tends, in turn, to undermine the national social contract in favor of segmentation into subnational communities based on factors such as class, ethnicity, sexual identity, and geographical region.

From this perspective, the Swedish social contract seems, if not quite an idyll, then at least in no imminent danger of being jettisoned. Its emphasis on individual freedom and its relatively weak demands that citizens identify with a restrictive ethnic national identity create opportunities for immigrants—even if such openness comes with conditions. Ultimately, if striving for freedom and social and gender equality is a universal tendency, the future remains hopeful.

The larger question, as we see it, is not whether Sweden's social contract can survive a greater measure of diversity in terms of race and ethnicity. More problematic is that Sweden, as we argue in chapter 13, has historically always found it difficult to accept religious pluralism. When issues of faith involve deeper underlying differences in relation to the family, sexuality, and child rearing, they come into conflict with Sweden's dominant secularism. This is not a particular problem for

Swedish Lutheranism, whose values in many respects not only resemble but are the historic basis of secularism. Yet other faiths, principally Islamism but also Catholicism, Orthodox Judaism, and some more evangelical Christian denominations, find themselves in a more conflictual relationship with statist individualism.

The challenges posed by immigration and diversity are further complicated by claims from both left and right that the nation-state is historically played out and that the world is now entering a postnational phase. The explicitly left-wing nationalism that was once the hallmark of social democracy has been replaced by ideals in which notions of human rights and global solidarity challenge the traditional social contract, based on social rights and existing within the framework of the national community. The right offers similar visions that, though primarily foregrounding the potential of global market liberalism as a project of universal freedom and prosperity, are also driven by the ideas of free movement and open borders. The goal of a global community is appealing—particularly when compared to the exclusionary logic of the nation-state—but the evidence suggests that it is, alas, too soon to dispense with the opportunities offered by the nation-state with regard to democracy, welfare policies, and economic control.

Exactly where this leaves us is unclear; Swedish statist individualism has established a delicate balance between ostensibly contradictory ideals. Echoing the slogan of the French Revolution, we might say that Swedish statist individualism has affirmed the individual's need for liberty, a collective desire for social equality, and a longing for fraternity—that is, national solidarity. It may well be that Swedes too easily take high levels of social trust for granted—like the air we breathe. But the question ought, perhaps, to be not whether we can have an equitable society without some kind of shared narrative, but how this shared narrative can be developed in a way that includes rather than excludes and looks forward in time rather than backward.

We do not know what the future holds for the balance between national democracy, solidarity, welfare, and cosmopolitan ideals such as unbounded humanity and global citizenship. But one advantage of the moral and political logic of Sweden's social contract is that it shows that supposedly national values are in fact the local expressions of universal principles. There is every reason to build on this legacy by recognizing the nation-state's continued existence and legitimacy while also working to sustain supranational institutions and a postnational vision.

So is Sweden a "model" worth studying? Or is it a curio—interesting, perhaps, but basically irrelevant? Or it is both? If we go back to the WVS data that we mention at the start of this chapter, we see that Sweden is instructive on several counts. On the one hand, it turns out that with regard to individualism, the world in general is moving in Sweden's direction. While Sweden may be an extreme outlier, the overall tendency suggests that it is not just a desirable model—for some—but something far more intriguing: a possible future, perhaps everyone's. On the other hand, if we move away from measures of individual freedom and look instead at the data on faith in and degree of corruption in institutions, the picture is very different. Here, too, Sweden stands out as having an unusually high level of faith in the state, authorities, and judiciary. But in this respect, it is much harder to argue that the world is moving, like Hegel's spirit of history, toward a Nordic journey's end.

If anything, it is the reverse. Looking only at the data for European Union countries, we see that people's faith in politicians and joint institutions is far lower than in Sweden and going down, not up. This means that the correlation between social trust and faith in political institutions that is characteristic of Sweden derives from a balance that, if not unique, is certainly unusual, between the project of individual freedom and a social contract defined by a positive attitude toward the community: the state, associations, the public right of way. Far from being part of a general universal movement, Sweden's social trust and faith in political institutions is the product of fortuitous historical circumstances that make it hard to apply to other countries.

The strength of statist individualism is that it provides an answer to a fundamental existential problem. Whether it will survive is an open question; we have no easy answers to its lack of pluralism, the more or less permanent unemployment, global competition, and the weakening of the institutions of national integration. In the present moment, however, it is hard to see any more convincing solutions to the asocial sociability that, according to Kant, is the hallmark of all people, including Swedes.

Social practices are hardy and collective memories long. While the forces of change seem at times to be raging furiously, it is important not to lose sight of the larger picture. The Nordic corner of the world offers considerable historical resources: a cooler sense of community

(*Gemeinschaft*) that leans toward an atomized *Gesellschaft* (society) but falls short of anomie and alienation, and a social contract that is able to embrace the other without dominating, a place where the law and not honor is the governing principle.

To the degree that Swedish statist individualism is an expression of these insights, it represents a practice rather than a self-consciously articulated theory. The aim of this book has been to uncover the underlying, partly hidden ideals of Swedish political culture and the historical roots of its foundational values.

ACKNOWLEDGMENTS

This English translation from the original Swedish book would not have been possible without Stephen Donovan. Locked down in London, he has not only managed to translate a text full of obscure Swedish historical concepts into elegant English but has also had to deal with no less than two anxious authors. Hopefully he has enjoyed our many e-mail exchanges over the North Sea as much as we have.

On behalf of University of Washington Press, copyeditor Kris Fulsaas helped to finalize the text. Her professionalism and thoroughness was an inspiration when we were forced to hunt down missing citations and add explanatory historical background. We hope she now feels comfortable with the four estates of the medieval Swedish parliament.

Rebecka Andersen at Ersta Sköndal Bräcke University College in Stockholm has also been of invaluable help. Taking time off from her doctoral research, she has made the manuscript fit for publication in more ways than we can enumerate, ranging from critical reading to attention to technical details.

Vanessa Barker at Stockholm University intervened to rescue our introduction at a time when our energies were flagging, combining her editorial skills and deep knowledge of the book's message with an eye on keeping our central questions and theses squarely at the center.

In the United States, the support from Mark Sandberg at University of California, Berkeley and Andrew Nestingen at University of Washington has helped pave the way for publication. The reading of the next-to-final manuscript, by Lisa Tiersten at Barnard College, served as a crucial check that we did not get lost in translation but spoke clearly to an English-speaking readership.

We also would like to reiterate our thanks to those who assisted in various way as we prepared the manuscript for the original Swedish edition in 2006: Roland Anrup, Roger Klinth, Ola Larsmo, Jan Larsson, Arne Ruth, Rolf Torstendahl, Carl Wennerlind, and Maciej Zaremba. Additionally, several experts on religion in Sweden provided useful advice as we added a new chapter on the legacy of Lutheranism for the second edition in 2015: Johan von Essen, Bengt Kristensson Uggla, Johannes Lindvall, Pekka Mellergård, Jonas Qvarsebo, Jayne Svennungsson, and Dominik Tierstrup.

Last but definitely not least, our heartfelt thanks to the Swedish Arts Council and the University of Washington Department of Scandinavian Studies's Fielding Fund for Excellence for making this English translation of our book finally possible. We hope that they will find their money well spent.

NOTES

INTRODUCTION

1. This is commonly known as the *folkhem* speech, held in the Swedish Parliament. During the speech Hansson mostly refers to citizens and democracy, but he also used the phrase "the people's or the citizen's home" (*"folk- eller medborgarhemmet"*). For reasons that will be explored later in this book, it was the concept of *folkhemmet* that caught on and has since been used to designate the nascent welfare system that the Social Democrats started to construct in the 1930s, but it is important to note that the concept of the folk (people) here refers primarily to *demos* and only secondarily to *ethnos*—that is, it is less about Sweden as an ethnic or racial community than about Sweden as a democratic community.

1. THE PEOPLE OF NIFELHEIM

1. Neander-Nilsson, *Är svensken människa*, 9.
2. Neander-Nilsson, *Är svensken människa*, 42, 45.
3. Neander-Nilsson, *Är svensken människa*, 50.
4. Neander-Nilsson, *Är svensken människa*, 82, 84.
5. Neander-Nilsson, *Är svensken människa*, 54–55.
6. Linnell and Löfgren, eds., *Svenska krusbär*; Alf W. Johansson, ed., *Vad är Sverige?*; Black and Pott, *Swedish Reflections*.
7. Sundbärg, *Emigrationsutredningen*.
8. Sundbärg, *Emigrationsutredningen*, 8.
9. Sundbärg, *Emigrationsutredningen*.
10. Levertin, *Dikter*, 12. Nifelheim, "the mist-covered world," lies in the far North, according to Norse mythology. It is a dreary, unpleasant place, sometimes also described as the realm of the dead.
11. Ottey, *Swedish Race in North America*, 28–30.
12. Söderbergh, *Svenskt*, 11.
13. Brandell, *Svensk folkkaraktär*, 63, 83, 86.
14. Gustaf Lundgren, ed., *Lasternas bok*, 53.
15. Gustaf Lundgren, ed., *Lasternas bok*, 53.

16. Scott, *The Swedes*, 12.
17. Austin, *On Being Swedish*, 53, 55–56.
18. Austin, *Being Swedish*, 148.
19. Austin, *Being Swedish*, 147; Hendin, *Suicide and Scandinavia*, 147.
20. Hendin, *Suicide and Scandinavia*, 73.
21. Daun, *Svensk mentalitet*, 92–93, 256. This book has been translated into English as *Swedish Mentality* (University Park: Pennsylvania State University Press, 1996).
22. Arnstberg, *Typiskt svenskt*, 88.
23. Liljeström and Özdalga, *Autonomy and Dependence in the Family*, 6.
24. Stridsberg, "Riskkapitalbolag ger få nya industrier."
25. Rojas, *I Ensamhetens labyrint*, 35.
26. Lennart Lundqvist, "Den underlige svensken."
27. Ahlsén, "Vänskap odlas i gemensam kultur."
28. Ludvig Nordström, "Behovet av en ny svensk fosterländskhet," 222.
29. Schneewind, *Invention of Autonomy*, 483–92; Reiss, ed., *Kant's Political Writings*, 37–38.
30. Kant, *Philosophy of Kant*, 120.

2. STATIST INDIVIDUALISM

1. Huntford, *New Totalitarians*, 348.
2. Enzensberger, *Ack, Europa*, 16–17.
3. Statist individualism was first discussed in Trägårdh, "Statist Individualism: On the Culturality of the Nordic Welfare State."
4. Heckscher, *Staten och organisationerna*, 255.
5. Hilding Johansson, *Folkrörelserna och det demokratiska statsskicket*, 244.
6. Rothstein, *Vad bör staten göra?* 225.
7. Middlekauff, *Glorious Cause*.
8. Shain, *Myth of American Individualism*, xvi.
9. McPherson, *Battle Cry of Freedom*; Levine and Foner, *Half Slave and Half Free*.
10. Trägårdh, *State and Civil Society in Northern Europe*.
11. Sheehan, "What Is German History?"; Iggers, *German Conception of History*; Walker, *German Home Towns*.
12. Applegate, *Nation of Provincials*; Confino, *Nation as a Local Metaphor*.
13. Lidtke, *Alternative Culture*; Roth, *Social Democrats in Imperial Germany*; Schorske, *German Social Democracy, 1905–17*.
14. Fölster, *Bortom de sju bergen*, 187.
15. For a critique of Geijer and this romantic narrative, see for example Hessler, "Aristokratifördömandet"; Roberts, *Essays in Swedish History*; Lönnroth, *Från svensk medeltid*; Frykman and Löfgren, *Den kultiverade människan*.
16. Trägårdh, "Concept of the People"; Trägårdh, "Statist Individualism: On the Culturality of the Nordic Welfare State"; Trägårdh, "Vad är en medborgare?"

17. Roberts, *Essays in Swedish History*, 4–5.
18. Österberg, "Vardagens sköra samförstånd," 145.
19. Zaremba, "Byalagets diskreta charm eller folkhemmets demokratiuppfattning," 97.
20. Quoted in Rothstein, *Den korporativa staten*, 63.
21. Rothstein, *Den korporativa staten*, 84.
22. Lukes, "Types of Individualism."
23. Zunz and Kahan. eds., *Tocqueville Reader*.
24. Tocqueville, *Democracy in America II*, 351.
25. Tocqueville, *Democracy in America I*, 6.
26. Mill, *On Liberty*, 121.
27. Tocqueville, *Democracy II*, 13.
28. Rousseau, *Social Contract*, 99.
29. Starobinski, *Jean-Jacques Rousseau*; Berman, *Politics of Authenticity*; Damrosch, *Jean Jacques Rousseau*.
30. Rousseau, *Confessions of Jean-Jacques Rousseau*, Kindle 554–56.
31. Berman, *Politics of Authenticity*, 92–99.
32. Cranston, "Introduction," 42.
33. Rousseau, *Social Contract*, 61.
34. One of the best works on these concepts is the Swedish sociologist Johan Asplund's *Esssä om Gemeinschaft och Gesellschaft*. Unfortunately, it is not available in English.
35. Antman, ed., *Systemskifte*, 16.
36. Åmark, *Hundra år av välfärdspolitik*; Berge, *Medborgarrätt och egenansvar*.

3. THE SWEDISH THEORY OF LOVE

1. Sundbärg, *Emigrationsutredningen*; Huntford, *New Totalitarians*.
2. Jeppson Grassman and Svedberg, "Medborgarskapets gestaltningar."
3. In 2015 the Italian-Swedish documentary filmmaker Erik Gandini released a film with the name *The Swedish Theory of Love*. The title and the film were inspired by our 2006 book, and one of us was featured in the film giving a lecture using this concept. It should be noted that Gandini's film, like the book by Neander-Nilsson, stressed the bleak aspects of Swedish culture such as alienation, loneliness, and the lack of warm community and family life.
4. Svallfors, *Vem älskar välfärdsstaten*.
5. Antman, "Inte utan jämlikhet," 17.
6. Modig and Ahlin, *Äldre med tydliga behov*.
7. Berman, *Politics of Authenticity*, 177–78; see also Eva-Lena Dahl, "Rousseaus civilisationskritik."
8. Therborn, *Between Sex and Power*; Shorter, *Making of the Modern Family*; Kertzer and Barbagli, eds., *History of the European Family*; Gaunt, *Familjeliv i norden*.
9. Hajnal, "European Marriage Patterns in Perspective." See also Laslett, "Family and Household as a Work Group and Kin Group, and Mackie, "Patterns of Social Trust in Western Europe and Their Genesis."

10. Mitterauer, *Ungdomstidens sociala historia*.
11. Gaunt, *Familjeliv i norden*, 173.
12. Hendin, *Suicide and Scandinavia*.
13. Gaunt, *Familjeliv i norden*, 153.
14. Odén, *De äldre i samhället—förr*, 9.
15. Gaunt, *Familjeliv i norden*, 173.
16. Gaunt, *Familjeliv i norden*, 173.
17. Mitterauer, *Ungdomstidens sociala historia*, 198–99.
18. Shorter, *Making of the Modern Family*, 102–6.
19. Gaunt, *Familjeliv i norden*, 137.
20. Gaunt, *Familjeliv i norden*, 41. See also Taussi Sjöberg, *Rätten och kvinnorna*, 155–62.
21. Qvist, *Konsten att blifva en god flicka*, 19.
22. Bradley, "Family Laws and Welfare States," 54–59.
23. Bradley, "Family Laws and Welfare States," 49–54. See also Moeller, *Protecting Motherhood*, and Steinmetz, *Regulating the Social*.
24. Bradley, "Family Laws and Welfare States," 39–48; Ronfani, "Family Law in Europe."
25. Ronfani, "Family Law in Europe"; Melby, *Inte ett ord om kärlek*.
26. Ronfani, "Family Law in Europe;" Melby, *Inte ett ord om kärlek*.
27. Ronfani, "Family Law in Europe."
28. There are some important differences, though. If one of the partners in a *sambo* relationship dies, the survivor has no right of inheritance without a will. This became a public issue when Stieg Larsson, the author of the worldwide best-selling Millennium trilogy, died. His fortune went to his brother and father, not the woman he was cohabiting with. In case of breakup of a *sambo* relationship, there are also different rules for how to divide the common property. But in both cases, voluntary agreements can be set up between the *sambos*.
29. Austin, *On Being Swedish*, 148.
30. Moeller, *Protecting Motherhood*; Steinmetz, *Regulating the Social*.
31. Gordon, *Pitied but Not Entitled*; Skocpol, *Protecting Soldiers and Mothers*.
32. Murray, *Losing Ground*. It should be noted that "welfare" as used in the United States and the United Kingdon differs in meaning from *välfärd* in the Swedish context. While "welfare" in English tends to suggest stigmatizing handouts to the poor and needy, *välfärd* in Swedish connotes universal social rights that apply to all citizens.
33. Melby, et al., eds., *Nordic Model of Marriage and the Welfare State*; Niels Finn Christiansen, Petersen, Edling, and Haave, eds., *Nordic Model of Welfare*; Åmark, *Hundra år av välfärdspolitik*.
34. Among these studies should be noted the following: European Values Study, World Values Survey, European Social Survey, the Eurobarometer, the Human Development Index, the Gender Empowerment Index, the Weighted Index of Social Progress, the Human Wellbeing Index, Transparency International's Corruption Index, and the World Bank Governance and Anti-Corruption Index, to mention only a few. See also Thorleif Pettersson and

Esmer, *Vilka är annorlunda?* and Ingelhart and Welzel, *Modernization, Cultural Change, and Democracy.*
35. Ingelhart and Welzel, *Modernization, Cultural Change, and Democracy.*
36. Thorleif Pettersson and Esmer, *Vilka är annorlunda?* 18.
37. Halman, Luijkx, and van Zandert, *Atlas of European Values.*
38. Björnberg and Bradshaw, "Conclusions," 291–92. See also Zetterberg, *Staten, familjen och hushållet.*
39. We return in later chapters to the various critiques of the Swedish social contract based on the logic of statist individualism and the Swedish theory of love by both Swedish and foreign researchers and politicians, including Burenstam Linder, *Den hjärtlösa välfärdsstaten*; Zetterberg, *Staten, familjen och hushållet*; and Popenoe, *Disturbing the Nest.*
40. Zaremba, *De rena och de andra*; Trägårdh, *Bemäktiga individerna.*

4. POVERTY AND PROGRESS

1. Almqvist, *Samlade skrifter*, vols. 8–10, 312; Geijer, *Samlade skrifter*, vol. 4, 30. All quotes from Almqvist (except the English translation of *Det går an (Sara Videbeck)* are from *Samlade skrifter*, vols. 1–15. All quotes from Geijer are from *Samlade skrifter*, vols. 1–12.
2. Geijer, *Samlade skrifter*, vol. 4, 34.
3. Almqvist, *Samlade skrifter*, vols. 8–10, 312.
4. Geijer, *Samlade skrifter*, vol. 4 (1926), 34.
5. Holmberg, *Sverige efter 1809*, 2.
6. Geijer, *Samlade skrifter*, vol. 4, 35.
7. Almqvist, *Samlade skrifter*, vols. 8–10, 317.
8. Ozkirimli, *Theories of Nationalism*; Anderson, *Imagined Communities*; Brubakers, *Citizenship and Nationhood*; Smith, *Ethnic Origins of Nations*; Gellner; *Nation and Nationalism*; Hettne, Sörlin, and Östergård, *Den globala nationalismen*; Reynolds, *Walt Whitman's America*; Kogan, *The "I" of History*; Sarti, *Mazzini*; Hall, *Social Construction of Nationalism*; Nordin, *Ett fattigt men fritt folk*; Sanders and Vind, *Grundtvig.*
9. Hobsbawm, *Nationer och nationalism*, 57.
10. Barnard, *Herder's Social and Political Thought*, 167–77; Hessler, *Geijer som politiker*, vol. 1 (1937), 75–77.
11. Trägårdh, "Crisis and the Politics of National Community," 88–89.
12. Henrik Berggren, "Jag hör Amerika sjunga."
13. Geijer, *Samlade skrifter*, vol. 8, 34; *Samlade skrifter*, vol. 9, 125.
14. Geijer, *Samlade skrifter*, vol. 7, 146–52; *Samlade skrifter*, vol. 8, 84.
15. Hessler, *Geijer som politiker*, vol. 1, 1–15; *Geijer som politiker*, vol. 2, 212–13.
16. Geijer, *Samlade skrifter*, vol. 2, 188. All quoted poetry is from this volume.
17. Geijer, *Samlade skrifter*, vol. 7, 118.
18. Witoszek, "Moral Community and the Crisis of the Enlightenment," 76.
19. Lönnroth, *Från svensk medeltid*, 12.

20. *Odalman* or *odalbonde* is an old Swedish word for a freeholder whose property could be passed on over generations. We have translated it here as "yeoman," which is technically correct but suggests a British social context. The more common and still used Swedish word for someone who cultivates the land is *bonde*. We have generally translated it as "peasant," which again is technically correct (like the Latin-derived "peasant," the Nordic word *bonde* indicates a person living on the land). But unlike English, in which "peasant" has become a historical term evoking a hierarchical feudal society, the term *bonde* is still used today to describe what in the English-speaking countries would be called a farmer. As we see it, this yet another example of the pervasiveness of the Swedish historical narrative of the free peasantry. That is not to say that all Swedish peasants were freeholders. While there were no feudal serfs, a fair number of peasants (depending on the historical period) were sharecroppers on noble or Crown lands.

21. Geijer, *Samlade skrifter*, vol. 2, 29–33.
22. Geijer, *Samlade skrifter*, vol. 2, 34–39.
23. Geijer, *Samlade skrifter*, vol. 2, 34–39.
24. Geijer, *Samlade skrifter*, vol. 3, 581.
25. Geijer, *Samlade skrifter*, vol. 7, 124.
26. Thompson, *Making of the English Working Class*.
27. Landquist, *Geijer*, 13; Delblanc and Lönnroth, *Den svenska litteraturen*, 3, 47.
28. Geijer, *Samlade skrifter*, vol. 4, 213; *Samlade skrifter*, vol. 9, 10.
29. Geijer, *Samlade skrifter*, vol. 7, 325; *Samlade skrifter*, vol. 9 (1931), 209.

30. The issue of how to translate the nineteenth-century concept of *personlighet* (or *persönlichkeit* in German, as used by Hegel and other German philosophers) is tricky. Following Warren Breckman, we have chosen to translate it as "personality." For a detailed discussion of this complex and vague concept, see Breckman, *Marx, the Young Hegelians, and the Origins of Radical Social Theory*, 12–14.

31. Geijer, *Samlade skrifter*, vol. 7, 325; *Samlade skrifter*, vol. 9, 209.
32. Geijer, *Samlade skrifter*, vol. 7, 331; *Samlade skrifter*, vol. 8, 386.
33. Ehnmark, *Minnets hemlighet*, 116.
34. Geijer, *Samlade skrifter*, vol. 2, 81.
35. Geijer, *Samlade skrifter*, vol. 2, 488–89.
36. Geijer, *Samlade skrifter*, vol. 2, 488–89.
37. Geijer, *Samlade skrifter*, vol. 2, 34–39.
38. Larsmo, *Andra sidan*, 159.

39. The term "Third Estate" as Geijer uses it here has nothing to with the four estates of the Swedish parliament. The Third Estate in prerevolutionary France consisted of all Frenchmen who were not nobles or priests, about 98 percent of the population. The French parliament, the Estates-General, was seldom consulted. In 1789 when it was called in, the Third Estate revolted and declared itself to be the National Assembly of all citizens.

40. Geijer, *Samlade skrifter*, vol. 9, 126; *Samlade skrifter*, vol. 5, 279–80.
41. Geijer, *Samlade skrifter*, vol. 9, 279–80; *Samlade skrifter*, vol. 6, 126.

42. Geijer, *Samlade skrifter*, vol. 9, 4–5.
43. Geijer, *Samlade skrifter*, vol. 9, 6.
44. Geijer, *Samlade skrifter*, vol. 9, 269–446; Wisselgren, *Samhällets kartläggare*, 35–44; Meurling, *Geijer och Marx*, 21–26.
45. Hessler, *Geijer som politiker*, vol. 2 (1947), 41–65.
46. Geijer, *Samlade skrifter*, vol. 8, 3.
47. Landquist, *Geijer*, 38–39.
48. Fryxell, *Om aristokrat-fördömandet i svensk historien*; Hessler, "Aristokratifördömandet."
49. Geijer, *Samlade skrifter*, vol. 9, 126.
50. Geijer, *Samlade skrifter*, vol. 9, 305.
51. Meurling, *Geijer och Marx*.
52. Ehnmark, *Minnets hemlighet*, 38.
53. Geijer, *Samlade skrifter*, vol. 3, 519.
54. Quoted in Jan Christensen, "Bönder och herrar," 32–33.
55. Jan Christensen, "Bönder och herrar," 32–33; Torbjörn Nilsson, "Liberalism på undantag."

5. LOVE AND INDEPENDENCE

1. Almqvist, *Sara Videbeck and The Chapel*, 105. *The Chapel* is another novel included in this English translation. All references to *Sara Videbeck* are from this English version, while all other Almqvist references are from his *Samlade skrifter* (*Collected Works*).
2. Burman, ed., *Carl Jonas Love Almqvist—diktaren, debattören, drömmaren*, 51.
3. Key, *Sveriges modernaste diktare*.
4. Henry Olsson, *Carl Jonas Love Almqvist till 1836*, 38.
5. Jacobson, *Almqvist: diktaren och hans tid*; Romberg, *Carl Jonas Love Almqvist: liv och verk*; Svedjedal, "Avfallens tid."
6. Romberg, *Carl Jonas Love Almqvist*, 61.
7. Henry Olsson, *Carl Jonas Love Almqvist till 1836*, 35.
8. Hajnal, "European Marriage Patterns in Perspective"; Laslett, "Family and Household as a Work Group and Kin Group"; Mackie, "Patterns of Social Trust in Western Europe and Their Genesis"; Gaunt, *Familjeliv i norden*; Mitterauer, *Ungdomstidens sociala historia*; Odén, *De äldre i samhället*; Shorter, *Making of the Modern Family*; Norman, ed., *Den utsatta familjen*.
9. Gaunt, *Familjeliv i norden*, 136.
10. Johannesson, "Den heliga familjen."
11. Frykman and Löfgren, *Den kultiverade människan*, 76–77, 79.
12. Ohlander and Strömberg, *Tusen svenska kvinnoår*, 141.
13. Kärnborg, *Fredrika Bremer*, 19.
14. Almqvist, *Samlade skrifter*, vol. 12, *Grimstahamns nybygge, Ladugårdslandet*.
15. Almqvist, *Samlade skrifter*, vol. 12, 65–113.
16. Almqvist, *Samlade skrifter*, vol. 12, 65–113.
17. Almqvist, *Samlade skrifter*, vol. 12, xx–xxi.

18. Romberg, *Carl Jonas Love Almqvist*, 9.
19. Almqvist, *Samlade skrifter* 2, 96–102.
20. Hammar, "Rousseau—åberopad i sin frånvaro."
21. Mijuskovic, *Loneliness in Philosophy, Psychology and Literature*; Jacobsson, *Almqvist*, 153–56.
22. Romberg, *Carl Jonas Love Almqvist*, 48–53.
23. Lundell, *Texter, noter, bilder*, 148.
24. Laurin, *Kvinnolynnen*, 54.
25. Almqvist, *Sara Videbeck* (*Samlade skrifter*, vol. 13), 6–7.
26. Almqvist, *Samlade skrifter*, vol. 12, *Den svenska fattigdomens betydelse, Arbetets ära*.
27. Westman Berg, *Studier i Carl Jonas Love Almqvists kvinnouppfattning*, 279.
28. The etymology of *göt*, *göter*, and *götisk* is disputed. In the nationalist discourse of the nineteenth century it was contended that the Swedish *göter* were identical with the Gothic tribes on the European continent. Few historians believe this today. Another theory is that they are related to the Geats of the *Beowulf* saga, but this is also disputed. We have with some hesitation chosen to translate *göt*, *göter*, and *götisk* with "goth,"goths," and "gothic" because they best evoke the intended meaning of Almquist, Geijer, and their contemporaries to an international audience. But it is a moot question and readers should remember that Swedish *göter* most probably were a separate tribe related neither to the famous sackers of Rome nor the Geats of *Beowulf*.
29. Almqvist, *Samlade skrifter*, vol. 12, 6.
30. Almqvist, *Samlade skrifter*, vol. 12, 1–25.
31. Almqvist, *Sara Videbeck* (*Samlade skrifter*, vol. 13), 120.
32. Almqvist, *Sara Videbeck* (*Samlade skrifter*, vol. 13), 127.
33. Almqvist, *Samlade skrifter*, vol. 16, *Europeiska missnöjets grunder*.
34. Almqvist, *Samlade skrifter*, vol. 16, *Europeiska missnöjets grunder*, 140.
35. Almqvist, *Samlade skrifter*, vol. 16, *Europeiska missnöjets grunder*, 127.
36. Almqvist, *Samlade skrifter*, vol. 16, 130.
37. Staberg, *Att skapa en ny man*, 82; Romberg, *Carl Jonas Love Almqvist*, 18.
38. Niels Finn Christiansen, Petersen, Edling, and Haave, eds., *Nordic Model of Welfare*, 25.

6. SUPERMAN AND OTHER PEOPLE

1. Strindberg, *Samlade verk*, vol. 20, *Tjänstekvinnans son I–II*, 183; Lagercrantz, *August Strindberg*, 21–27; Lamm, *August Strindberg*, 11–19.
2. Strindberg, *Samlade verk*, vol. 6, *Röda Rummet*; *Samlade verk*, vol. 5, *Mäster Olof*. All Strindberg citations are from the *Samlade verk* (*Collected Works*).
3. Ahlström, *Det moderna genombrottet*; Delblanc and Lönnroth, *Den svenska litteraturen*; Fulsås and Rem, *Ibsen, Scandinavia and the Making of a World Drama*, 237–42.
4. Ibsen, *An Enemy of the People*.

5. Stenström, *Den ensamme*.
6. Stenström, *Den ensamme*, 31–32, 49.
7. Statistiska centralbyrån, *Historisk statistik för Sverige, del 1*, 66, 200.
8. Johnson, *Det svenska teleundret*, 7.
9. Björck, *Verner von Heidenstam*, 7–8.
10. Tommy Möller, *Svensk politisk historia 1809–1975*, 31.
11. Ahlström, *Det moderna genombrottet*, 41.
12. Strindberg, *Samlade verk*, vol. 16, *Giftas I*, 11–12. *Giftas I* is available in English as *Married: Twenty Stories of Married Life*.
13. Strindberg, "Nationalitet och svenskhet," 194–212.
14. Zöller, *Schweden—Land und Volk*.
15. Strindberg, "Nationalitet och svenskhet," 194–212.
16. Strindberg, *Samlade verk*, vols. 13–14, *Svenska öden och äventyr I–II*.
17. Lagercrantz, *August Strindberg*, 111; Strindberg, *Samlade verk*, vol. 20, *Tjänstekvinnans son I*, 182.
18. Strindberg, *Samlade verk*, vol. 13, *Svenska öden och äventyr I*, 64.
19. Strindberg, *Samlade verk*, vol. 13, *Svenska öden I*, 87.
20. Strindberg, *Samlade verk*, vol. 14, *Svenska öden II*, 34.
21. Starobinski, *Jean-Jacques Rousseau*, 20.
22. Strindberg, *Samlade verk*, vol. 20, *Tjänstekvinnans son*, 123.
23. Strindberg, *Samlade verk*, vol. 16, *Giftas I*, 21.
24. Strindberg, *Samlade verk*, vol. 16, *Giftas I*, 18.
25. Strindberg, *Samlade verk*, vol. 16, *Giftas I*, 21.
26. Strindberg, *Samlade verk*, vol. 16, *Giftas I*, 21.
27. Lagercrantz, *August Strindberg*, 234.
28. Lagercrantz, *August Strindberg*, 272.
29. Lagercrantz, *August Strindberg*, 128.
30. Strindberg, *Samlade verk*, vol. 16, *Giftas I*, 81–99.
31. Meidal, "August Strindberg," 18.
32. Meidal, "Från poet till folktribun."
33. Leche Löfgren, *Ellen Key*; Ambjörnsson, "Ellen Key"; Boëthius, Hildebrand, and Nilzén, eds., *Svenskt biografiskt lexikon*, 90–98.
34. Lindén, *Om kärlek*, 17.
35. Manns, *Den sanna frigörelsen*, 134–56.
36. Strindberg, *Samlade verk*, vol. 57, *Svarta fanor*.
37. Key, *Livslinjer 1*, 73–74.
38. Key, "Om patriotismen," 251.
39. Key, *Tankebilder, del 1*, 155.
40. Key, *Tankebilder, del 1*, 155.
41. Key, *Tankebilder, del 1*, 147.
42. *Aftonbladet*, November 1, 1900, quoted in Lindén, *Om kärlek*, 153.
43. Key, *Barnets århundrade*, vol. 1, 18.
44. Key, *Barnets århundrade*, vol. 1, 35; see also Lagergren, *På andra sidan välfärdsstaten*, 80–81, for a discussion of this point.
45. Lindén, *Om kärlek*, 188.
46. Borland, *Nietzsche's Influence on Swedish Literature*; Brandl, *Persönlichkeitsidealismus und Willenskult*.

47. Henrik Berggren, *Seklets ungdom*, 89–90; Stenkvist, *Proletärskalden*, 104–42; Wizelius, "Heroer och människor," 62–372.
48. Brandl, *Persönlichkeitsidealismus und Willenskult*, 16–18.
49. Geijer, *Samlade skrifter*, vol. 2, 35.
50. Key, *Tal till Sveriges ungdom*, 24.
51. Key, *Livslinjer 1: Kärleken och äktenskapet*, vols. 1–2, 277.
52. Key, *Livslinjer 1: Kärleken och äktenskapet*, vols. 1–2, 265.
53. Key, *Livslinjer 1: Kärleken och äktenskapet*, vols. 1–2, 266.
54. Key, *Livslinjer 1: Kärleken och äktenskapet*, vols. 1–2, 321–69.
55. Key, *Livslinjer 1: Kärleken och äktenskapet*, vols. 1–2, 342.
56. Key, *Livslinjer 1: Kärleken och äktenskapet*, vols. 1–2, 330.
57. Key, *Livslinjer 1: Kärleken och äktenskapet*, vols. 1–2, 366.
58. Lindén, *Om kärlek*, 184–88.
59. Key, *Barnets århundrade*, vol. 1, 4.
60. Key, *Barnets århundrade*, vol. 1, 4.
61. Henrik Berggren, *Seklets ungdom*, 40–47.
62. Key, *Skönhet för alla*, 14; Ambjörnsson, "Ellen Key," 493–94.
63. Sejersted, *Socialdemokratins tidsålder*, 12.

7. A BOUNDED COMMUNITY

1. Kjellén, "Nationalitetsidén," 276.
2. Kjellén, *Politiska essayer*, vol. 2, 22.
3. Trägårdh, "Concept of the People"; Lagergren, *På andra sidan välfärdsstaten*; Sten O. Karlsson, *Det intelligenta samhället*, 477–90; Jan Larsson, *Hemmet vi ärvde*, 60–73.
4. Boëthius, Hildebrand, and Nilzén, eds., *Svenskt biografiskt lexikon*, 203–6; Elvander, *Harald Hjärne och konservatismen*, 257–326.
5. Björck, *Heidenstam och sekelskiftets Sverige*; Broberg, "När svenskarna uppfann Sverige"; Hobsbawm, *Nationer och nationalism*; Rosenblad, *Nation, nationalism och identitet*; Strahl, *Nationalism och socialism*.
6. Nasaw, *Chief: The Life of William Randolph Hearst*, 130–42.
7. Mann, *History of Germany*, 516.
8. Stråth, *Union och demokrati*, 390–95.
9. Mann, *History of Germany*, 511.
10. From Roosevelt's "Corollary to the Monroe Doctrine."
11. Ironically, Norway had never been part of the Swedish Empire. It had been given to Sweden as compensation for the loss of German territories in the peace treaty of Kiel in 1814 after the first defeat of Napoleon.
12. Stråth, *Union och demokrati*.
13. Björck, *Heidenstam och sekelskiftets Sverige*, 11.
14. Elvander, *Harald Hjärne och konservatismen*, 208–13.
15. Kjellén-Björkquist, *Rudolf Kjellén*, 39.
16. Kjellén-Björkquist, *Rudolf Kjellén*, 42.
17. Kjellén-Björkquist, *Rudolf Kjellén*, 269–72.
18. Kjellén, "Nationalitetsidén," 278.

19. Kjellén, "Nationalitetsiden," 278.
20. Björck, *Heidenstam och sekelskiftets Sverige*, 62.
21. Kjellén, "Nationalitetsidén," 282.
22. Kjellén, "Nationalitetsidén," 278.
23. Kjellén, "Nationalitetsidén," 282.
24. Alf W. Johansson, ed., *Vad är Sverige?*; Linnell and Löfgren, eds., *Svenska krusbär*.
25. Torsten Dahl and Bohman, *Svenska män och kvinnor*, vol. 7, 322–24; Daun, "Gustav Sundbärg och det svenska folklynnet"; Forsman, "Gustaf Sundbärg och det svenska folklynnet."
26. Laurin, *Folklynnen*, 493.
27. Edling, *Det fosterländska hemmet*, 190–215.
28. Sundbärg, *Emigrationsutredningen: Bil. 16: Det svenksa folklynnet*, 43.
29. Sundbärg, *Emigrationsutredningen: Bil. 16*, 26.
30. Sundbärg, *Emigrationsutredningen: Bil. 16*, 70–79.
31. Sundbärg, *Emigrationsutredningen: Bil. 16*, 28.
32. Sundbärg, *Emigrationsutredningen: Bil. 16*, 39.
33. Sundbäreg, *Emigrationsutredningen: Bil. 16*, 92.
34. Sundbärg, *Emigrationsutredningen: Bil. 16*, 29, 32, 37, 46, 117, B43.
35. Björck, *Heidenstam och sekelskiftets Sverige*, 190.
36. Heidenstam, *Samlade verk*, vol. 23, 8–9.
37. Böök, *Verner von Heidenstam*, 114–16; Engberg, *Jag förstår inte vad världen är*.
38. Schiöler, *Vännerna Strindberg och Heidenstam*, 4.
39. Gedin, *Verner von Heidenstam*, 578–59; Stenkvist, *Nationalskalden*.
40. Borland, *Nietzsche's Influence on Swedish Literature*.
41. Heidenstam, *Samlade verk*, vol. 19, 13.
42. *Social Tidskrift: Organ för studenter och arbetare*, 217.
43. The Great Strike of 1909 ended in a resounding defeat for the Swedish labor movement. It sharpened class antagonisms and diminished the appeal of the kind of nationalist-democratic rhetoric that had made Heidenstam popular among working-class activists. Instead they supported Strindberg in his radical attacks on his former friend.
44. Heidenstam, *Samlade verk*, vol. 19, 11.
45. Heidenstam, *Samlade verk*, vol. 19, 11.
46. Heidenstam, *Samlade verk*, vol. 23, 49.
47. Key, "Om patriotismen," 248.

8. SWEDEN FOR THE SWEDES!

1. Later historical research has shown that the peasants weren't represented at the Riksdag of 1435. All the four estates were in place at the Riksdag of 1527, however.
2. Hansson, *Demokrati*, 261–67.
3. Lundberg, *Folkstyre eller fogdevälde*, 24.
4. Linderborg, *Socialdemokraterna skriver historia*, 324.

5. Strahl, *Nationalism och socialism*; Trägårdh, "Concept of the People"; Trägårdh, "Crisis and the Politics of National Community"; Linderborg, *Socialdemokraterna skriver historia*.
6. Isaksson, *Per Albin 1*, 18–21.
7. Isaksson, *Per Albin 1*, 20.
8. Boëthius, Hildebrand, and Nilzén, eds., *Svenskt biografiskt lexikon*, vol. 28, 67–77.
9. Selander, *Lärobokskunskap*, 56–57.
10. Trägårdh, "Concept of the People," 195–210.
11. Odhner, *Lärobok i fädnerslandets historia*, 97.
12. Lönnroth, "Den svenska riksdagens uppkomst."
13. Hansson, *Demokrati*, 132–33.
14. Isaksson, *Per Albin 1*, 48–53.
15. Isaksson, *Per Albin 1*, 49.
16. Lindström, *Tyskland och socialdemokratin*, 11–13.
17. Henrik Berggren, *Seklets ungdom*, 176–78.
18. Karleby, *Socialismen inför verkligheten*.
19. Karleby, *Socialismen inför verkligheten*, 93; Sten O. Karlsson, *Det intelligenta samhället*, 490–500.
20. Lindström, "Socialism, nation och stat," 280–302.
21. Lindström, "Socialism, nation och stat," 293.
22. Lindström, "Socialism, nation och stat," 294.
23. Lindström, "Socialism, nation och stat," 297.
24. Lindström, *En socialist*, 207; Sten O. Karlsson, *Det intelligenta samhället*, 500–514.
25. Hansson, *Demokrati*, 7–18.
26. Linderborg, *Socialdemokraterna skriver historia*, 285–98.
27. Ambjörnsson, *Den skötsamme arbetaren*; Lundkvist, *Folkrörelserna i det svenska samhället*; Enquist, *Lewis resa*.
28. Sewell, *Work and Revolution in France*, 239–42.
29. *Social-demokraten*, February 26, 1886, cited in Henrik Berggren, *Seklets ungdom*, 77–8.
30. Ambjörnsson, *Den skötsamme arbetaren*, 157.
31. Ambjörnsson, *Den skötsamme arbetaren*, 157.
32. *Fram* magazine, July 1905.
33. *Fram* magazine, August 1910.
34. Sävström, *En talmans levnadsminnen*, 61.
35. Hansson, "Den 'gamla' ungdomsrörelsen," 22.
36. Henrik Berggren, *Seklets ungdom*, 285.
37. *Fram* valnummer 3, 1908, cited in Henrik Berggren, *Seklets ungdom*, 245.
38. Lundkvist, *Folkrörelserna i det svenska samhället*, 67.
39. Enquist, *Lewis resa*, 15–16.
40. Ambjörnsson, *Den skötsamme arbetaren*.
41. Brunnsviks folkhögskola, *Brunnsviks folkhögskolas*, 36; Henrik Berggren, "Proletärerna vid Mimers brunn."
42. Ambjörnsson, *Den skötsamme arbetaren*, 75.

43. Henrik Berggren, "Proletärerna vid Mimers brunn."
44. Kjellén-Björkquist, *Rudolf Kjellén*, 230.
45. Rydén, "Medborgarkunskap," 153.
46. Brevskolan och Folkberedskapen, "Den svenska livsformen," 312.
47. Cullberg, "Den svenska linjen."
48. Karleby, *Socialismen inför verkligheten*, 21.
49. Karleby, *Socialismen inför verkligheten*, 4.
50. Geijer, *Samlade skrifter*, vol. 2, 34–39.
51. Källström, *Den gode nihilisten*; Hägerström, *Socialfilosofiska uppsatser*.
52. Hägerström, *Socialfilosofiska uppsatser*, 107.
53. Runcis, *Steriliseringar i folkhemmet*; Zaremba, *De rena och de andra*; Broberg and Tydén, *Oönskade i folkhemmet*.
54. Runcis, *Steriliseringar i folkhemmet*, 58–97.
55. Hansson, *Demokrati*, 220.
56. Thomasson, *Sweden*.
57. Ruth, "Second New Nation."
58. Ludvig Nordström quoted in Ruth, "Second New Nation," 83.
59. Henrik Berggren, *Seklets ungdom*.
60. Henrik Berggren, "I skuggan av det förflutna," 21–22.
61. Kungliga Skolöverstyrelesen, *Läroplan för grundskolan*, 254.

9. NATIONALIZING THE CHILD

1. Pedersen, *Family, Dependence and the Origins of the Welfare State*; Bock and Thane, eds., *Maternity and Gender Policies*; Koven and Michel, eds., *Mothers of a New World*.
2. Paul, "Eugenics and the Left"; Kevles, *In the Name of Eugenics*; Stepan, *Hour of Eugenics*; Broberg and Tydén, *Oönskade i folkhemmet*; Runcis, *Steriliseringar i folkhemmet*, Zaremba, *De rena och de andra*.
3. Witoszek, "Moral Community and the Crisis of the Enlightenment," 54–59.
4. Plato, *The Republic*, "Marriage and the Family," 236–52.
5. Sandin, "Barndomens omvandling."
6. Myrdal and Myrdal, *Kris i befolkningsfrågan*, 299.
7. Mral, "'Den nya kvinnan'."
8. Mral, "'Den nya kvinnan'."
9. Therborn, *Between Sex and Power*, 162–66.
10. Sten O. Karlsson, *Arbetarfamiljen och det nya hemmet*, 109.
11. Sten O. Karlsson, *Arbetarfamiljen och det nya hemmet*, 101–11.
12. Mral, "'Den nya kvinnan'," 78.
13. Bok, *Alva Myrdal*, 50.
14. Vinterhed, *Kärlek i tjugonde seklet*.
15. Mral, "'Den nya kvinnan'."
16. Alva Myrdal, *Folk och familj*, 27–44.
17. Alva Myrdal, *Nation and Family*, 13. This passage is not included in the Swedish edition.
18. Alva Myrdal, *Folk och familj*, 13.

19. Alva Myrdal, *Folk och familj*, 25–27.
20. Bok, *Alva Myrdal*, 69, 107.
21. Bok, *Alva Myrdal*, 20.
22. Bok, *Alva Myrdal*, 23.
23. Alva Myrdal, "Den nya familjen," quoted in Yvonne Hirdman, ed., *Alva Myrdal*, 158–59.
24. Myrdal and Myrdal, *Kris i befolkningsfrågan*, 351–52.
25. Alva Myrdal, *Folk och familj*, 146.
26. Alva Myrdal, *Folk och familj*, 146.
27. Hirdman, "Utopia in the Home."
28. Quoted in Ohlander, "Det osynliga barnet?" 182.
29. Schüllerqvist, "Från kosackval till kohandel."
30. Torbjörn Nilsson, *Mellan arv och utopi*, 347–48.
31. Rothstein, *Just Institutions Matter*.
32. Rothstein, *Vad bör staten göra?* 218.
33. Jönsson and Lindblom, *Politik och kärlek*, 83; Gustav Möller, "Memoarkoncept 2."
34. Strindberg, *Samlade verk*, vols. 13–14, *Svenska öden och äventyr I–II*, 173.
35. Åmark, *Hundra år av välfärdspolitik*, 124–27.
36. Åmark, *Hundra år av välfärdspolitik*, 87.
37. Alva Myrdal, *Folk och familj*, 162.
38. Alva Myrdal, *Folk och familj*, 183.
39. Alva Myrdal, *Folk och familj*, 184.
40. Murray, *Losing Ground*; Gordon, *Pitied but Not Entitled*; Skocpol, *Protecting Soldiers and Mothers*.
41. Alva Myrdal, *Nation and Family*, 398. Chapter 22 was titled "One Sex a Social Problem."
42. Alva Myrdal quoted in Thorsell, "Könsrollsfrågan och barnomsorgen," 96.
43. Myrdal and Klein, *Kvinnans två roller*.
44. Brun-Gulbrandsen, et al., *Kvinnors liv och arbete*.

10. ASOCIAL, UNNATURAL, INHUMAN

1. Strömstedt, *Astrid Lindgren*, 249.
2. Ulla Lundqvist, *Århundradets barn*.
3. Strömstedt, *Astrid Lindgren*, 102.
4. Strömstedt, *Astrid Lindgren*, 102.
5. Strömstedt, *Astrid Lindgren*, 251.
6. See Blume, *Pippi Långstrumps Verwandlung zur "dame-bien-élevée,"* for how Pippi was "tamed" for domestic French consumption through tendentious mistranslations.
7. Henrik Berggren, "I skuggan av det förflutna."
8. This can be compared with Georges Bataille's analysis of sovereign versus servile man in *The Accursed Share* and the discussion in the final chapter of his book.

9. Ohlander and Strömberg, *Tusen svenska kvinnoår*, 183.
10. Statistiska centralbyrån, *Statistisk årsbok för Sverige årgång 36, 42, 49*, 1949, 1955, 1957.
11. Åmark, *Hundra år av välfärdspolitik*, 258–60.
12. Statistiska centralbyrån, *Statistisk årsbok för Sverige årgång 36, 49*, 1949, 1957.
13. Eva Moberg, *Kvinnor och människor*, 113.
14. On the politics of gender equality during the 1960s and 1970s, see Florin and Nilsson, *"Något som liknar en oblodig revolution"*; Florin, Sommestad, and Wikander, eds., *Kvinnor mot kvinnor*; and Svanström and Östberg, *Än män då?*
15. Eva Moberg, "Kvinnans villkorliga frigivning," 196.
16. Eva Moberg, "Kvinnans villkorliga frigivning," 195.
17. Eva Moberg, "Kvinnans villkorliga frigivning," 197.
18. Eva Moberg, "Kvinnans villkorliga frigivning," 197.
19. Eva Moberg, *Kvinnor och människor*, 109.
20. Christina Carlsson, *Kvinnosyn och kvinnopolitik*.
21. Eva Moberg, *Kvinnor och människor*, 111.
22. Eva Moberg, *Kvinnor och människor*, 113.
23. Eva Moberg, *Kvinnor och människor*, 113.
24. Norberg, *Motståndsmannen Vilhelm Moberg*.
25. See Eva Moberg, *Kvinnor och människor*, in which she responds to a number of articles criticizing her writings.
26. Stina Engström in Eva Moberg, *Kvinnor och människor*, 53.
27. Baude, ed., *Visionen om jämställdhet*, 10.
28. Dahlström in Brun-Gulbrandsen, et al., *Kvinnors liv och arbete*.
29. Baude, ed., *Visionen om jämställdhet*, 11.
30. Romanus, "Ett nätverk för jämställdhet."
31. Romanus, "Ett nätverk för jämställdhet," 26.
32. Siv Thorsell quoted in Hederberg, "Hörnet Flöjelgatan-Alviksvägen," 21.
33. Barbro Backberger quoted in Vestbro, "Från liberal rörelse till socialistisk kamp mot patriarkatet," 61.
34. Romanus, "Ett nätverk för jämställdhet," 28.
35. Florin, "Skatten som befriar."
36. On LO, family policy, and issues concerning gender and gender equality, see Hirdman, *Med kluven tunga*; Waldemarson, *Mjukt till formen, hårt till innehållet*; Ingemar Lindberg, *Den nya familjens tid*.
37. SAP and LO, *Rådslag 65. Din mening om*.
38. Lyttkens, "Införande av särbeskattning i Sverige," 73.
39. Lyttkens, "Införande av särbeskattning i Sverige," 79.
40. Troedsson in Högerns Ungdomsförbund, *Hög tid för ny familjepolitik*, 31.
41. Troedsson in Högerns Ungdomsförbund, *Hög tid för ny familjepolitik*, 44.
42. Troedsson cited in Lyttkens, "Införande av särbeskattning," 81.
43. Sveriges liberala studentförbund, *Solidarisk familjepolitik*. See also Folkpartiets ungdomsförbund, *Radikal familjepolitik*, which contains contributions

from a number of young liberals who later became influential: Gunvor Hildén, Ingmar Mundebo, Gabriel Romanus, Carl Tham, Ola Ullsten. See also Drangel, "Folkpartiet och jämställdhetsfrågan."
44. Lyttkens, "Införande av särbeskattning," 88.
45. The last remnants of joint taxation disappeared only with the tax reforms of 1990.
46. Elvander, *Svensk skattepolitik 1945–1970*.
47. Familjeskatteberedningen (Fi), *Individuell beskattning*.
48. Familjeskatteberedningen (Fi), *Individuell beskattning*.
49. Quoted from governmental commission Familjeskatteberedningen (Fi), *Individuell beskattning*, 63–65.
50. On the women's wing of the Social Democratic Party, see Gunnel Karlsson, *Från broderskap till systerskap*.
51. Nancy Eriksson, *Bara en hemmafru*. For a discussion of the reception and debate over the book, see Florin, "Skatten som befriar."
52. Nancy Eriksson, *Bara en hemmafru*, 36–37.
53. Sveriges socialdemokratiska kvinnoförbund, *Familjen i framtiden*, 5.
54. Sveriges socialdemokratiska kvinnoförbund, *Familjen i framtiden*, 5.
55. Sveriges socialdemokratiska kvinnoförbund, *Familjen i framtiden*, 6.
56. Sveriges socialdemokratiska kvinnoförbund, *Familjen i framtiden*, 6.
57. Eva Moberg, *Kvinnor och människor*.
58. Sveriges socialdemokratiska kvinnoförbund, *Familjen i framtiden*, 35.
59. Sveriges socialdemokratiska kvinnoförbund, *Familjen i framtiden*, 26.
60. Sveriges socialdemokratiska kvinnoförbund, *Familjen i framtiden*, 35.
61. Sveriges socialdemokratiska kvinnoförbund, *Familjen i framtiden*, 40.
62. Sveriges socialdemokratiska kvinnoförbund, *Familjen i framtiden*, 36, 41.
63. Sveriges socialdemokratiska kvinnoförbund, *Familjen i framtiden*, 42, 44–45.
64. Sveriges socialdemokratiska kvinnoförbund, *Familjen i framtiden*, 46.
65. SOU, *Reformer inom studiemedelssystemet*, 36.
66. Staffan Nilsson in SOU, *Reformer inom studiemedelssystemet*, 26.
67. Staffan Nilsson in SOU, *Reformer inom studiemedelssystemet*, 26.
68. SOU, *Studiestöd: alternativa utvecklingslinjer*, "Tilläggsdirektiv, Bilaga 1," 225.
69. SOU, *Studiestöd: alternativa utvecklingslinjer*, "Tilläggsdirektiv, Bilaga 1," 242.
70. Romanus, "Ett nätverk för jämställdhet."
71. SOU, *Familj och äktenskap, Utredningsuppdraget*.
72. SOU, *Familj och äktenskap, Utredningsuppdraget*.
73. SOU, *Familj och äktenskap, Utredningsuppdraget*.
74. SOU, *Familj och äktenskap, Utredningsuppdraget*.
75. SOU, *Delbetänkande av familijesakkunniga*.
76. SOU, *Delbetänkande av familijesakkunniga*.
77. Persson, *Daghemsfrågan*, 5.
78. Persson, *Daghemsfrågan*, 5.
79. Thorsell, "Könsrollsfrågan och barnomsorgen," 98.

80. Romanus, "Ett nätverk för jämställdhet," 32.
81. Florin and Nilsson, *"Något som liknar en oblodig revolution."* The phrase is taken from Leijon, *Swedish Women—Swedish Men.*
82. Eva Sundström, *Gender Regimes,* 7–17; Landler, "Quoth the Raven."
83. Wikander, *Kvinnoarbete i Europa 1798–1950,* 194.
84. Florin and Nilsson, *"Något som liknar en oblodig revolution."* See also Kulawik, "Maskulinism och välfärdsstatens framväxt i Sverige och Tyskland."

11. JUST A HOUSEWIFE

1. Thorsell, "Könsrollsfrågan och barnomsorgen," 98.
2. Mannheimer, *Rapport om kvinnor,* 12–13.
3. Sten Carlsson, et al., *Den svenska historien 15,* 143–45.
4. Gunnar Sträng quoted in Brita Nordström, "Familjepolitisk horisont," 25.
5. Brita Nordström, "Familjepolitisk horisont," 25.
6. Lyttkens, "Införande av särbeskattning i Sverige," 90.
7. For a discussion of Nordström, Eriksson, and the Family Campaign, see Florin, "Skatten som befriar."
8. Lyttkens, "Införande av särbeskattning i Sverige," 90.
9. Wieselgren, Nordström, et al., *Rädda familjen.*
10. Barbro Backberger quoted in Brita Nordström, "Familjepolitisk horisont," 21.
11. Florin, "Skatten som befriar."
12. Wieselgren, "Kulturpolitisk översikt," 16.
13. Wieselgren, "Kulturpolitisk översikt," 19.
14. Brita Nordström, "Familjepolitisk horisont," 22.
15. Brita Nordström, *Ska familjen krossas?* 25–26.
16. Brita Nordström, *Ska familjen krossas?* 12–13.
17. Rousseau, *Social Contract.*
18. Wieselgren, Nordström, et al., *Rädda familjen,* 112.
19. Personal communication from Tom Hardt to Lars Trägårdh.
20. Rubin, "En ny front mot familjens fundamentalister."
21. Anne Marie Berggren, "Likhet eller särart—harmoni eller konflikt?" 84–91.
22. Lyttkens, "Införande av särbeskattning i Sverige," 91.
23. Spruill, *Divided We Stand.*
24. Ingemar Lindberg, *Den nya familjens tid.*
25. Klinth, *Göra pappa med barn,* 185.
26. Klinth, *Göra pappa med barn,* 185.
27. Birgitta Dahl, "Familjepolitiken och jämlikheten."
28. Birgitta Dahl, "Familjepolitiken och jämlikheten."
29. Klinth, *Göra pappa med barn,* 162–63.
30. Klinth, *Göra pappa med barn,* 181.
31. Klinth, *Göra pappa med barn,* 181.
32. Brita Nordström, *Ska familjen krossas?* 68.
33. Brita Nordström, *Ska familjen krossas?* 8, 99.

34. Florin, "Skatten som befriar."
35. Cited in Klinth, *Göra pappa med barn*, 207.
36. Eva Moberg quoted in Klinth, *Göra pappa med barn*, 207.
37. See Klinth, *Göra pappa med barn*, 215.
38. Klinth, *Göra pappa med barn*, 215.
39. Klinth, *Göra pappa med barn*, 217.
40. This negative effect has been remarked on, for example, in the commission on parental leave that SOU presented in 2005, *Reformerad föräldraförsäkring* (SOU 2005:73). We wrote an article pointing out the problem in 1994: Berggren and Trägårdh, "Ge papporna halva tiden."
41. Wästberg, "Efter folkpartiets landsmöte," 37.
42. Wästberg, "Efter folkpartiets landsmöte," 37.
43. Nonetheless, fathers have gradually begun to use their right to parental leave. By 2020 the number stands at 30 percent, compared to 0.5 percent in the early 1970s.
44. Wiegert, *Dagis—Nej tack!*
45. Wiegert, *Dagis—Nej tack!* 100.
46. Wiegert, *Dagis—Nej tack!* 17.
47. Wiegert, *Dagis—Nej tack!* 48.
48. Wiegert, *Dagis—Nej tack!* 19.
49. Haas, *Equal Parenthood and Social Policy*, 35.
50. Hernes, *Welfare State and Woman Power*; Sainsbury, *Gender, Equality and Welfare States*.
51. Leira, *Welfare States and Working Mothers*; Leira, "The 'Woman-friendly' Welfare State?"; Leira, *Working Parents and the Welfare State*.
52. See for example the Gender Empowerment Measurement, www.rrojasdatabank.info/hdr20072008tab29.pdf.
53. Ruggie, *The State and Working Women*; Eduards, "Toward a Third Way."
54. Haas, *Equal Parenthood and Social Policy*, 44.
55. Burenstam Linder, *Den hjärtlösa välfärdsstaten*, 33–35, 12.
56. Langby, *Vinter i välfärdslandet*.
57. Henrik Berggren, *Landet utanför*, 17–18.
58. Quote from Eisenhower taken from David Jenkins, *Sweden and the Price of Progress*, 15.
59. Huntford, *New Totalitarians*, 221.
60. Wolfe, "Day-care Dilemma," 15.
61. Wolfe, "Day-care Dilemma," 23.
62. Popenoe, *Disturbing the Nest*.
63. Popenoe, "Family Decline in the Swedish Welfare State."
64. Sandqvist and Andersson, "Thriving Families in the Swedish Welfare State."
65. Burenstam Linder, *Den hjärtlösa välfärdsstaten*.

12. COMPETING VISIONS OF COMMUNITY

1. Vilhelm Moberg's epic of Swedish emigration to North America was published in four volumes during the 1950s and later translated into English:

The Emigrants (*Utvandrarna*; 1949), *Unto a Good Land* (*Invandrarna*; 1952), *The Settlers* (*Nybyggarna*; 1956), and *The Last Letter Home* (*Sista brevet hem*; 1959). See also Norberg, *Motståndsmannen Vilhelm Moberg.*
2. Trägårdh, *State and Civil Society in Northern Europe.*
3. Berggren, *Underbara dagar framför oss,* 526–37; Tobisson, *Löntagarfonder.*
4. Petersson, Westholm, and Blomberg, *Medborgarnas makt.*
5. Trägårdh, *State and Civil Society in Northern Europe*; Trägårdh, "Rethinking the Nordic Welfare State."
6. Antman, ed., *Systemskifte,* 23.
7. Arvidsson and Berntson, *Makten, socialismen och demokratin.* The book was debated a few later in the SSU journal *Tvärdrag*: see Bengtsson and Pettersson, "Alternativ till stark stat."
8. Alsing in Antman, ed., *Systemskifte,* 96.
9. Koselleck, *Critique and Crisis*; Habermas, *Structural Transformation of the Public Sphere.*
10. Jansson, *Adertonhundratalets associationer.*
11. Lundkvist, *Folkrörelserna i det svenska samhället 1850–1920.*
12. Childs, *Sweden.*
13. Adamson, ed., *När botten stack upp*; Salomon, *Rebeller i takt med tiden.*
14. Isling, *Folkrörelserna i ny roll?* 12–13.
15. Isling, *Folkrörelserna i ny roll?* 14.
16. Tommy Svensson, *Ung och radikal,* 54.
17. *Frihet,* 1974.
18. Håkan Bengtsson, *Vägval,* 99.
19. Gustafsson in Isling, *Folkrörelserna i ny roll?* 35.
20. Isling, *Folkrörelserna i ny roll?* 178.
21. Ahlmark in Isling, *Folkrörelserna i ny roll?* 175–76.
22. Isling, *Folkrörelserna i ny roll?*
23. Editorial published in *Aftonbladet* July 6, 1975, quoted in Isling, *Folkrörelserna i ny roll?* 59–61.
24. Engqvist in Jesper Bengtsson, *Det måttfulla upproret,* 62.
25. *Tvärdrag,* 1984, 12–14.
26. Bernhardsson and Kolk, *Det nödvändiga uppbrottet,* 14.
27. Andersson, *Självförvaltning och rörelsetradition.*
28. *Tvärdrag,* 1984, 4–5.
29. Håkan Bengtsson, *Vägval,* 150.
30. Håkan Bengtsson, *Vägval,* 153.
31. Håkan Bengtsson, ed., *En ny socialdemokrati.*
32. Burenstam Linder, *Den hjärtlösa välfärdsstaten.*
33. Berger and Neuhaus, *To Empower People.* When the book first was published in 1977, the term *civil society* was not used, but when it was republished in 1996, the concept of *civil society* replaced the more cumbersome notion of *mediating structures.*
34. Linder, *Demokratins små plattformar.*
35. Arvidsson and Berntson, *Det civila samhället.*
36. Berntson, "Det gemensamma och det enskilda."

37. Zetterberg, *Den svenska socialstaten*; Zetterberg and Ljungberg. *Vårt land*.
38. Moderata samlingspartiet, *Idéer för vår framtid*.
39. Zetterberg in Antman, ed., *Systemskifte*, 66.
40. Zetterberg, "Civila samhället, demokratin och välfärdsstaten."
41. Dahlkvist, "'Det civila samhället' i samhällsteori och samhällsdebatt."
42. Habermas, *Structural Transformation of the Public Sphere*; Cohen and Arato, *Civil Society and Political Theory*; Keane, ed., *Civil Society and the State*.
43. Rothstein, *Den korporativa staten*.
44. Antman, ed., *Systemskifte*, 86–87, 90.
45. Antman, ed., *Systemskifte*, 90.
46. Antman, ed., *Systemskifte*.
47. Linde in Antman, ed., *Systemskifte*, 115.
48. Linde in Antman, ed., *Systemskifte*, 111.
49. Antman and Thorwaldsson, *Hur förena jämlikhet med individens frihet?*
50. Antman and Thorwaldsson, *Hur förena jämlikhet med individens frihet?*
51. Lundström and Wijkström, *Nonprofit Sector in Sweden*; Jeppson Grassman, "Frivilliga insatsero Sverige"; Jeppson Grassman and Svedberg, "Frivilligt socialt arbete i Sverige."
52. Baer, "Voluntary Association Involvement in Comparative Perspective"; Schofer and Fourcade-Gourinchas, "Structural Contexts of Civic Engagement."
53. Rothstein, *Vad bör staten göra?* 224–25.
54. Rothstein, *Vad bör staten göra?* 218.
55. Somers, "Narrating and Naturalizing Civil Society," 259.
56. Wuthnow, *Saving America?*; Putnam, *Bowling Alone*.
57. Henriksen, Strømsnes, and Svedberg, eds., *Civic Engagement in Scandinavia*.
58. Blix and Jordahl, *Privatizing Welfare Services*.
59. Wijkström and Einarsson, "Comparing Swedish Foundations."
60. Henriksen, Strømsnes, and Svedberg, eds., *Civic Engagement in Scandinavia*.
61. Moyn, *Last Utopia*; Hoffmann, "Human Rights and History."
62. Trägårdh, "Scaling up Solidarity from the National to the Global."

13. A LUTHERAN MODERNITY?

1. The Swedish Church still retains a favored legal position in comparison with other religious denominations.
2. Bexell, *Sveriges kyrkohistoria 7*, 117–19, 166–77.
3. Blomquist and Rothstein, *Välfärdsstatens nya ansikte*; Furhammar, *Såpor, sex, och svenska krusbär*; Arvidsson, *Fritt fall*; Bohm and Hesselbon, S J, *Televerket och Posten—Bättre som bolag?*

4. Aurelius, *Luther i Sverige.*
5. Stolt, "Luther—glädjedödaren," 3.
6. Wingren, "Utan Luther stannar Sverige," 51.
7. Billing, *Den svenska folkkyrkan.*
8. Österlin, "Nationalism och nationalkyrklighet i svenska tradition," 321.
9. Aurelius, *Luther i Sverige.*
10. Aurelius, *Luther i Sverige*, 60.
11. Quoted in Aurelius, *Luther i Sverige*, 60.
12. Aurelius, *Luther i Sverige*, 60.
13. Ulf L. Larsson, *Värner Rydén*, 142–45; Ulf L. Larsson, "Bilden av Sverige."
14. Claesson, "Folkhemmets kyrka," 17.
15. Jan Olof Olsson, *1914*; Torbjörn Aronson, "Den unge Manfred Björkquist."
16. Söderblom, *Religionen och staten*, 200.
17. Aronson, "Den unge Manfred Björkquist," 180–84, 205–32.
18. Björkquist quoted in Aronson, "Den unge Manfred Björkquist, 210.
19. Björkquist quoted in Aronson, "Den unge Manfred Björkquist," 215.
20. Björkquist quoted in Aronson, "Den unge Manfred Björkquist," 216.
21. Aronson, "Den unge Manfred Björkquist," 207.
22. Björkquist quoted in Aronson, "Den unge Manfred Björkquist," 219
23. Björkquist quoted in Aronson, "Den unge Manfred Björkquist," 221.
24. Gunnarsson, "Kyrkan, nazismen och demokratin," 44.
25. Billing, *Kyrka och stat i vårt land i detta nu*, 27.
26. Gunnarsson, "Kyrkan, nazismen och demokratin," 109.
27. Billing, *Den svenska folkkyrkan*, 76.
28. Billing, *Den svenska folkkyrkan*, 77.
29. Billing, *Den svenska folkkyrkan*, 79–80.
30. Billing, *Den svenska folkkyrkan*, 83–5.
31. Billing, *Den svenska folkkyrkan*, 87.
32. Billing, *Den svenska folkkyrkan*, 87–92.
33. Billing, *Den svenska folkkyrkan*, 114.
34. Whitford, "Luther's Political Encounters," 188–89.
35. McKim, ed., *Cambridge Companion to Martin Luther.*
36. Per Svensson, *Dr Luther och Mr Hyde.*
37. Whitford, "Luther's Political Encounters," 184–86; Per Svensson, *Dr Luther och Mr Hyde*, 13–65.
38. Whitford, "Luther's Political Encounters," 184–86; Per Svensson, *Dr Luther och Mr Hyde*, 13–65.
39. Tegborg and Andrén, *Sveriges kyrkohistoria 3*, 65–68.
40. Lindkvist, et al,. *Concise History of Sweden*, 61–64.
41. Pleijel, *Hustavlans värld*, 16–17; Nyman, *Förlorarnas historia*, 16–19.
42. Larson, *Reforming the North*, 78–86.
43. Larson, *Reforming the North*, 6–7.
44. Larson, *Reforming the North*, 251.
45. Lindkvist, et al., *Concise History of Sweden*, 61–64.
46. Aronsson, "Bönder gör politik."

47. Lindkvist, et al., *Concise History of Sweden*, 89–91.
48. Per Svensson, *Dr Luther och Mr Hyde*.
49. Wannenwetsch, "Luther's Moral Theology," 120–21.
50. Bluhm, "Nietzsche's Final View of Luther and the Reformation."
51. Foucault, *Discipline and Punish*, 30.
52. Luther, *Lilla och stora katekesen*, 14.
53. Pleijel, *Hustavlans värld*, 23; Aronsson, "Mentalitet, norm, verklighet."
54. Aronsson, "Bönder gör politik," 63.
55. Brilkman, "Undersåten som förstod," 1–18.
56. Hallingberg, *Läsarna*, 26–54.
57. Hallingberg, *Läsarna*, 26–54.
58. Hammar and Flodell, *Religionsblindhet*, 17–18.
59. Carter Lindberg, "Luther's Struggles with Social-ethical Issues," 168.
60. Stolt, "Luther—glädjedödaren."
61. Luther quoted in Stolt, "Luther—glädjedödaren," 10.
62. Astrid Norberg quoted in Gerle, ed., *Luther som utmaning*, 37.
63. McKim, ed., *Cambridge Companion to Martin Luther*, 15–16.
64. Carter Lindberg, "Luther's Struggle with Social-ethical Issues," 169.
65. Derek Wilson, quoted in Per Svensson, *Dr Luther och Mr Hyde*.
66. Becker and Wöβmann, "Luther and the Girls."
67. Becker and Wöβmann, "Luther and the Girls."
68. Becker and Wöβman, "Luther and the Girls."
69. Hammar and Flodell, *Religionsblindhet*, 18.
70. Aronson, *Väckelserörelser i Sverige 1700–2000*.
71. Tegborg and Lenhammar, eds., *Sveriges kyrkohistoria 5*, 32–61.
72. Witoszek, "Fugitives from Utopia."
73. Säfström, "Religious Origins of Democratic Pluralism," 8.
74. Säfström, "Religious Origins of Democratic Pluralism," 58.
75. Gunnar Westin quoted in Hallingberg, *Läsarna*, 418.
76. Jarlert, *Sveriges kyrkohistoria 6*, 125–87.
77. Letter from Geijer to Bremer, December 15, 1841, quoted in Hallingberg, *Läsarna*, 34.
78. Geijer, quoted in Hallingberg, *Läsarna*, 34.
79. Hallingberg, *Läsarna*; the reference is to Fourier.
80. Letter from Tegner, quoted in Hallingberg, *Läsarna*, 53.
81. Enquist, *Lewis resa*, 16.
82. Tegborg and Jarlert, eds., *Sveriges kyrkohistoria 6*, 168.
83. Bredberg, *Bibelsyn och församlingstanke*, 69–89.
84. Hallingberg, *Läsarna*.
85. Gerle, *Luther som utmaning*.
86. Ambjörnsson, 1983, quoted in Hallingberg, *Läsarna*, 33.
87. Per Svensson, *Dr Luther och Mr Hyde*.
88. Åhlén, *Uppsalahistorier*.
89. Claesson, "Att lösa klimatproblem med Luther eller Calvin," 197.
90. Trägårdh, "Concept of the People"; Henrik Berggren, *Seklets ungdom*; Linderborg, *Socialdemokraterna skriver historia*; Isaksson, *Per Albin 4*; Jan Larsson, *Hemmet vi ärvde*.

91. Linnea Lundgren, *A Risk or a Resource?*
92. Pehrsson, "Vår kyrkas sociala uppgifter med särskild hänsyn till den nya lagstiftningen på detta område."
93. Cavanaugh, "Killing for the Telephone Company."
94. MacIntyre quoted in Cavanaugh, "Killing for the Telephone Company," 263.
95. Cavanaugh, "Church, Pluralism, and the Christian Theory of Love"; Trägårdh, "Statist Individualism."

14. CODA

1. Tocqueville, *Democracy in America I*, 5.
2. Welzel, *Freedom Rising*.
3. Bauman, *Liquid Love;* Castells, *Rise of the Network Society*.
4. Mauss, *The Gift*; Durkheim, *Elementary Forms of Religious Life*.
5. Bataille, *The Accursed Share*; Bataille, *Erotism*.
6. Miller, *The Passion of Michel Foucault*.
7. Interview with Michel Foucault by Yngve Lindung in *Bonniers Litterära Magasin*, March 1968.
8. A parliamentarian from the center-right Moderate Party (Moderaterna) even brought a motion to abolish *jantelagen*—as if it were a piece of Social Democratic legislation. As one perceptive commentator on this book's manuscript put it, "Sandemose's text is being misused fairly dramatically, since his original point was about how violence, repression, and cruelty are internalized through a multigenerational structure of hazing."
9. Judt, *Postwar*.
10. Broberg and Tydén, *Oönskade i folkhemmet*; Runcis, *Steriliseringar i folkhemmet*; Zaremba, *De rena och de andra*.
11. Baldwin, *Contagion and the State*; Baldwin, *Disease and Democracy*.
12. Trägårdh, *Bemäktiga individerna*.
13. Petersson, Westholm, and Blomberg, *Medborgarnas makt*.
14. Rothstein, *Vad bör staten göra?* 256–58.
15. Tönnies, *Community and Society*.
16. Durkheim, *Elementary Forms of Reglegious Life*; Weber, *Protestant Ethic*; Marx, *Economic and Philosophic Manuscripts*.
17. Riesman, *Lonely Crowd*; Lasch, *Culture of Narcissism*; Habermas, *Theory of Communicative Action*; Bauman, *Individualized Society*; Putnam, *Bowling Alone*.
18. Bauman, *Liquid Love*.
19. See World Values Survey, European Social Survey, Eurobarometer, and other surveys that measure trust.
20. van Hoorn, "Individualist–Collectivist Culture and Trust Radius."
21. Trägårdh, "Statsindividualismen och civilsamhället"; Larsen, *Rise and Fall of Social Cohesion*.
22. Trägårdh, "Statsindividualismen och civilsamhället."
23. Bourdieu, "Forms of Capital."
24. Morel, Palier, and Palme, eds., *Toward a Social Investment Welfare State?*

25. *The Economist*, "The Next Supermodel."
26. Björnberg and Bradshaw, "Conclusions," 283–95; Popenoe, "Marriage and Family"; Therborn, *Between Sex and Power*, 201; Statistiska centralbyrån, *Statistisk årsbok för Sverige årgång 92* (2005), 96, 733.
27. Popenoe, "Marriage and Family," 11.
28. Klinenberg, *Going Solo*.
29. Pettersson and Esmer, *Vilka är annorlunda?*
30. Trägårdh, "Statsindividualismen."

BIBLIOGRAPHY

Note: The following abbreviations are found throughout this bibliography.

LO: Landsorganisationen (Swedish Trade Union Confederation)
SNS: Studieförbundet Näringsliv och Samhälle (Center for Business and Policy Studies)
SOU: Statens offentliga utredningar (Official Reports of the Swedish Government)
SSU: Sveriges socialdemokratiska ungdomsförbund (youth wing of the Social Democratic Party)

Adamson, Monica, ed. *När botten stack upp: Om de utslagnas kamp för frihet och människovärde*. Hedemora: Gidlund, 2004.

Åhlén, Bengt. *Uppsalahistorier*. Stockholm: Wahlström & Widstrand, 1948.

Ahlsén, Pernilla. "Vänskap odlas i gemensam kultur." *Dagens Nyheter*, December 29, 2005.

Ahlström, Gunnar. *Det moderna genombrottet i nordens litteratur*. Stockholm: Rabén & Sjögren, 1973.

Almqvist, Carl Jonas Love. *Samlade skrifter (Collected Works)*. 16 vols. Stockholm: Bonniers, 1920–1938.

———. *Sara Videbeck (Det går an) and The Chapel*. New York: American-Scandinavian Foundation, 1919.

Almqvist, Kurt, and Kay Glans. *The Swedish Success Story?* Stockholm: Axel and Margaret Ax:son Johnson Foundation, 2001.

Åmark, Klas. *Hundra år av välfärdspolitik: Välfärdsstatens framväxt i Norge och Sverige*. Umeå: Boréa, 2005.

Ambjörnsson, Ronny. *Den skötsamme arbetaren: Idéer och ideal i ett norrländskt sågverksamhälle 1880–1936 (The Conscientious Worker)*. Stockholm: Carlssons, 1988.

———. *Ellen Key: En europeisk intellektuell*. Stockholm: Bonnier, 2012.

———. "Ellen Key: Miljö, liv, idéer." In *Hemmets århundrade*, Ellen Key. Stockholm: Aldus, 1976.

Anderson, Benedict. *Den föreställda gemenskapen: Reflexioner kring nationalismens ursprung och spridning* (*Imagined Communities: Reflections on the Origin and Spread of Nationalism*). London: Verso, 1991.

Andersson, Widar. *Självförvaltning och rörelsetradition: En bok om stadsdelen Eriksbo*. Kristianstad: Kristianstads boktr, 1982.

Antman, Peter. "Inte utan jämlikhet." In *Hur förena jämlikhet med individens frihet?* edited by Peter Antman and Karl-Petter Thorwaldsson. Stockholm: Utbildningsförlaget Brevskolan, 1994.

Antman, Peter, ed. *Systemskifte*. Stockholm: Carlssons, 1993.

Antman, Peter, and Karl-Petter Thorwaldsson. *Hur förena jämlikhet med individens frihet?* Stockholm: Utbildningsförlaget Brevskolan, 1994.

Applegate, Celia. *A Nation of Provincials: The German Idea of Heimat*. Berkeley: University of California Press, 1990.

Arnstberg, Karl-Olov. *Typiskt svenskt: 8 essäer om det nutida Sverige*. Stockholm: Carlssons, 2005.

Aronson, Torbjörn. "Den unge Manfred Björkquist: Hur en vision av kristendomens möte med kultur och samhälle växer fram." PhD diss., Uppsala University, 2008.

———. *Väckelserörelser i Sverige 1700–2000*. Uppsala: Areopagus/Livets ords förlag, 2014.

Aronsson, Peter. "Bönder gör politik: Det lokala självstyret som social arena i tre Smålandssocknar, 1680–1850." PhD diss., Lund University, 1992.

———. "Mentalitet, norm, verklighet: Hustavlan i lokalsamhället." In *Hilding Pleijel symposium: 19 oktober 1893–19 oktober 1993: Ett hundraårsjubileum*. Lund: Lund University Press, 1995.

Arvidsson, Claes. *Fritt fall*. N.p.: Från penna till papper bokförlag, 2017.

Arvidsson, Håkan, and Lennart Berntson. *Det civila samhället*. Stockholm: Timbro, 1990.

———. *Makten, socialismen och demokratin: Om det förstatligade samhället* (*Power, Socialism, and Democracy*). Lund: Zenit, 1980.

Aspers, Patrik, and Emil Uddhammar, eds. *Framtidens dygder*. Stockholm: City University Press, 1999.

Asplund, Johan. *Essä om Gemeinschaft och Gesellschaft*. Göteborg: Bokförlaget Korpen, 1991.

Aurelius, Carl Axel. *Luther i Sverige: Svenska Lutherbilder under tre sekler*. Skellefteå: Artos, 1994.

———. "Vilken Luther: Om Lutherbilden i Sverige." In *Luther och Sverige*, edited by Carl-Axel Aurelius, Torgny Bohlin, Birgit Stolt, and Gustaf Wingren. Linköping: Akademi för kyrka och kultur i Linköpings stift, 1994.

Austin, Paul Britten. *On Being Swedish*. London: Secker & Warburg, 1968.

Baer, Douglas. "Voluntary Association Involvement in Comparative Perspective." In *State and Civil Society in Northern Europe: The Swedish Model Reconsidered*, edited by Lars Trägårdh, 67–125. New York: Berghahn Books, 2006.

Baldwin, Peter. *Contagion and the State in Europe, 1830–1930*. Cambridge, UK: Cambridge University Press, 1999.

———. *Disease and Democracy: The Industrialized World Faces AIDS*. Berkeley: University of California Press, 2005.

Barnard, F. M. *Herder's Social and Political Thought: From Enlightenment to Nationalism*. Oxford: Clarendon Press, 1965.

Bataille, Georges. *The Accursed Share: An Essay on General Economy*. Vols. 2–3. New York: Zone Books, 1991.

———. *Erotism: Death and Sensuality*. London: Calder, 1962.

Baude, Annika. "Inledning." In *Visionen om jämställdhet*, edited by Annika Baude. Stockholm: SNS förlag, 1992.

Baude, Annika, ed. *Visionen om jämställdhet*. Stockholm: SNS förlag, 1992.

Bauman, Zygmunt. *Det individualiserade samhället (The Individualized Society)*. Cambridge, UK: Polity Press, 2001.

———. *Liquid Love. On the Frailty of Human Bonds*. Cambridge, UK: Polity Press, 2003.

Becker, Sascha O., and Ludger Wößmann. "Luther and the Girls: Religious Denomination and the Female Education Gap in 19th-Century Prussia." IZA (Institut zur Zukunft der Arbeit; Institute for the Study of Labor) Discussion Paper Series no. 3837, Bonn, 2008.

Bengtsson, Håkan. *Vägval: Idéutvecklingen i SSU*. Stockholm: SSU, 1992.

Bengtsson, Håkan, ed. *En ny socialdemokrati (A New Social Democracy)*. Stockholm: Tidens förlag, 1992.

Bengtsson, Håkan, and Henry Pettersson. "Alternativ till stark stat: 'civilt samhälle'?" *Tvärdrag: en tidning för debatt och kritik*, no. 1–2 (1984).

Bengtsson, Jesper. *Det måttfulla upproret*. Stockholm: Norstedts, 2004.

Berge, Anders. *Medborgarrätt och egenansvar: De sociala försäkringarna i Sverige 1901–1935*. Lund: Arkiv, 1995.

Berger, Peter, and Richard John Neuhaus. *To Empower People: From State to Civil Society*. Washington, DC: American Enterprise Institute, 1996.

———. *To Empower People: The Role of Mediating Structures in Public Policy*. Washington, DC: American Enterprise Institute, 1977.

Berggren, Anne Marie. "Likhet eller särart—harmoni eller konflikt? En analys av kvinnorörelsens idéer." PhD diss., Göteborg University, 1987.

Berggren, Henrik. "I skuggan av det förflutna: Om att växa upp i det modernaste av samhällen." In *Det förflutna—ett främmande land*. Stockholm: Moderna Tider/Forskningsrådsnämnden, 1994.

———. "Jag hör Amerika sjunga." In *Demokratiska perspektiv*, by Walt Whitman, Introduction. Umeå: Text och kultur, 2006.

———. *Landet utanför. Del 1: Sverige och kriget 1939–1940*. Stockholm: Norstedts, 2018.

———. "'Min ras, min rot, min stam': Rickard Lindström och den svenska arbetarklassen." In *Vad är Sverige? Röster om svensk nationell identitet*, edited by Alf W. Johansson. Stockholm: Prisma, 2001.

———. "Proletärerna vid Mimers brunn." *Historisk tidskrift* 2 (1988).

———. *Seklets ungdom: Politik, retorik och modernitet 1900–1939*. Stockholm: Tiden, 1995.

———. *Underbara dagar framför oss: En biografi över Olof Palme*. Stockholm: Norstedt, 2010.

Berggren, Henrik, and Lars Trägårdh. "Ge papporna halva tiden." *Dagens Nyheter*, December 29, 1994.

———. "Pippi Longstocking: The Autonomous Child and the Moral Logic of the Swedish Welfare State." In *Swedish Modernism: Architecture, Consumption and the Welfare State*, edited by Helena Mattson and Sven-Olov Wallenstein. London: Black Dog, 2010.

Berman, Marshall. *The Politics of Authenticity: Radical Individualism and the Emergence of Modern Society*. New York: Atheneum, 1970.

Bernhardsson, Bo, and Jaan Kolk. *Det nödvändiga uppbrottet (The Necessary Break)*. Stockholm: Rabén & Sjögren, 1980.

Berntson, Lennart. "Det gemensamma och det enskilda." In *Det civila samhället*, edited by Håkan Arvidsson. Stockholm: Timbro, 1990.

Bexell, Oloph. *Sveriges kyrkohistoria 7: Folkväckelsens och kyrkoförnyelsens tid*. Stockholm: Verbum med Svenska kyrkans forskningsråd, 2003.

Billing, Einar. *Den svenska folkkyrkan*. Stockholm: Sveriges Kristliga Studentrörelse, 1930.

———. *Kyrka och stat i vårt land i detta nu*. Stockholm: Sveriges Kristliga Studentrörelse, 1942.

Björck, Staffan. *Heidenstam och sekelskiftets Sverige*. Stockholm: Natur och kultur, 1946.

———. *Verner von Heidenstam*. Stockholm: Natur och kultur, 1959.

Björnberg, Ulla, ed. *European Parents in the 1990s: Contradictions and Comparisons*. New Brunswick, NJ: Transaction Publishers, 1992.

Björnberg, Ulla, and Jonathan Bradshaw. "Conclusions." In *Social Policy, Employment and Family Change in Comparative Perspective*, edited by Jonathan Bradshaw and Aksel Hatland. Northampton, MA: Edward Elgar, 2006.

Black, Judith, and Jim Pott. *Swedish Reflections: From Beowulf to Bergman*. London: Arcadia, 2003.

Blix, Mårten, and Henrik Jordahl. *Privatizing Welfare Services: Lessons from the Swedish Experiment*. Oxford: Oxford University Press, 2021.

Blomquist, Paula, and Bo Rothstein. *Välfärdsstatens nya ansikte*. Stockholm: Agora, 2000.

Bluhm, Heinz. "Nietzsche's Final View of Luther and the Reformation." *Concordia Theological Monthly* 27, no. 10 (1956): 765–75.

Blume, Svenja. *Pippi Långstrumps Verwandlung zur "dame-bien-élevée": Die anpassung eines Kinderbuchs an ein fremdes kulturelles system: Eine analyse der französicschen Übersetzung von Astrid Lindgrens Pippi Långstrump (1945–1948)*. Hamburg: Kovac, 2001.

Bock, Gisela, and Pat Thane, eds. *Maternity and Gender Policies: Women and the Rise of European Welfare States 1880s–1950s*. London: Routledge, 1994.

Boëthius, B., B. Hildebrand, and G. Nilzén, eds. *Svenskt biografiskt lexikon*. Stockholm: Svenskt biografiskt lexikon, 1918–present.

Bohm, Peter, and Per Ove Hesselbon. *SJ, Televerket och Posten—Bättre som bolag? Rapport till Expertgruppen för studier i offentlig ekonomi (ESO)*. Stockholm: Allmänna förlaget, 1991.

Bok, Sissela. *Alva Myrdal: A Daughter's Memoir*. Reading, MA: Addison-Wesley, 1991.

Böök, Fredrik. *Verner von Heidenstam*. Stockholm: Bonnier, 1959.

Borland, Harold. *Nietzsche's Influence on Swedish Literature: With Special Reference to Strindberg, Ola Hansson, Heidenstam and Fröding*. Serie A, Humanistiska Skrifter. Göteborg: Göteborgs kungliga vetenskaps och vitterhets-samhälles handlingar, 1956.

Bourdieu, Pierre. "The Forms of Capital." In *Handbook of Theory and Research for the Sociology of Education*, edited by John G. Richardson. Westport, CT: Greenwood Press, 1986.

Bradley, David. "Family Laws and Welfare States." In *The Nordic Model of Marriage and the Welfare State*, edited by Kari Melby, et al. Copenhagen: Nordic Council of Ministers, 2000.

Bradshaw, Jonathan, and Aksel Hatland, eds. *Social Policy, Employment and Family Change in Comparative Perspective*. Northampton, MA: Edward Elgar, 2006.

Brandell, Gustaf. *Svensk folkkaraktär: Bidrag till svenska folkets psykologi*. Stockholm: Effellve, 1944.

Brandl, Horst. *Persönlichkeitsidealismus und Willenskult: Aspekte der Nietzsche-rezeption in Schweden*. Heidelberg: Winter, 1977.

Breckman, Warren. *Marx, the Young Hegelians, and the Origins of Radical Social Theory*. Cambridge, UK: Cambridge University Press, 1999.

Bredberg, William. *Bibelsyn och församlingstanke*. Stockholm: Gummesson, 1968.

Brevskolan och Folkberedskapen. "Den svenska livsformen." In *Vad är Sverige? Röster om svensk nationell identitet*, edited by Alf W. Johansson. Stockholm: Prisma, 2001.

Brilkman, Kajsa. "Undersåten som förstod: Den svenska reformatoriska samtalsordningen och den tidigmoderna integrationsprocessen." PhD diss., Lund University, 2013.

Broberg, Gunnar. "När svenskarna uppfann Sverige: Anteckningar till ett hundraårsjubileum." In *Tänka, tycka, tro*, edited by Gunnar Broberg, Ulla Wikander, and Klas Åmark. Stockholm: Ordfront, 1993.

Broberg, Gunnar, and Mattias Tydén. *Oönskade i folkhemmet: Rashygien och sterilisering i Sverige*. Stockholm: Gidlunds, 1991.

Brohed, Ingmar, ed. *Kyrka och nationalism i Norden: Nationalism och skandinavism i de nordiska folkkyrkorna under 1800-talet*. Lund: Lund University Press, 1998.

Brubakers, Roger. *Citizenship and Nationhood in Germany and France*. Cambridge, MA: Harvard University Press, 1992.

Brun-Gulbrandsen, Sverre, Edmund Dahlström, Gösta Dahlström, Harriet Holter, Stina Thyberg, and Per Olav Tiller. *Kvinnors liv och arbete: Svenska och norska studier av ett aktuellt samhällsproblem (Women's Lives and Work)*. Stockholm: SNS förlag, 1962.

Brunnsviks folkhögskola. *Brunnsviks folkhögskolas minnesskrift 1906–1931*. Sörvik: Brunnsviks folkhögskola, 1931.

Burenstam Linder, Staffan. *Den hjärtlösa välfärdsstaten (The Heartless Welfare State)*. Stockholm: Timbro, 1983.

Burman, Lars, ed. *Carl Jonas Love Almqvist—diktaren, debattören, drömmaren: Föreläsningar och essäer. Utgiven av Almqvist-sällskapet*. Hedemora: Gidlund, 2001.

Carlsson, Christina. *Kvinnosyn och kvinnopolitik: En studie av svensk socialdemokrati 1880–1910*. Lund: Arkiv, 1986.

Carlsson, Sten. *Bonde-präst-ämbetsman: Svensk ståndscirkulation från 1680 till våra dagar*. Stockholm: Prisma, 1962.

Carlsson, Sten, et al. *Den svenska historien 15: Våra dagars Sverige*. Stockholm: Bonniers, 1992.

Castells, Manuel. *The Rise of the Network Society*. Oxford: Blackwell, 2000.

Cavanaugh, William T. "The Church, Pluralism, and the Christian Theory of Love." In *Between the State and the Eucharist: Free Church Theology in Conversation with William T. Cavanaugh*, edited by Joel Halldorf and Fredrik Wenell. Eugene, OR: Pickwick Publications, 2014.

———. "Killing for the Telephone Company: Why the Nation-state Is Not the Keeper of the Common Good." *Modern Theology* 20, no. 2 (April 2004).

Childs, Marquis. *Sweden: The Middle Way*. New Haven, CT: Yale University Press, 1936.

Christensen, Jan. "Bönder och herrar: Bondeståndet i 1840-talets liberala representationsdebatt: Exemplen Gustaf Hierta and J. P. Theorell." PhD diss., Göteborg University, 1997.

Christiansen, Niels Finn, Klaus Petersen, Nils Edling, and Per Haave, eds. *The Nordic Model of Welfare: A Historical Reappraisal*. Copenhagen: Museum Tusculanum Press, 2006.

Claesson, Urban. "Att lösa klimatproblem med Luther eller Calvin." In *Luther som utmaning: Om frihet och ansvar*, edited by Elisabeth Gerle. Stockholm: Verbum, 2008.

———. "Folkhemmets kyrka: Harald Hallén och folkkyrkans genombrott: En studie av socialdemokrati, kyrka och nationsbygge med särskild hänsyn till perioden 1905–1933." PhD diss., Uppsala University, 2004.

Cohen, Jean, and Andrew Arato. *Civil Society and Political Theory*. Cambridge, MA: Harvard University Press, 1992.

Confino, Alon. *The Nation as a Local Metaphor: Württemberg, Imperial Germany, and National Memory, 1871–1918*. Chapel Hill: University of North Carolina, 1997.

Cranston, Michael. "Introduction." In *The Social Contract*, Jean-Jacques Rousseau. New York: Penguin, 1968.

Cullberg, John. "Den svenska linjen." *Svensk Tidskrift*, 1942.

Daedalus. *Journal of the American Academy of Sciences* 113, no. 2 (Spring 1984). Cambridge, MA: MIT Press.

Dahl, Birgitta. "Familjepolitiken och jämlikheten." *Tiden*, no. 1 (1966). Stockholm: Sveriges socialdemokratiska arbetarparti.

Dahl, Eva-Lena. "Rousseaus civilisationskritik." In *Kulturen och människan: Två avhandlingar*, Jean-Jacques Rousseau. Göteborg: Daidalos, 1992.

Dahl, Torsten, and Nils Bohman. *Svenska män och kvinnor: Biografisk uppslagsbok.* Vol. 7, *Sibylla-Tjällgren.* Stockholm: Bonnier, 1954.

Dahlkvist, Mats. "'Det civila samhället' i samhällsteori och samhällsdebatt: En kritisk analys." In *Civilt samhälle kontra offentlig sektor,* edited by Lars Trägårdh. Stockholm: SNS, 1995.

Damrosch, Leo. *Jean Jacques Rousseau: Restless Genius.* Boston: Houghton Mifflin, 2005.

Daun, Åke. "Gustav Sundbärg och det svenska folklynnet." In *Vad är Sverige? Röster om svensk nationell identitet,* edited by Alf W. Johansson. Stockholm: Prisma, 2001.

———. *Svensk mentalitet: Ett jämförande perspektiv.* Stockholm: Rabén & Sjögren, 1989.

Delblanc, Sven, and Lars Lönnroth. *Den svenska litteraturen: Det liberala genombrottet 1830–1890.* Stockholm: Bonniers, 1988.

Drangel, Louise. "Folkpartiet och jämställdhetsfrågan." In *Liberal ideologi och politik 1934–1984.* Stockholm: Folk och samhälle, 1984.

Durkheim, Emile. *The Elementary Forms of Religious Life.* New York: Oxford University Press, 2001.

Economist, The. "The Next Supermodel: Why the World Should Look at the Nordic Countries." February 2–8, 2013.

Edling, Nils. *Det fosterländska hemmet: Egnahemspolitik, småbruk och hemideologi kring sekelskiftet 1900.* Stockholm: Carlssons, 1996.

Eduards, Maud. "Toward a Third Way: Women's Politics and Welfare Policies in Sweden." *Social Research* 58, no. 3 (1991).

Ehnmark, Anders. *Minnets hemlighet: En bok om Erik Gustaf Geijer.* Stockholm: Norstedts, 1999.

Elvander, Nils. *Harald Hjärne och konservatismen: Konservativ idédebatt i Sverige 1865–1922.* Stockholm: Almqvist & Wiksell, 1961.

———. *Svensk skattepolitik 1945–1970.* Stockholm: Rabén & Sjögren, 1972.

Engberg, Magnus. *Jag förstår inte vad världen är: Verner von Heidenstam i biografi, brev och bilder.* Linköping: G. Ekström, 2005.

Enquist, Per Olov. *Lewis resa.* Stockholm: Norstedts, 2001.

Enzensberger, Hans Magnus. *Ack, Europa: Iakttagelser från sju länder.* Stockholm: Norstedts, 1988.

Eriksson, Marianne. *Är EG, en kvinnofälla?* Göteborg: Nej till EG (Europeiska gemenskapen), 1993.

Eriksson, Nancy. *Bara en hemmafru: Ett debattinlägg om kvinnan i familjen.* Stockholm: Forum, 1964.

Esping Andersen, Gøsta. *The Three Worlds of Welfare Capitalism.* Cambridge, UK: Polity Press, 1990.

Etzioni, Amitai. *The Spirit of Community: Rights, Responsibilities, and the Communitarian Agenda*. New York: Simon & Schuster, 1993.

Familjeskatteberedningen (Fi; Committee on Joint Taxation). *Individuell beskattning: Betänkande. Del 1, Motiv och förslag*. Report 4 (Fi 1969:4). Stockholm: Finansdepartementet, 1969.

Florén, Anders, Stellan Dahlgren, and Jan Lindegren. *Kungar och krigare: Tre essäer om Karl X Gustav, Karl XI och Karl XII*. Stockholm: Atlantis, 1992.

Florin, Christina. "Skatten som befriar: Hemmafruar mot yrkeskvinnor i 1960-talets särbeskattningsdebatt." In *Kvinnor mot kvinnor: Om systerskapets svårigheter*, edited by Christina Florin, Lena Sommestad, and Ulla Wikander. Stockholm: Norstedts, 1999.

Florin, Christina, and Bengt Nilsson. *"Något som liknar en oblodig revolution-" Jämställdhetens politisering under 1960- och 70-talen*. Umeå: Umeå University, 2000.

Florin, Christina, Lena Sommestad, and Ulla Wikander, eds. *Kvinnor mot kvinnor: Om systerskapets svårigheter*. Stockholm: Norstedts, 1999.

Folkpartiets ungdomsförbund. *Radikal familjepolitik*. Stockholm: Selig, 1964.

Fölster, Kaj. *Bortom de sju bergen: Tyska bilder 1958–1994*. Stockholm: Bonniers, 1994.

Forsman, Ingrid. "Gustaf Sundbärg och det svenska folklynnet." Undergraduate ethnology research paper. Institutet för folklivsforskning, Stockholm University, 1984.

Foucault, Michel. *Mental Illness and Psychology*. New York: Harper, 1976.

———. *Discipline and Punish: The Birth of the Prison*. New York: Vintage Books, 1995.

Frykman, Jonas, and Orvar Löfgren. *Den kultiverade människan*. Lund: Liber, 1979.

Fryxell, Anders. *Om aristokrat-fördömandet i svenska historien jemnte granskning av tvenne blad i prof. Geijers trenne föreläsningar*. Stockholm: printed by the author, 1845.

Fulsås, Narve, and Tore Rem. *Ibsen, Scandinavia and the Making of a World Drama*. Cambridge, UK: Cambridge University Press, 2018.

Furhammar, Leif. *Såpor, sex, och svenska krusbär*. Stockholm: Ekerlid, 2006.

Gaunt, David. *Familjeliv i norden*. Stockholm: Gidlund, 1996.

Gedin, Per. *Verner von Heidenstam: ett liv*. Stockholm: Bonnier, 2006.

Geijer, Erik Gustaf. *Samlade skrifter (Collected Works)*. 12 vols. Stockholm: Norstedts, 1923–1931.

Gellner, Ernest. *Nations and Nationalism*. Malden, MA: Blackwell Publishing, 2006.

Gerle, Elisabeth, ed. *Luther som utmaning: Om frihet och ansvar*. Stockholm: Verbum, 2008.

Goos, Maarten, Alan Manning, and Anna Salamons. "Explaining Job Polarization: Routine Biased Technological Change and Offshoring." *American Economic Review* 104, no. 8 (2014): 2509–26.

Gordon, Linda. *Pitied but Not Entitled: Single Mothers and the History of Welfare 1880–1935*. New York: Free Press, 1994.

Gunnarsson, Lars. "Kyrkan, nazismen och demokratin: åsiktsbildning kring svensk kyrklighet 1919–1945." PhD diss., Stockholm University, 1995.

Haas, Linda. *Equal Parenthood and Social Policy: A Study of Parental Leave in Sweden*. Albany: State University of New York Press, 1992.

Habermas, Jürgen. *Between Facts and Norms: Contributions to a Discourse Theory of Law and Democracy*. London: Polity Press, 1996.

———. *The Structural Transformation of the Public Sphere*. Cambridge, MA: MIT Press, 1989.

———. *The Theory of Communicative Action*. Vol. 2, *Lifeworld and System: A Critique of Functionalist Reason*. Cambridge, UK: Polity Press, 1987.

Hägerström, Axel. *Socialfilosofiska uppsatser*. Stockholm: Bonniers, 1939.

Hajnal, John. "European Marriage Patterns in Perspective." In *Population in History: Essays in Historical Demography*, edited by V. D. Glass and D. E. Eversley. London: Arnold, 1965.

Hall, Patrick. *The Social Construction of Nationalism: Sweden as an Example*. Lund: Lund University Press, 1998.

Hallingberg, Gunnar. *Läsarna: 1800-talets folkväckelse och det moderna genombrottet*. Stockholm: Atlantis, 2010.

Halman, Loek, Ruud Luijkx, and Marga van Zandert. *Atlas of European Values*. Leiden, the Netherlands: Brill, 2005.

Hammar, Inger. "Emancipation och religion: den svenska kvinnorörelsens pionjärer i debatt om kvinnans kallelse ca 1860–1900." PhD diss., Lund University, 1999.

———. "Rousseau—åberopad i sin frånvaro." *Scandia* 68 (2002).

Hammar, Inger, and Sven Arne Flodell. *Religionsblindhet*. Stockholm: Stiftelsen Sverige och kristen tro, 2006.

Hansson, Per Albin. *Demokrati: Tal och uppsatser*. Stockholm: Tiden, 1935.

———. "Den 'gamla' ungdomsrörelsen: Hågkomster från brytningstiden." In *Skånes ungdom: Skånes socialdemokratiska ungdomsdistrikt 1918–1938*. Malmö: Framtiden, 1938.

Heckscher, Gunnar. *Staten och organisationerna*. Stockholm: Kooperativa förbundets bokförlag, 1946.

Hederberg, Hans. "Hörnet Flöjelgatan-Alviksvägen." In *Visionen om jämställdhet*, edited by Annika Baude. Stockholm: SNS, 1992.

Heidenstam, Verner von. *Samlade verk (Collected Works)*. 23 vols. Stockholm: Bonnier, 1943–1944.

Hendin, Herbert. *Suicide and Scandinavia: A Psychoanalytic Study of Culture and Character*. New York: Grune & Stratton, 1964.

Henriksen, Lars Skov, Kristin Strømsnes, and Lars Svedberg, eds. *Civic Engagement in Scandinavia: Volunteering, Informal Help and Giving in Denmark, Norway and Sweden*. Cham: Springer, 2019.

Hernes, Helga Maria. *Welfare State and Woman Power: Essays in State Feminism*. Oslo: Norwegian University Press, 1987.

Hessler, Carl Arvid. "Aristokratifördömandet." *Scandia* 15 (1943).

———. *Geijer som politiker*. 2 vols. Stockholm: Geber, 1937, 1947.

Hettne, Björn, Sverker Sörlin, and Uffe Østergård. *Den globala nationalismen: Nationalstatens historia och framtid*. Stockholm: SNS, 1998.

Hirdman, Yvonne, ed. *Alva Myrdal: "Något kan man väl göra": Texter 1932–1982*. Stockholm: Carlssons, 2002.

———. *Att lägga livet tillrätta*. Stockholm: Carlssons förlag, 1989.

———. *Med kluven tunga: LO och genusordningen*. Stockholm: Atlas, 1998.

———. "Utopia in the Home." *International Journal of Political Economy* 22, no. 2 (1992).

Hobsbawm, Eric. *Nationer och nationalism*. Stockholm: Ordfront, 1994. Originally published as *Nations and Nationalism since 1780: Programme, Myth, Reality*. Cambridge, UK: Cambridge University Press, 1990.

Hoffmann, Stefan-Ludwig. "Human Rights and History." *Past and Present*, no. 232 (August 2016).

Högerns Ungdomsförbund. *Hög tid för ny familjepolitik*. Stockholm: Högerns Ungdomsförbund, 1962.

Holmberg, Åke. *Sverige efter 1809: Politisk historia under 150 år*. Stockholm: Bonniers, 1959.

Huntford, Roland. *The New Totalitarians*. London: Allen Lane, 1971.

Ibsen, Henrik. *An Enemy of the People*. London: Hart-Davis, 1963.

Iggers, Georg. *The German Conception of History: The National Tradition of Historical Thought from Herder to the Present*. Middletown, CT: Wesleyan University Press, 1968.

Inglehart, Ronald, and Christian Welzel. *Modernization, Cultural Change, and Democracy: The Human Development Sequence*. Cambridge, UK: Cambridge University Press, 2005.

Isaksson, Anders. *Per Albin 1: Vägen mot folkhemmet*. Stockholm: Wahlström & Widstrand, 1985.

———. *Per Albin 4: Landsfadern*. Stockholm: Wahlström & Widstrand, 2000.

Isling, Åke. *Folkrörelserna i ny roll?* Stockholm: Sober, 1978.

Jacobson, Magnus. *Almqvist: Diktaren och hans tid*. Lund: Historiska medier, 2002.

Jansson, Torkel. *Adertonhundratalets associationer: Forskning och problem kring ett sprängfullt tomrum eller sammanslutningsprinciper och föreningsformer mellan två samhällsformationer c:a 1800–1870 (Associations of the Nineteenth Century)*. Stockholm: Almqvist & Wiksell International, 1985.

Jenkins, David. *Sweden and the Price of Progress*. New York: Coward-McCann, 1986.

Jeppson Grassman, Eva. "Frivilliga insatser i Sverige: En befolkningsstudie." In *Frivilligt socialt arbete: Kartläggning och kunskapsöversikt*. SOU report 82. Stockholm: SOU, 1993.

Jeppson Grassman, Eva, and Lars Svedberg. "Frivilligt socialt arbete i Sverige—både mer och mindre." In *Medmänsklighet att hyra? Åtta forskare om ideell verksamhet*, edited by Erik Amnå. Örebro: Libris, 1995.

———. "Medborgarskapets gestaltningar." In *Civilsamhället*, edited by Erik Amnå, SOU report 84. Stockholm: Fakta info direkt, 1999.

Johannesson, Erik. "Den heliga familjen: Om borgerlig familjekult under 1800-talet." In *Den utsatta familjen: Liv, arbete och samlevnad i olika nordiska miljöer under de senaste tvåhundra åren*, edited by Hans Norman. Stockholm: LT:s förlag, 1983.

Johansson, Alf W. "Inledning: Svensk nationalism och identitet efter andra världskriget." In *Vad är Sverige? Röster om svensk nationell identitet*, edited by Alf W. Johansson. Stockholm: Prisma, 2001.

Johansson, Alf W., ed. *Vad är Sverige? Röster om svensk nationell identitet*. Stockholm: Prisma, 2001.

Johansson, Hilding. *Folkrörelserna och det demokratiska statsskicket i Sverige*. Lund: Gleerup, 1952.

Johansson Heinö, Andreas. *Gillar vi olika? Hur den svenska likhetsnormen hindrar integrationen*. Stockholm: Timbro, 2012.

Johnson, Anders. *Det svenska teleundret: Entreprenörer, ingenjörer och andra hjältar*. Stockholm: Ekerlid, with NetCom, 2000.

Jönsson, Nine Christine, and Paul Lindblom. *Politik och kärlek: En bok om Gustav Möller och Else Kleen*. Stockholm: Tiden, 1987.

Judt, Tony. *Postwar: A History of Europe since 1945*. New York: Penguin Press, 2005.

Källström, Staffan. *Den gode nihilisten: Axel Hägerström och striderna kring Uppsalafilosofin*. Stockholm: Rabén & Sjögren, 1986.

Kant, Immanuel. *Perpetual Peace: A Philosophical Essay*. 1795. Reprint, Bristol, UK: Thoemmes Press, 1992.

———. *The Philosophy of Kant: Immanuel Kant's Moral and Political Writings*. New York: Modern Library, 1949.

Karleby, Nils. *Socialismen inför verkligheten: Studier över socialdemokratisk åskådning och nutidspolitik*. Stockholm: Tiden, 1926.

Karlsson, Gunnel. *Från broderskap till systerskap: Det socialdemokratiska kvinnoförbundets kamp för inflytande och makt i SAP*. Lund: Arkiv, 1996.

Karlsson, Sten O. *Arbetarfamiljen och det nya hemmet: Om bostadshygienism och klasskultur i mellankrigstidens Göteborg*. Stockholm: Symposion, 1993.

———. *Det intelligenta samhället: En omtolkning av socialdemokratins idéhistoria*. Stockholm: Carlsson, 2001.

Kärnborg, Ulrika. *Fredrika Bremer*. Stockholm: Natur och kultur, 2001.

Keane, John, ed. *Civil Society and the State*. London: Verso, 1988.

Kertzer, David I., and Marzio Barbagli, eds. *The History of the European Family*. 3 vols. New Haven, CT: Yale University Press, 2001.

Kevles, Daniel. *In the Name of Eugenics*. New York: Knopf, 1985.

Key, Ellen. *Barnets århundrade: Studie (The Century of the Child)*. 2 vols. Stockholm: Bonniers, 1900.

———. *Livslinjer 1: Kärleken och äktenskapet (Lifelines)*. 2 vols. Stockholm: Bonniers, 1914, 1916.

———. "Om patriotismen: Öppet brev till min vän Verner von Heidenstam." In *Svenska Krusbär*, edited by Björn Linnell and Mikael Löfgren. Stockholm: Bonnier Alba, 1995.

———. *Skönhet för alla: fyra uppsatser (Four Essays)*. Stockholm: Verdandi, 1913. Facsimile, Stockholm: Rekolid, 1996.

———. *Sveriges modernaste diktare: Carl Jonas Ludvig Almqvist*. Stockholm: Walström & Widstrand, 1897.

———. *Tal till Sveriges ungdom*. Stockholm: Fram, 1910.

———. *Tankebilder, del 1: Kvinnorna—livsbehov—individualitet*. Stockholm: Bonniers, 1922.

Kjellén, Rudolf. "Nationalitetsidén." In *Svenska krusbär*, edited by Björn Linnell and Mikael Löfgren. Stockholm: Bonnier Alba, 1995.

———. *Politiska essayer*. 2 vols. Stockholm: Geber, 1912, 1915.

Kjellén-Björkquist, Ruth. *Rudolf Kjellén: En människa i tiden kring sekelskiftet*. 2 vols. Stockholm: Verbum, 1970.

Klinenberg, Eric. *Going Solo: The Extraordinary Rise and Surprising Appeal of Living Alone*. New York: Penguin, 2012.

Klinth, Roger. *Göra pappa med barn: Den svenska pappapolitiken 1960–95*. Umeå: Borea, 2002.

Koblik, Steven. *Från fattigdom till överflöd*. Stockholm: Wahlström & Widstrand, 1973.

Kogan, Vivian. *The "I" of History: Self-fashioning and National Consciousness in Jules Michelet*. Chapel Hill: North Carolina Studies in the Romance Languages and Literatures, 2006.

Koselleck, Reinhart. *Critique and Crisis*. Cambridge, MA: MIT Press, 1988.

Koven, Seth, and Sonya Michel, eds. *Mothers of a New World: Maternalist Politics and the Origins of Welfare States*. New York: Routledge, 1993.

Kulawik, Teresa. "Maskulinism och välfärdsstatens framväxt i Sverige och Tyskland." *Kvinnovetenskaplig Tidskrift*, no. 3 (1999).

Kungliga Skolöverstyrelsen. *Läroplan för grundskolan*. Stockholm: Kungliga Skolöverstyrelsen, 1962.

Lagercrantz, Olof. *August Strindberg*. Stockholm: Wahlström & Widstrand, 1985.

Lagergren, Fredrika. *På andra sidan välfärdsstaten: En studie i politiska idéers betydelse*. Eslöv: Symposion, 1999.

Lamm, Martin. *August Strindberg*. Lund: Berling, 1963.

Landler, Mark. "Quoth the Raven: I Bake Cookies, Too." *New York Times*, April 23, 2006.

Landquist, John. *Geijer: En levnadsteckning*. Stockholm: Norstedts, 1954.

Langby, Elisabeth. *Vinter i välfärdslandet (Winter in the Welfare Society)*. Stockholm: Askelin & Hägglund, 1984.

Larsen, C. A. *The Rise and Fall of Social Cohesion: The Construction and De-construction of Social Trust in the US, UK, Sweden and Denmark*. Oxford: Oxford University Press, 2013.

Larsmo, Ola. *Andra sidan: Om skrivande*. Stockholm: Bonniers, 2001.

Larson, James L. *Reforming the North: The Kingdoms and Churches of Scandinavia, 1520–1545*. Cambridge, UK: Cambridge University Press, 2010.

Larsson, Jan. *Hemmet vi ärvde: Om folkhemmet, identiteten och den gemensamma framtiden*. Stockholm: Arena, 1994.

Larsson, Ulf L. "Bilden av Sverige: Värner Rydéns bok om medborgarkunskap." In *Vad är Sverige? Röster om svensk nationell identitet*, edited by Alf W. Johansson. Stockholm: Prisma, 2001.

——. *Värner Rydén—En av Brantings män*. Stockholm: Hjalmarson & Högberg, 2000.

Lasch, Christopher. *The Culture of Narcissism: American Life in an Age of Diminishing Expectations*. New York: Warner Books, 1979.

———. *The True and Only Heaven: Progress and Its Critics*. New York: W. W. Norton, 1991.

Laslett, Peter. "Family and Household as a Work Group and Kin Group: Areas of Traditional Europe Compared." In *Family Forms in Historic Europe*, edited by Richard Wall. Cambridge, UK: Cambridge University Press, 1983.

Laurin, Carl G. *Folklynnen*. Stockholm: Norstedts, 1916.

———. *Kvinnolynnen*. Stockholm: Norstedts, 1916.

Leche Löfgren, Mia. *Ellen Key*. Stockholm: Natur och kultur, 1930.

Leijon, Anna-Greta. *Swedish Women—Swedish Men*. Stockholm: Swedish Institute, 1968.

Leira, Arnlaug. *Welfare States and Working Mothers: The Scandinavian Experience*. Cambridge, UK: Cambridge University Press, 1992.

———. "The 'Woman-friendly' Welfare State? The Case of Norway and Sweden." In *Women and Social Policies in Europe*, edited by Jane Lewis. Brookfield, VT: Edward Elgar, 1993.

———. *Working Parents and the Welfare State: Family Change and Policy Reform in Scandinavia*. Cambridge, UK: Cambridge University Press, 2002.

Levertin, Oscar. *Dikter: Tredje samlingen*. Stockholm: Bonniers, 1925.

Levine, Bruce, and Eric Foner. *Half Slave and Half Free: The Roots of Civil War*. New York: Hill & Wang, Noonday Press, 1992.

Lidtke, Vernon. *The Alternative Culture: Socialist Labor in Imperial Germany*. New York: Oxford University Press, 1985.

Liljeström, Rita, and Elisabeth Özdalga. *Autonomy and Dependence in the Family*. Transactions vol. 11. Istanbul: Swedish Research Institute in Istanbul, 2002.

Lindberg, Carter. "Luther's Struggle with Social-ethical Issues." In *The Cambridge Companion to Martin Luther*, edited by Donald K. McKim. Cambridge, UK: Cambridge University Press, 2003.

Lindberg, Ingemar. *Den nya familjens tid: Omläggningen av den svenska familjepolitiken under första hälften an 1970-talet—och några reflektioner trettio år senare*. LO:s välfärdsprojekt. Stockholm: LO, 2001.

Lindén, Claudia. *Om kärlek: Litteratur, sexualitet och politik hos Ellen Key*. Stockholm: Symposion, 2002.

Linder, P. J. Anders. *Demokratins små plattformar: Om nätverk och gruppsamverkan (The Little Platoons of Democracy: Notes on Networks and Group Cooperation)*. Stockholm: Timbro, 1988.

Linderborg, Åsa. *Socialdemokraterna skriver historia: Historieskrivning som ideologisk maktresurs 1892–2000*. Stockholm: Atlas, 2001.

Lindkvist, Thomas, Maria Sjöberg, Susanna Hedenborg, and Lars Kvarnström. *A Concise History of Sweden from the Viking Age to the Present*. Lund: Studentlitteratur, 2018.

Lindström, Rickard. *En socialist: Fragment ur en självbiografi*. Stockholm: Bonniers, 1930.

———. *Socialism, nation och stat*. Eskilstuna: Frihet, 1928.

———. "Socialism, nation och stat." In *Vad är Sverige? Röster om svensk nationell identitet*, edited by Alf W. Johansson. Stockholm: Prisma, 2001.

———. *Tyskland och socialdemokratin: Vad ha vi att lära?* Stockholm: Tiden, 1933.

Lindung, Yngve. Interview with Michel Foucault. *Bonniers Litterära Magasin*, March 1968.

Linnell, Björn, and Mikael Löfgren, eds. *Svenska krusbär: En historiebok om Sverige och svenskar*. Stockholm: Bonniers, 1995.

Lönnroth, Erik. "Den svenska riksdagens uppkomst." *Scandia* 15 (1943).

———. *Från svensk medeltid: Kyrkofurstar och riksbyggare i maktsträvan från Vikingatid till Gustav Vasa*. Stockholm: Bonniers, 1959.

Lukes, Steven. "Types of Individualism." In *Dictionary of the History of Ideas*, vol. 2, edited by Philip P. Wiener. New York: Scribner, 1973.

Lundberg, Gunnar. *Folkstyre eller fogdevälde*. Stockholm: Tiden, 1934.

Lundell, Ulf. *Texter, noter, bilder*. Stockholm: Wahlström & Widstrand, 1996.

Lundgren, Gustaf, ed. *Lasternas bok: Våra kulturfel*. Stockholm: Natur och kultur, 1946.

Lundgren, Linnea. *A Risk or a Resource? A Study of the Swedish State's Shifting Perception and Handling of Minority Religious Communities between 1952–2019*. Stockholm: Ersta Sköndal Bräcke University College, 2021.

Lundkvist, Sven. *Folkrörelserna i det svenska samhället 1850–1920*. Uppsala: Almqvist & Wiksell International, 1967.

Lundqvist, Lennart. "Den underlige svensken." *Svenska Dagbladet*, April 12, 1998.

Lundqvist, Ulla. *Århundradets barn: Fenomenet Pippi Långstrump och dess förutsättningar*. Stockholm: Rabén & Sjögren, 1979.

Lundström, Tommy, and Filip Wijkström. *The Nonprofit Sector in Sweden*. Manchester, UK: Manchester University Press, 1997.

Luther, Martin. *Lilla och stora katekesen: Särtryck ur Lutherska kyrkans bekännelseskrifter (Concordia pia)*. Lund: C. W. K. Gleerup, 1895.

Lyttkens, Sonja. "Införande av särbeskattning i Sverige." In *Visionen om jämställdhet*, edited by Annika Baude. Stockholm: SNS, 1992.

Mackie, Gerry. "Patterns of Social Trust in Western Europe and Their Genesis." In *Trust in Society*, edited by Karen S. Cook. New York: Russell Sage, 2001.

Malmborg, Mikael af. *Sverige och den västeuropeiska integrationen 1945–1959*. Lund: Lund University Press, 1994.

Mann, Golo. *The History of Germany since 1789*. London: Penguin, 1988. First published as *Deutsche Geschichte des 19. und 20. jahrhunderts*, Frankfurt am Main: S. Fischer Verlag, 1958.

Mannheimer, Carin. *Rapport om kvinnor*. Stockholm: Bonnier, 1969.

Manns, Ulla. *Den sanna frigörelsen: Fredrika Bremerförbundet 1884–1921*. Eslöv: Symposion, 1997.

———. *Upp systrar, väpnen er: Kön och politik i svensk 1800-talsfeminism*. Stockholm: Atlas akademi, 2005.

Marcusdotter, Eva. "Låt inte Timbro stjäla fler vänsterprojekt." *Broderskap*, no. 94–41 (1994).

Marx, Karl. *Economic and Philosophic Manuscripts of 1844*. New York: Prometheus Books, 1988.

Mauss, Marcel. *The Gift: The Form and Reason for Exchange in Archaic Societies*. New York: W. W. Norton, 2000.

McKim, Donald K., ed. *The Cambridge Companion to Martin Luther*. Cambridge, UK: Cambridge University Press, 2003.

McPherson, James. *Battle Cry of Feedom: The Civil War Era*. New York: Oxford University Press, 1988.

Meidal, Björn. "August Strindberg—'Oh, så osvenskt'?" In *Vad är Sverige? Röster om svensk nationell identitet*, edited by Alf W. Johansson. Stockholm: Prisma, 2001.

———. "Från profet till folktribun: Strindberg och Strindbergsfejden 1910–12 ("From prophet to tribune: August Strindberg and the Strindberg feud 1910–12"). Diss. Stockholm: Tiden, 1982.

Melby, Kari. *Inte ett ord om kärlek: äktenskap och politik i Norden ca. 1850–1930*. Göteborg: Makadam, with Center for Danish Studies at Lund University, 2006.

Melby, Kari, et al., eds. *The Nordic Model of Marriage and the Welfare State*. Copenhagen: Nordic Council of Ministers, 2000.

Meurling, Per. *Geijer och Marx: Studier i Erik Gustaf Geijers sociala filosofi*. Stockholm: Tiden, 1983.

Micheletti, Michele. *Det civila samhället och staten*. Stockholm: Fritzes, 1994.

Middlekauff, Robert. *The Glorious Cause: The American Revolution 1763–1789*. New York: Oxford University Press, 2005.

Mijuskovic, Ben Lazare. *Loneliness in Philosophy, Psychology and Literature*. Assen, the Netherlands: Van Gorcum, 1979.

Mill, John Stuart. *On Liberty*. London: Walter Scott Publishing, 1859. Project Gutenberg e-book. www.gutenberg.org/files/34901/34901-h/34901-h.htm.

Miller, James. *The Passion of Michel Foucault*. New York: Simon & Schuster, 1993.

Mitterauer, Michael. *Ungdomstidens sociala historia*. Göteborg: Röda bokförlaget, 1998.

Moberg, Eva. "Kvinnans villkorliga frigivning." In *Visionen om jämställdhet*, edited by Annika Baude, Appendix. Stockholm: SNS, 1992.

———. *Kvinnor och människor (Women and Human Beings)*. Stockholm: Bonniers, 1962.

Moberg, Vilhelm. *The Emigrants (Utvandrarna)*. New York: Simon & Schuster, 1951. Reprint, St. Paul: Minnesota Historical Society Press, 1995.

———. *The Last Letter Home (Sista brevet hem)*. London: Reinhardt, 1961. Reprint, St. Paul: Minnesota Historical Society Press, 1995.

———. *The Settlers (Nybyggarna)*. 1961. Reprint, St. Paul: Minnesota Historical Society Press, 1995.

———. *Unto a Good Land (Invandrarna)*. New York: Simon & Schuster, 1954. Reprint, St. Paul: Minnesota Historical Society Press, 1995.

Moderata samlingspartiet. *Idéer för vår framtid*. Stockholm: Moderata samlingspartiet, 1990.

Modig, Arne, and David Ahlin. *Äldre med tydliga behov av hjälp lämnas ensamma*. TEMO (Testhuset Marknad-Opinion) report T-111919, November 10, 2005.

Moeller, Robert G. *Protecting Motherhood: Women and the Family in the Politics of Postwar West Germany*. Berkeley: University of California Press, 1993.

Möller, Gustav. "Memoarkoncept 2," unpublished ms., n.d. Gerda Möllers arkiv. Arbetarrörelsens arkiv och bibliotek, Stockholm.

Möller, Tommy. *Svensk politisk historia 1809–1975*. Lund: Studentlitteratur, 2004.

Morel, Nathalie, Bruno Palier, and Joakim Palme, eds. *Toward a Social Investment Welfare State? Ideas, Policies and Challenges*. Bristol, UK: Policy Press, 2012.

Moyn, Samuel. *The Last Utopia: Human Rights in History*. Cambridge, MA: Belknap Press of Harvard University Press, 2010.

Mral, Birgitte. "'Den nya kvinnan:' Alva Myrdal och medierna på 30-talet." Uppsala: Avdelningen för retorik (Department of Rhetoric), Universitet Litteraturvetenskapliga institutionen, 1994.

Murray, Charles. *Losing Ground: American Social Policy, 1950–1980*. New York: Basic Books, 1984.

Myrdal, Alva. "Den nya familjen." *Vi* 35 (1964).

———. *Folk och familj*. Stockholm: Kooperativa förbundets förlag, 1944.

———. *"Något kan man väl göra": Texter 1932–1982*. Stockholm: Carlssons, 2002.

———. *Nation and Family: The Swedish Experiment in Democratic and Population Policy*. New York: Harper, 1941.

Myrdal, Alva, and Viola Klein. *Kvinnans två roller (Women's Two Roles)*. Stockholm: Tiden, 1957.

Myrdal, Gunnar, and Alva Myrdal. *Kris i befolkningsfrågan (The Crisis in the Population Question)*. Stockholm: Bonniers, 1934.

Nasaw, David. *The Chief: The Life of William Randolph Hearst*. Boston: Houghton Mifflin, 2000.

Neander-Nilsson, Sanfrid. *Är svensken människa?* Stockholm: Fahlcrantz & Gumaelius, 1946.

Nilsson, Staffan. "Särskilt yttrande." *Reformer inom studiemedelssystemet*. SOU report 87, 1971.

Nilsson, Torbjörn. "Liberalism på undantag—bland adliga fritänkare och borgerliga statsvänner i svenskt 1800-tal." *En skrift från Bertil Ohlininstitutet*, no. 5. Stockholm: Bertil Ohlin-institutet, 1996.

———. *Mellan arv och utopi: Moderaternas vägval under hundra år, 1904–2004*. Stockholm: Santérus, 2004.

Norberg, Johan. *Motståndsmannen Vilhelm Moberg*. Stockholm: Timbro, 1997.

Nordin, Jonas. *Ett fattigt men fritt folk: Nationell och politisk självbild i Sverige från sen stormaktstid till slutet av frihetstiden*. Eslöv: Symposion, 2000.

Nordström, Brita. "Familjepolitisk horisont." In *Rädda familjen: En bok om familjepolitik (Save the Family)*, edited by Jon Peter Wieselgren, Brita Nordström, et al. Uppsala: Pro Veritate, 1972.

———. *Ska familjen krossas? (Will the Family Be Destroyed?)* Uppsala: Pro Veritate, 1973.

Nordström, Ludvig. "Behovet av en ny svensk fosterländskhet." In *Svenska krusbär*, edited by Björn Linnell and Mikael Löfgren. Stockholm: Bonniers, 1995.

Norman, Hans, ed. *Den utsatta familjen: Liv, arbete och samlevnad i olika nordiska miljöer under de senaste tvåhundra åren.* Stockholm: LT:s förlag, 1983.

Nyman, Magnus. *Förlorarnas historia: Katolskt liv i Sverige från Gustav Vasa till drottning Kristina.* Stockholm: Veritas, 2002.

Odén, Birgitta. *De äldre i samhället—förr: Fem föreläsningar.* Lund: Projektet Äldre i Samhället, 1985.

Odhner, C. T. *Lärobok i fädnerslandets historia.* Stockholm: Nya tiden, 1902.

Ohlander, Ann-Sofie. "Det osynliga barnet? Kampen om den socialdemokratiska familjepolitiken." In *Socialdemokratins samhälle*, edited by Klaus Misgeld, Karl Molin, and Klas Åmark. Stockholm: Tiden, 1989.

Ohlander, Ann-Sofie, and Ulla-Britt Strömberg. *Tusen svenska kvinnoår: Svensk kvinnohistoria från vikingatid till nutid.* Stockholm: Rabén Prisma, 1996.

Olsson, Henry. *Carl Jonas Love Almqvist till 1836.* Stockholm: Geber, 1937.

Olsson, Jan Olof. *1914.* Stockholm: Bonnier, 1964.

Olsson, Sven E. *Social Policy and Welfare State in Sweden.* Lund: Arkiv, 1990.

Österberg, Eva. "Bönder och centralmakt i det tidigmoderna Sverige: konflikt—kompromiss—politisk kultur." *Scandia* 55 (1989).

———. "Folklig mentalitet och statlig makt." *Scandia* 58 (1992).

———. "Vardagens sköra samförstånd: Bondepolitik i den svenska modellen från Vasatid till Frihetstid." In *Tänka, tycka, tro*, edited by Gunnar Broberg, Ulla Wikander, and Klas Åmark. Stockholm: Ordfront, 1993.

Österlin, Lars. "Nationalism och nationalkyrklighet i svenska tradition." In *Kyrka och nationalism i Norden: Nationalism och skandinavism i de nordiska folkkyrkorna under 1800-talet*, edited by Ingmar Brohed. Lund: Lund University Press, 1998.

Ottey, Abram. *The Swedish Race in North America.* Philadelphia: Olney Printing, 1940.

Özkirimli, Umut. *Theories of Nationalism: A Critical Introduction.* London: Palgrave, 2017.

Paul, Diane. "Eugenics and the Left." *Journal of the History of Ideas*, no. 44 (1984).

Pedersen, Susan. *Family, Dependence and the Origins of the Welfare State: Britain and France 1914—1945.* Cambridge, UK: Cambridge University Press, 1993.

Pehrsson, Per. "Vår kyrkas sociala uppgifter med särskild hänsyn till den nya lagstiftningen på detta område." Inledningsföredrag. Vår kyrkas uppgifter i närvarande tidsläge: Förhandlingar vid Allmänna svenska prästföreningens femte allmänna möte (Introductory remarks at the Fifth General Meeting of the Association of Swedish Priests). Gävle: printed by the author, 1916.

Persson, Gustav. *Daghemsfrågan—Ett arbetsmarknadsproblem*. Stockholm: LO, 1962.

Petersson, Olof, Anders Westholm, and Göran Blomberg. *Medborgarnas makt*. Stockholm: Carlssons, 1989.

Pettersson, Thorleif, and Yilmaz Esmer. *Vilka är annorlunda? Om invandrares möte med svensk kultur*. Norrköping: Integrationsverket, 2006.

Plato. *The Republic*. London: Penguin Books, 1987.

Pleijel, Hilding. *Hustavlans värld: Kyrkligt folkliv i äldre tiders Sverige (A World of Household Codes)*. Stockholm: Verbum, 1970.

Popenoe, David. *Disturbing the Nest: Family Change and Decline in Modern Societies*. New York: Aldine de Gruyter, 1988.

———. "Family Decline in the Swedish Welfare State." *The Public Interest*, no. 102 (1991).

———. "Marriage and Family: What Does the Scandinavian Experience Tell Us?" In *The National Marriage Project, the State of Our Unions: The Social Health of Marriage in America*. New Brunswick, NJ: Rutgers University, 2005.

Putnam, Robert D. *Bowling Alone: The Collapse and Revival of American Community*. New York: Touchstone, 2000.

Qvist, Gunnar. *Konsten att blifva en god flicka: Kvinnohistoriska uppsatser*. Stockholm: Liber, 1978.

Reiss, Hans, ed. *Kant's Political Writings*. Cambridge, UK: Cambridge University Press, 1970.

Reynolds, David. *Walt Whitman's America: A Cultural Biography*. New York: Knopf, 1995.

Riesman, David. *The Lonely Crowd*. New Haven, CT: Yale University Press, 1950.

Roberts, Michael. *Essays in Swedish History*. London: Weidenfeld & Nicolson, 1967.

———. *Sverige under frihetstiden 1719–1772*. Stockholm: Tiden, 1995.

Rojas, Mauricio. *I ensamhetens labyrint: Invandring och svensk identitet*. Stockholm: Brombergs, 2001.

Romanus, Gabriel. "Ett nätverk för jämställdhet." In *Visionen om jämställdhet*, edited by Annika Baude. Stockholm: SNS förlag, 1992.

Romberg, Bertil. *Carl Jonas Love Almqvist: Liv och verk*. Stockholm: Ordfront, 1993.

Ronfani, Paola. "Family Law in Europe." In *The History of the European Family*, vol. 3, *Family Life in the Twentieth Century*, edited by David I. Kertzer and Marzio Barbagli. New Haven, CT: Yale University Press, 2001.

Roosevelt, Theodore. "Corollary to the Monroe Doctrine." Theodore Roosevelt's Annual Message to Congress for 1904 [electronic record]; House Records HR 58A-K2; Records of the US House of Representatives; Record Group 233; Center for Legislative Archives; National Archives at College Park, MD. www.ourdocuments.gov/doc.php?doc=56.

Rosenberg, Göran. *The Reluctant Nation*. London: Counterpoint, 2012.

Rosenblad, Jan Gunnar. *Nation, nationalism och identitet: Sydafrika i svensk sekelskiftesdebatt*. Nora: Nya doxa, 1992.

Roth, Gunther. *The Social Democrats in Imperial Germany: A Study in Working-class Isolation and National Integration*. Totowa, NJ: Bedminster Press, 1963.

Rothstein, Bo. *Den korporativa staten (The Corporatist State)*. Stockholm: Norstedts, 1992.

———. *Just Institutions Matter: The Moral and Political Logic of the Universal Welfare State*. Cambridge, UK: Cambridge University Press, 1998.

———. *Vad bör staten göra?* Stockholm: SNS, 1994.

Rousseau, Jean-Jacques. *The Confessions of Jean-Jacques Rousseau*. Geneva: Jean-Jacques Rousseau, 1782. Project Gutenberg e-book. Kindle. www.gutenberg.org/ebooks/3913.

———. *The Social Contract*. London: Penguin, 1968.

Rubin, Birgitta. "En ny front mot familjens fundamentalister." *Dagens Nyheter*, January 28, 1994.

Ruggie, Mary. *The State and Working Women: A Comparative Study of Britain and Sweden*. Princeton, NJ: Princeton University Press, 1984.

Runcis, Maja. *Steriliseringar i folkhemmet*. Stockholm: Ordfront, 1998.

Ruth, Arne. "The Second New Nation: The Mythology of Modern Sweden." *Dædalus* 113, no. 2 (1984).

Rydén, Verner. "Medborgarkunskap" ("Civic Education"). In *Vad är Sverige? Röster om svensk nationell identitet*, edited by Alf W. Johansson. Stockholm: Prisma, 2001.

Säfstrom, Mark. "The Religious Origins of Democratic Pluralism: Paul Peter Waldenström and the Politics of the Swedish Awakening 1868–1917." PhD diss., University of Washington, Seattle, 2010.

Sainsbury, Diane. *Gender, Equality and Welfare States*. Cambridge, UK: Cambridge University Press, 1996.

Salomon, Kim. *Rebeller i takt med tiden: FNL-rörelsen och 60-talets politiska ritualer*. Stockholm: Rabén Prisma, 1996.

Sanders, Hanne, and Ole Vind. *Grundtvig—nyckeln till det danska*. Göteborg: Makadam med centrum för Danmarksstudier vid Lunds universitet, 2001.

Sandin, Bengt. "Barndomens omvandling—från särart till likart." In *Barnets bästa: En antologi om barndomens innebörder och välfärdens organisering*, edited by Bengt Sandin and Gunilla Halldén. Stockholm: Symposion, 2003.

Sandqvist, Karin, and Bengt-Erik Andersson. "Thriving Families in the Swedish Welfare State." *The Public Interest*, no. 109 (Fall 1992).

SAP (Social Democratic Worker's Party) and LO. *Rådslag 65. Din mening om: Familjen i morgondagens samhälle*. Stockholm: Sakom Tryck, 1965.

Sarti, Roland. *Mazzini: A Life for the Religion of Politics*. Westport, CT: Praeger, 1997.

Sävström, August. *En talmans levnadsminnen*. Stockholm: Lindfors, 1949.

Schiöler, Tomas. *Vännerna Strindberg och Heidenstam*. Stockholm: Strindbergsmuséet, 1997.

Schneewind, J. B. *The Invention of Autonomy: A History of Modern Moral Philosophy*. Cambridge, UK: Cambridge University Press, 1998.

Schofer, Evan, and Marion Fourcade-Gourinchas. "The Structural Contexts of Civic Engagement: Voluntary Association Membership in Comparative Perspective." *American Sociological Review* 66 (2001).

Schorske, Carl. *German Social Democracy, 1905–1917: The Development of the Great Schism*. Cambridge, MA: Harvard University Press, 1955.

Schück, Herman. "Sweden as an Aristocratic Republic." *Journal of Scandinavian History* 9, no. 1 (1984).

Schüllerqvist, Bengt. "Från kosackval till kohandel: SAP:s väg till makten (1928–33)." ("The Rise to Power of the Swedish Social Democrats: Organizational Changes in the Swedish Labor Movement 1928–33"). Diss. Stockholm: Tiden, 1992.

Scott, George Walton. *The Swedes: A Jigsaw Puzzle*. London: Sigwick & Jackson, 1967.

Sejersted, Francis. *Socialdemokratins tidsålder: Sverige och Norge under 1900-talet*. Nora: Nya doxa, 2005.

Selander, Staffan. *Lärobokskunskap: Pedagogisk textanalys med exempel från läroböcker i historia 1841–1985*. Lund: Studentlitteratur, 1988.

Sewell, William. *Work and Revolution in France: The Language of Labor from the Old Regime to 1848*. Cambridge, UK: Cambridge University Press, 1980.

Shain, Barry Allan. *The Myth of American Individualism: The Protestant Origins of American Political Thought*. Princeton, NJ: Princeton University Press, 1994.

Sheehan, James. "What Is German History? Reflections on the Role of the Nation in German History and Historiography." *Journal of Modern History* 53 (1981).

Shorter, Edward. *The Making of the Modern Family.* New York: Basic Books, 1975.

Skocpol, Theda. *Protecting Soldiers and Mothers: The Political Origins of Social Policy in the United States.* Cambridge, UK: Belknap, 1992.

Smith, Anthony D. *The Ethnic Origins of Nations.* Oxford: Blackwell, 1986.

Social tidskrift: Organ för studenter och arbetare. Stockholm, 1908.

Söderbergh, Gotthard. *Svenskt.* Stockholm: Bonniers, 1929.

Söderblom, Nathan. *Religionen och staten (Religion and the State).* Stockholm: Norstedt, 1918.

Somers, Margaret. "Narrating and Naturalizing Civil Society and Citizenship Theory: The Place of Political Culture and the Public Sphere." *Sociological Theory* 13, no. 3 (1995): 229–74.

Sørerensen, Øysten, and Bo Stråth, eds. *The Cultural Construction of Norden.* Oslo: Scandinavian University Press, 1997.

SOU. *Delbetänkande av familjesakkunniga.* Report 37, 1977 (SOU 1977:37).

———. *Familj och äktenskap, Utredningsuppdraget.* Report 41, 1972 (SOU 1972:41).

———. *Reformerad föräldraförsäkring—Kärlek, omvård, trygghet.* Report 73, 2005 (SOU 2005:73).

———. *Reformer inom studiemedelssystemet.* Report 87, 1971 (SOU 1971:87).

———. *Studiestöd: alternativa utvecklingslinjer, Tilläggsdirektiv, Bilaga 1.* Report 31, 1977 (SOU 1977:31).

———. *Studiestöd: alternativa utvecklingslinjer, Bilaga 22 (Sammanfattning av utvecklingstendenserna inom det studiesociala området i några länder).* Report 31, 1977 (SOU 1977:31).

Spruill, Marjorie. *Divided We Stand: The Battle over Women's Rights and Family Values that Polarized American Politics.* New York: Bloomsbury, 2017.

Staberg, Jakob. *Att skapa en ny man: C. J. L. Almqvist och MannaSamfund 1816–1824.* Eslöv: Symposion, 2002.

Starobinski, Jean. *Jean-Jacques Rousseau: Transparency and Obstruction.* Chicago: University of Chicago Press, 1988.

Statistiska centralbyrån. *Historisk statistik för Sverige, del 1.* Stockholm: Statistiska centralbyrån, 1969.

———. *Historisk statistik. Översiktstabeller.* Stockholm: Statistiska centralbyrån, 1960.

———. *Statistisk årsbok för Sverige årgång 36, 42, 49, 51, 92*. Stockholm: Statistiska centralbyrån, 1949, 1955, 1957, 1962, 2005.

Steinmetz, George. *Regulating the Social: The Welfare State and Local Politics in Imperial Germany*. Princeton, NJ: Princeton University Press, 1993.

Stenkvist, Jan. *Nationalskalden: Heidenstam och politiken från och med 1909*. Stockholm: Norstedts, 1982.

———. *Proletärskalden: Exemplet Ragnar Jändel*. Stockholm: Gidlunds, 1985.

Stenström, Thure. *Den ensamme: En motivstudie i det moderna genombrottets litteratur*. Stockholm: Natur och kultur, 1961.

Stepan, Nancy. *The Hour of Eugenics: Race, Gender and Nation in Latin America*. Ithaca, NY: Cornell University Press, 1991.

Stolt, Birgitta. "Luther—glädjedödaren." In *Luther och Sverige*. edited by Carl Axel Aurelius, Torgny Bohlin, Birgit Stolt, and Gustaf Wingren. Linköping: Akademi för kyrka och kultur i Linköpings stift, 1994.

Strahl, Christer. *Nationalism och socialism: Fosterlandet i den politiska idédebatten i Sverige 1890–1914*. Växjö: Smålandsposten, 1983.

Stråth, Bo. *Union och demokrati: De förenade rikena Sverige och Norge 1814–1905*. Nora: Nya doxa, 2005.

Stridsberg, Lennart. "Riskkapitalbolag ger få nya industrier." *Dagens Nyheter*, July 15, 1993.

Strindberg, August. *Married: Twenty Stories of Married Life*. Translated by Ellie Schleussner. London: printed by the author, 1913.

———. "Nationalitet och svenskhet." In *Svenska Krusbär*, edited by Björn Linnell and Mikael Löfgren. Stockholm: Bonnier Alba, 1995.

———. *The Red Room: Scenes from the Lives of Artists and Authors*. Stockholm: Norstedts, 2019.

———. *Samlade verk (Collected Works)*. 72 vols. Nationalupplagan (national ed.). Stockholm: Norstedts, 1981–2013.

Strömstedt, Margareta. *Astrid Lindgren—en levnadsteckning*. Stockholm: Rabén & Sjögren, 1977.

Sundbärg, Gustav. *Emigrationsutredningen: Bil. 16: Det svenska folklynnet*. Stockholm: Nordiska bokh, 1911.

Sundström, Eva. *Gender Regimes: Family Policies and Attitudes to Female Employment. A Comparison of Germany, Italy and Sweden*. Umeå: Sociologiska institutionen, 2003.

Sundström, Marianne. "The Growth in Full-Time Work Among Swedish Women in the 1980s." *Acta Sociologica* 36 (1993).

Svallfors, Stefan. *Vem älskar välfärdsstaten: Attityder, organiserade intressen och svensk välfärdspolitik*. Lund: Arkiv, 1989.

Svanström, Yvonne, and Kjell Östberg. *Än män då? Kön och feminism i Sverige under 150 år.* Stockholm: Atlas, 2004.

Svedjedal, Johan. "Avfallens tid: Om Almqvist och Geijer." *Ord och Bild* 3–4 (1997).

Svensson, Per. *Dr Luther och Mr Hyde: Om tro och makt då och nu.* Stockholm: Cordia, 2008.

Svensson, Tommy. *Ung och radikal: SSU från 1950- till 1980-talet.* Stockholm: SSU, 1987.

Sveriges liberala studentförbund. *Solidarisk familjepolitik.* Fakta och åsikt (Facts and Opinions) 6. Helsingborg: Bertil Höst AB, 1962.

Sveriges socialdemokratiska kvinnoförbund. *Familjen i framtiden: En socialistisk familjepolitik.* Stockholm: AB Litopress, 1972.

Taussi Sjöberg, Marja. *Rätten och kvinnorna: Från släktmakt till statsmakt på 1500- och 1600-talen.* Stockholm: Atlantis, 1996.

Tegborg, Lennart, and Åke Andrén, eds. *Sveriges kyrkohistoria 3: Reformationstid.* Stockholm: Verbum med Svenska kyrkans forskningsråd, 1999.

Tegborg, Lennart, and Anders Jarlert, eds. *Sveriges kyrkohistoria 6: Romantikens och liberalismens tid.* Stockholm: Verbum med Svenska kyrkans forskningsråd, 2001.

Tegborg, Lennart, and Harry Lenhammar, eds. *Sveriges kyrkohistoria 5: Individualismens och upplysningens tid.* Stockholm: Verbum i samarbete med Svenska kyrkans forskningsråd, 2000.

Therborn, Göran. *Between Sex and Power: The Family in the World 1900–2000.* London: Routledge, 2004.

Thomasson, Richard. *Sweden: Prototype of Modern Society.* New York: Random House, 1970.

Thompson, E. P. *The Making of the English Working Class.* Harmondsworth, UK: Penguin Books, 1977.

Thorsell, Siv. "Könsrollsfrågan och barnomsorgen." In *Visionen om jämställdhet*, edited by Annika Baude. Stockholm: SNS, 1992.

Tobisson, Lars. *Löntagarfonder: så nära men ändå inte.* Stockholm: Dialogos, 2016.

Tocqueville, Alexis de. *Democracy in America I.* New York: Colonial Press, 1900.

———. *Democracy in America II.* London: Longman, Green, Longman and Roberts, 1862.

Tönnies, Ferdinand. *Community and Society.* New Brunswick, NJ: Transaction Publishers, 1988.

Torstendahl, Rolf. *Bureaucratisation in Northwestern Europe 1880–1985: Domination and Governance.* London: Routledge, 1991.

———. *Mellan nykonservatism och liberalism: Idébrytningar inom högern och bondepartierna 1918–1934*. Stockholm: Svenska bokförlaget. 1969.

Trägårdh, Lars. *Bemäktiga individerna: Om domstolarna, lagen och de individuella rättigheterna i Sverige*. SOU report 103, 1998. Stockholm: SOU, 1999.

———. "The Concept of the People and the Construction of Popular Political Culture in Germany and Sweden 1848–1933." PhD diss., University of California, Berkeley, 1993.

———. "Crisis and the Politics of National Community: Germany and Sweden, 1933–2000." In *Culture and Crisis: The Case of Germany and Sweden*, edited by Lars Trägårdh and Nina Witoszek. New York: Berghahn Books, 2002.

———. "Rethinking the Nordic Welfare State Through a Neo-Hegelian Theory of State and Civil Society." *Journal of Political Ideologies* 15, no. 3 (2010): 227–39.

———. "Scaling up Solidarity from the National to the Global: Sweden as Welfare State and Moral Superpower." In *Sustainable Modernity: The Nordic Model and Beyond*, edited by Nina Witoszek and Atle Midttun. London: Routledge, 2018.

———. *State and Civil Society in Northern Europe: The Swedish Model Reconsidered*. New York: Berghahn Books, 2006.

———. "Statist Individualism: On the Culturality of the Nordic Welfare State." In *The Cultural Construction of Norden*, edited by Øystein Sørensen and Bo Stråth. Oslo: Scandinavian University Press, 1997.

———. "Statist Individualism: The Swedish Theory of Love and Its Lutheran Imprint." In *Between the State and the Eucharist: Free Church Theology in Conversation with William T. Cavanaugh*, edited by Joel Halldorf and Fredrik Wenell. Eugene, OR: Pickwick Publications, 2014.

———. "Statsindividualismen och civilsamhället." In *Civilsamhället klämt mellan stat och kapital*, edited by Lars Trägårdh, Per Selle, Lars Skov Henriksen, and Hanna Hallin. Stockholm: SNS förlag, 2013.

———. "Swedish Model or Swedish Culture." *Critical Review* 4, no. 4 (1990).

———. "Vad är en medborgare?" *Dagens Nyheter*, September 28, 2002.

Trägårdh, Lars, Susanne Wallman Lundåsen, Dag Wollebaek, and Lars Svedberg. *Den svala svenska tilliten: Förutsättningar och utmaningar*. Stockholm: SNS förlag, 2013.

van Hoorn, André. "Individualist–Collectivist Culture and Trust Radius: A Multilevel Approach." *Journal of Cross-Cultural Psychology* 46, no. 2 (2015): 269–76.

Vestbro, Dick Urban. "Från liberal rörelse till socialistisk kamp mot patriarkatet." In *Visionen om jämställdhet*, edited by Annika Baude. Stockholm: SNS, 1992.

Vinterhed, Kerstin. *Kärlek i tjugonde seklet: En biografi över Alva och Gunnar Myrdal*. Stockholm: Atlas, 2003.

Waldemarson, Ylva. *Mjukt till formen, hårt till innehållet: LO:s kvinnoråd 1947–1967*. Stockholm: Atlas, 1998.

Walker, Mack. *German Home Towns*. Ithaca, NY: Cornell University Press, 1971.

Wannenwetsch, Berd. "Luther's Moral Theology." In *The Cambridge Companion to Martin Luther*, edited by Donald K. McKim. Cambridge, UK: Cambridge University Press, 2003.

Wästberg, Olle. "Efter folkpartiets landsmöte: Familjepolitik i folkpartiet." *Liberal debatt*, no. 8 (1975).

Weber, Max. *The Protestant Ethic and the Spirit of Capitalism*. New York: Charles Scribner's Sons, 1958.

Welzel, Christian. *Freedom Rising*. Cambridge, UK: Cambridge University Press, 2013.

Westman Berg, Carin. *Studier i Carl Jonas Love Almqvists kvinnouppfattning*. Göteborg: Gumpert, 1962.

Whitford, David M. "Luther's Political Encounters." In *The Cambridge Companion to Martin Luther*, edited by Donald K. McKim. Cambridge, UK: Cambridge University Press, 2003.

Wiegert, Monica. *Dagis—Nej tack! (Day-care Centers—No Thanks!)* Simrishamn: Vår framtids förlag, 1982.

Wieselgren, Jon Peter. "Kulturpolitisk översikt." In *Rädda familjen: En bok om familjepolitik*, edited by Jon Peter Wieselgren, Brita Nordström, et al. Uppsala: Pro Veritate, 1972.

Wieselgren, Jon Peter, Brita Nordström, et al. *Rädda familjen: En bok om familjepolitik*. Uppsala: Pro Veritate, 1972.

Wijkström, Filip, and Stefan Einarsson. "Comparing Swedish Foundations: A Carefully Negotiated Space of Existence." *American Behavioral Scientist* 62, no. 13 (2018): 1889–1918.

Wikander, Ulla. *Kvinnoarbete i Europa 1798–1950: Genus, makt och arbetsdelning*. Stockholm: Atlas, 1999.

Wilentz, Sean. *The Rise of American Democracy: Jefferson to Lincoln*. New York: W. W. Norton, 2005.

Wingren, Gustaf. "Utan Luther stannar Sverige." In *Luther och Sverige*, edited by Carl Axel Aurelius, Torgny Bohlin, Birgit Stolt, and Gustaf Wingren. Linköping: Akademi för kyrka och kultur i Linköpings stift, 1994.

Wisselgren, Per. *Samhällets kartläggare: Lorénska stiftelsen, den sociala frågan och samhällsvetenskapens formering 1830–1920.* Eslöv: Symposion, 2000.

Witoszek, Nina. "Fugutives from Utopia: The Scandinavian Enlightenment Reconsidered." In *The Cultural Construction of Norden,* edited by Øystein Sørensen and Bo Stråth. Oslo: Scandinavian University Press, 1997.

———. "Moral Community and the Crisis of the Enlightenment: Sweden and Germany in the 1920s and 1930s." In *Culture and Crisis: The Case of Germany and Sweden,* edited by Lars Trägårdh and Nina Witoszek. New York: Berghahn Books, 2002.

Wizelius, Ingemar. "Heroer och människor." *Tiden,* no. 6 (1941): 362–72.

Wolfe, Alan. "The Day-care Dilemma: A Scandinavian Perspective." *The Public Interest,* no. 95 (1989).

Wuthnow, Robert. *Saving America? Faith-based Services and the Future of Civil Society.* Princeton, NJ: Princeton University Press, 2004.

Zaremba, Maciej. "Byalagets diskreta charm eller folkhemmets demokratiuppfattning." In *Du sköna gamla värld,* Sekretariatet för framtidsstudier. Stockholm: Forskningsrådsnämnden, Framtidsstudier, 1987.

———. *De rena och de andra: Om tvångssteriliseringar, rashygien och arvsynd.* Stockholm: Bokförlaget DN *(Dagens Nyheter),* 1999.

Zetterberg, Hans. "Civila samhället, demokratin och välfärdsstaten." In *Civilt samhälle kontra offentlig sektor,* edited by Lars Trägårdh. Stockholm: SNS förlag, 1995.

———. *Den svenska socialstaten—ett forskningsprojekt.* Stockholm: City University Press, 1992.

———. *Staten, familjen och hushållet.* Delrapport 1, Moderaternas familjepolitiska grupp, Stockholm, August 2005.

Zetterberg, Hans, and Carl Johan Ljungberg. *Vårt land—den svenska socialstaten.* Stockholm: City University Press, 1997.

Zöller, Egon. *Schweden—Land und Volk: Schilderungen aus seiner Natur, seinem geistigen, und wirthschaftlichen Leben.* Lindau: printed by the author, 1882.

Zunz, Olivier, and Alan S. Kahan, eds. *The Tocqueville Reader: A Life in Letters and Politics.* Oxford: Blackwell, 2002.

INDEX

abortion, 41, 42, 214, 217
Åkerman, Brita, 191
alienation, 27, 29, 49, 75, 89, 127, 132, 173, 233, 236, 239, 250, 295–96, 302–4, 315
Almqvist, Carl Jonas Love, 37, 88, 96, 98, 107–8, 114, 116, 125, 132, 136, 140, 142, 177, 189, 210, 231; and Alva Myrdal, 166, 172–75; and Ellen Key, 74, 107–10, 114, 116; and Erik Gustaf Geijer, 53–57, 71–76, 84, 86, 89–90, 95, 97, 107, 122–23; and family, 57, 72; and independence 53–54, 83, 84, 107, 123, 200; and individualism, 57, 74–75, 89; and Jean-Jacques Rousseau, 37, 80–82; and liberalism, 74, 75, 88, 90; and love, 73–74, 80–87, 98, 109, 200; and marriage, 75–76, 79, 81–83, 85–87; and peasant culture, 54, 57, 71–72, 79, 90–91, 107; and Swedishness, 53–55, 57, 74–75, 200; and women, 80, 81, 84, 86, 87, 90
Åmark, Klas, 179
Ambjörnsson, Ronny, 144, 147, 148, 290
anomie, 302–3, 315
antisemitism, 57, 117
Antman, Peter, 30, 256, 257
Arato, Andrew, 255
aristocracy, nobility, 19, 21–27, 55–56, 68, 71, 90, 97, 121, 131, 139, 144, 161, 277–79
Aristotle, 82
Arnstberg, Karl-Olov, 10
Arvidsson, Håkan, 240, 248, 251
asocial sociability, 12–14, 296, 314
atomism, atomistic, 27, 37, 61, 150, 237, 250

Aurelius, Carl Axel, 267
Austin, Paul Britten, 9, 10, 43, 294
authenticity, 80, 81, 101, 108–9
autonomy: and August Strindberg, 102, 107; and Carl Jonas Love Almqvist, 88; and children, 187, 311; and community, xi, 14, 149, 238, 260, 296; and dependence, 45; and elderly, 35; and Ellen Key, 107, 113, 114; and equality, xi, 29, 32, 40, 212, 261, 296; and Erik Gustaf Geijer, x, 62, 65; and family, 42, 187, 198; and Germany, 20; and Immanuel Kant, x, 13; and individualism, xi, 11, 260, 296; and Jean-Jacques Rousseau 28, 217; and love, xi, 34, 48; and national community 149, 164; ; and self-realization, 36, 47, 148; and self-reliance, 10, 148; and social contract, x–xi; and solidarity, 32, 199, 212, 217; and state, xi, 49, 133, 296, 298; and statist individualism, xi; and Sweden, 11, 14, 20, 42, 47, 48, 211; and United States, 19; and welfare state, 30, 32, 213, 258, 303; and women, 194, 198, 199

Backberger, Barbro, 193, 215
Baldwin, Peter, 300–302
Bataille, Georges, 298
Baude, Annika, 191–92
Bauman, Zygmunt, 304
Bengtsson, Håkan A., 244, 247–48
Berger, Peter, 250
Bergman, Ingmar, 9, 214, 252, 294
Berntson, Lennart, 240, 248, 251
Bildt, Carl, 232
Billing, Einar, 268, 271–74, 276–78, 282

373

Billing, Gottfrid, 271
Bismarck, Otto von, 20–21, 30, 41
Björck, Staffan, 8, 9, 121
Björkquist, Manfred, 123, 268–71, 290
Bjørnson, Bjørnstjerne, 128
Bok, Sissela (born Myrdal), 168, 172
Bonnevie, Margareta 191
Böök, Fredrik, 127–28
Boström, C. J., 69
Bourdieu, Pierre, 306
bourgeoisie, 21, 25, 40, 71, 76, 93–94, 139, 144, 148, 249
Bradley, David, 41
Brandell, Georg, 8
Brandes, Georg, 93, 100, 107
Branting, Hjalmar, 267
Bremer, Fredrika, 76, 79, 186, 287
Brilkman, Kajsa, 281
bureaucracy, 24, 243, 248, 251
Burenstam Linder, Staffan, 231, 235–36, 250

Calvin, Jean, 263, 279, 291
charity, charity organizations, 27, 30, 32, 47, 136, 148, 170, 178, 186, 259
children's ombudsman, 35
children's rights, xii, 43, 47, 292
Childs, Marquis, 232–33, 242
Christian II, 22, 266, 277
Christianity, 59, 61, 75, 89, 92, 97, 99, 106, 120, 132, 147, 262, 267, 269, 271–72, 279, 281, 287–88
civil servants, 24, 90, 170, 308
civil society, x, 25, 270, 297, 304; and Alexis de Tocqueville, 27, 259; and debate in Sweden, 238–41, 244–46, 248–52, 254–57, 260, 262; and Erik Gustaf Geijer, 69; and Germany, 21, 44–45, 235, 292; and Social Democratic Youth Movement (SSU), 244–45, 248–49; and Sweden, 17–18, 20, 30–31, 34, 44, 49, 257–62, 291–93, 301, 308; and Timbro, 240–41, 249–52, 254–55; and the United States, 19–20, 26, 44–46, 259, 292–93
Claesson, Urban, 268, 291
class society, 131, 142, 145, 148–49, 166, 233
co-habitation (*sambo*), 43
Cohen, Jean, 255
collectivism, 11, 30, 130–31, 252
common will, 28–29
communitarianism, 304; and Sweden, 29, 250–52, 254, 260, 291, 305, 309, 312; and the United States, 46–47, 240, 263, 312
conformism, 11, 17, 24, 237, 298–99
conservatism, 56, 59, 74, 104, 116, 121, 226, 254–55, 281
Conservative Party, 191, 195
Constant, Benjamin, 56, 64
cooperatives, 137, 171–72, 241–42, 244, 291
corporations, 67–69, 307
corporatism, 17, 18, 239, 242, 256, 302

Dahl, Birgitta, 219–20
Dahlkvist, Mats, 254
Dahlström, Edmund, 182, 191
Daun, Åke, 10
day care, 205, 231; and Alva Myrdal, 171, 181; and Brita Nordström, 223, 228; Eva Moberg, 190, 221, 224–25; extension of, 201–2, 207–8, 225, 235; and Germany, 310; and Monica Wiegert, 227–29; and Nancy Eriksson, 212; and Sweden, 192, 194–95, 201–2, 210, 213, 220, 222–23, 226, 234, 257, 302; and United States, 259
Denmark, xi, 21, 40, 42–43, 45, 124, 135, 214, 265, 266
division of powers, 19, 152
divorce, 40–42, 47–48, 96, 108–10, 168, 206, 210, 214, 226, 235, 296, 309, 311
Durkheim, Émile, 298, 303

economic democracy, 176, 244
egoism, 25, 32, 36, 64, 81, 89, 105, 108
Ehnmark, Anders, 62–63, 65, 70
Eisenhower, Dwight D., 232
Eklund, J. A., 268
elderly, care of, 35, 39, 165, 202, 234
Elvander, Nils, 196
emigration, 5, 123–24, 189
empowerment (*egenmakt*), 239, 246, 252, 257, 260, 284, 291
Engberg, Arthur, 267
Engelbrekt Engelbrektsson, 21, 119, 134–35, 137, 145, 154, 156, 223, 266–67
Engels, Friedrich, 189
Engqvist, Lars, 244, 246
Enlightenment, 12, 25, 56, 58–61, 68, 286
Enquist, Per Olov, 147, 288
estates, 22, 23–24, 57–58, 67–69, 82, 90, 121, 280, 287
eugenics, 106, 162

Index

family: campaign, 214–15, 218, 223–24; history, 38; law, 41–42, 199, 203, 205–6, 208, 215; modern, 218; nuclear, 76, 168, 184, 201, 216, 264; patriarchal, 29, 173, 217, 309; policy, 41–43, 166, 177, 186, 190, 192–93, 195–96, 198–99, 205, 207, 209, 215–17, 219, 221, 224, 227, 234, 309, 310. *See also* taxation
fascism, 4, 17, 135, 162
fatherhood, 87
feminism, 104, 113, 177, 188, 197, 210, 228, 230, 236
Ferguson, Adam, 239
Fichte, Johann Gottlieb, 70
Finland, 5, 40, 54, 265
Flaubert, Gustave, 78
Florin, Christina, 208
Folkets hus (People's Hall), 242
Folkets Park (People's Park), 242
folkhemmet (people's home), 14, 17, 24, 31, 138, 140, 149, 154, 162, 164, 184, 242, 256, 261, 264, 271, 298, 304; and Church of Sweden, 268–70, 291; and debate about, 237–39, 255, 260, 299; and Martin Luther, 271; and Per Albin Hansson, 116, 135–36, 142, 156, 237, 249, 255, 270; and Rudolf Kjellén, 116, 255, 269
Fölster, Kaj (born Myrdal), 21, 168
Forsslund, Karl Erik, 146
Foucault, Michel, 280, 298–99
Fourier, Charles, 90, 288
France, 19, 25–26, 40, 55, 58, 71, 81, 94, 117, 170
France, Anatole, 66
free churches, 24, 146, 268, 270–71, 289–90
French revolution, 25, 56, 65, 161, 296, 313
Fryxell, Anders, 68
Fröding, Gustaf, 119

Garbo, Greta, 169
Gaunt, David, 39, 40
Geijer, Erik Gustaf, x, 5, 64, 92, 95–97, 99, 107, 111–12, 114, 116, 120–21, 124–25, 129, 139–40, 156, 172, 210, 242, 266, 287–88; and Carl Jonas Love Almqvist, 53–57, 71–76, 84, 86, 89–90, 95, 97, 107, 122–23; and Christianity, 59, 61, 62, 75; and Enlightenment, 58–61, 68; and family, 76, 164; and Georg Wilhelm Friedrich Hegel, 63, 70; and history 56–57, 59–62, 65, 67–68, 70–71, 121, 137, 139, 152, 153; and independence, 64–67; and individualism, 57, 58, 60–72, 89, 107, 132, 142, 297; and law, 115, 132, 149, 151–53; and liberalism 57, 58, 60, 70, 76, 121; and nationalism, 70, 71, 121; and parliamentary reform, 62, 71, 72; and personality principle, 62–63, 65, 67–69, 98; and state, 64, 67–70, 151, 297; and Swedishness, 53, 54, 70, 142; and Thomas Hobbes 63, 64; and turn to liberalism in 1838, 57–59; and women's suffrage, 66–67
Gemeinschaft, 20, 29, 251, 303–4, 315
gender: equality, 10, 35, 77, 182, 188, 191–92, 194–95, 197–98, 204–5, 213, 218–22, 224, 226, 228–30, 234, 285, 292, 294–95, 309, 311–12; norms, 88; order, 81, 88, 172, 230, 236
Gerle, Elisabeth, 289
Germany, 20, 41, 56, 94–95, 117–18, 135, 138, 140, 142, 209, 236, 271; and Catholic Church, 20, 285; and family, 30, 41, 45, 180–81, 310; and Martin Luther, 264, 276, 281; and protestantism, 263–64, 285; and social contract, 30, 45; and Sweden, xi, 17–18, 21, 23, 44, 46, 55, 57, 112, 119, 235, 255, 276, 293; and United States, 21, 44, 106, 118, 208, 255, 264, 292
Gesellschaft, 30, 241, 251, 303–4, 315
globalization, 297, 307
Great Britain, 20, 23–24, 40, 55, 61, 81, 90, 94, 117, 169–70, 214, 246, 258, 286
Greider, Göran, 255–56, 260
Grundtvig, Nikolaj, 55
guilds, 26, 57, 67, 69, 83–84, 90, 97, 146, 241, 301
Gullberg, Hjalmar, 169
Gunnarsson, Lars, 271
Gustafsson, Hans, 244
Gustav Vasa (Gustav I), 21, 22, 135, 266–67, 272, 276–77
Gustav II Adolf, 119, 265–66, 268, 273, 278, 287
Gustav III, 81
Gustav IV Adolf, 81

Habermas, Jürgen, 255, 304
Hägerström, Axel, 152
Hajnal, John, 37

Hallén, Harald, 268, 270, 291
Hallingberg, Gunnar, 289
Hammar, Inger, 81, 285
Hammarlund, Jan, 218
Hansson, Ola, 100
Hansson, Per Albin, xii, 116, 135, 154, 156, 237, 269; and childhood, 136–38; and Erik Gustaf Geijer, 142; and peasants, 134; and popular movements, 143–45
Hardt, Tom, 218
health care, 165, 202, 209, 219, 245, 257, 260, 293, 300–301, 307–8
Heckscher, Gunnar, 17, 18, 24
Hedenius, Ingemar, 185
Hegel, Georg Wilhelm Friedrich, 24, 63, 70, 130, 235, 241, 279, 314
Heidenstam, Verner von, 5, 7, 100, 102, 123, 127–30, 255; and aristocracy, 131–32; and Ellen Key, 105, 131; and Erik Gustaf Geijer, 129; and family, 128; and individualism, 127–29, 130–32; and labor movement, 130; and nationalism, 127–28, 200
Hendin, Herbert, 9, 10, 38
Henry VIII, 272
Herder, Johann Gottfried von, 56
Hierta, Lars Johan, 74
Hirdman, Yvonne, 175, 177
Hitler, Adolf, 4, 20, 21, 135, 140, 142, 264
Hjärne, Harald, 123
Hjortzberg, Olle, 265, 266
Hobbes, Thomas, 49, 63, 64, 70, 131, 274, 298
Hobsbawm, Eric, 56
Höglund, Zeth, 145
Höjer, Karl, 178
homosexuality, 42–43, 200, 218, 243, 295, 311
housewives, 40, 79, 168–69, 175, 183, 185–86, 193, 197–99, 208, 212–14, 216, 223, 227, 236
Hugo, Yngve, 129
human rights, 24, 62, 152, 217, 261, 307, 312, 313
Huntford, Roland, 16–17, 33, 232–33, 299
Huxley, Aldous, 16

Ibsen, Henrik, 93, 95, 99
Iceland, 43, 59, 170, 235, 265
immigration, 11–12, 29, 61, 263, 312, 313
independence: and Alva Myrdal, 172; and Carl Jonas Love Almquist, 75; and children, 10, 38–40, 103, 114, 169, 211; and civic duty, 146, 148, 149; economic, 84, 189, 195, 199–201, 217, 220, 224; and egoism, 32, 48; and equality, 64, 65, 130; and Erik Gustaf Geijer, 60–62, 64–65, 68; and Eva Moberg, 186–87, 189–90, 220; and freedom, 64, 294; and Gustav Möller, 179; and individualism, 12, 32, 47, 75, 77, 103, 107; and Jean-Jacques Rousseau, 27–29, 36–37, 217; and loneliness, 32, 48, 101, 294; and love, 36, 38, 48, 73, 80, 172; and peasants, 72, 89, 91, 95; personal, 11, 197, 210, 234, 236; political, 15, 107, 111, 146; and selfishness, 32, 48; and self-sufficiency, 10, 125, 153, 189, 222; and state, 46, 68, 70; and Sweden, 11, 29, 31, 43, 47, 83, 105, 132, 156; and women, 35, 73, 169, 195, 201, 205, 211, 222; and work, 49, 84
individualism, 147; egalitarian, 147; rugged, 312; statist, xi–xii, 16–17, 32–33, 37, 47, 212, 218–20, 222–23, 230–33, 235, 237–38, 249, 260–61, 263–64, 291, 297–98, 302–3, 306–9, 311, 313–15
inequality, 25, 97, 109, 256
internationalism, 116, 131, 139
Isaksson, Anders, 136
Italy, 4, 17, 55, 135, 209

Jansson, Albert (later Reimer, father of Alva Myrdal), 172
Jansson, Torkel, 241
Jantelagen, 299–300. *See also* social control
Jarl, Birger, 149
Jaurès, Jean, 139
Jefferson, Thomas, 19
Johansson, Hilding, 18
Judt, Tony, 300

Kant, Immanuel, x, xi, 35, 70, 105, 314; and asocial sociability, x, xi, 12–13, 185, 296; and social contract, 13–14, 185
Karl IX (earlier Duke Karl), 272, 273
Karl XI, 142, 277, 278
Karl XII, 102, 119, 286
Karleby, Nils, 138–39, 150–51, 246
Karlsson, Sten O., 168
Kärnborg, Ulrika, 78
Kautsky, Karl, 138
Key, Ellen, 5, 37, 74, 132, 145, 166, 172, 183, 184, 210, 283, 299; and Alva

Myrdal, 172–75, 177, 183, 187; and August Strindberg, 37, 103, 104, 107, 111, 114–16, 145, 184, 299; and Carl Jonas Love Almqvist, 74, 107–10, 114, 116; and child-rearing, 103, 112–14; and egoism 105, 106; and Erik Gustaf Geijer, 111, 114–16, 121; and eugenics 106, 153; and family, 110; and feminism, 104; and Friedrich Nietzsche, 106–8, 111–12; and individualism, 105–8, 111; and marriage, 103, 108–12, 114; and Rudolf Kjellén 116, 121; and Verner von Heidenstam, 105, 131

Key, Emil, 103

kindergarten. *See* day care

Kjellén, Rudolf, 116–17, 149, 255, 269; and break-up of the Swedish-Norwegian Union, 119; and Ellen Key, 116, 121; and geopolitics, 117; and individualism, 116, 120; and loneliness, 120; and nationalism, 116–17, 121–23, 126, 131; and people's home (*folkhemmet*), 116; and Social Democracy, 120; and state, 121, 130, 132

Klein, Viola, 181, 191

Klinenberg, Eric, 310

Kling, Herman, 204, 206

Klinth, Roger, 219, 221

Lagercrantz, Olof, 100

Landquist, John, 67

Langby, Elisabeth, 232

Lasch, Christopher, 304

Laurin, Carl G., 7, 83, 123

lawlessness, 60, 107, 276, 299

Le Play, Frédéric, 38

Levertin, Oscar, 7, 123

Lidbom, Carl, 204

Lindberg, Ingemar, 219

Linde, Leif, 257

Lindén, Claudia, 106, 112

Linder, P. J. Anders, 250

Linderborg, Åsa, 135, 142

Lindgren, Astrid, 183, 184, 210

Lindström, Rickard 138–40

Ling, Per Henrik, 59

local democracy, 242, 246, 249, 302

Locke, John, 19, 239, 274, 298

Löfgren, Orvar, 78

Lo-Johansson, Ivar, 9

Lönnroth, Erik, 137

Louise, Swedish Crown Princess, 169

love, Swedish theory of, xi–xii, 33–34, 36

Lundberg, Gunnar, 134

Lundell, Ulf, 83

Lundkvist, Sven, 242

Lundqvist, Ulla, 183

Lundstedt, Vilhelm, 152

Luther, Käthe (Katharina von Bora), 283

Luther, Martin, 81, 263–67, 271–72, 274–85, 289–91

Luxemburg, Rosa, 138

Lyttkens, Sonja, 195–96, 214–15, 218

Magnus Ladulås, 149

Mannheimer, Carin, 213

market economy, 143, 157, 166, 171, 208, 233, 246, 307–8

marriage law, 69, 90, 109, 114, 172. *See also* family: law

marriage pattern, European, 37–39, 76–78, 284

Marx, Karl, 26, 61, 62, 70, 90, 144, 151, 152, 304

matriarchy, 98, 110, 112, 172

Mauss, Marcel 298

Mazzini, Giuseppe, 55

Meidal, Björn, 102

Meurling, Per, 70

Michelet, Jules, 55

Mill, John Stuart, 26, 56

minority rights, 24

Mitterauer, Michael, 38

Moberg, Eva, 166, 182, 195, 199, 210, 215, 220–21, 224–25, 229; and Alva Myrdal, 186; and gender equality, 186–92

Moberg, Vilhelm, 189, 237

Möller, Gustav, 177–81, 186

Montesquieu, Charles de, 19, 70, 95

Morris, William, 114

motherhood, 111, 174, 187–88, 209

Müntzer, Thomas, 275

Mussolini, Benito, 4, 143

Myrdal, Alva, 21, 41, 167–69, 176, 178, 181–84, 186–88, 191, 199, 210; and Carl Jonas Love Almqvist, 166, 170, 172–73, 175, 177; and children, 166, 171, 174, 175; and Ellen Key, 172–75, 177, 183, 187; and family, 166, 172–74, 179, 210; and individualism, 172, 179; and Jean-Jacques Rousseau, 172–73, 187; and law, 170; and love, 173; and paternalism, 180; and population question, 167, 169, 175–76; and state, 175, 179; and sterilizations, 171

Myrdal, Gunnar, 21, 41, 166–69, 175–77, 181

Myrdal family, 21, 167–69, 172

narcissism, 234, 303
national character, 3, 5, 7–9, 12–15, 53, 95, 97, 122–23, 126–27, 131, 149, 185
national community: and democracy, 55, 118, 139, 153, 255, 291; ethnic national community, 29, 118, 121, 271; and *folkhemmet*, 149, 153; and human rights, 313; and individualism, 124, 126, 142, 164, 238; organic, 121, 291; and political culture, 238; and state, 29, 161, 164, 238, 307; and United States, 57
nationalism, 56, 61, 118–19, 132, 136, 161–62, 176, 268, 296; conservative, 116, 122; democratic, 118, 125, 131; left-wing, 118, 140, 143, 267, 313; liberal, 56, 75, 118, 124, 136, 142; right-wing, 116–19, 121–22
nation-state, 118, 139, 161–62, 164, 254–55, 261, 263, 276, 289, 293, 296, 306–8, 313
natural rights, 142, 150, 153
Neander-Nilsson, Sanfrid, 3–5, 235–36
neoliberalism, 31, 181, 189, 239–40, 251, 252, 261, 308
Neuhaus, Richard John, 250
Nietzsche, Friedrich, 100, 106–8, 111–12, 128–29, 144, 147, 152, 279, 299
night courting, 39–40, 43, 77
Nilsson, Staffan, 203
nobility. *See* aristocracy, nobility
Norberg, Johan, 189
Nordström, Brita, 214–17, 223–24, 228, 235
Nordström, Ludvig, 12, 154
Norway, xi, 5, 21, 40, 42, 43, 61, 118–19, 130, 170, 265–66, 276

Odhner, C. T., 136–37
Ohlander, Ann-Sofie, 218
Olsson, Henry, 75
Ossiannilsson, K. G., 145
Österberg, Eva, 23, 278
Östman, Karl, 144
Ottey, Abram, 7
Özdalga, Elisabeth, 11

Palm, August, 143
Palme, Joakim, 307
Palme, Olof, 202, 220–21, 232
parental leave, 47, 216, 219–20, 222, 225–30, 310
paternity leave, 228

patriarchy, 25, 29, 36, 77–78, 165, 183, 210, 217, 231, 309; and Alva Myrdal, 172–73; and August Strindberg, 97; and Carl Jonas Love Almqvist, 76, 83, 86–87, 89; and and Erik Gustaf Geijer, 57–59, 61, 66–67, 72, 89; European marriage pattern, 40–42; and Germany, 41, 209; and Martin Luther, 264, 282–84
patriotism, 10, 55, 57, 59, 105, 121, 123, 126–27, 129–32, 136, 139, 149–50, 167, 269
pauperism, 62
peasantry, 21–22, 54, 78, 89, 137, 140, 154, 276, 278; estate, 23, 25, 71; *odalbonde(n)*, 60, 297
Peasant's Party (Bondeförbundet), 140
Peasants' War, 55–56, 276
Pehrsson, Per, 293
pensions, 94, 165, 178, 184, 206
people's home. *See folkhemmet*
personality principle (*personlighets-principen*), 62–63, 65, 67–69, 92, 98, 120
Persson, Gustav, 192, 194, 207
Petersen, Emilie, 288
Petri, Olaus, 266, 272
Pettersson, Thorleif, 47
pietism, pietistic, 59, 147, 285–86, 288
Plato, 28, 164
political culture, 16–17, 20–21, 23–25, 33, 57, 71, 232, 238, 259, 297, 309–10, 315
Popenoe, David, 234–35, 309
popular movements, 18, 24–25, 136–38, 146–49, 156, 178, 191, 238–46, 248–49, 255–57, 260, 270–71, 290
population question, 164, 167, 169–70, 176
preschool. *See* day care
prostitution, 108, 189, 216, 301
protestantism, 263–65, 283–85, 287, 292
public sector, 31, 45, 229–30, 238, 244–49, 251–52, 256–60, 308
Putnam, Robert, 304, 306

Reagan, Ronald, 246
religion, 20, 43, 47, 64, 147, 166, 185, 262–64, 267, 269, 277, 279–81, 288–92, 296, 311
religious communities, 18, 20, 23, 259, 292
Riesman, David, 304
Roberts, Michael, 23
Rojas, Mauricio, 11

Romanus, Gabriel, 192, 194, 204, 208
Ronfani, Paola, 42
Roosevelt, Theodore, 119, 143
Rosenius, Carl Olof, 287, 290
Rothstein, Bo, 24, 260; and Alva Myrdal, 177–78; and civil society, 258; and corporatism, 17–18, 256; and universal welfare politics, 258
Rousseau, Jean-Jacques, 37, 70, 97, 178, 187; and Alexis de Tocqueville, 27–29, 37, 49, 218; and Alva Myrdal, 172–73, 187; and August Strindberg, 37, 97–98, 130; and authenticity, 81; and Brita Nordström, 217; and Carl Jonas Love Almqvist, 37, 80–82; and dependence, 27–28, 36–37, 130; and Ellen Key, 37; and equality, 29, 81, 130; and love 36–37, 80; and Sweden, 250
Ruskin, John, 114
Ruth, Arne, 136
Rydén, Värner, 149, 267

Säfström, Mark Daniel, 286
Saint-Simon, Henri de, 56, 58, 66, 90
Samuelsson, Kurt, 196
Sandin, Bengt, 165
Sandlund, Maj-Britt, 192
Sandqvist, Karin, 235
Scandinavia, 53, 55, 71, 92–94, 115, 118, 154, 259; and Enlightenment, 286; and family, 41, 43, 204, 310; and family history, 38–39; and literature, 59, 92–94; and marriage laws, 41–43, 114; and protestantism, 59, 265, 276; and Sweden, 31, 42
Schlafly, Phyllis, 218
schooling, 99, 162, 165, 187, 259, 261, 263, 267; expansion of, 57, 90, 156; and Martin Luther, 281–82, 284, 289; and social investment, 307–8; and Sweden, 34, 288, 292, 300, 307
Scott, George, 287
Scott, George Walton, 9
secularism, 48, 234, 264, 267, 271, 291, 294, 311–13
segregation, 222, 245–46, 249, 261
Sejersted, Frances, 115
Selander, Sten, 134
selfishness, 25, 32, 36, 67, 80
self-realization: and autonomy, 47, 107; and childhood, 9; and citizenship, 99; and community, 92–93, 235, 295; and egoism, 89, 247, 299; and family policy, 42; individual right to, 84, 92–93, 114–15, 143, 147; and love, 295; and motherhood, 9, 174, 188, 209; and women, 99–100, 102–3, 111–12, 229, 296; and work, 9, 229–30
Servetus, Michael, 279
servility, xi, 13, 297
sexuality, 41, 82, 104, 153, 169, 175, 283, 312
Shain, Barry Allan, 19
Sigismund, 272
single mothers, 31, 180, 209, 223
single parents, 46
Smith, Adam, 239
sobriety (skötsamhet), 148, 168, 171, 299
social capital, 20, 256, 258, 304, 306
social contract, xi, 32, 230, 291, 303; and Ellen Key, 112; and Eva Moberg, 187, 221; and Germany, 21, 236; and Immanuel Kant, 13–14, 185; and Jean-Jacques Rousseau, 28–29, 98; and religion, 263; and Sweden, 14, 17, 29, 33, 36, 47, 49, 178, 291–92, 297–98, 301, 307–8, 311–15
social control, 38, 40, 89, 94, 299, 306
Social Democratic Party, 24, 138, 143, 154, 169, 171, 194; and agrarian socialism, 146; and Christian socialism, 144; and church, 267–68, 291; and civil society, 248–49, 257, 259; and family policy, 190, 192, 200, 205, 214, 224, 226; and housewives, 197, 199, 214; and nationalism, 134–35, 137, 139, 142, 149; and 1968 movement, 239; and rule of law, 149–51; and self-management, 239, 247–48, 257; and socialism, 138, 176; and state, 151, 156, 165, 190, 239, 242, 291, 300; and taxation, 196, 206, 249; and utopian legacy, 171; and wage-earner's fund, 238; women's association of, 176, 192, 196–200, 205, 210, 214, 221, 227; youth wing of, 145, 239, 246–49
social economy, 257
social engineering, 32–33, 41, 49, 99, 164, 175, 177, 232, 236, 289
social insurance, 30–32, 46, 205, 219, 241
social rights, x, 32, 46, 177, 179, 241, 301, 302, 313; general, 179; safety net as, 170
Söderberg, Gotthard, 7
Söderblom, Nathan, 266, 268–70

solidarity: and alienation, 49;
  collective, 282; and community,
  29, 147, 220, 241, 244, 291;
  and democracy 124, 139, 164;
  and equality, 32, 108, 202, 212,
  294; ethnic, 47, 118; and family,
  164, 168, 217; global, 313; and
  individual autonomy, 29, 32, 108,
  111, 116, 126, 199, 217, 304;
  international, 125, 135; national,
  25, 59, 132, 164, 286, 298, 313;
  reciprocal, 168; social, ix, 143,
  198, 306; and state, 199, 254, 304;
  and trust, 292, 306; and unions,
  148, 241; voluntary, 137; and
  work, 145, 147
Staaff, Karl, 268
Staberg, Johan, 88
Stalin, Josef, 143
state church, 166, 262–64, 267, 269,
  271, 273–74, 278, 285–90
Stehouwer, Jan, 38
Stenström, Thure, 93
Stolpe, Sven, 8
Stolt, Birgit, 283
Sträng, Gunnar, 196–97, 214–15, 224
Stridsberg, Lennart, 11
Strindberg, August, 5, 102, 105, 112,
  116, 128, 132, 173, 178, 210; and
  Carl Jonas Love Almqvist, 37,
  95, 97–98, 107; and Ellen Key,
  37, 103–4, 107, 111, 114–16,
  145, 184, 299; and Erik Gustaf
  Geijer, 95–97, 99, 107, 111;
  and family, 92, 100, 108; and
  feminism, 99, 103; and Friedrich
  Nietzsche, 100, 107, 108, 299;
  and individualism 95, 99; and
  Jean-Jacques Rousseau, 37, 97–98,
  130; and loneliness, 93, 100, 101;
  and nature, 97; and peasants,
  94–95; and radical individualism,
  99, 102–3; and Verner von
  Heidenstam, 100, 128
Ström, Fredrik, 217
student loans, 202–3, 208
subsidiarity, 20, 45, 244, 278
Sundbärg, Gustaf, 5, 7–9, 33, 123–27,
  131–32, 140
Svedberg, Lars, 258
Svensson, Per, 290
Sweden Democrats, 297
Swedish model, 14, 233, 256, 308, 310
Swedish welfare state, 15, 32, 37, 47, 49,
  180, 222, 230, 250, 306, 308, 311
Szebehely, Marta, 35

taxation, 307; individual, 42, 166,
  193–200, 206, 210, 212, 214–15,
  222, 224, 227, 310; joint, 110, 193,
  195–96, 208, 218, 226–27, 310
Tegnér, Esaias, 54, 59, 288
temperance, 129, 137, 144, 146–48, 157,
  241–42, 268, 270, 290
Thatcher, Margaret, 246
Therborn, Göran, 167
Thomas, Bishop, 223, 266
Thorsell, Siv, 192–93, 207–8
Thorwaldsson, Karl-Petter, 257
Timbro, 238, 240, 249–52, 254–56
Tingsten, Herbert, 185
Tocqueville, Alexis de, 58, 70, 90,
  242–43, 259; and democracy,
  26–27, 49, 295; and dependence,
  26; and equality, 27, 29, 69, 295;
  and Erik Gustaf Geijer, 69; and
  history, 27; and individualism,
  26–27, 295; and Jean-Jacques
  Rousseau, 27–29, 37, 49, 218; and
  state, 49, 63, 130, 218
Tönnies, Ferdinand, 251, 303, 304
Troedsson, Ingegerd, 195
Trolle, Gustaf, 277
trust, 83, 192, 238, 265, 288, 292, 299,
  303, 305, 306, 312–14

unemployment, 156, 197, 205, 314
United States, 19–21, 24, 36, 117, 178,
  180, 204, 218–19, 242, 246, 305,
  310; and civil society, 26, 259;
  and Germany, xi, 106, 118; and
  individualism, 20, 46–47, 55, 57,
  61, 180, 312; and protestantism,
  263–64; and religion, 20, 23, 119,
  286, 292; and state, 45, 235, 310;
  and Sweden, xi, 11, 17–18, 20, 23,
  44, 124, 232, 235, 240, 259; and
  taxation, 208
universalism, 179, 261, 269, 292–93

voluntary associations, x, 34, 69, 149,
  166, 238, 254, 259, 290

Waldenström, Paul Peter, 286, 289
Wallin, J. O., 266, 287
Wästberg, Olle, 192, 226
Weber, Max, 24, 303, 304
Welzel, Christian, 295
Wennström, Elsy, 167
Westerberg, Bengt, 227
Westman-Berg, Karin, 83
Whitman, Walt, 55, 57
Wiegert, Monica, 227–29, 231, 235, 236

Wieselgren, Jon Peter, 216
Wijkström, Filip, 258
Wingren, Gustaf, 265
Wolfe, Alan, 234
Wollstonecraft, Mary, 76
women's movement, 103, 105, 188, 218, 221, 243
work ethic, 31, 264–65, 290
working class, 104, 131, 136–40, 142–45, 148, 168, 176, 178, 188, 190, 197, 214, 229, 256, 267, 269
World Values Survey, 47–48, 295, 311

Zaremba, Maciej, 23
Zetterberg, Hans: and civil society, 251, 252, 254, 255, 260; and communitarianism, 251, 252; and Timbro, 251, 252, 254, 255, 260
Zola, Émile, 93, 101, 117

www.ingramcontent.com/pod-product-compliance
Lightning Source LLC
Chambersburg PA
CBHW031751220426
43662CB00007B/360